INUYASHA

VOL. 52

Shonen Sunday Edition

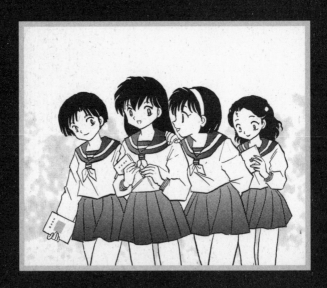

STORY AND ART BY
RUMIKO TAKAHASHI

CONTENTS

SCROLL ONE
THE BOW'S POWER
5

SCROLL TWO
HELL
23

SCROLL THREE
KAGOME'S POWER
41

SCROLL FOUR
THE CORRECT WISH
59

SCROLL FIVE
THE JEWEL'S WILL
77

SCROLL SIX
PERIL
97

SCROLL SEVEN
THE BORROWED BODY
115

SCROLL EIGHT
MAGATSUHI
133

SCROLL NINE
MAGATSUHI'S TRUE BODY
151

SCROLL TEN
BAKUSAIGA
169

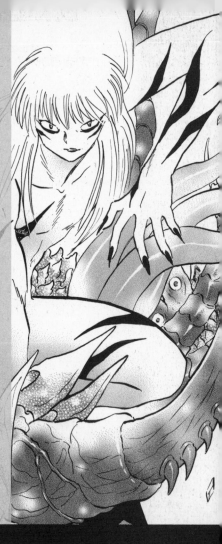

Long ago, in the "Warring States" era of Japan's Muromachi period, dog-like half demon Inuyasha attempted to steal the Shikon Jewel—or "Jewel of Four Souls"—from a village. The village priestess, Kikyo, put a stop to his thievery with an enchanted arrow. Pinned to a tree, Inuyasha fell into a deep sleep, while mortally wounded Kikyo took the jewel with her into her funeral pyre. Years passed...

In the present day, Kagome, a Japanese high school girl, is pulled down into a well and transported into the past. There she discovers trapped Inuyasha—and frees him.

When the Shikon Jewel mysteriously reappears, demons attack. In the ensuing battle, the jewel *shatters*!

Now Inuyasha is bound to Kagome with a powerful spell, and the grudging companions must battle to reclaim the shattered shards of the Shikon Jewel to keep them out of evil hands...

LAST VOLUME Sesshomaru imbeds a Shikon shard from Kanna's magic mirror in Tenseiga's blade and attacks Inuyasha. Byakuya teleports the brothers to another dimension where no friends can come to their aid—and Naraku tries to ensure that they never return! In the end, Tetsusaiga absorbs the Meido Zangetsuha, and Tenseiga leads them back to the world of the living.
   Plus, Shippo enters a fox-demon competition and quickly moves up in the ranks. But then Naraku possesses the priestess Hitomiko and dispatches her to kill Kagome!

CHARACTERS

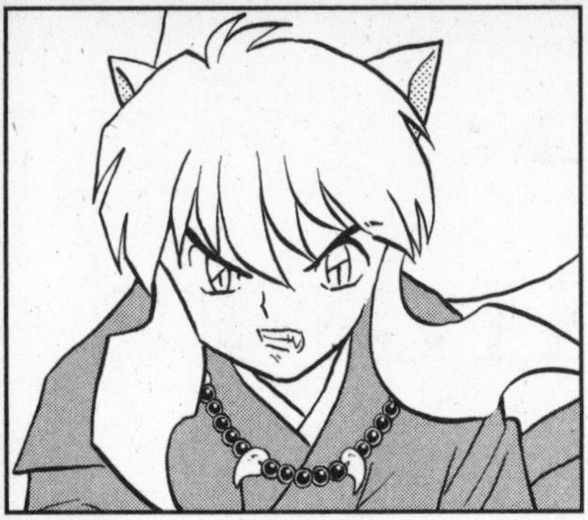

INUYASHA
Half-demon hybrid, son of a human mother and demon father. His necklace is enchanted, allowing Kagome to control him with a word.

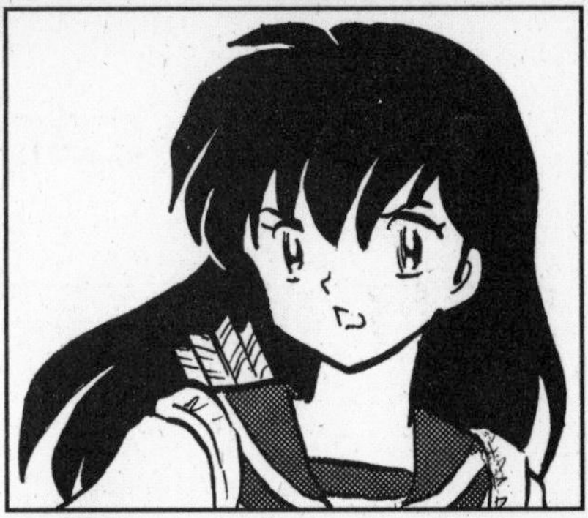

KAGOME
Modern-day Japanese schoolgirl who can travel back and forth between the past and present through an enchanted well.

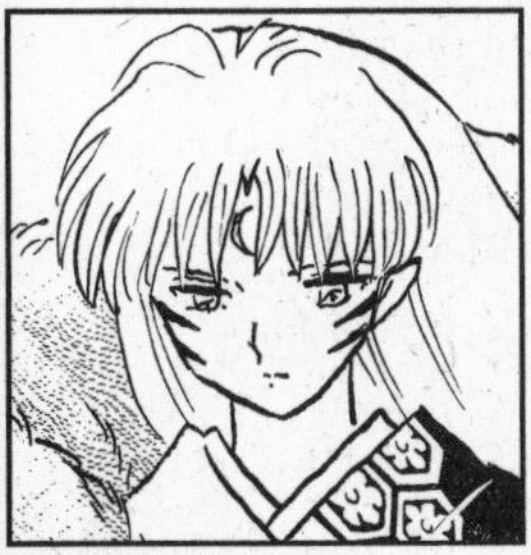

SESSHOMARU
Inuyasha's pureblood-demon half brother. They have the same demon father. Sesshomaru covets the sword left to Inuyasha by their father.

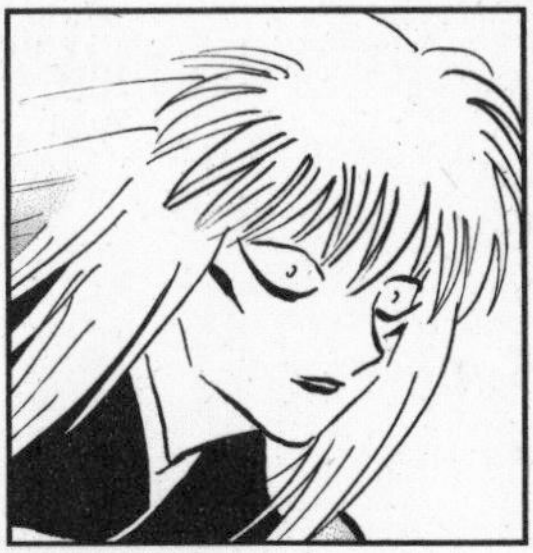

MAGATSUHI
A monstrous demon who dwells inside the Shikon Jewel but can sometimes escape to wreak havoc on everyone, including Naraku.

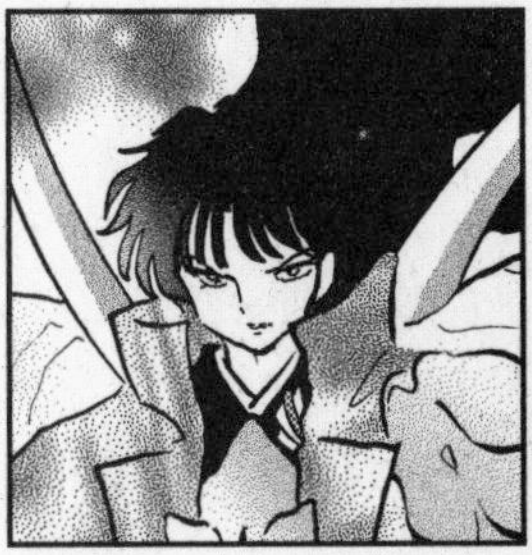

NARAKU
Enigmatic demon mastermind behind the miseries of nearly everyone in the story. He has the power to create multiple incarnations of himself from his body.

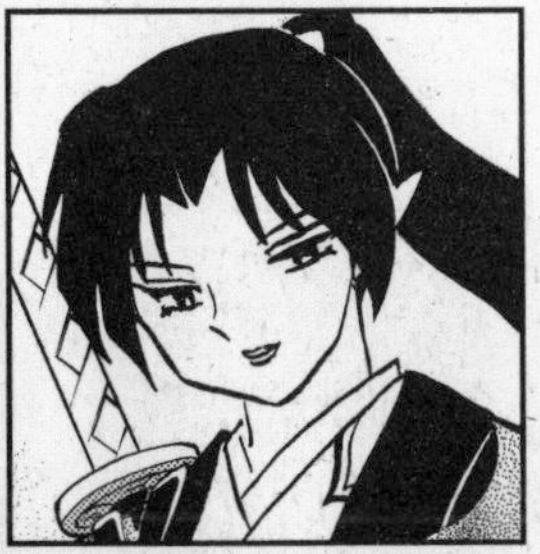

BYAKUYA
A powerful sorcerer and master of illusions created by Naraku.

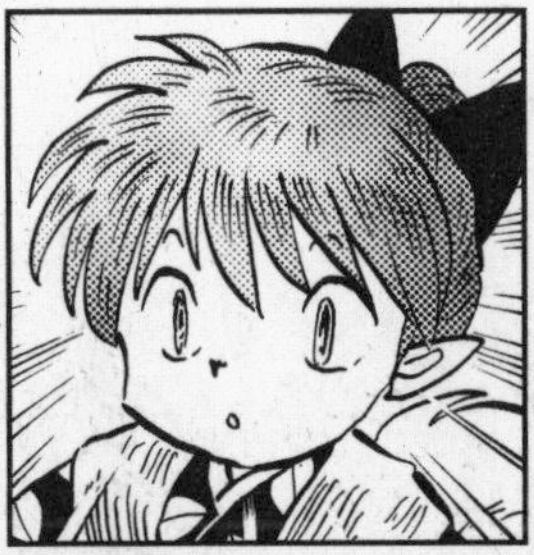

SHIPPO
A tactless fox demon who can perform a little, usually inept, magic.

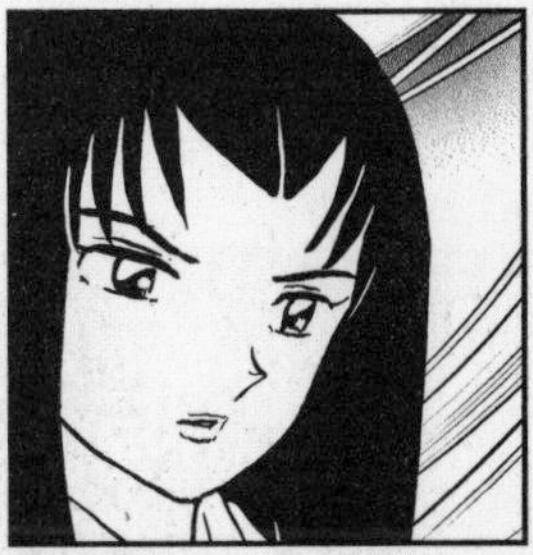

HITOMIKO
A priestess possessed by Naraku and instructed to destroy Kagome.

SCROLL 1

THE BOW'S POWER

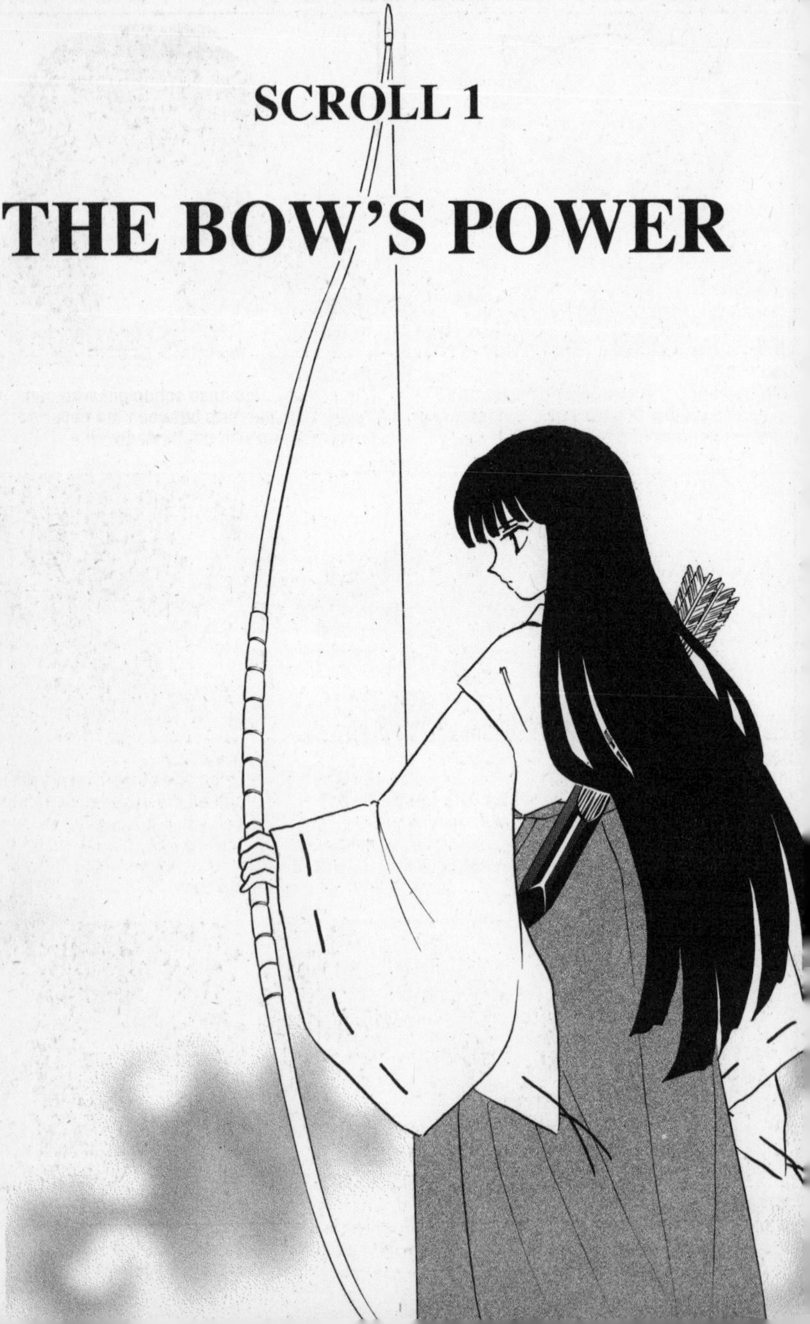

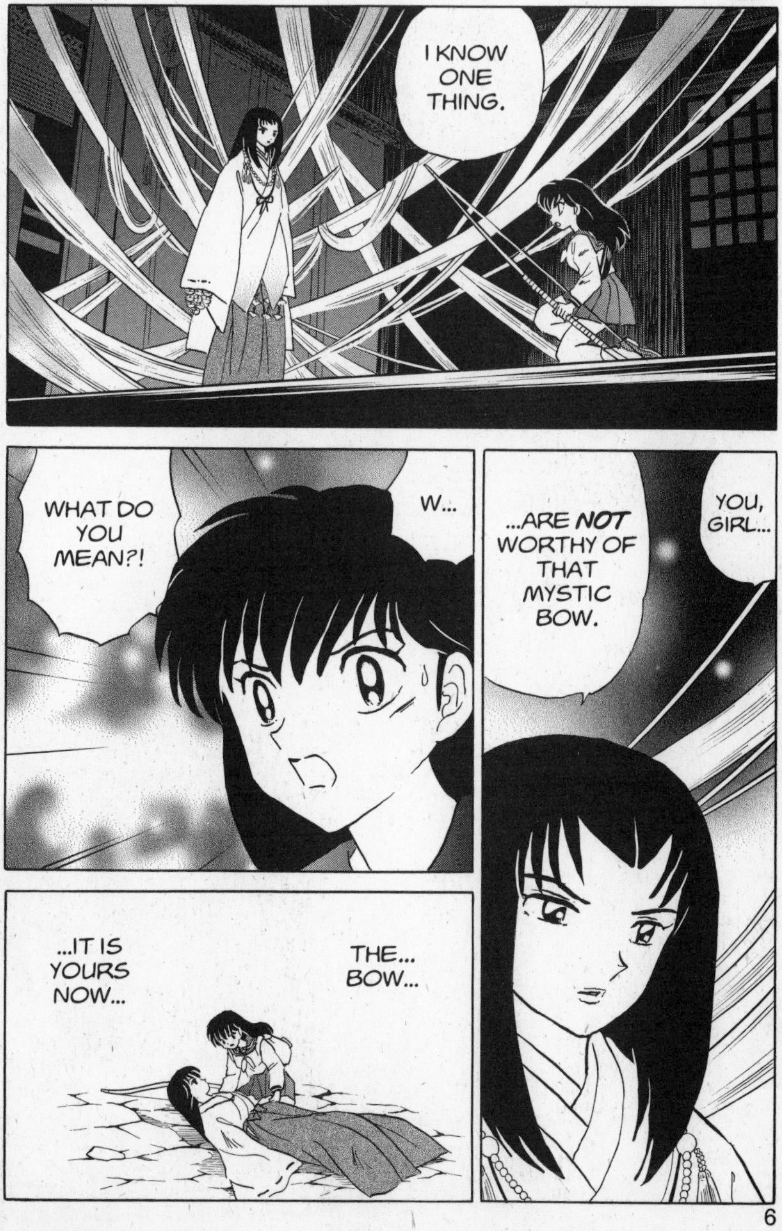
I KNOW ONE THING.
YOU, GIRL...
...ARE **NOT** WORTHY OF THAT MYSTIC BOW.
W...
WHAT DO YOU MEAN?!
THE... BOW...
...IT IS YOURS NOW...

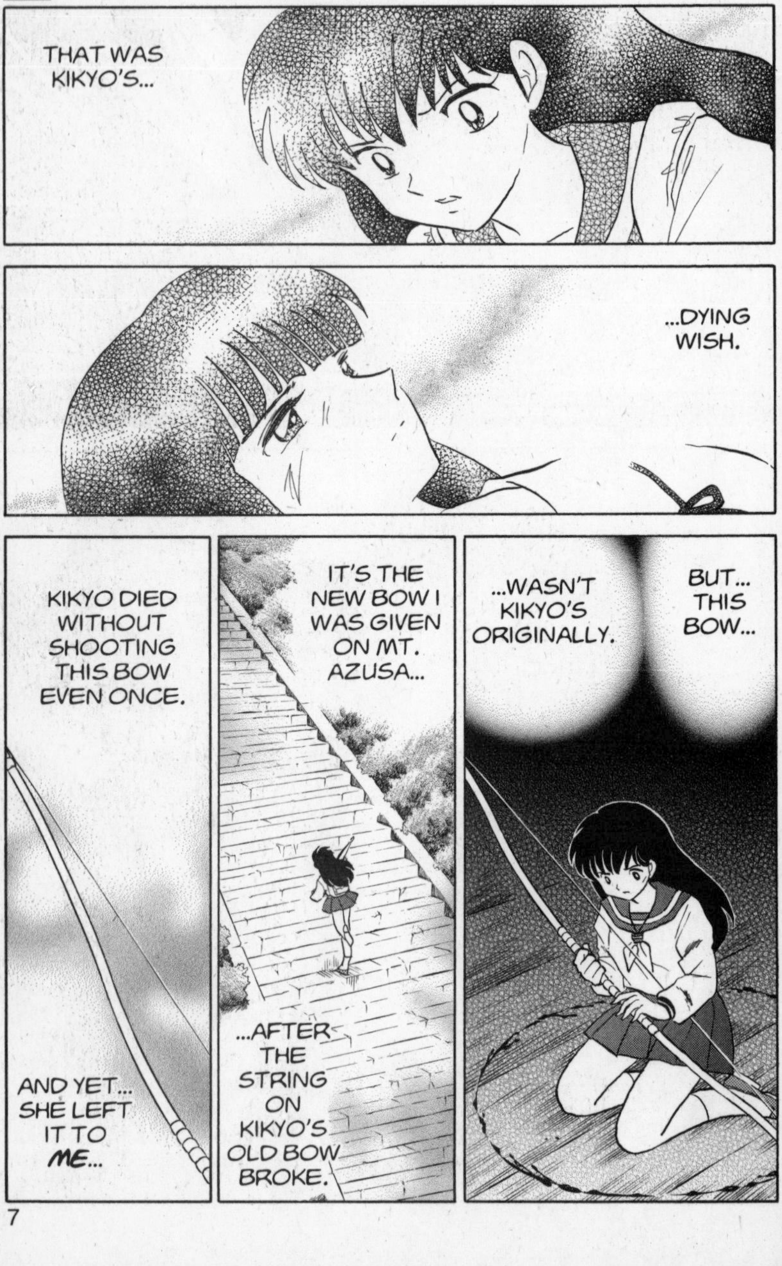
THAT WAS KIKYO'S...
...DYING WISH.
BUT... THIS BOW...
...WASN'T KIKYO'S ORIGINALLY.
IT'S THE NEW BOW I WAS GIVEN ON MT. AZUSA...
...AFTER THE STRING ON KIKYO'S OLD BOW BROKE.
KIKYO DIED WITHOUT SHOOTING THIS BOW EVEN ONCE.
AND YET... SHE LEFT IT TO *ME*...

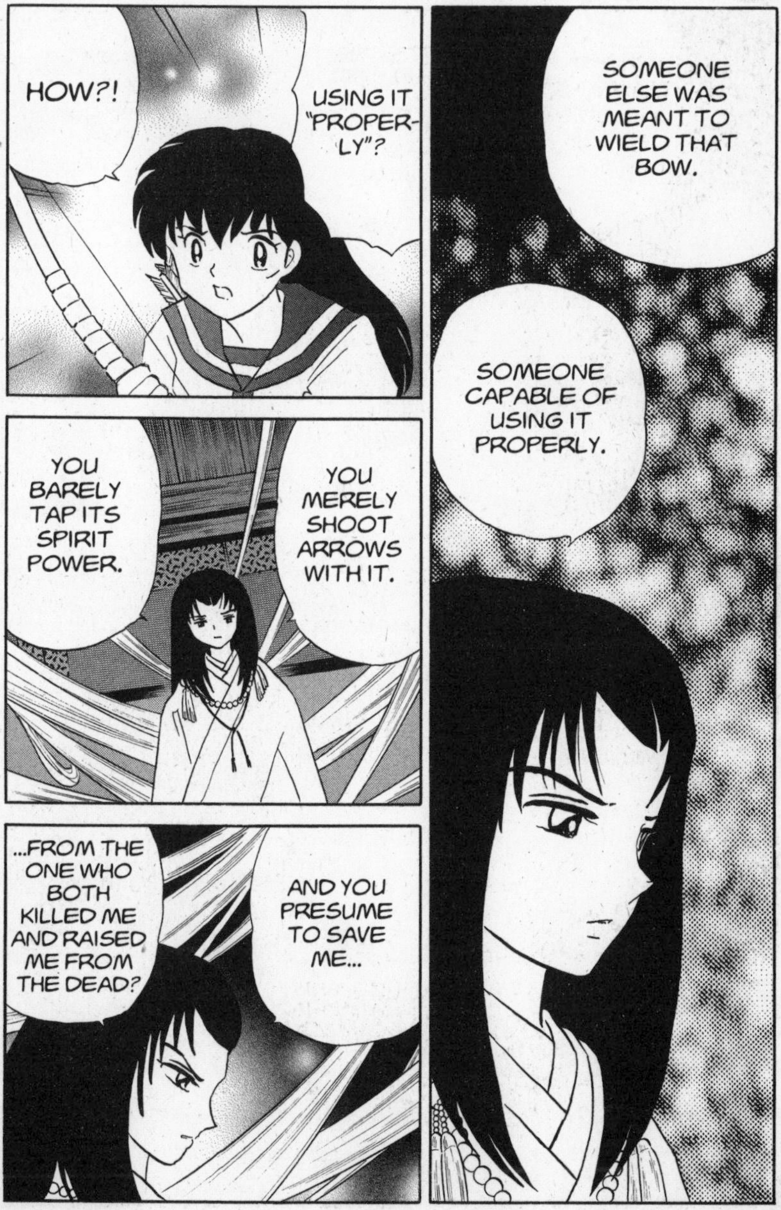
SOMEONE ELSE WAS MEANT TO WIELD THAT BOW.
SOMEONE CAPABLE OF USING IT PROPERLY.
USING IT "PROPER-LY"?
HOW?!
YOU MERELY SHOOT ARROWS WITH IT.
YOU BARELY TAP ITS SPIRIT POWER.
AND YOU PRESUME TO SAVE ME...
...FROM THE ONE WHO BOTH KILLED ME AND RAISED ME FROM THE DEAD?

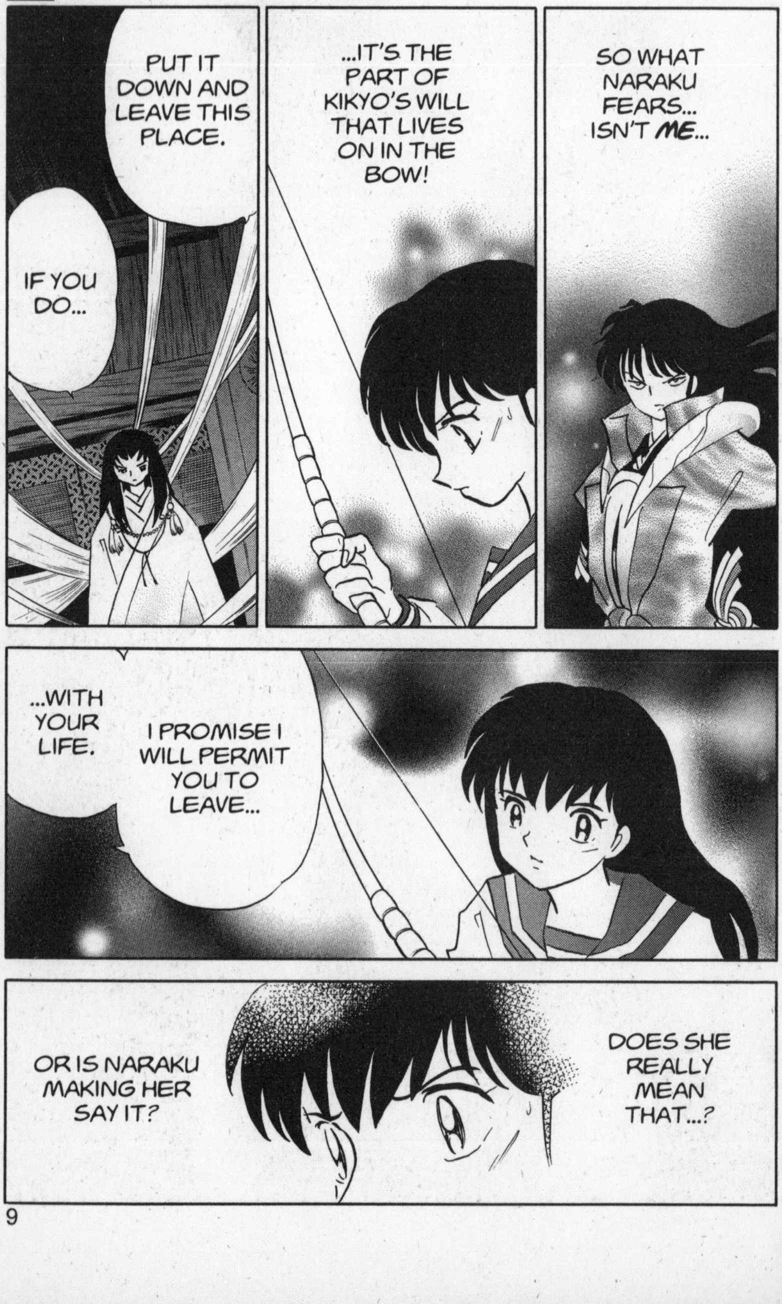
SO WHAT NARAKU FEARS... ISN'T *ME*...
...IT'S THE PART OF KIKYO'S WILL THAT LIVES ON IN THE BOW!
PUT IT DOWN AND LEAVE THIS PLACE.
IF YOU DO...
I PROMISE I WILL PERMIT YOU TO LEAVE...
...WITH YOUR LIFE.
DOES SHE REALLY MEAN THAT...?
OR IS NARAKU MAKING HER SAY IT?

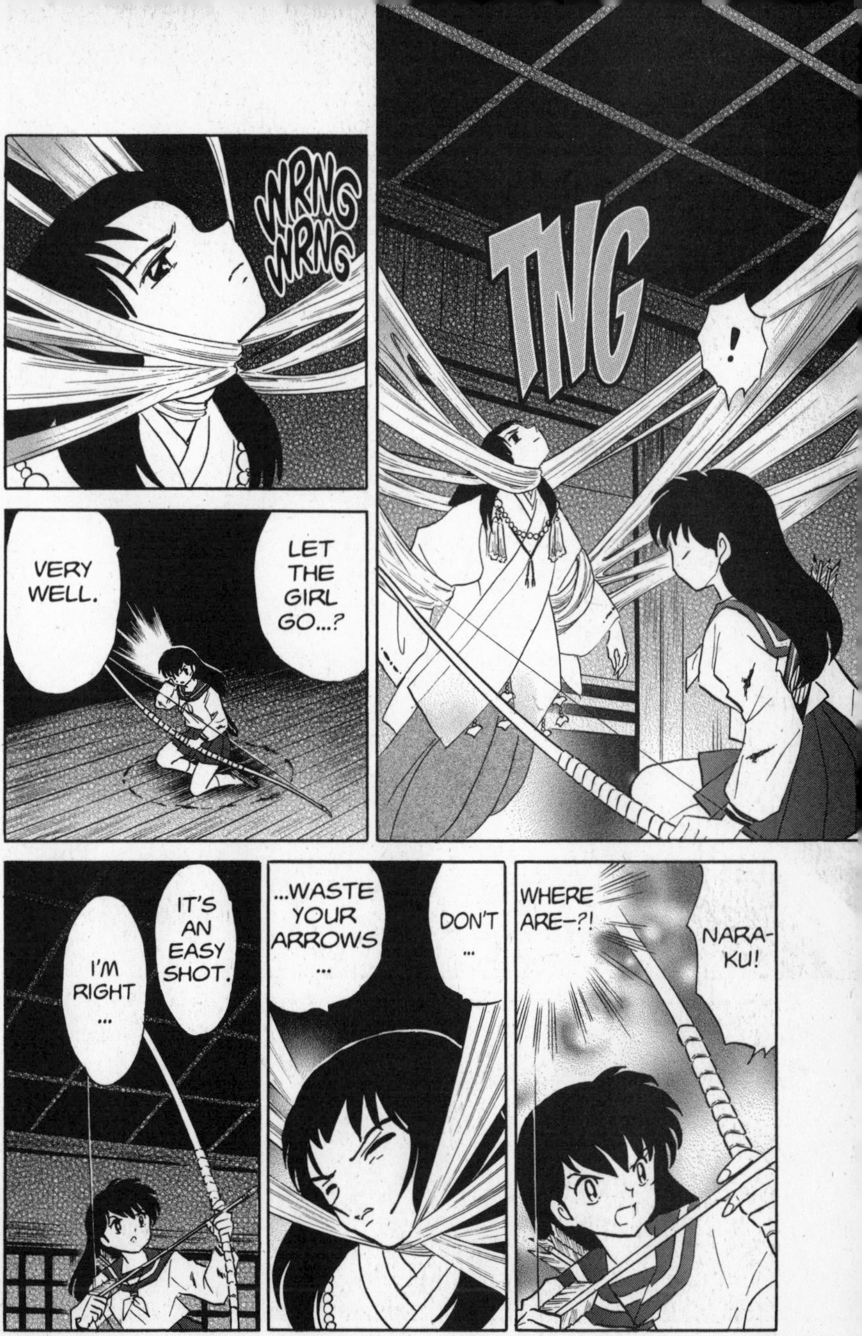
TING
!
WRNG WRNG
LET THE GIRL GO...?
VERY WELL.
NARAKU!
WHERE ARE-?!
DON'T ...
...WASTE YOUR ARROWS ...
IT'S AN EASY SHOT.
I'M RIGHT ...

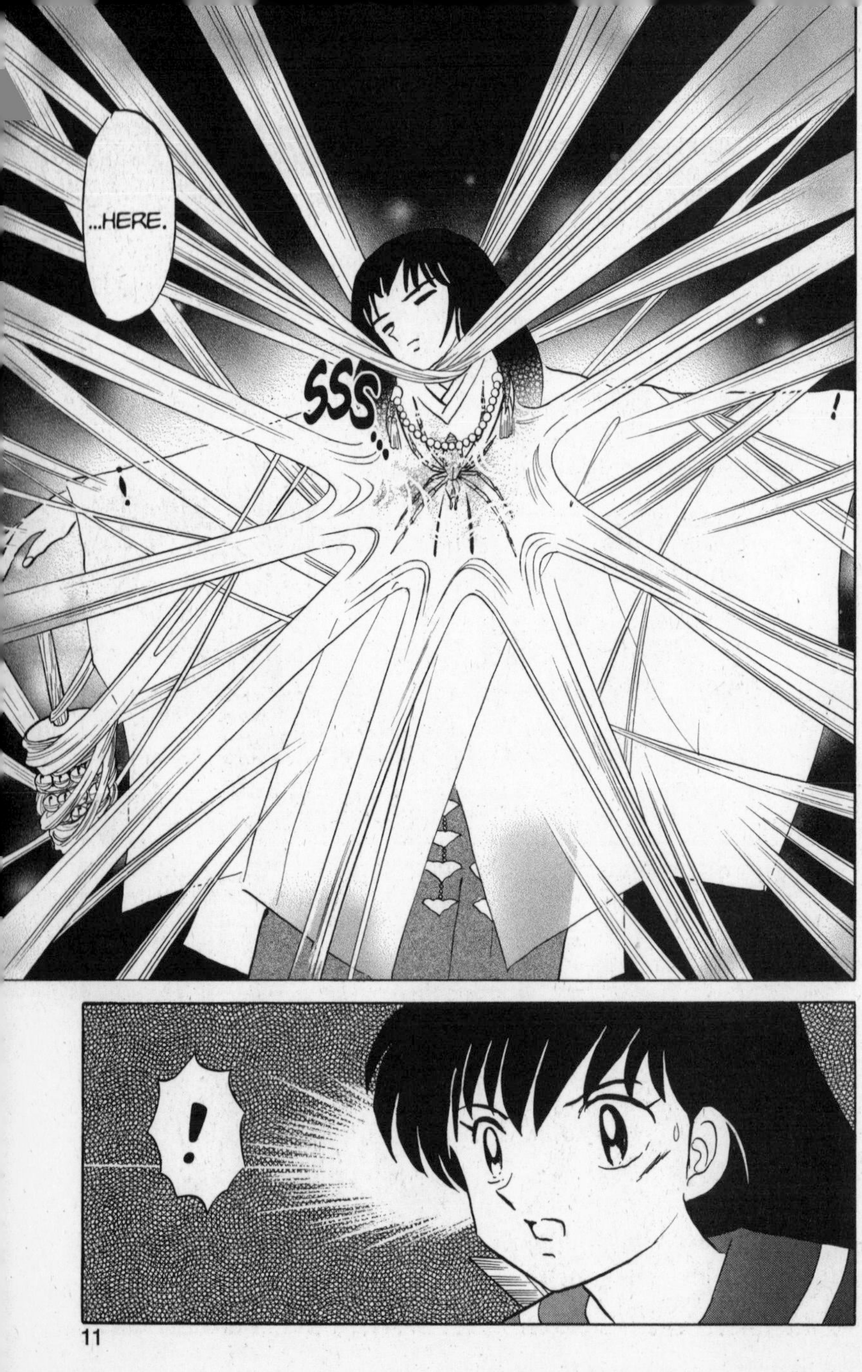
...HERE.
SSS...
!
!
!

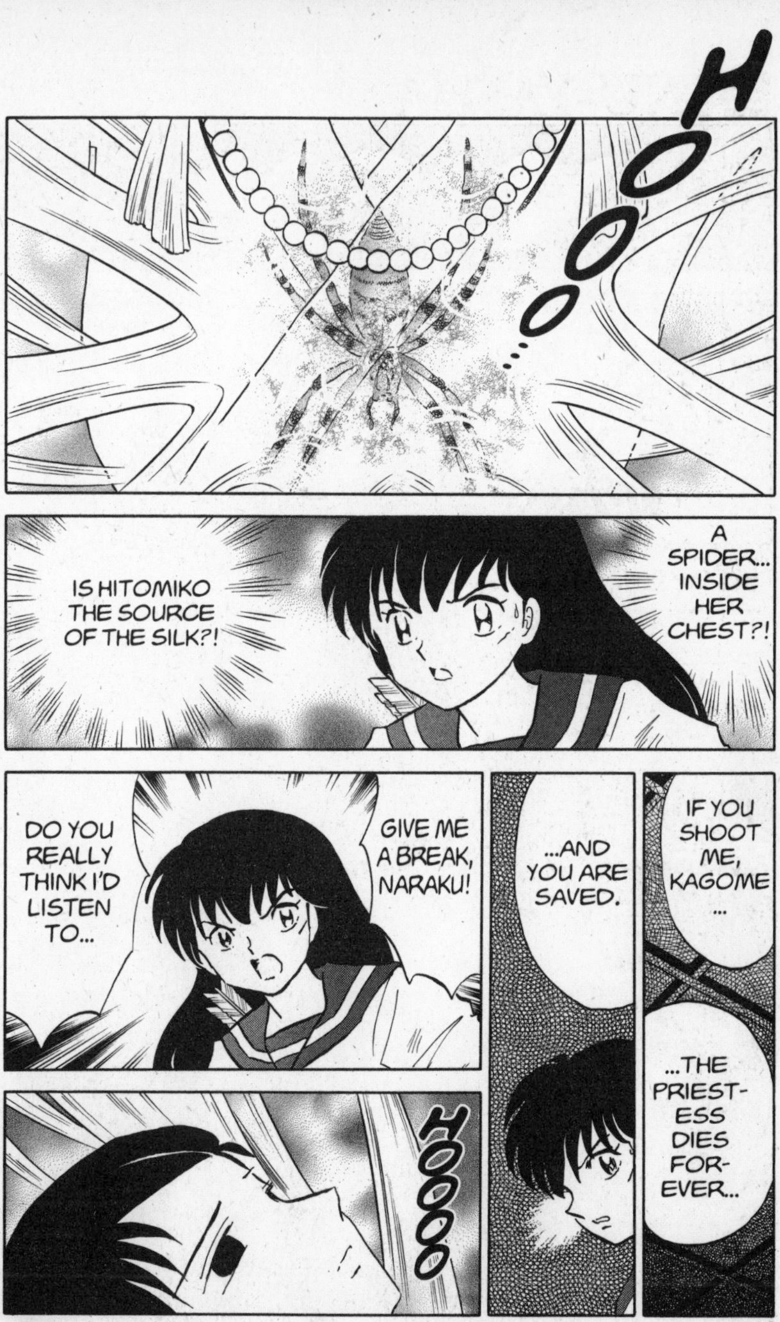
HOOOOO...
A SPIDER... INSIDE HER CHEST?!
IS HITOMIKO THE SOURCE OF THE SILK?!
IF YOU SHOOT ME, KAGOME ...
...THE PRIEST-ESS DIES FOR-EVER...
...AND YOU ARE SAVED.
GIVE ME A BREAK, NARAKU!
DO YOU REALLY THINK I'D LISTEN TO...
HOOOOO

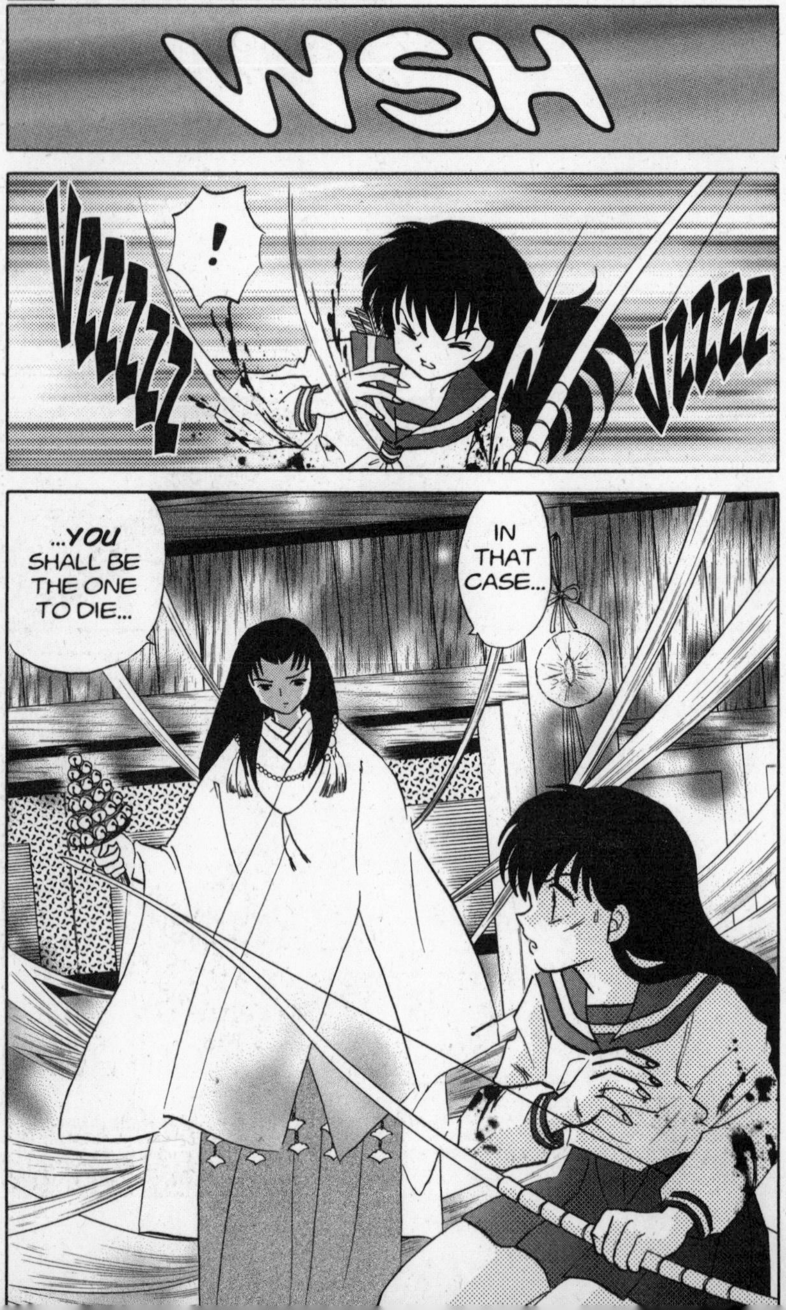
WSH
VZZZZZ
!
VZZZZZZZ
IN THAT CASE...
...YOU SHALL BE THE ONE TO DIE...

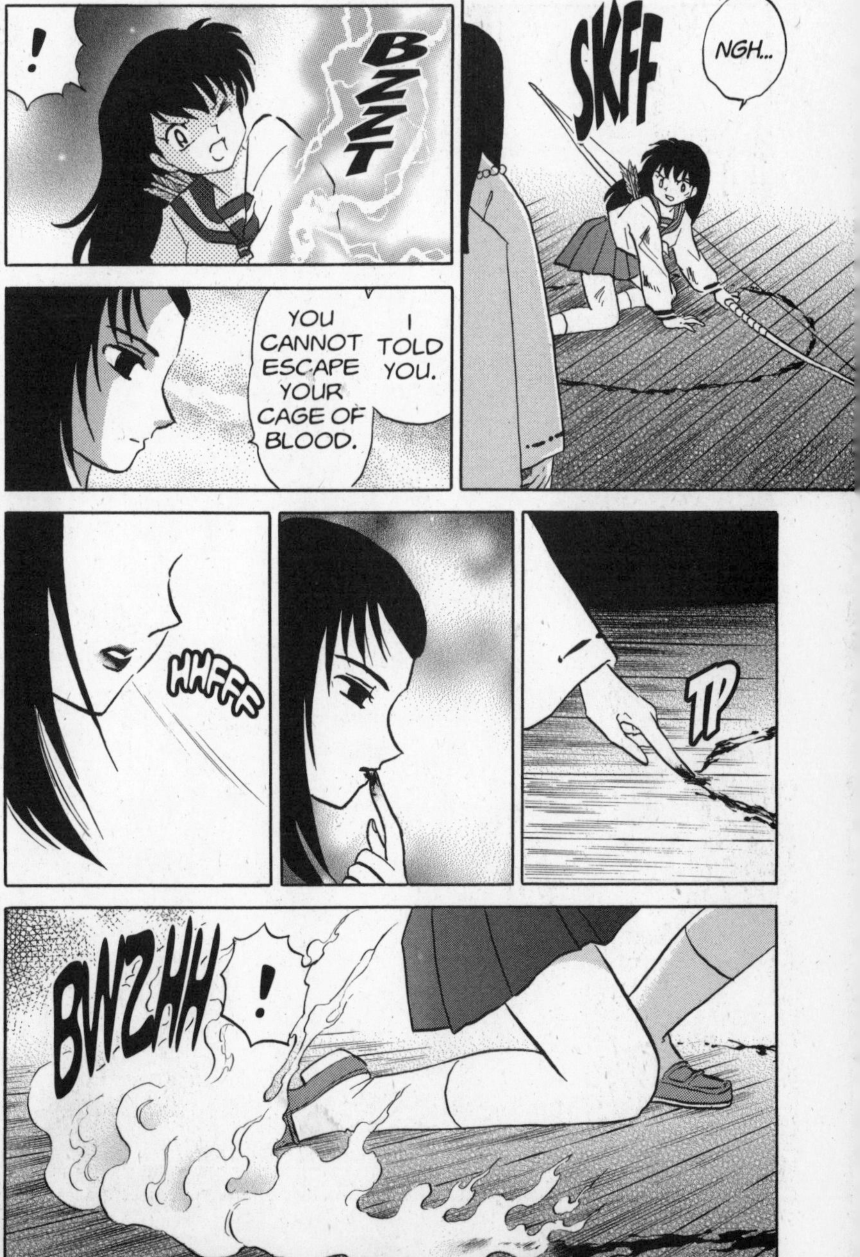
SKFF
NGH...
BZZT
!
I TOLD YOU.
YOU CANNOT ESCAPE YOUR CAGE OF BLOOD.
TP
HHFFF
!
BWZHH

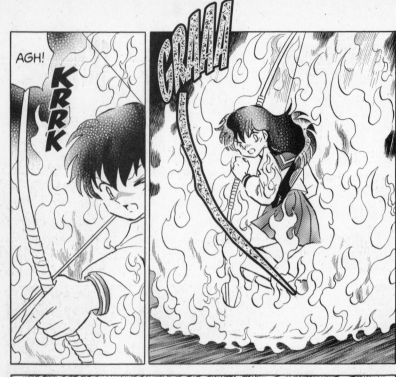

AGH!

KRRK

GRAAA

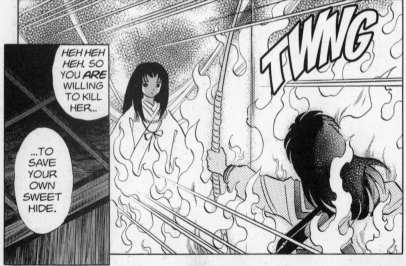

HEH HEH HEH. SO YOU **ARE** WILLING TO KILL HER...

...TO SAVE YOUR OWN SWEET HIDE.

TWNG

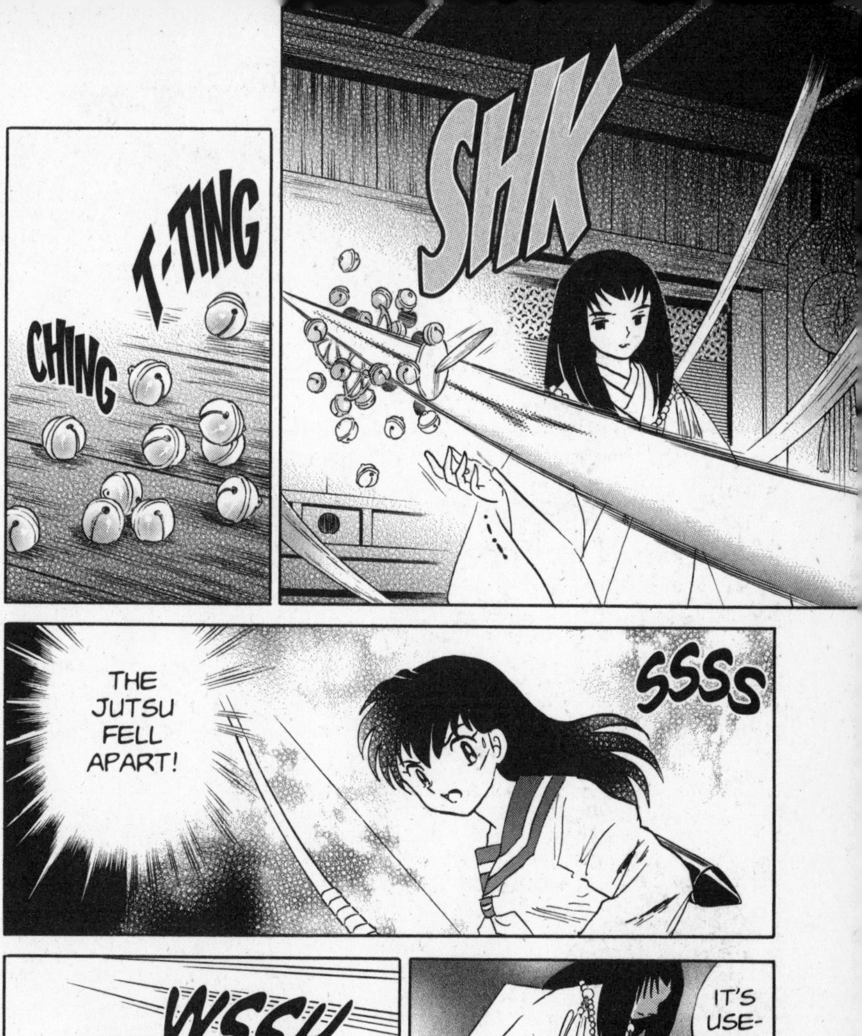
SHK
T-TING
CHING
SSSS
THE JUTSU FELL APART!
IT'S USE-LESS.
TING
WSSH

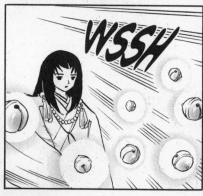

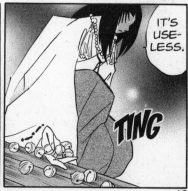

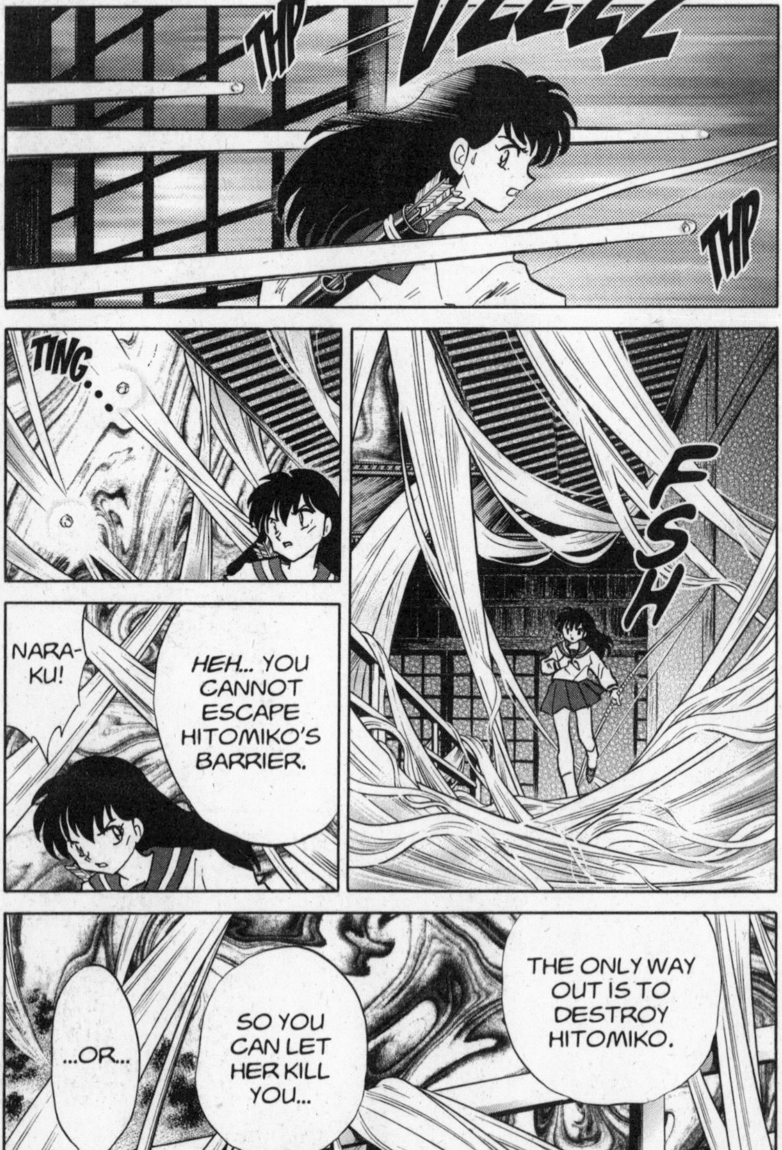
VZZZZ
THP
THP
FSH
TING...
HEH... YOU CANNOT ESCAPE HITOMIKO'S BARRIER.
NARA-KU!
THE ONLY WAY OUT IS TO DESTROY HITOMIKO.
SO YOU CAN LET HER KILL YOU...
...OR...

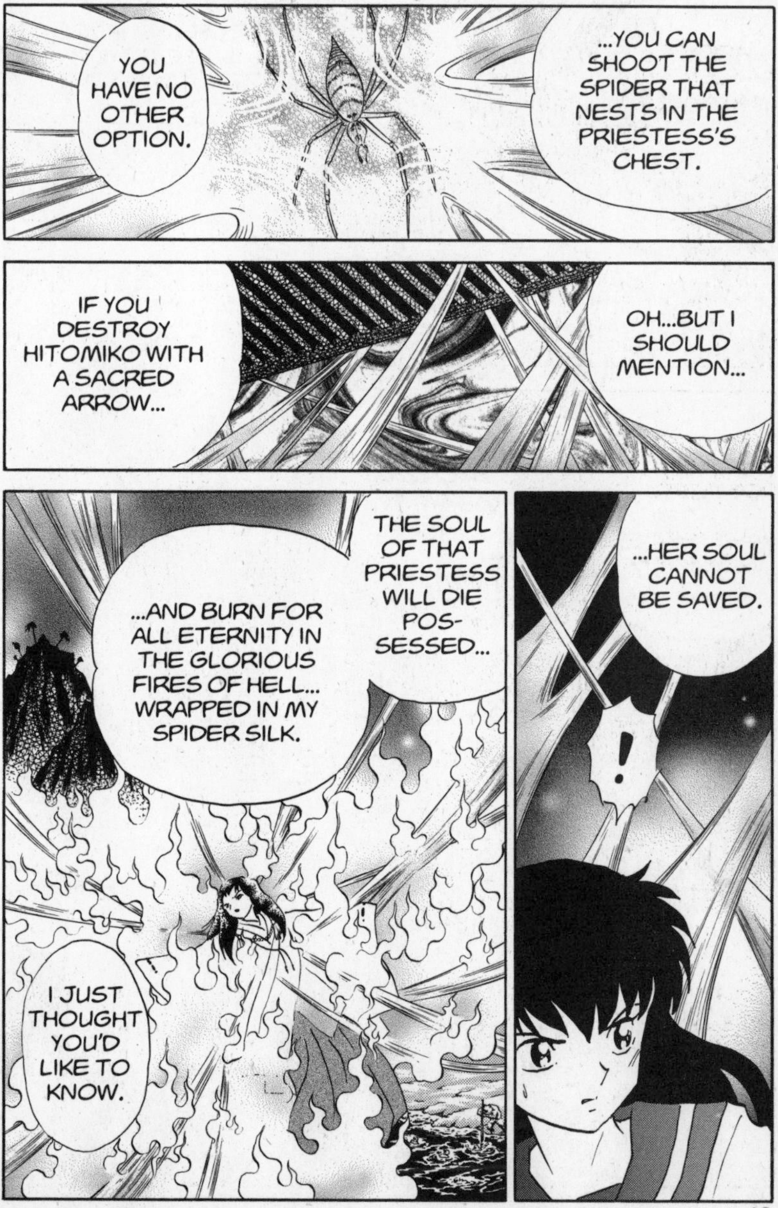
...YOU CAN SHOOT THE SPIDER THAT NESTS IN THE PRIESTESS'S CHEST.
YOU HAVE NO OTHER OPTION.
OH...BUT I SHOULD MENTION...
IF YOU DESTROY HITOMIKO WITH A SACRED ARROW...
...HER SOUL CANNOT BE SAVED.
!
THE SOUL OF THAT PRIESTESS WILL DIE POS-SESSED...
...AND BURN FOR ALL ETERNITY IN THE GLORIOUS FIRES OF HELL... WRAPPED IN MY SPIDER SILK.
I JUST THOUGHT YOU'D LIKE TO KNOW.

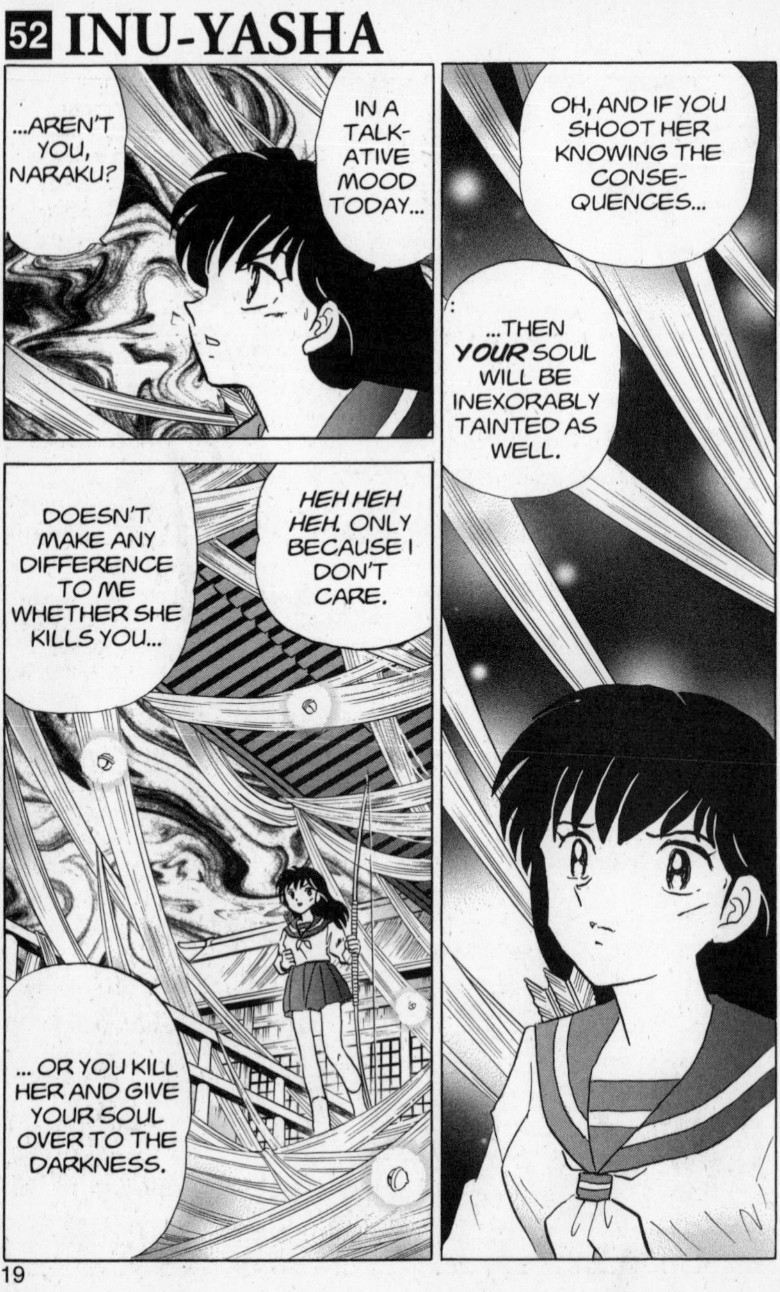
OH, AND IF YOU SHOOT HER KNOWING THE CONSE- QUENCES...
...THEN ***YOUR*** SOUL WILL BE INEXORABLY TAINTED AS WELL.
IN A TALK- ATIVE MOOD TODAY...
...AREN'T YOU, NARAKU?
HEH HEH HEH. ONLY BECAUSE I DON'T CARE.
DOESN'T MAKE ANY DIFFERENCE TO ME WHETHER SHE KILLS YOU...
... OR YOU KILL HER AND GIVE YOUR SOUL OVER TO THE DARKNESS.

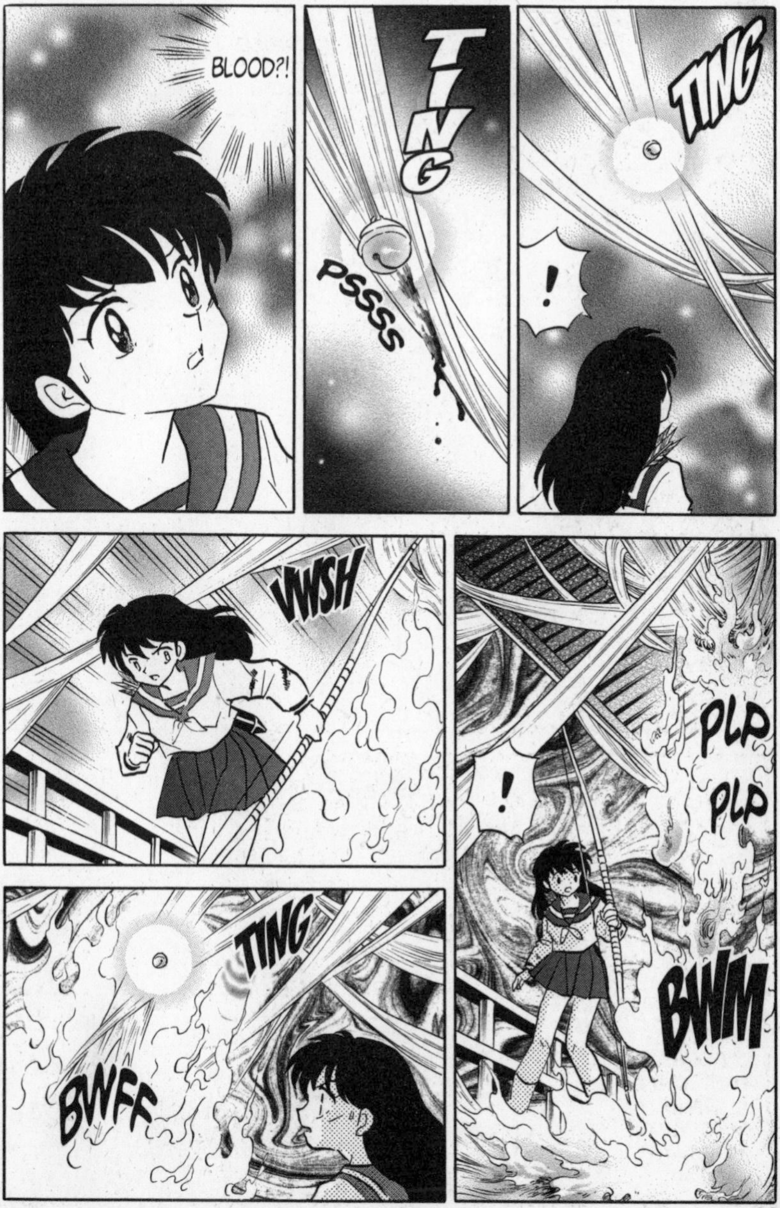
TING
!
TING
PSSSS
BLOOD?!
PLP
PLP
!
BWM
VWSH
TING
BWFF

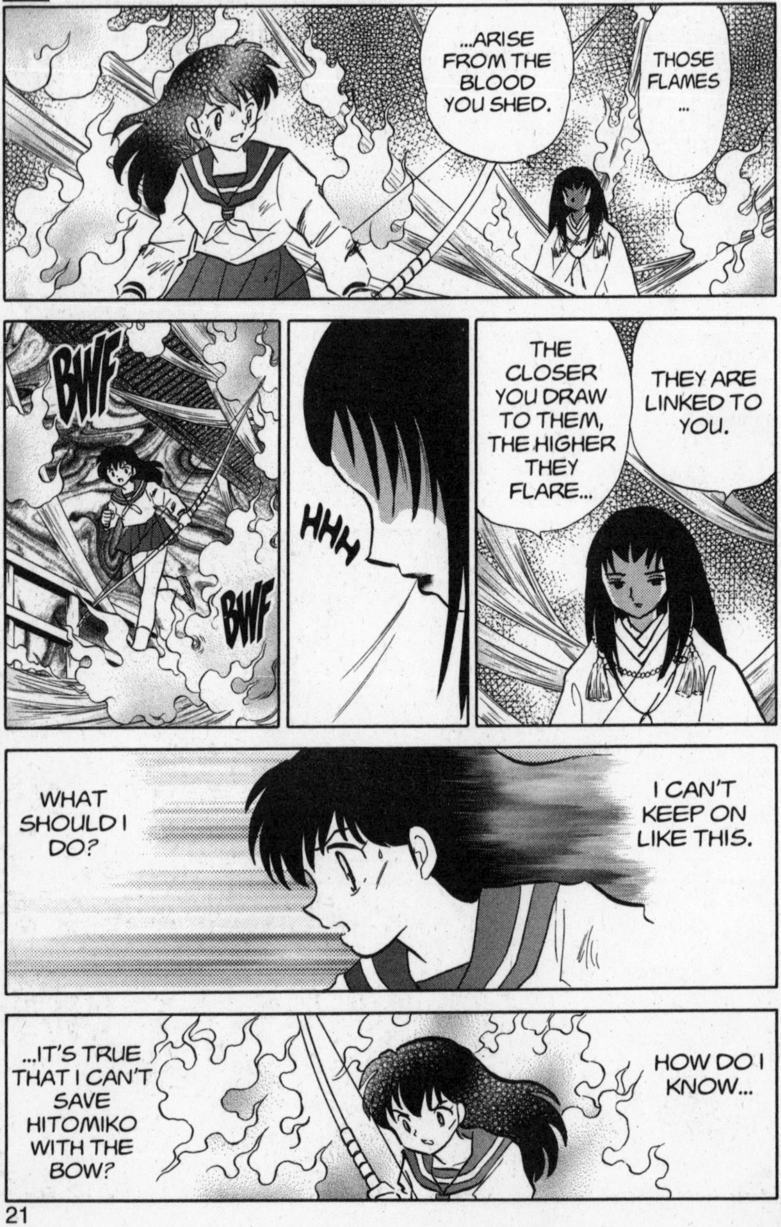
THOSE FLAMES ...
...ARISE FROM THE BLOOD YOU SHED.
THEY ARE LINKED TO YOU.
THE CLOSER YOU DRAW TO THEM, THE HIGHER THEY FLARE...
HHH
BWF
BWF
I CAN'T KEEP ON LIKE THIS.
WHAT SHOULD I DO?
HOW DO I KNOW...
...IT'S TRUE THAT I CAN'T SAVE HITOMIKO WITH THE BOW?

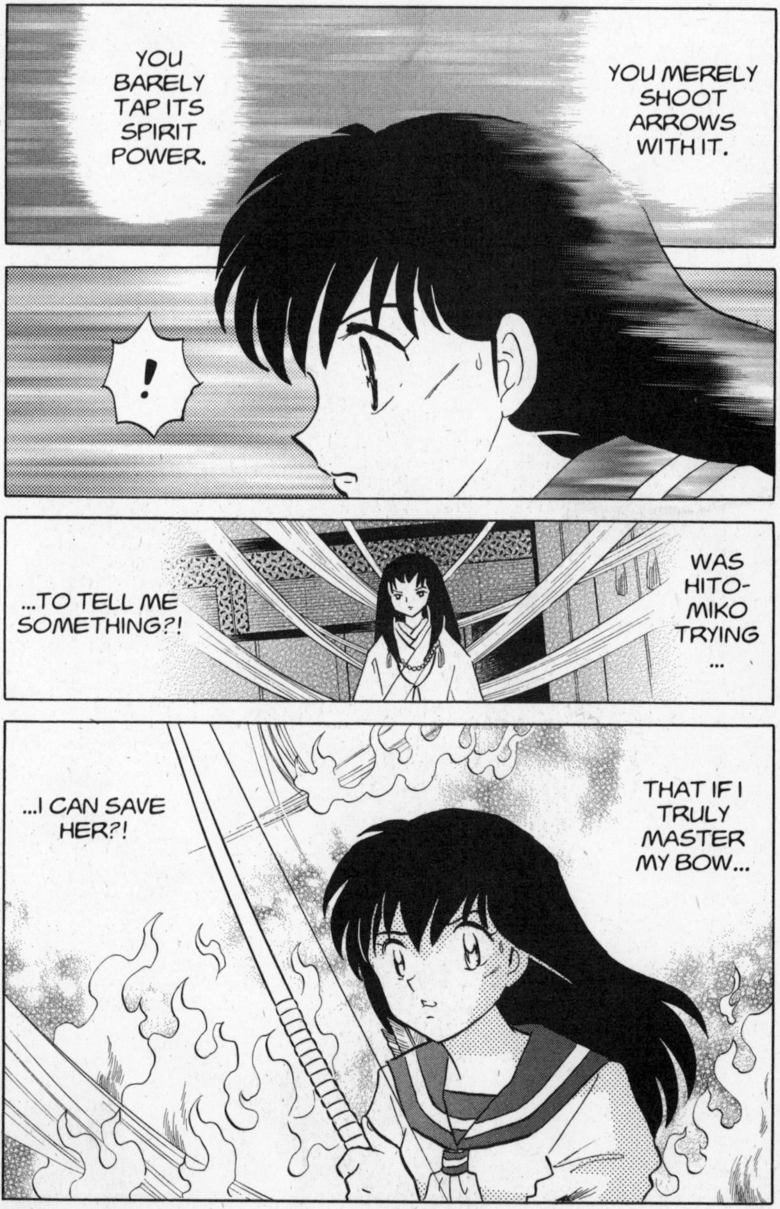
YOU MERELY SHOOT ARROWS WITH IT.
YOU BARELY TAP ITS SPIRIT POWER.
!
WAS HITO-MIKO TRYING ...
...TO TELL ME SOMETHING?!
THAT IF I TRULY MASTER MY BOW...
...I CAN SAVE HER?!

SCROLL 2

HELL

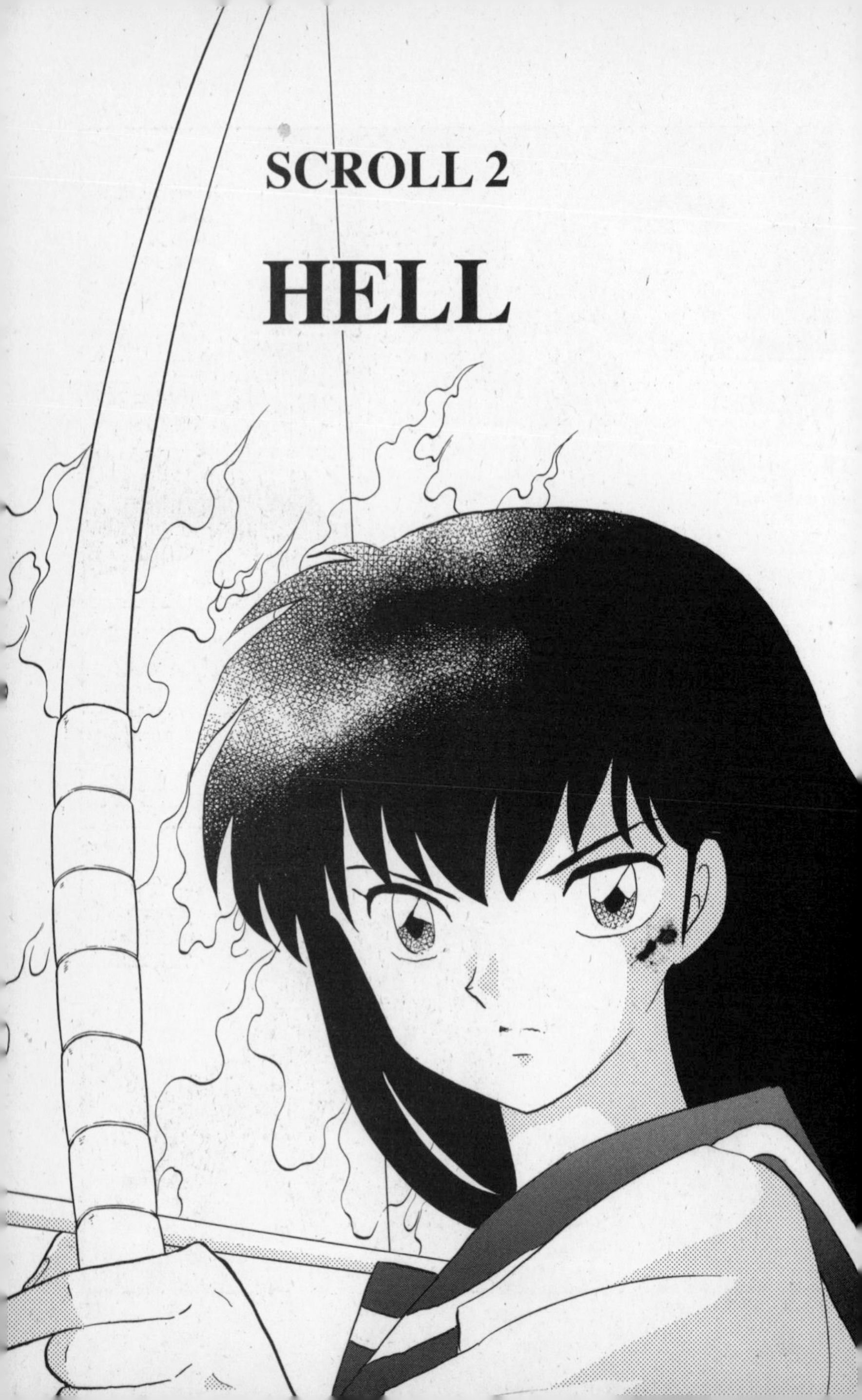

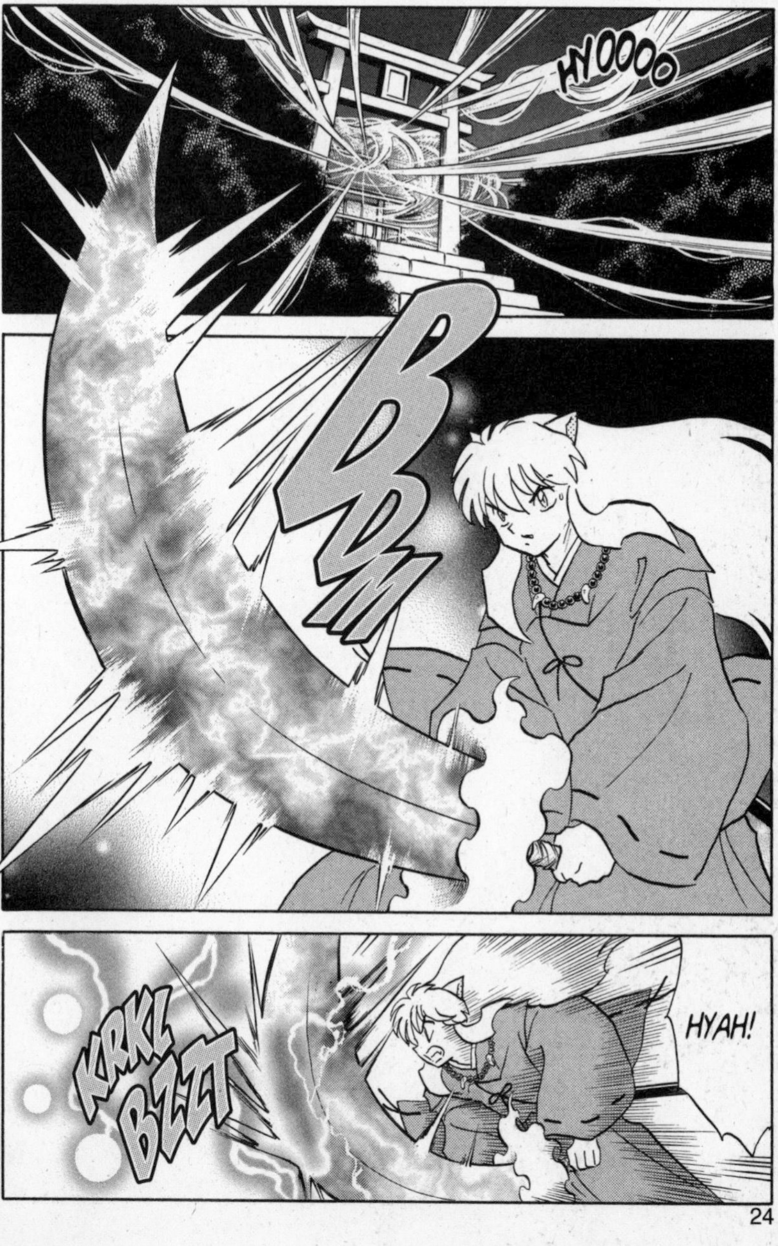
HYOOOO
BDUM
HYAH!
KRKL
BZZT

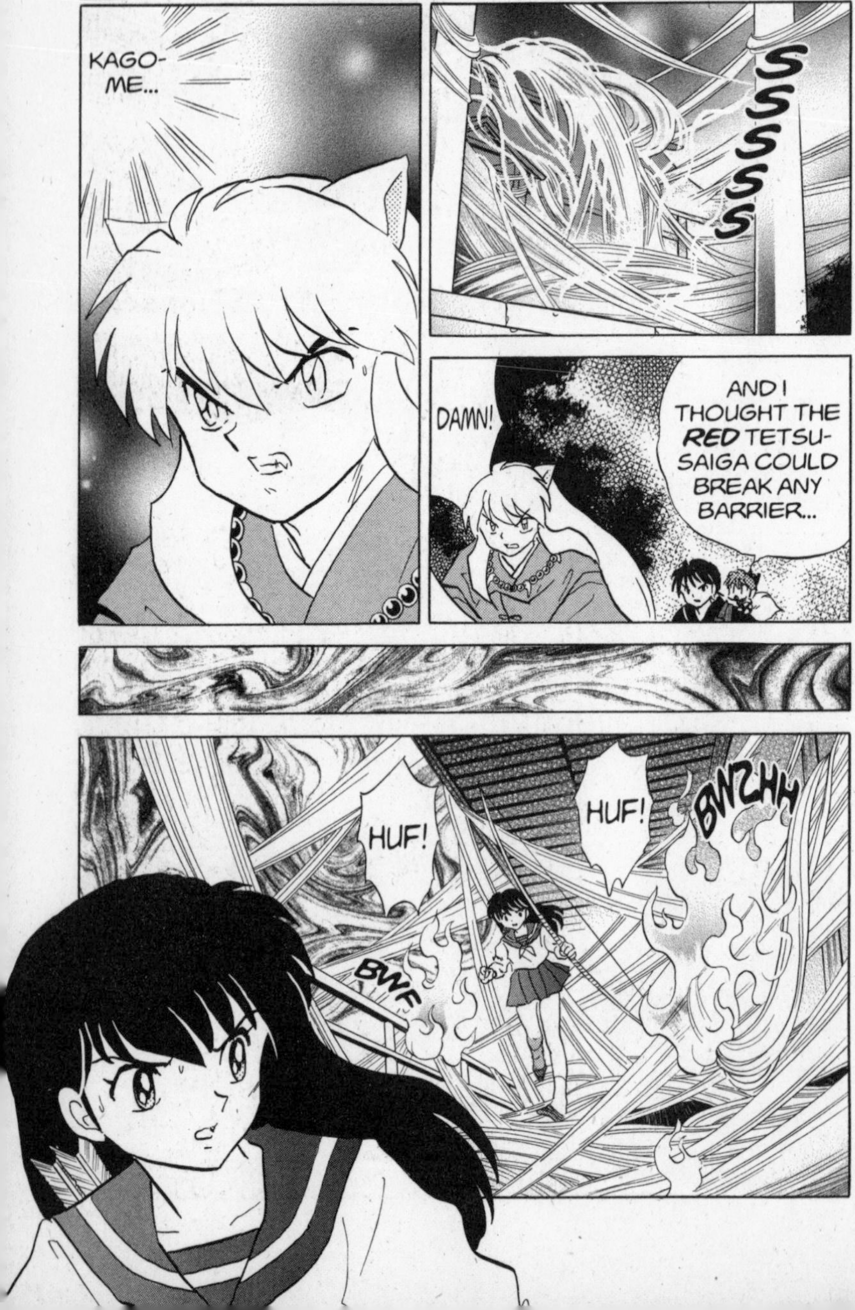
SSSSSS
AND I THOUGHT THE RED TETSU-SAIGA COULD BREAK ANY BARRIER...
DAMN!
KAGO-ME...
BWZHH
HUF!
HUF!
BWF

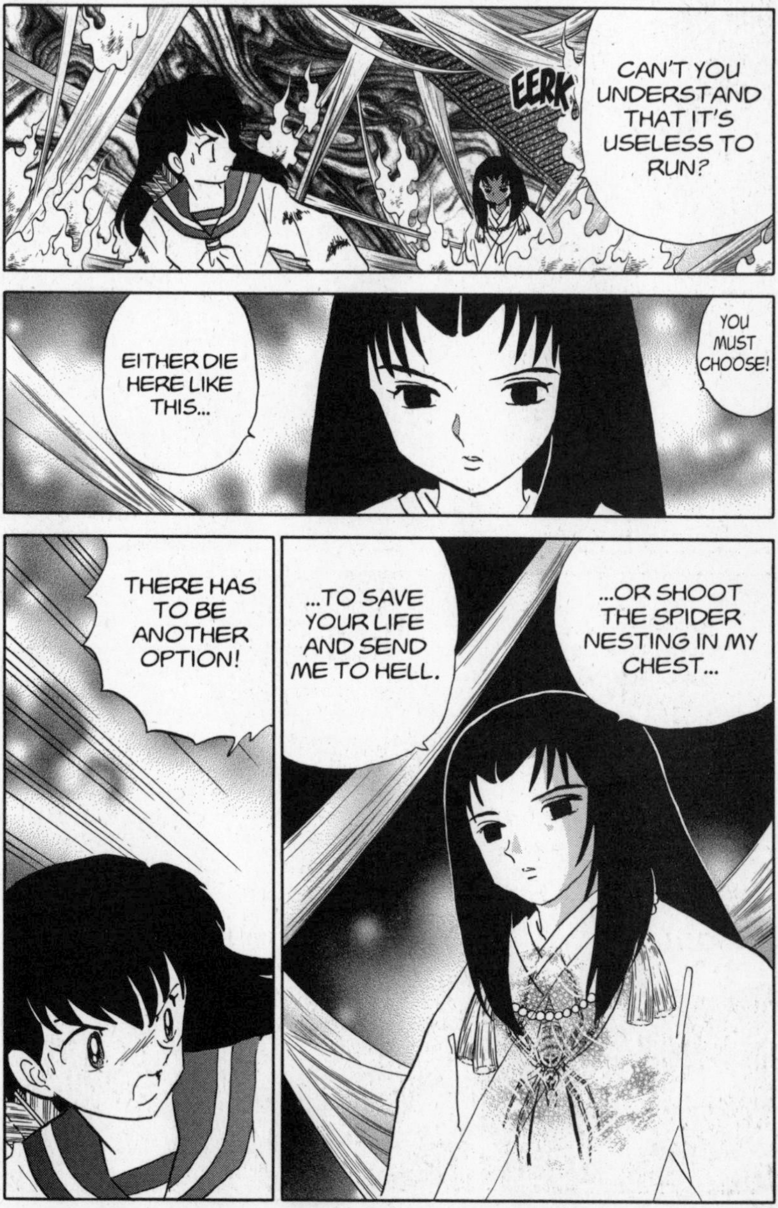
CAN'T YOU UNDERSTAND THAT IT'S USELESS TO RUN?
EERK
YOU MUST CHOOSE!
EITHER DIE HERE LIKE THIS...
...OR SHOOT THE SPIDER NESTING IN MY CHEST...
...TO SAVE YOUR LIFE AND SEND ME TO HELL.
THERE HAS TO BE ANOTHER OPTION!

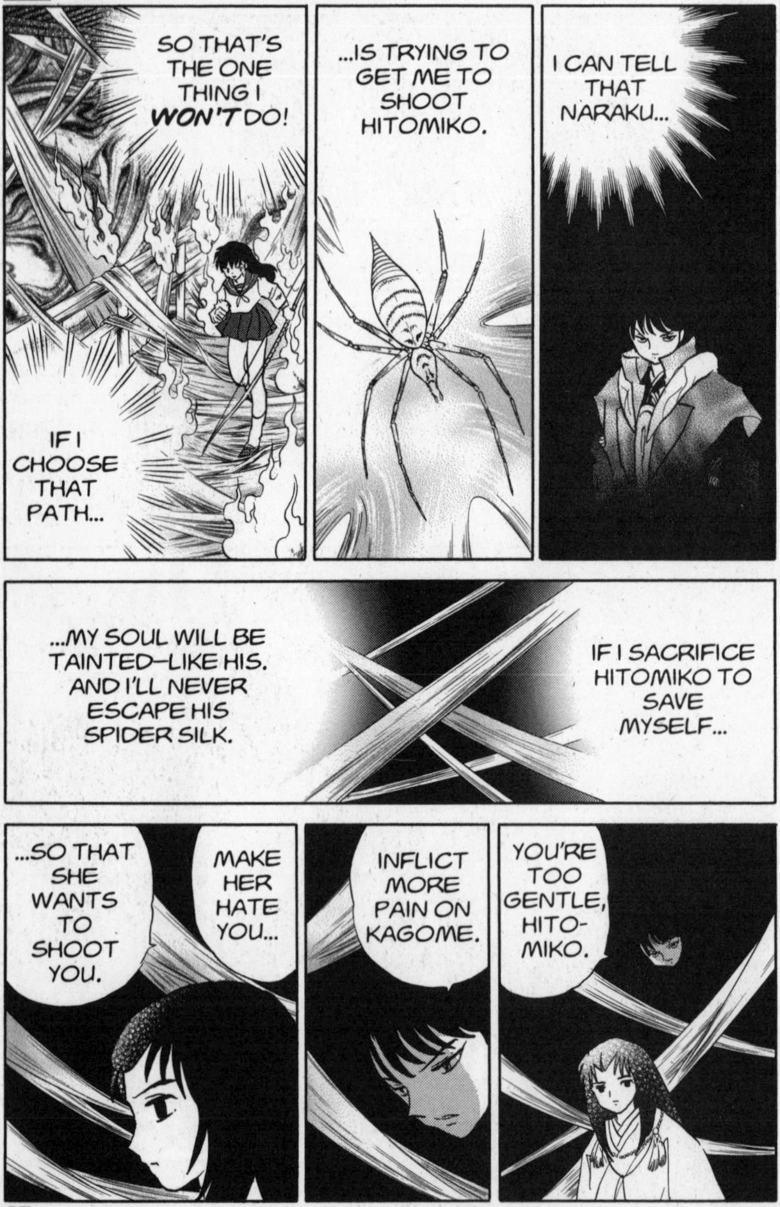
I CAN TELL THAT NARAKU...
...IS TRYING TO GET ME TO SHOOT HITOMIKO.
SO THAT'S THE ONE THING I *WON'T* DO!
IF I CHOOSE THAT PATH...
IF I SACRIFICE HITOMIKO TO SAVE MYSELF...
...MY SOUL WILL BE TAINTED—LIKE HIS. AND I'LL NEVER ESCAPE HIS SPIDER SILK.
YOU'RE TOO GENTLE, HITO-MIKO.
INFLICT MORE PAIN ON KAGOME.
MAKE HER HATE YOU...
...SO THAT SHE WANTS TO SHOOT YOU.

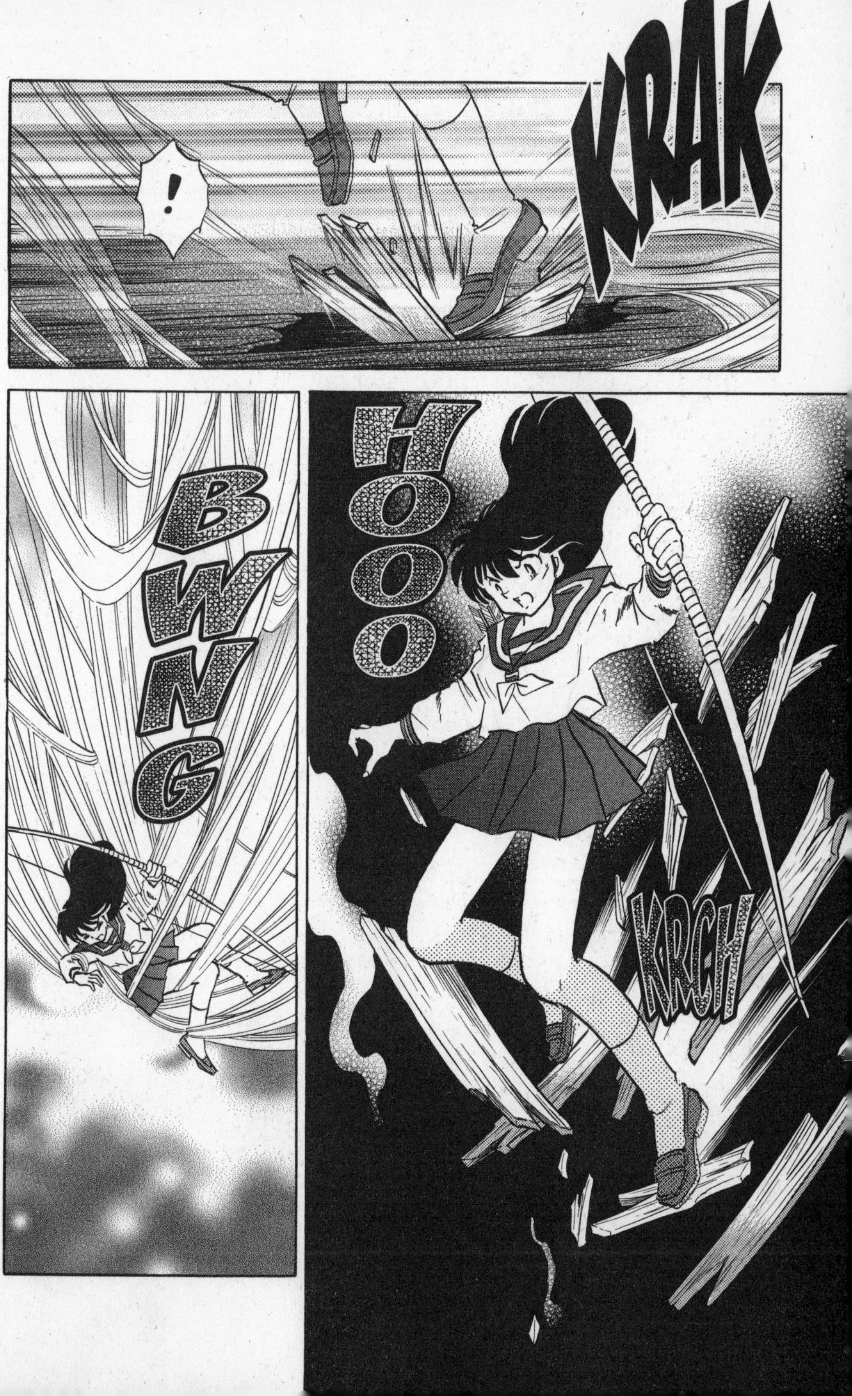
KRAK
!
HOOO
KRCH
BWNG

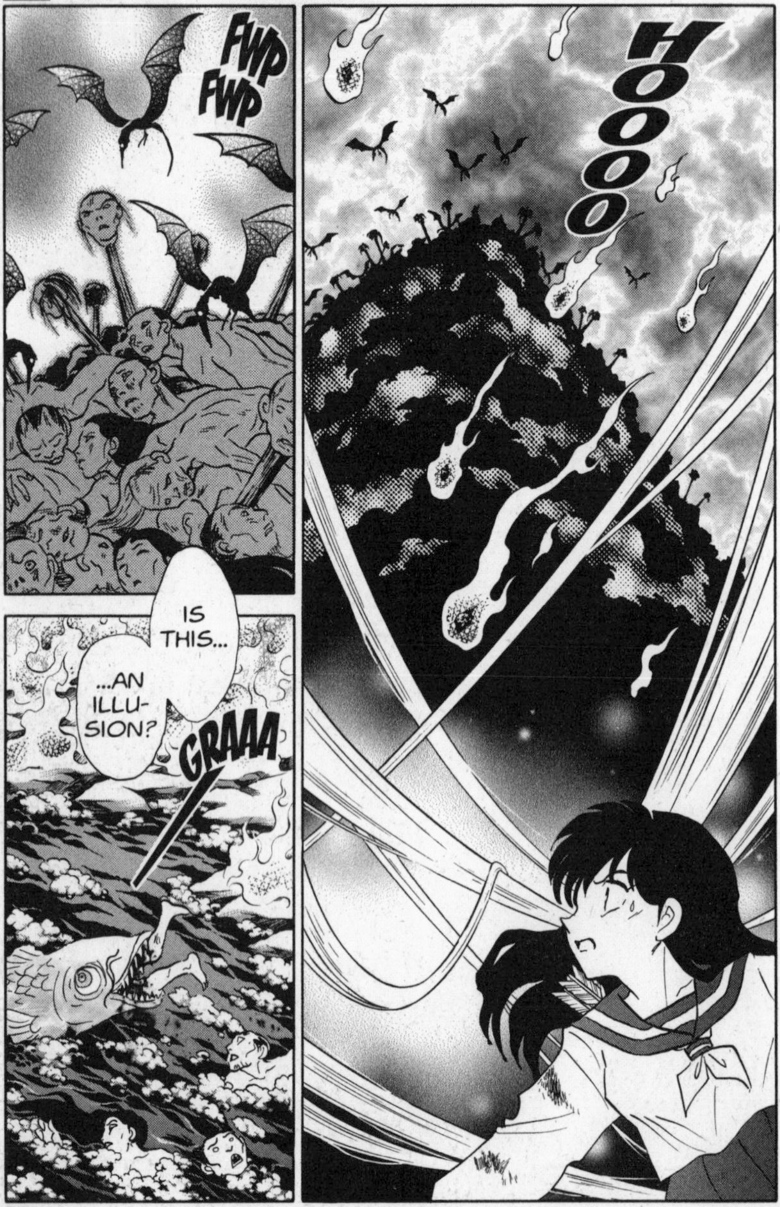
HOOOOO
FWP FWP
IS THIS...
...AN ILLUSION?
GRAAA

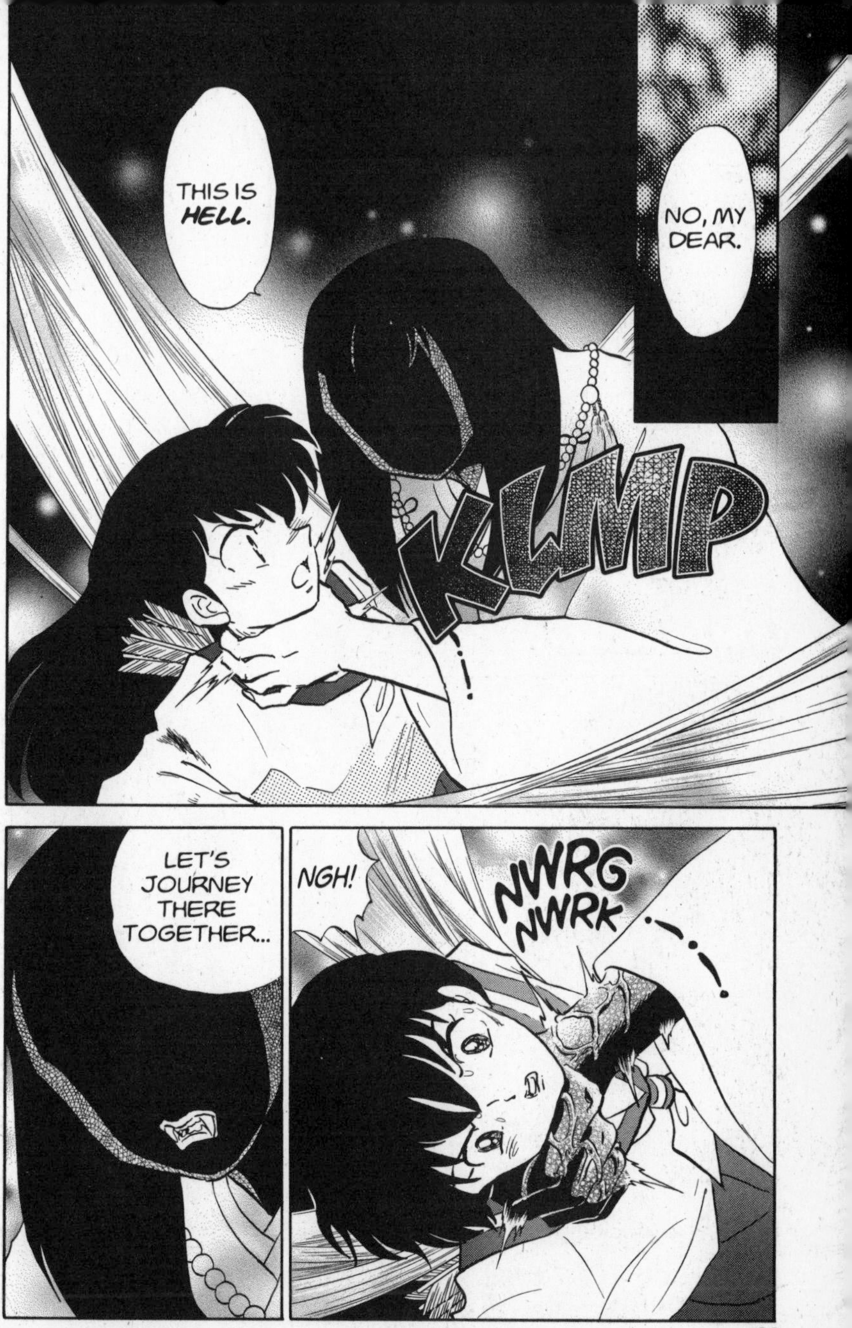
NO, MY DEAR.
THIS IS HELL.
KLUMP
NWRG NWRK
NGH!
LET'S JOURNEY THERE TOGETHER...

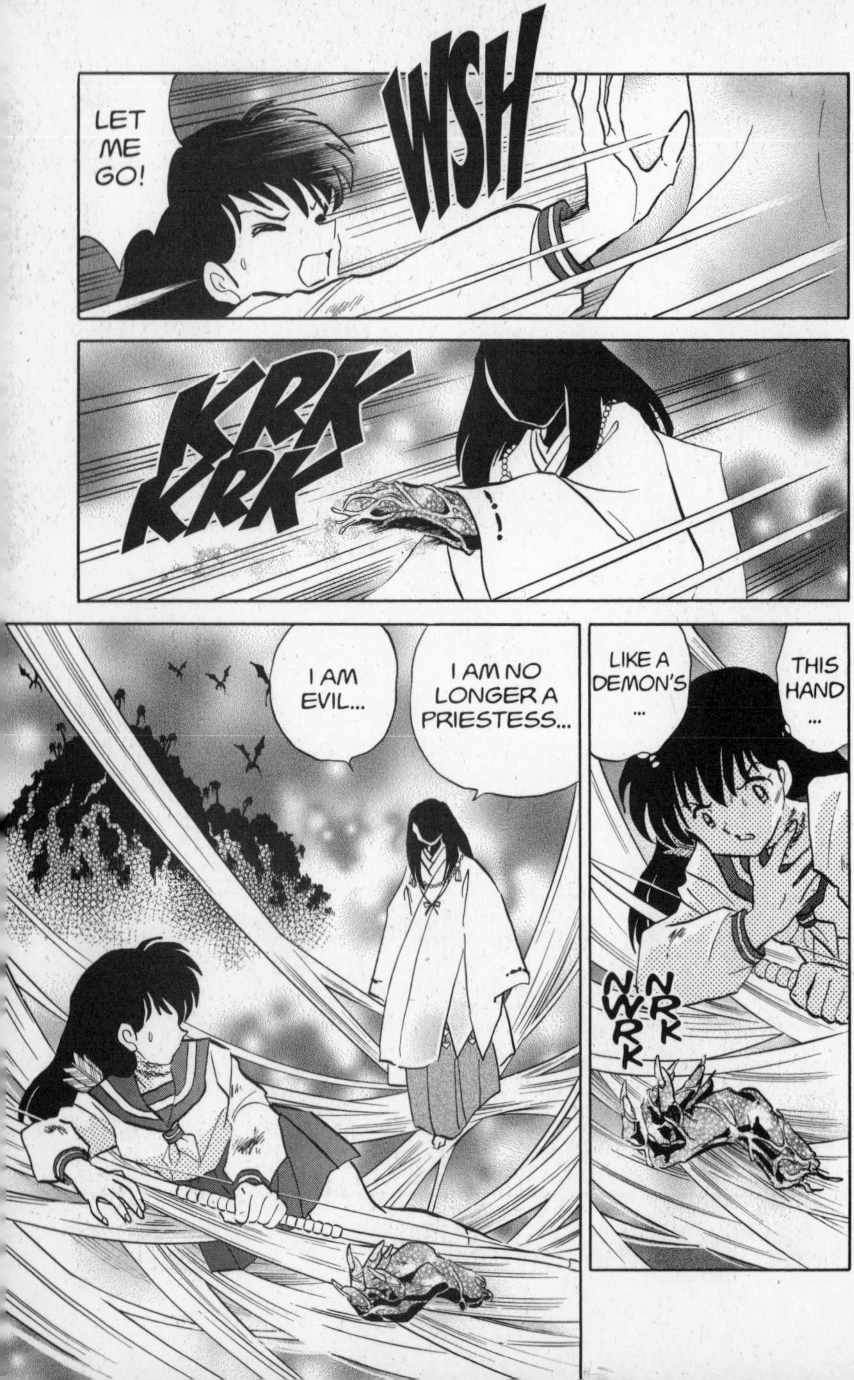
WSH
LET ME GO!
KRK KRK
THIS HAND...
LIKE A DEMON'S...
NRK
NWRK
I AM NO LONGER A PRIESTESS...
I AM EVIL...

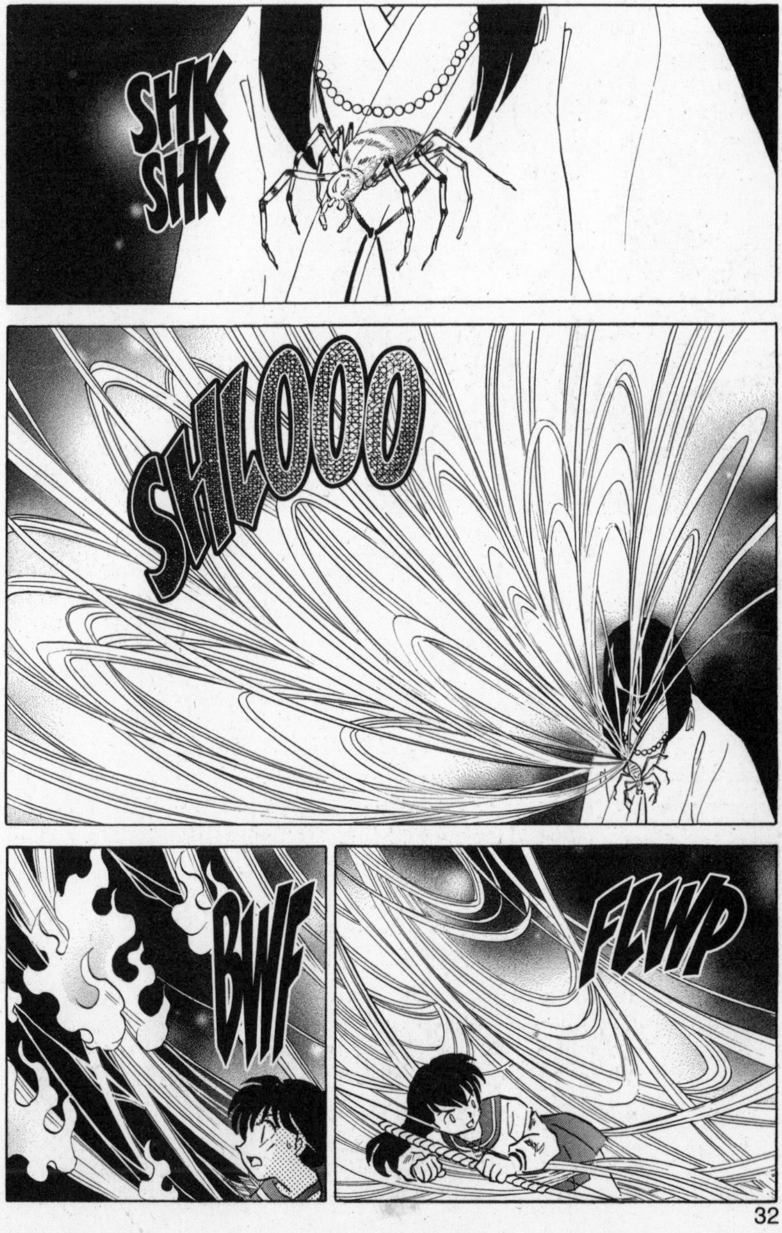
SHK
SHK
SHLOOO
FLWP
BWF

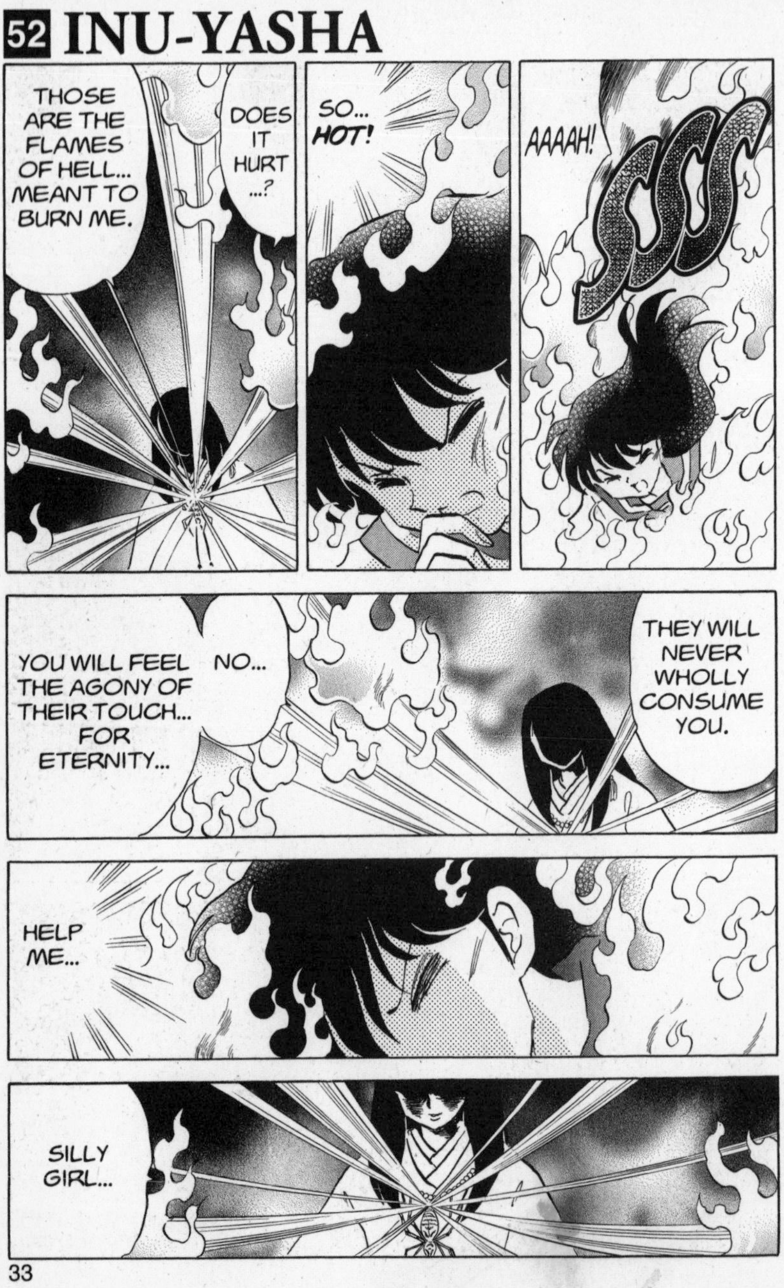
AAAAH!
SO... HOT!
DOES IT HURT ...?
THOSE ARE THE FLAMES OF HELL... MEANT TO BURN ME.
THEY WILL NEVER WHOLLY CONSUME YOU.
NO...
YOU WILL FEEL THE AGONY OF THEIR TOUCH... FOR ETERNITY...
HELP ME...
SILLY GIRL...

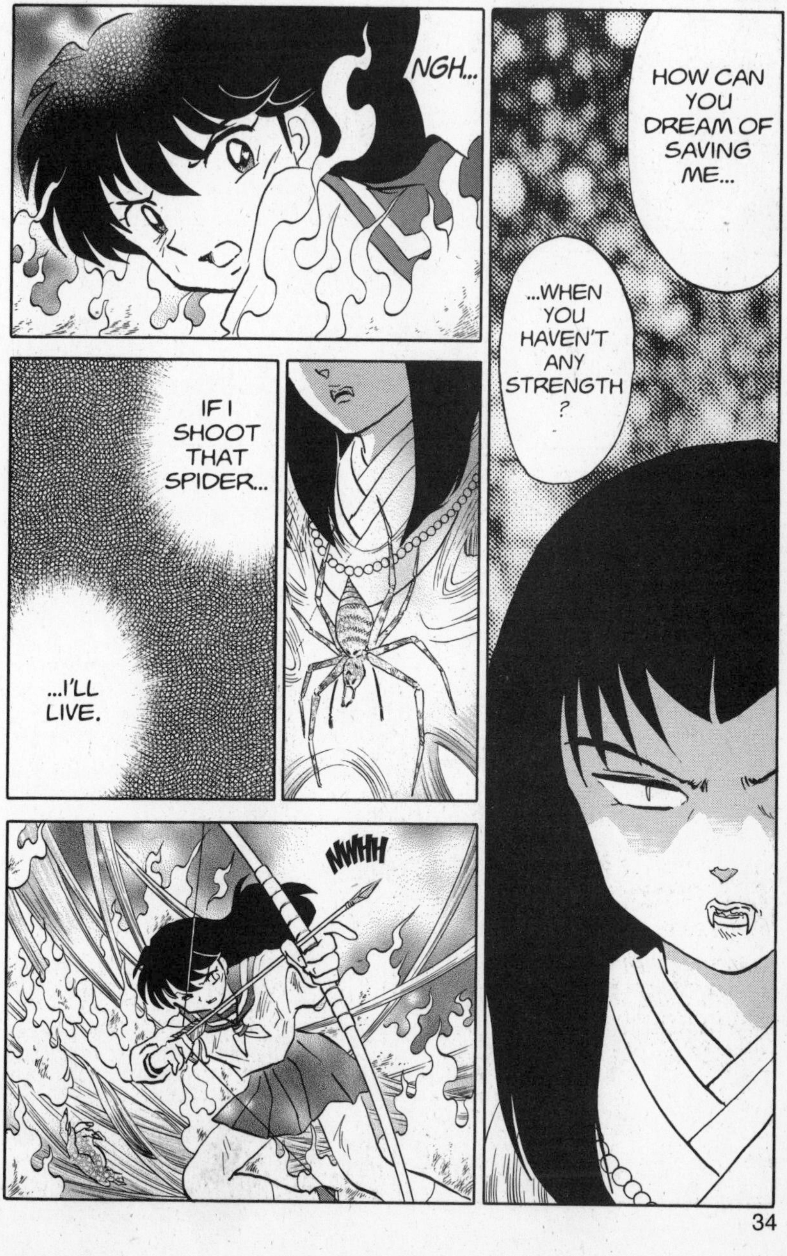
HOW CAN YOU DREAM OF SAVING ME...
...WHEN YOU HAVEN'T ANY STRENGTH?
NGH...
IF I SHOOT THAT SPIDER...
...I'LL LIVE.
NWHH

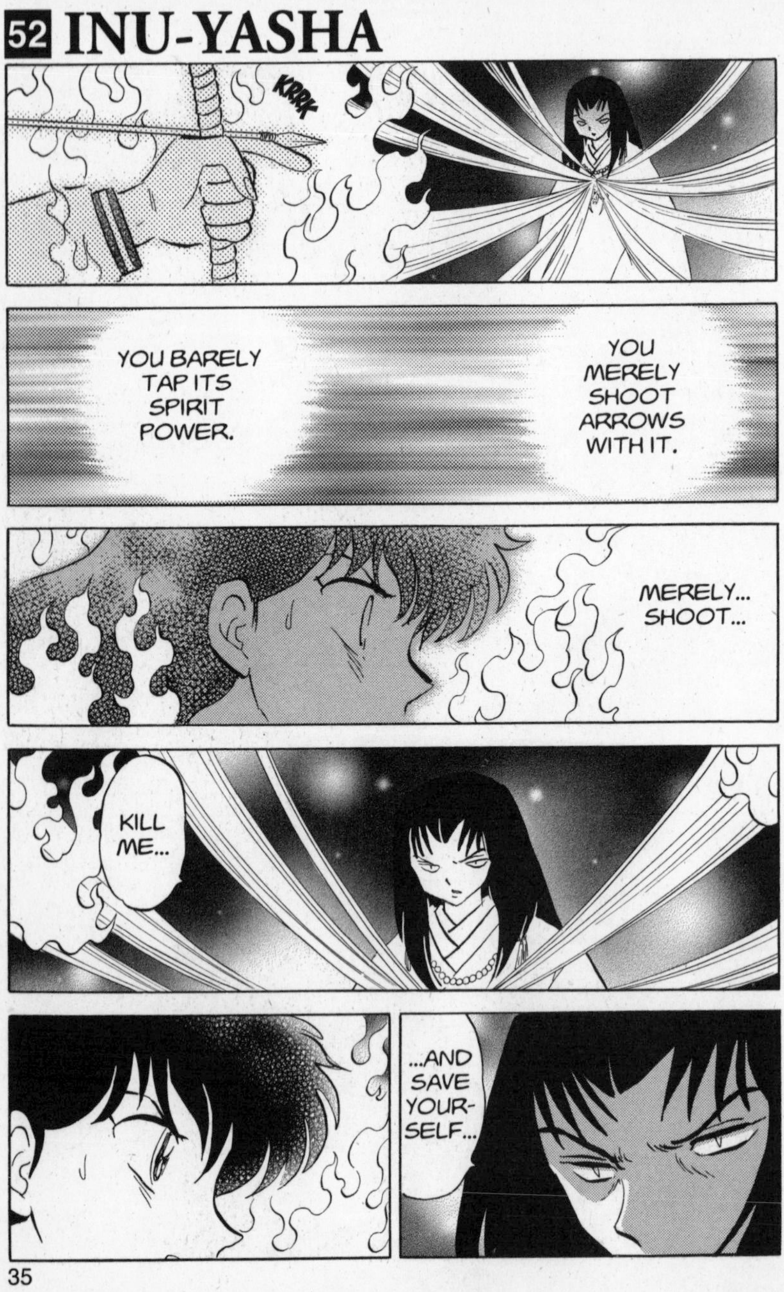
KRRK
YOU MERELY SHOOT ARROWS WITH IT.
YOU BARELY TAP ITS SPIRIT POWER.
MERELY... SHOOT...
KILL ME...
...AND SAVE YOUR-SELF...

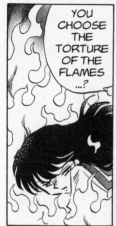

DRWP
YOU WON'T?
WHAT A FOOL ...
YOU CHOOSE THE TORTURE OF THE FLAMES ...?
...
WHEN HER HAND THROTTLED ME...
I FELT EMOTIONS FLOWING INTO ME...
THERE WAS FEAR... BUT SOME-THING ELSE TOO...

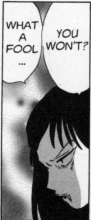

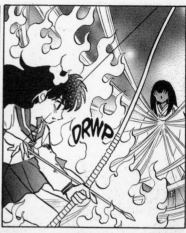

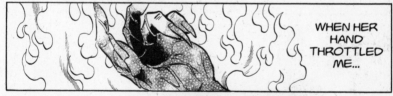

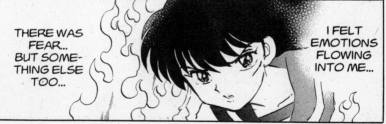

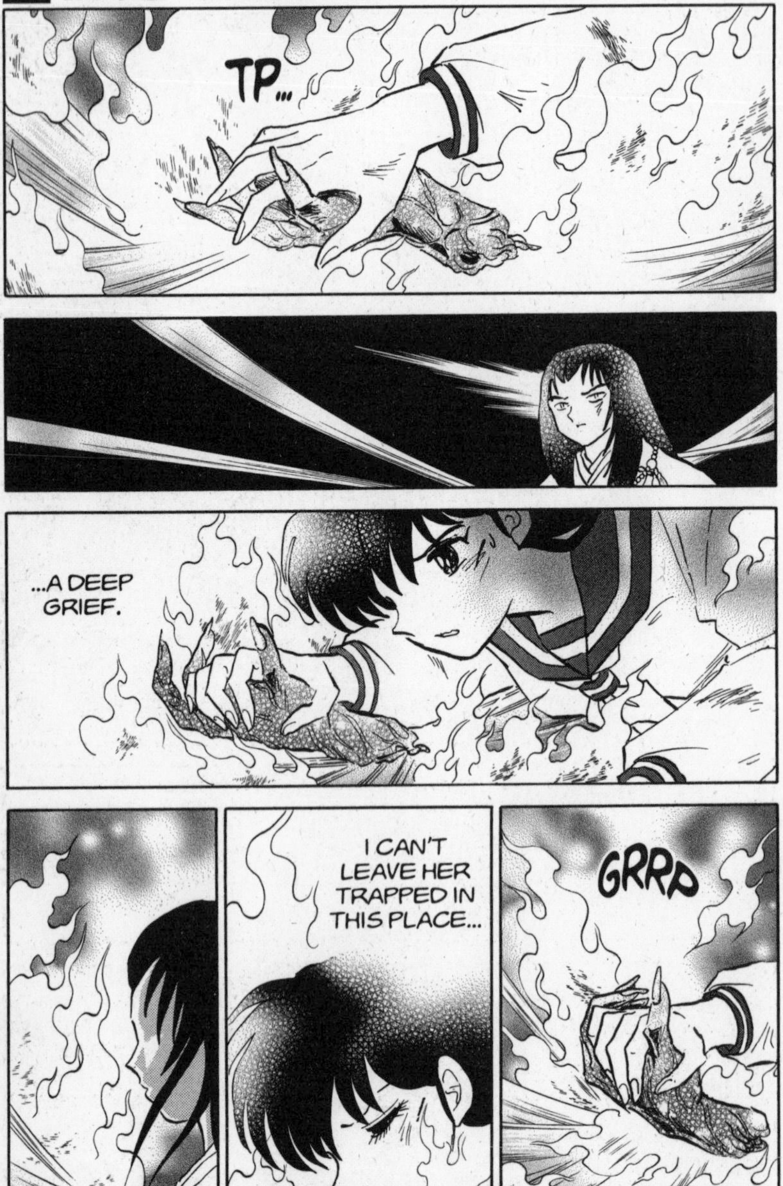

TP...
...A DEEP GRIEF.
GRRP
I CAN'T LEAVE HER TRAPPED IN THIS PLACE...

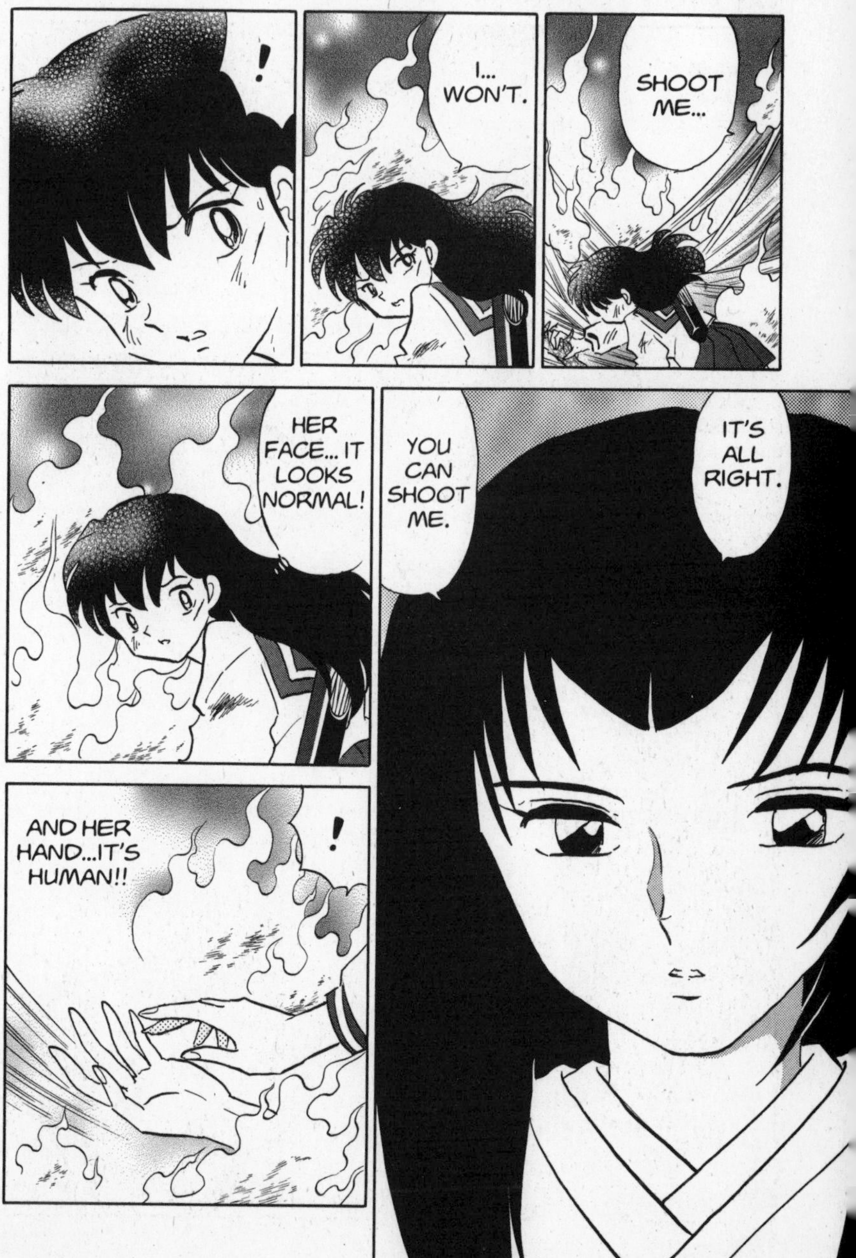
SHOOT ME...
I... WON'T.
!
IT'S ALL RIGHT.
YOU CAN SHOOT ME.
HER FACE... IT LOOKS NORMAL!
AND HER HAND...IT'S HUMAN!!
!

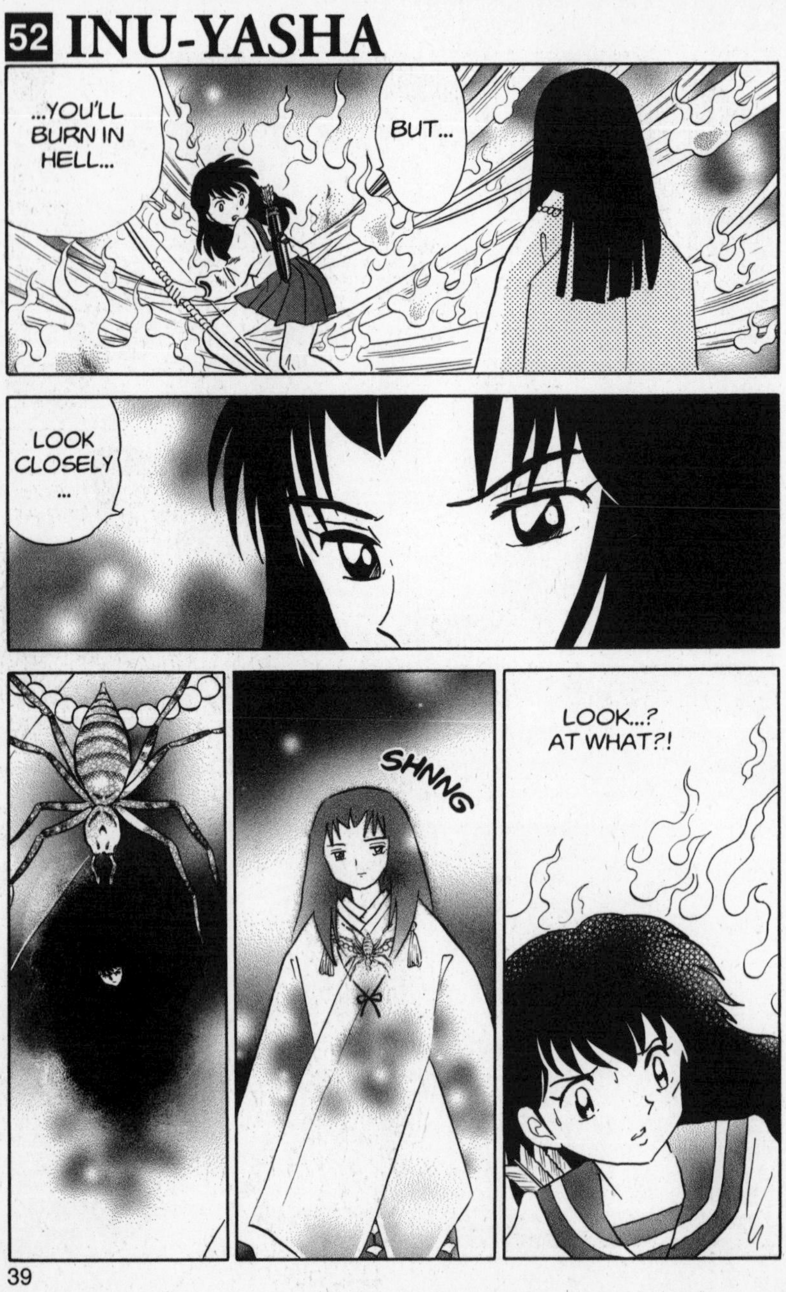
BUT...
...YOU'LL BURN IN HELL...
LOOK CLOSELY ...
LOOK...? AT WHAT?!
SHNNG

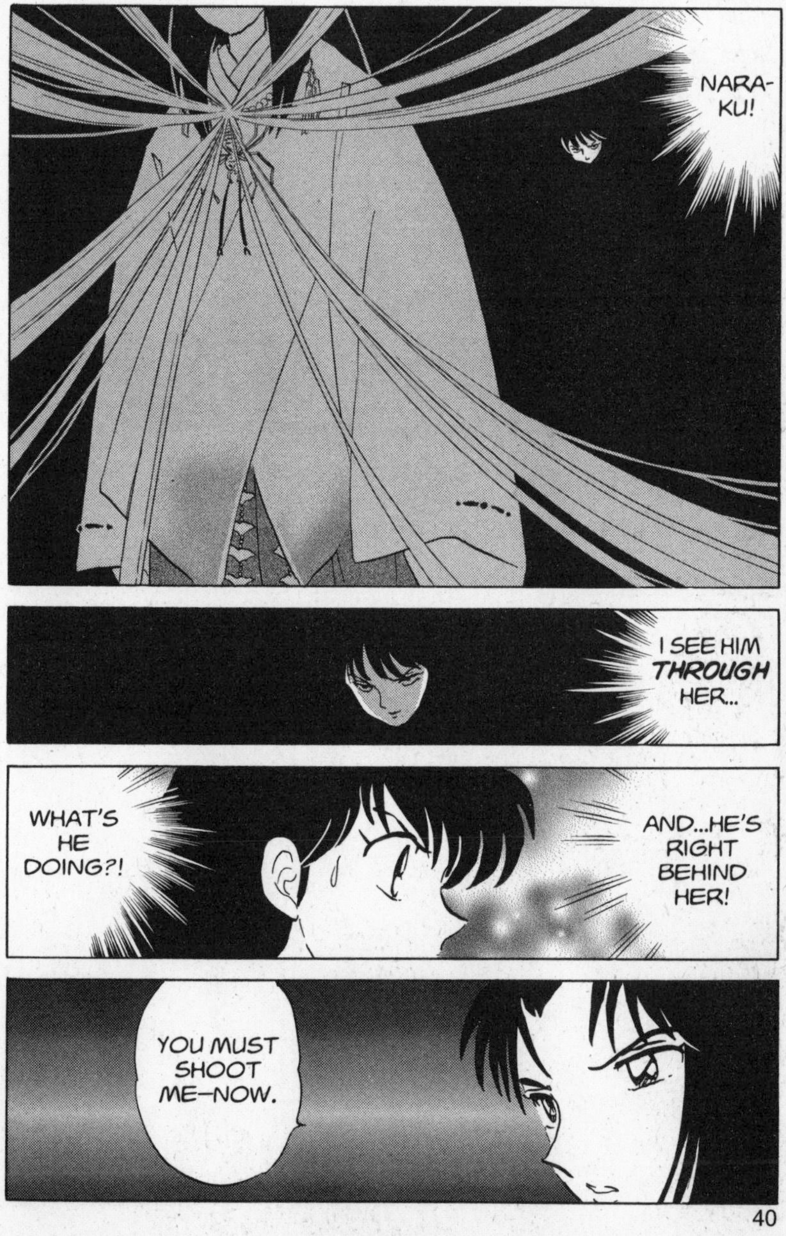
NARAKU!
I SEE HIM THROUGH HER...
AND...HE'S RIGHT BEHIND HER!
WHAT'S HE DOING?!
YOU MUST SHOOT ME—NOW.

SCROLL 3

KAGOME'S POWER

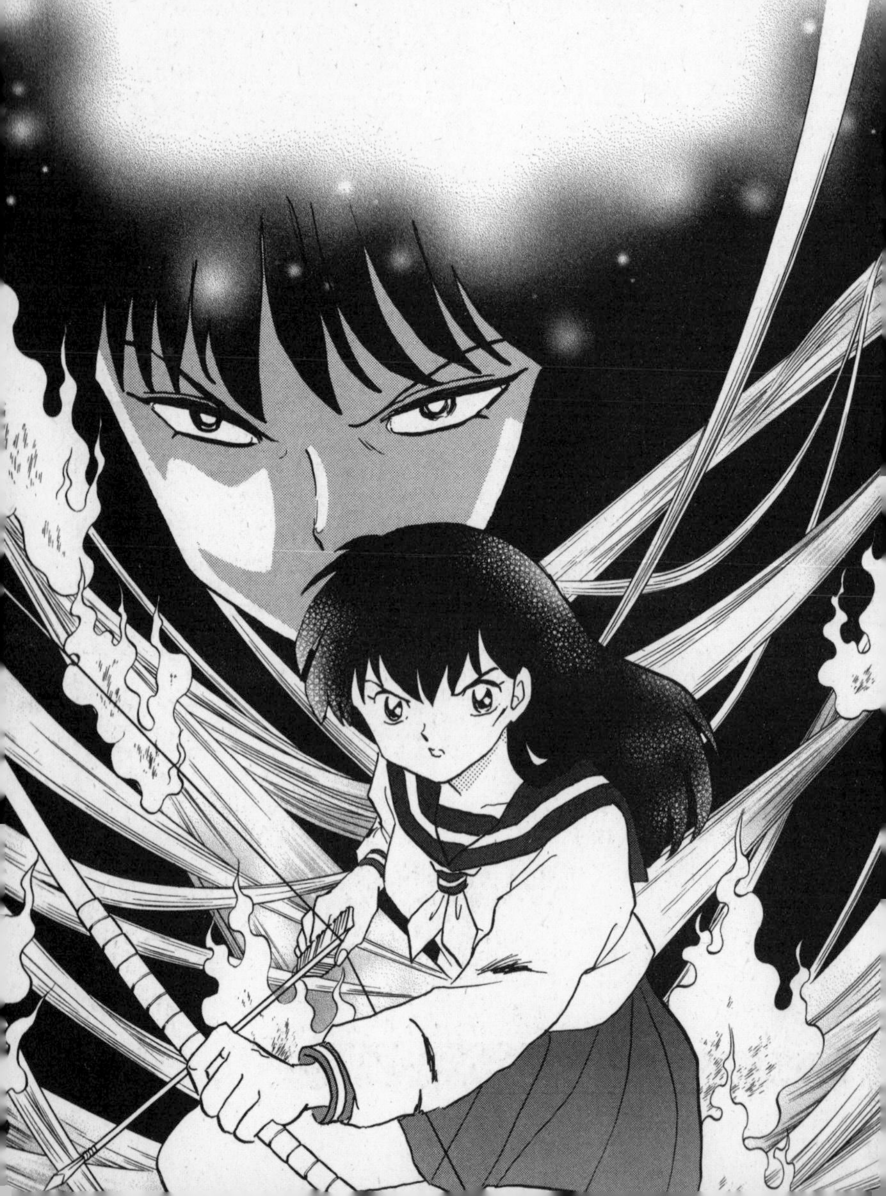

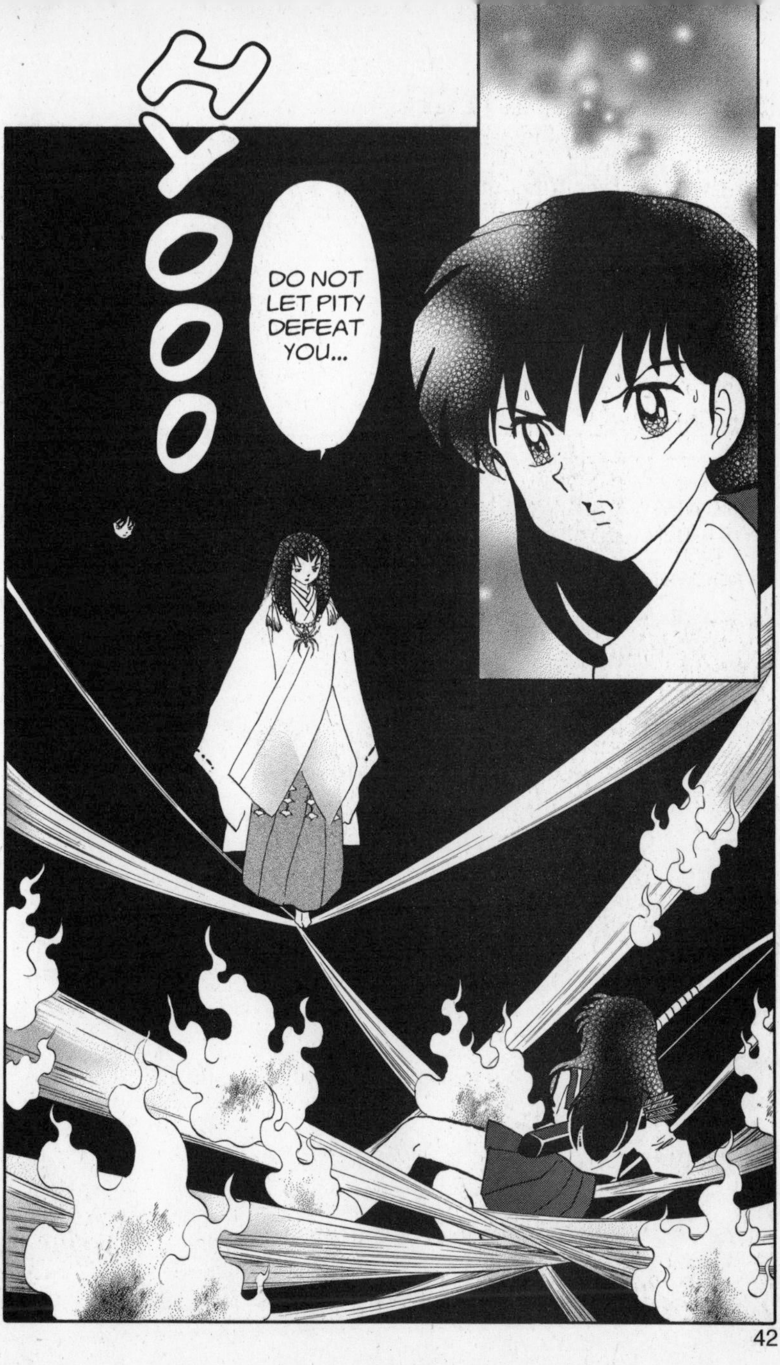
HYOOO
DO NOT LET PITY DEFEAT YOU...

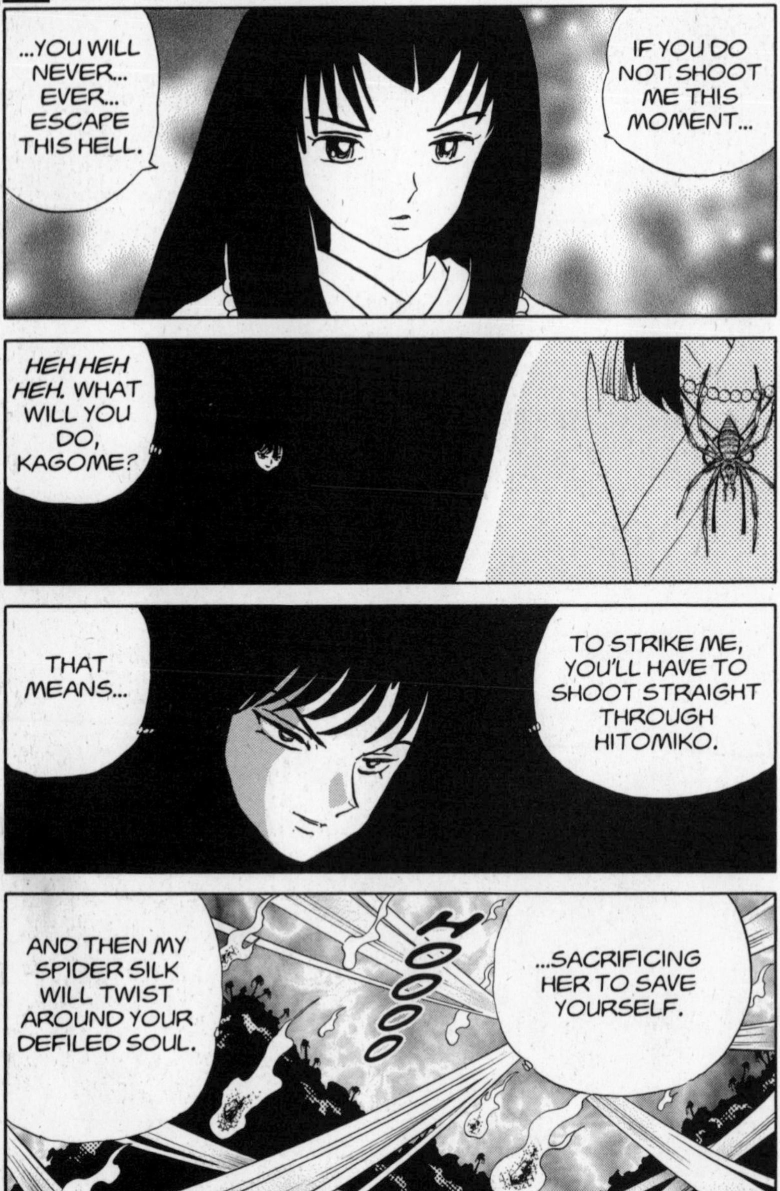
IF YOU DO NOT SHOOT ME THIS MOMENT...
...YOU WILL NEVER... EVER... ESCAPE THIS HELL.
HEH HEH HEH. WHAT WILL YOU DO, KAGOME?
TO STRIKE ME, YOU'LL HAVE TO SHOOT STRAIGHT THROUGH HITOMIKO.
THAT MEANS...
...SACRIFICING HER TO SAVE YOURSELF.
HOOOO
AND THEN MY SPIDER SILK WILL TWIST AROUND YOUR DEFILED SOUL.

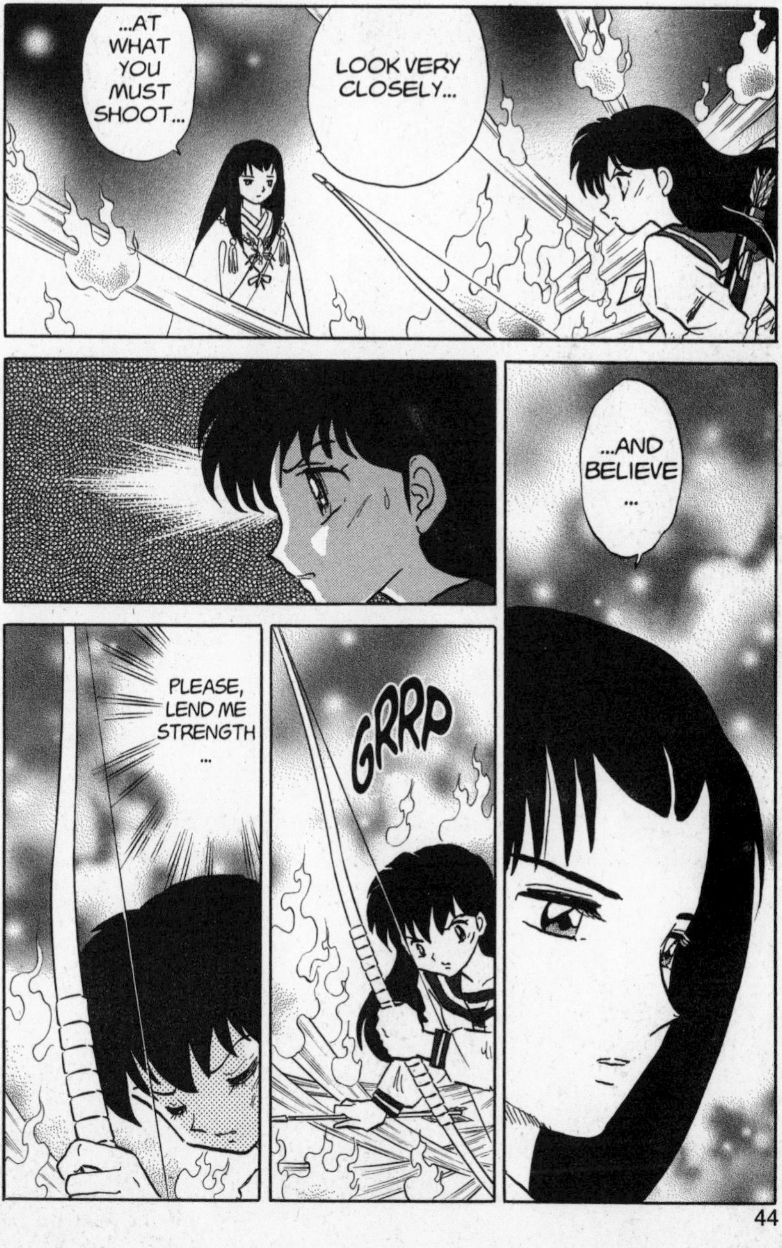
LOOK VERY CLOSELY...
...AT WHAT YOU MUST SHOOT...
...AND BELIEVE ...
GRRP
PLEASE, LEND ME STRENGTH ...

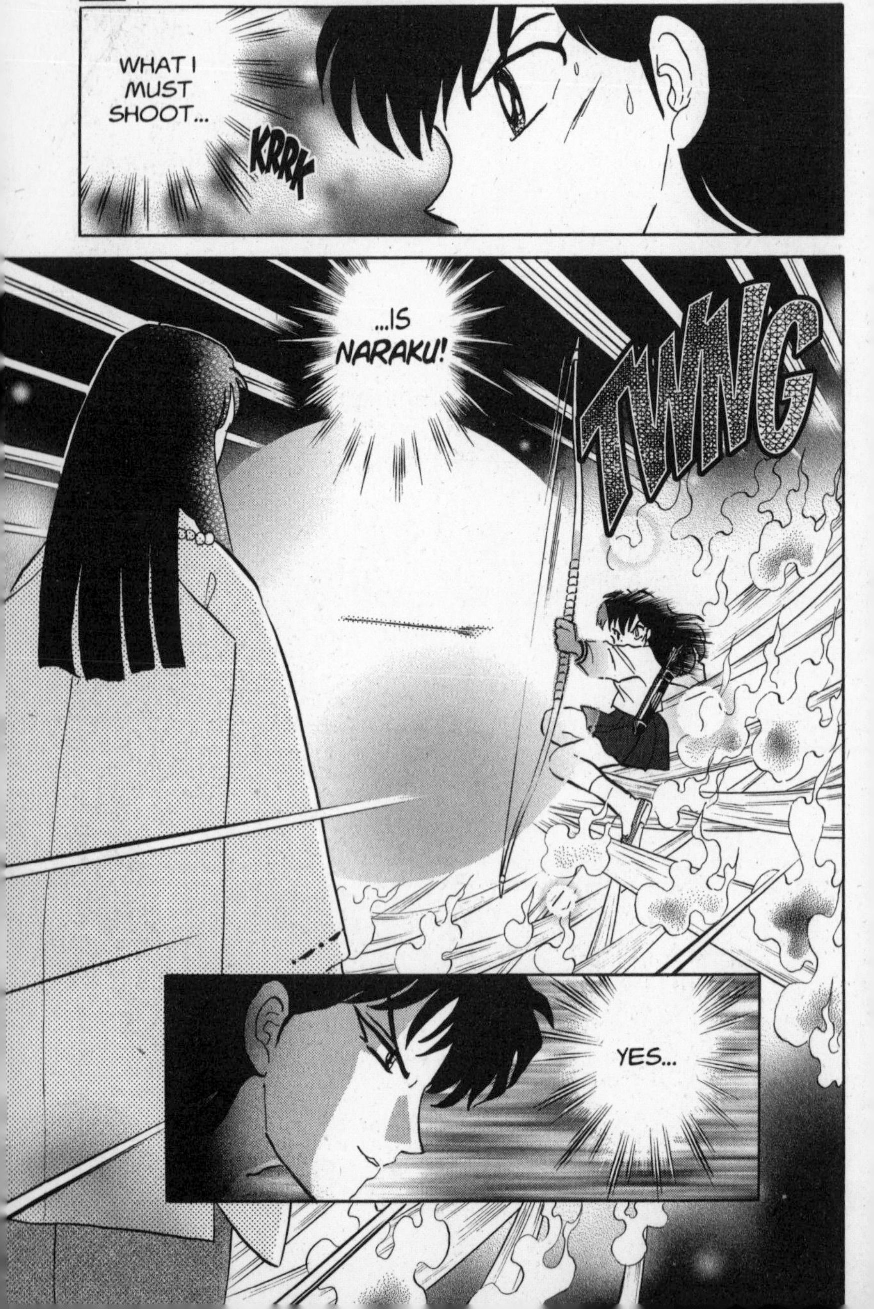
WHAT I MUST SHOOT...
KRRRK
...IS NARAKU!
TWING
YES...

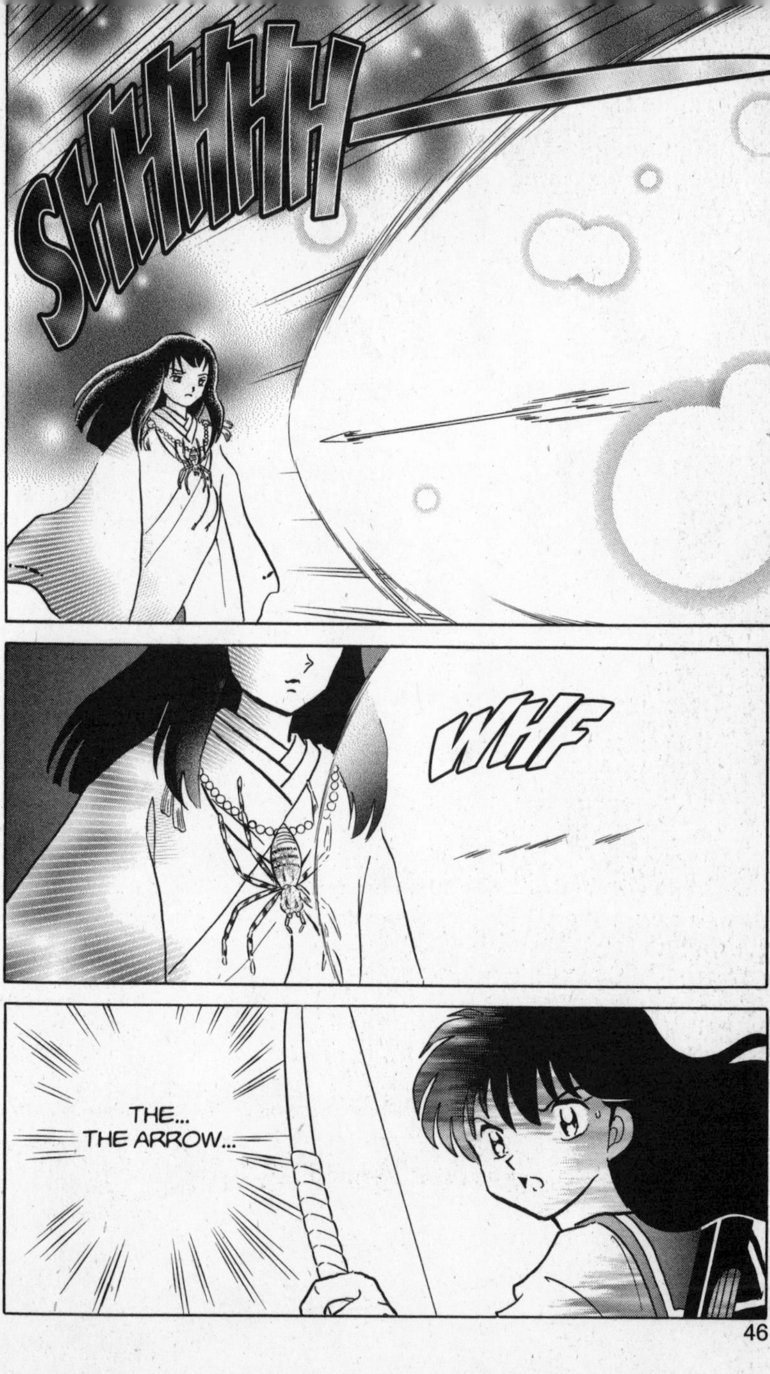
SHHHHHH
WHF
THE...
THE ARROW...

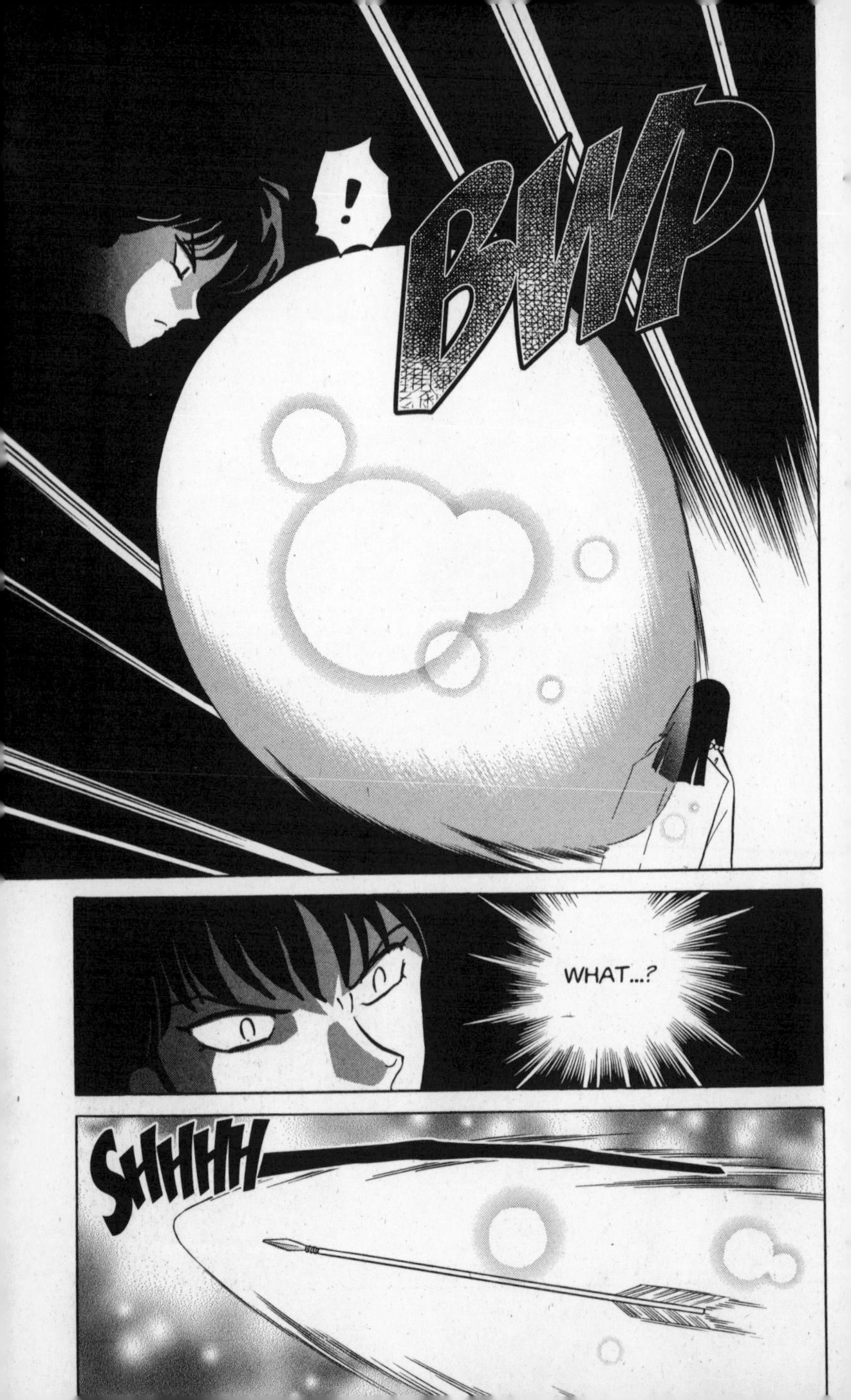
BMP
!
WHAT...?
SHHHH

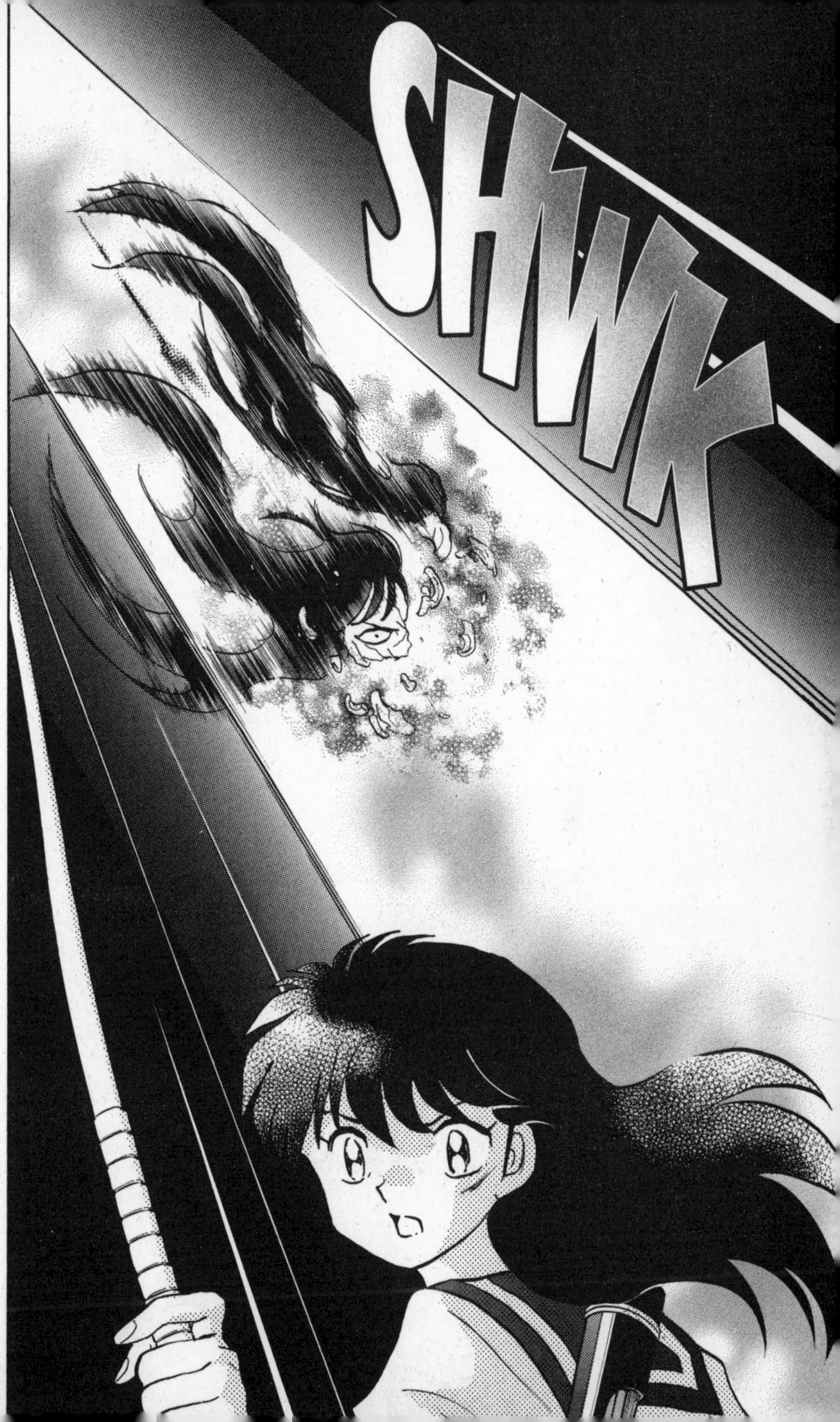
SHWK

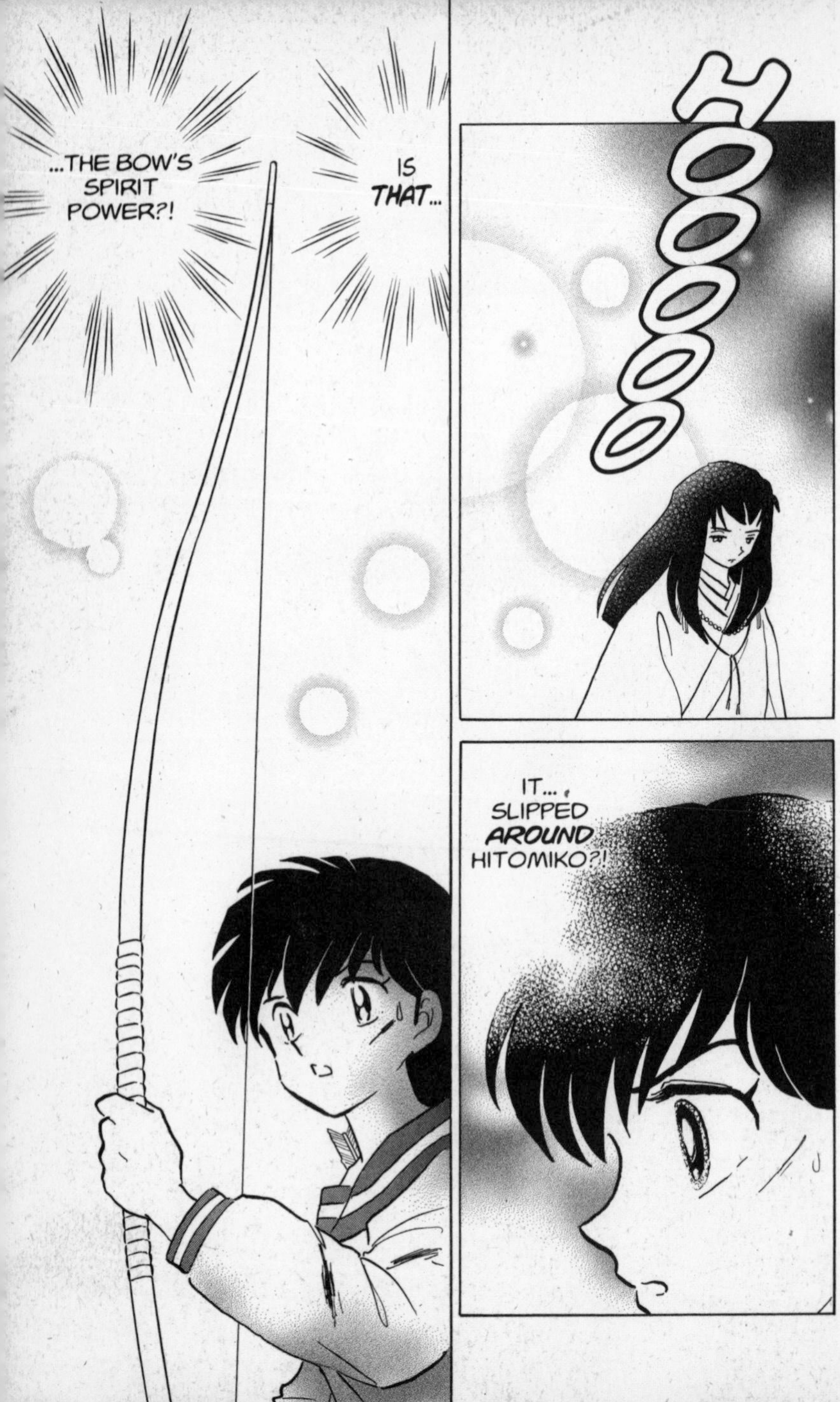
HOOOOOO
IT... SLIPPED AROUND HITOMIKO?!
IS THAT...
...THE BOW'S SPIRIT POWER?!

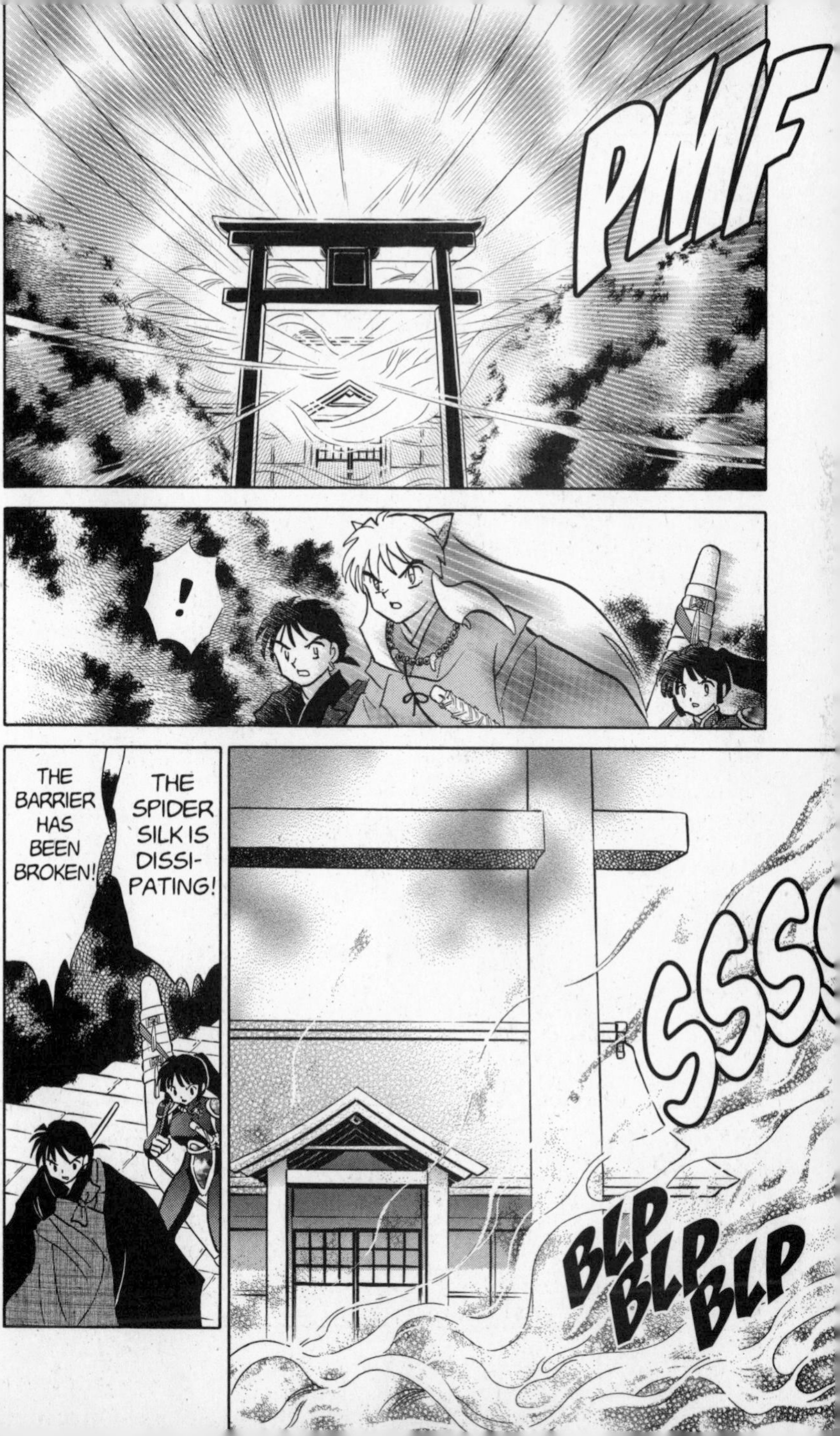
PMF
!
SSSS
BLP BLP BLP
THE SPIDER SILK IS DISSIPATING!
THE BARRIER HAS BEEN BROKEN!

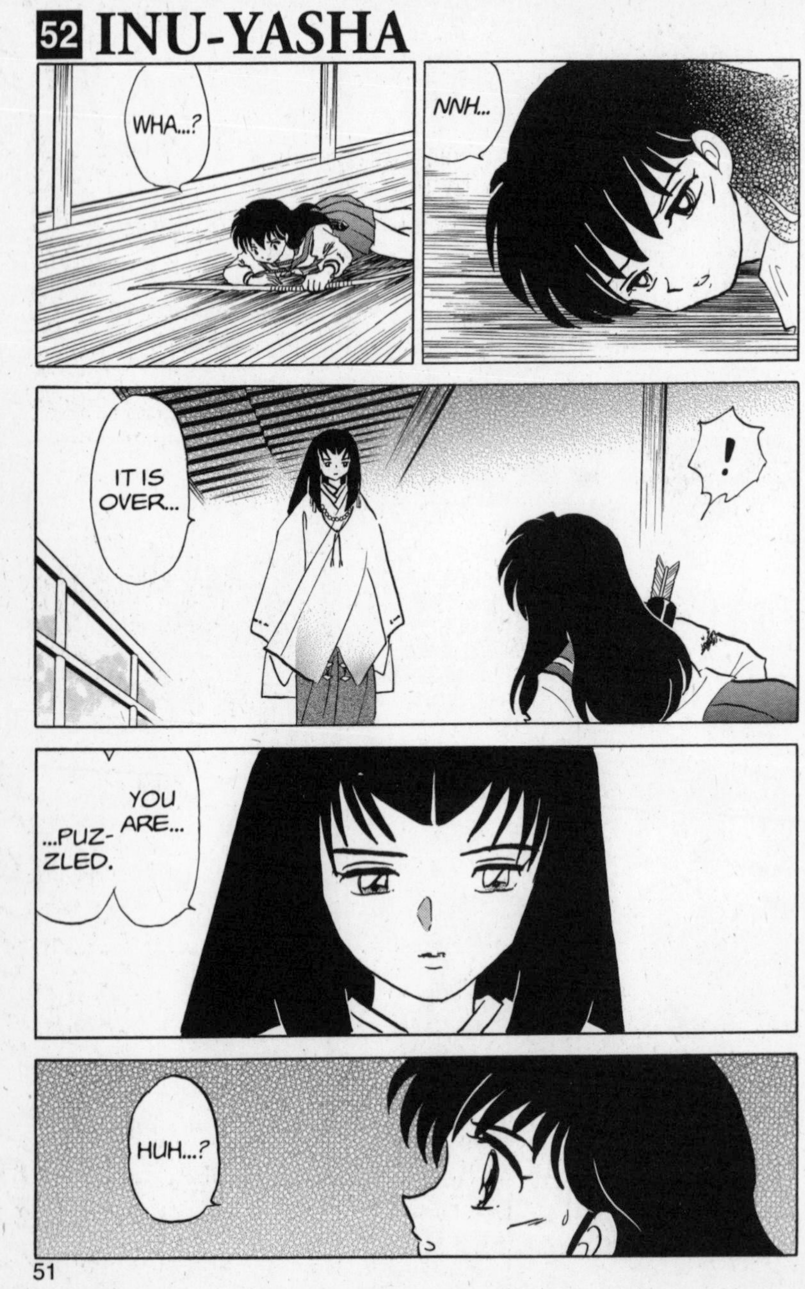
NNH...
WHA...?
!
IT IS OVER...
YOU ARE... ...PUZ-ZLED.
HUH...?

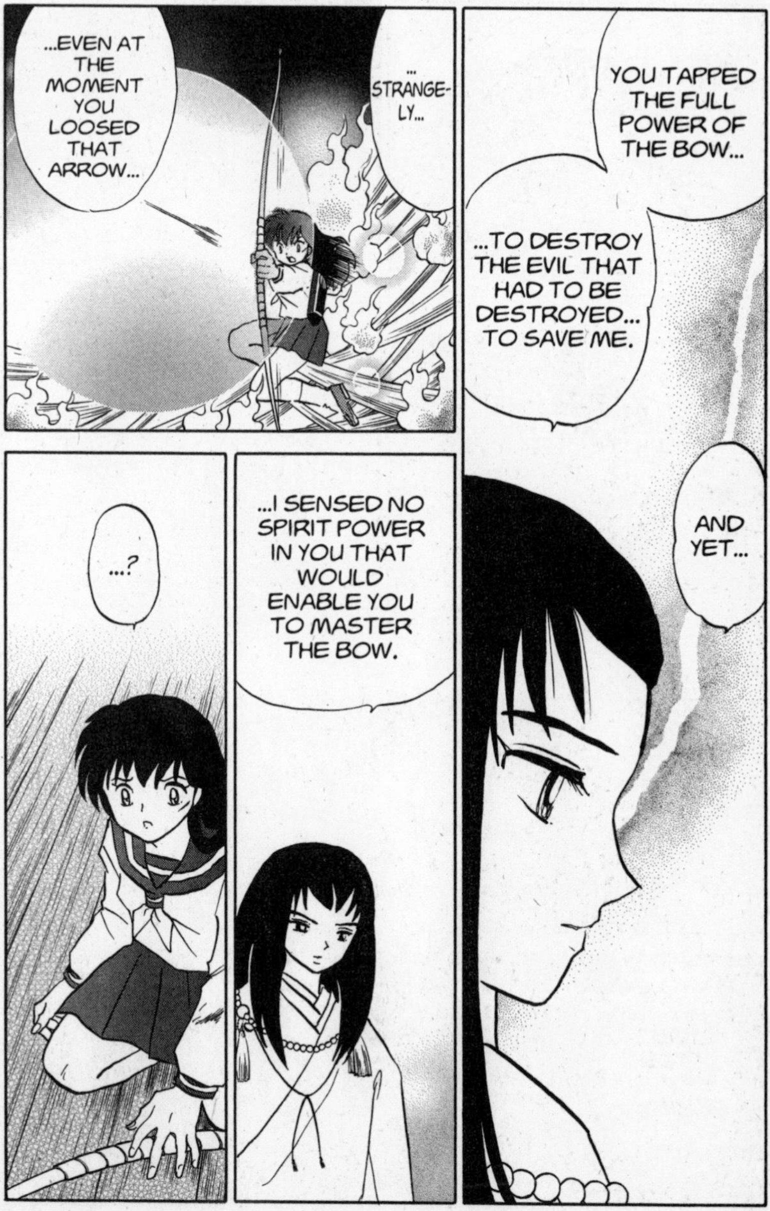
YOU TAPPED THE FULL POWER OF THE BOW...
...TO DESTROY THE EVIL THAT HAD TO BE DESTROYED... TO SAVE ME.
AND YET...
...STRANGE-LY...
...EVEN AT THE MOMENT YOU LOOSED THAT ARROW...
...I SENSED NO SPIRIT POWER IN YOU THAT WOULD ENABLE YOU TO MASTER THE BOW.
...?

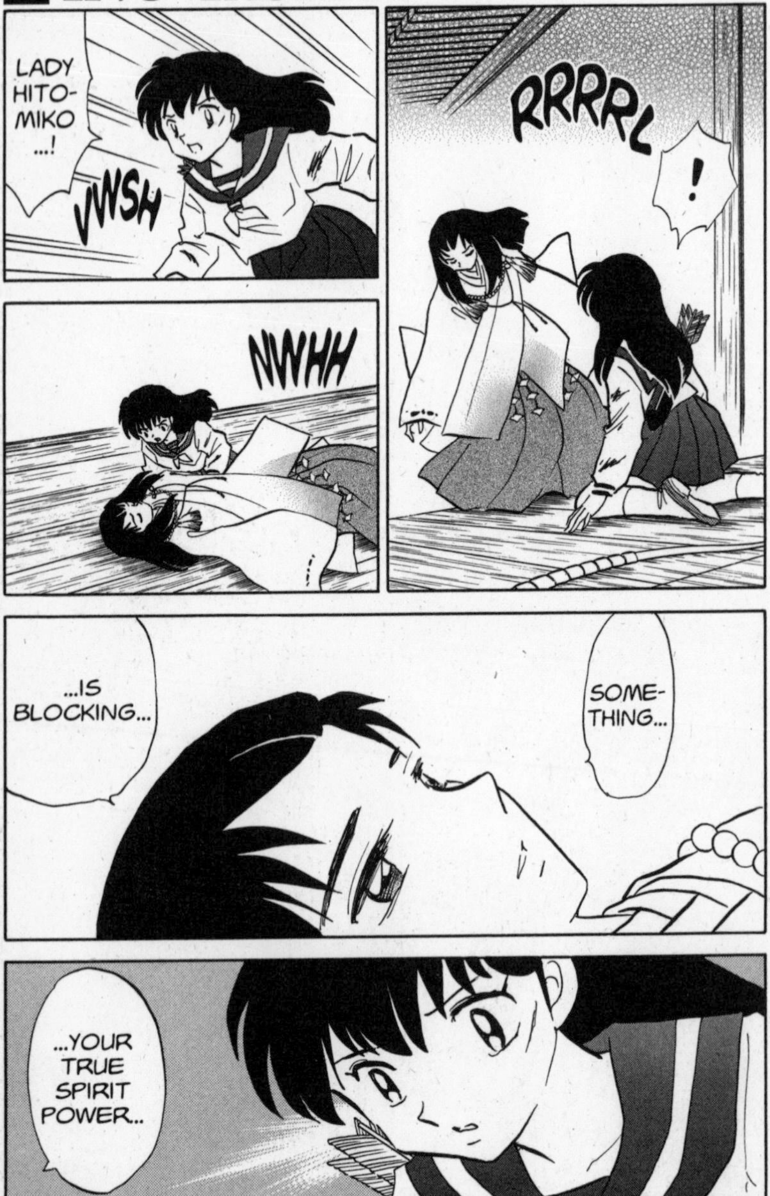
RRRRL
!
LADY HITOMIKO ...!
VWSH
NWHH
SOMETHING...
...IS BLOCKING...
...YOUR TRUE SPIRIT POWER...

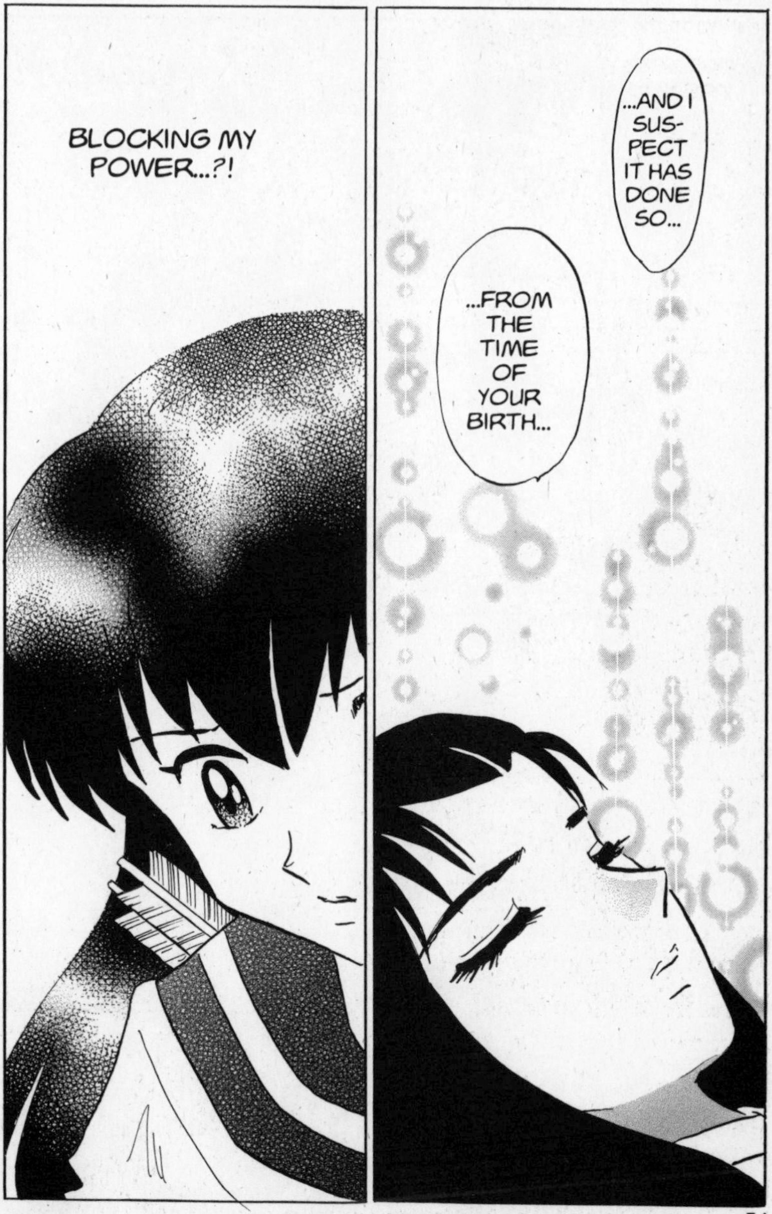
...AND I SUS-PECT IT HAS DONE SO...
...FROM THE TIME OF YOUR BIRTH...
BLOCKING MY POWER...?!

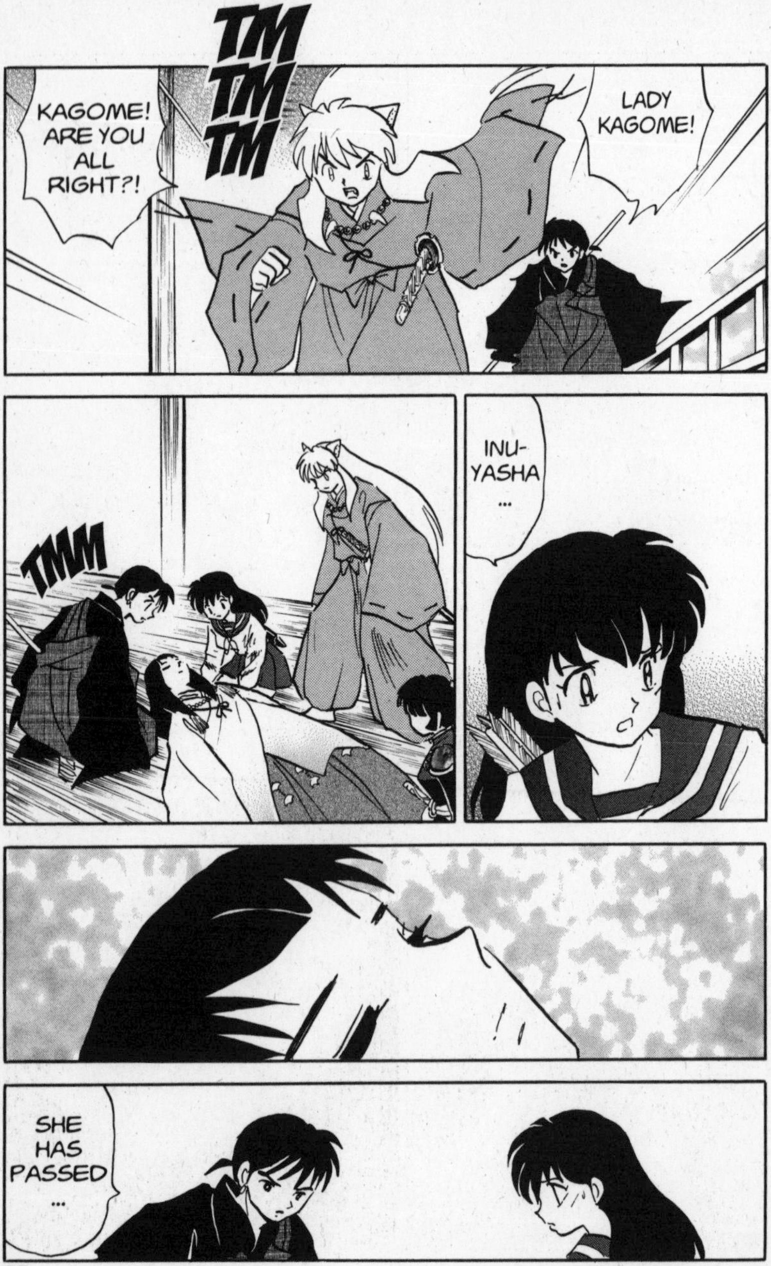
LADY KAGOME!
TM TM TM
KAGOME! ARE YOU ALL RIGHT?!
INU-YASHA ...
TMM
! !
SHE HAS PASSED ...

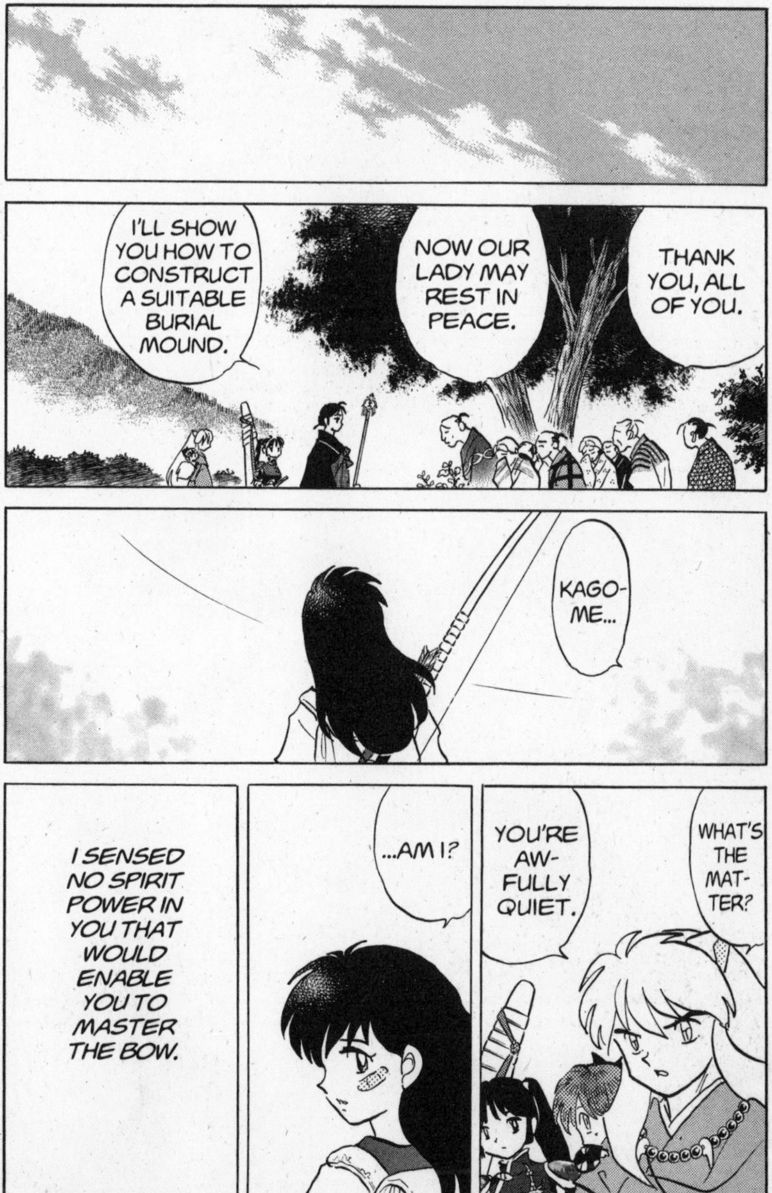
THANK YOU, ALL OF YOU.
NOW OUR LADY MAY REST IN PEACE.
I'LL SHOW YOU HOW TO CONSTRUCT A SUITABLE BURIAL MOUND.
KAGO-ME...
WHAT'S THE MAT-TER?
YOU'RE AW-FULLY QUIET.
...AM I?
I SENSED NO SPIRIT POWER IN YOU THAT WOULD ENABLE YOU TO MASTER THE BOW.

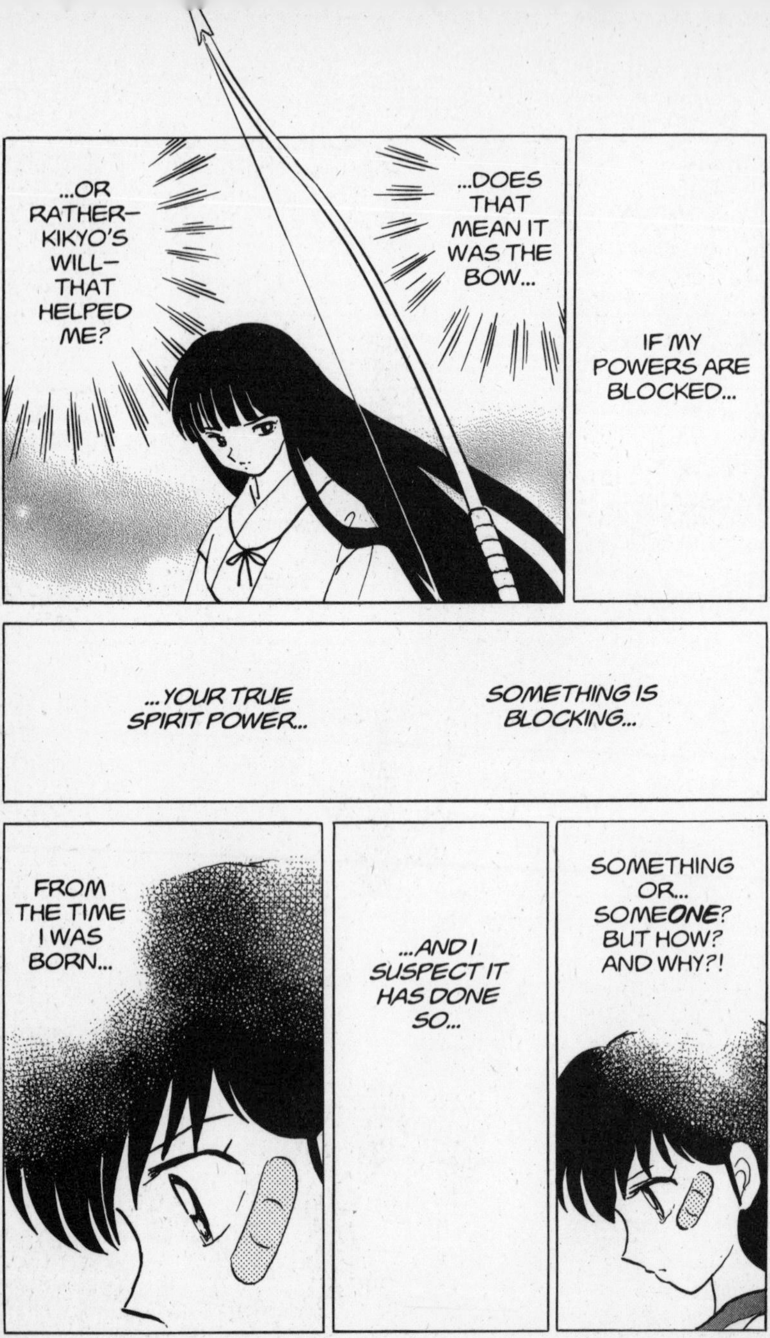
IF MY POWERS ARE BLOCKED...
...DOES THAT MEAN IT WAS THE BOW...
...OR RATHER— KIKYO'S WILL— THAT HELPED ME?
SOMETHING IS BLOCKING...
...YOUR TRUE SPIRIT POWER...
SOMETHING OR... SOME*ONE*? BUT HOW? AND WHY?!
...AND I SUSPECT IT HAS DONE SO...
FROM THE TIME I WAS BORN...

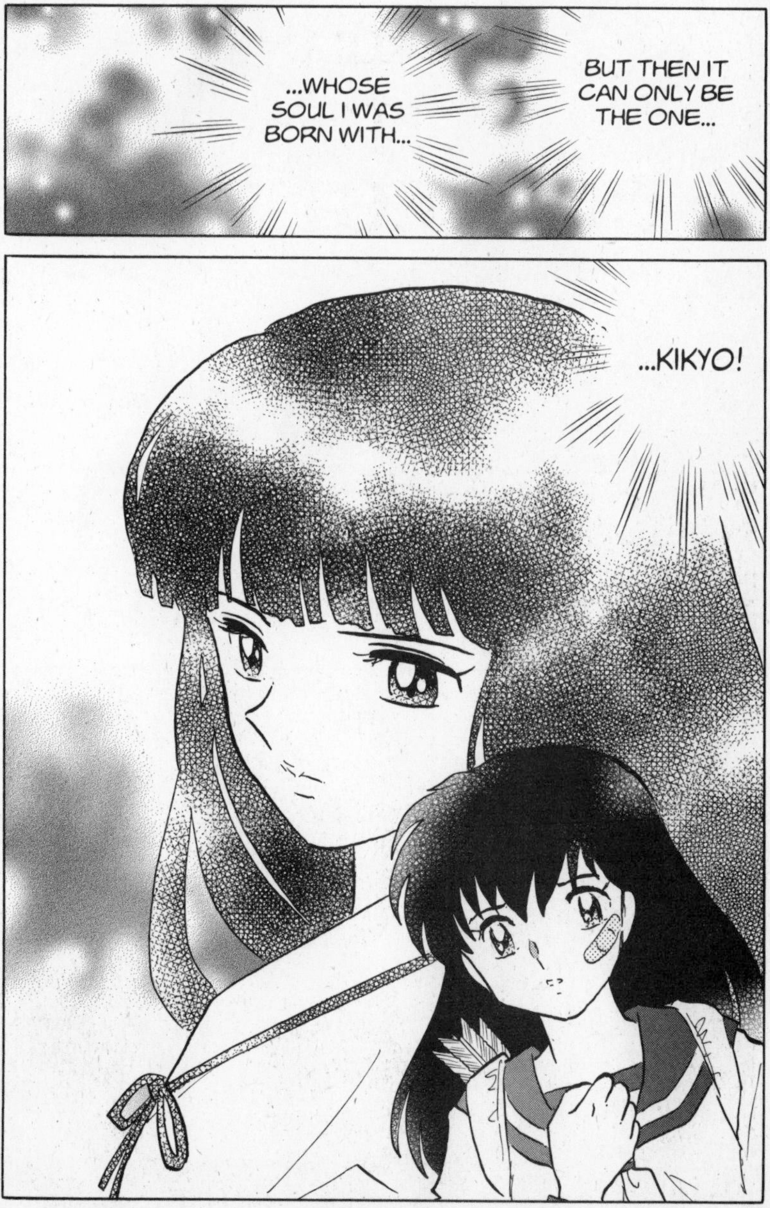
BUT THEN IT CAN ONLY BE THE ONE...
...WHOSE SOUL I WAS BORN WITH...
...KIKYO!

SCROLL 4
THE CORRECT WISH

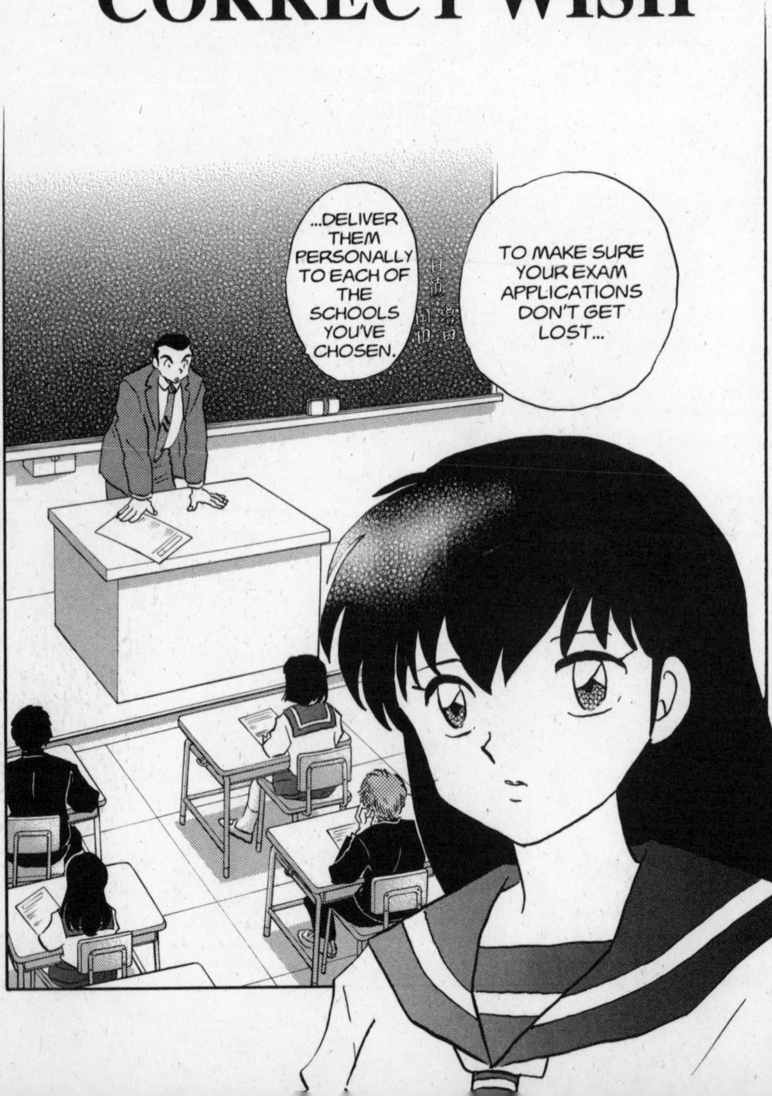
TO MAKE SURE YOUR EXAM APPLICATIONS DON'T GET LOST...
...DELIVER THEM PERSONALLY TO EACH OF THE SCHOOLS YOU'VE CHOSEN.

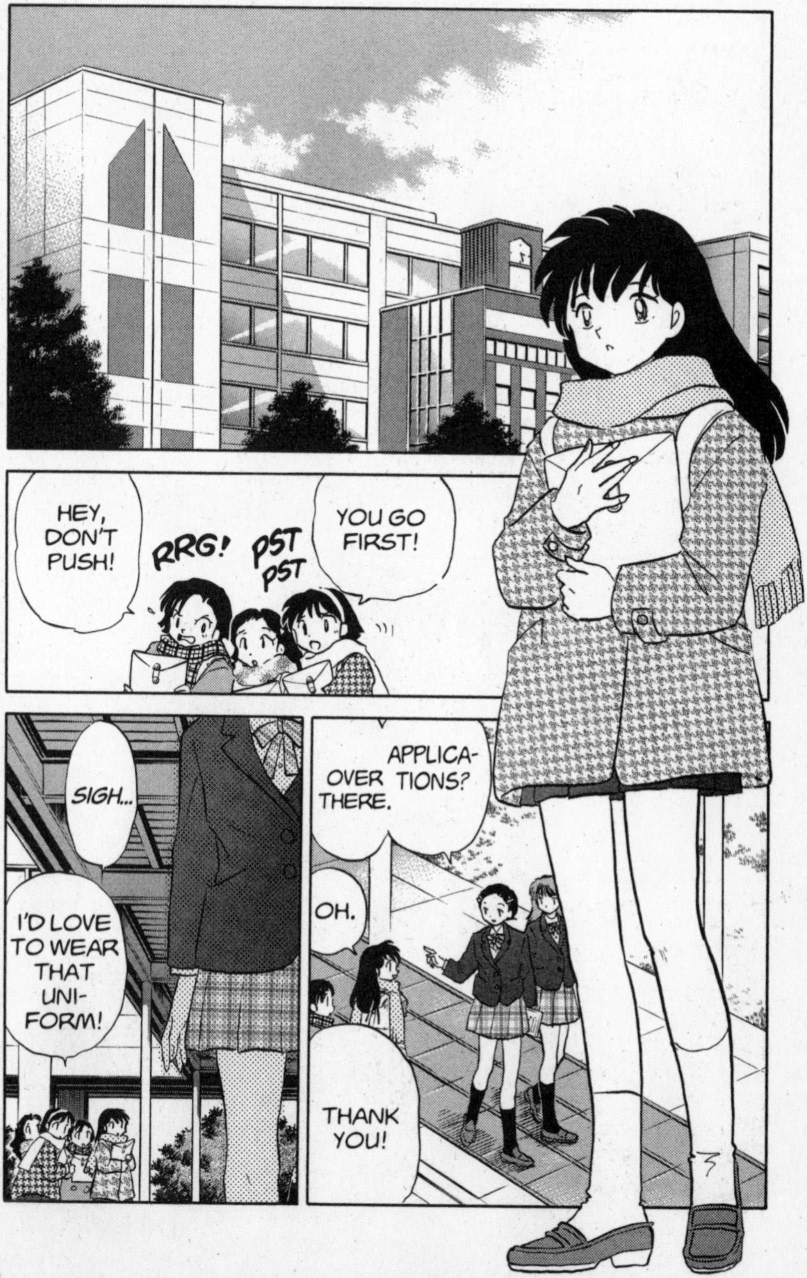
YOU GO FIRST!
PST PST
RRG!
HEY, DON'T PUSH!
APPLICATIONS?
OVER THERE.
OH.
THANK YOU!
SIGH...
I'D LOVE TO WEAR THAT UNIFORM!

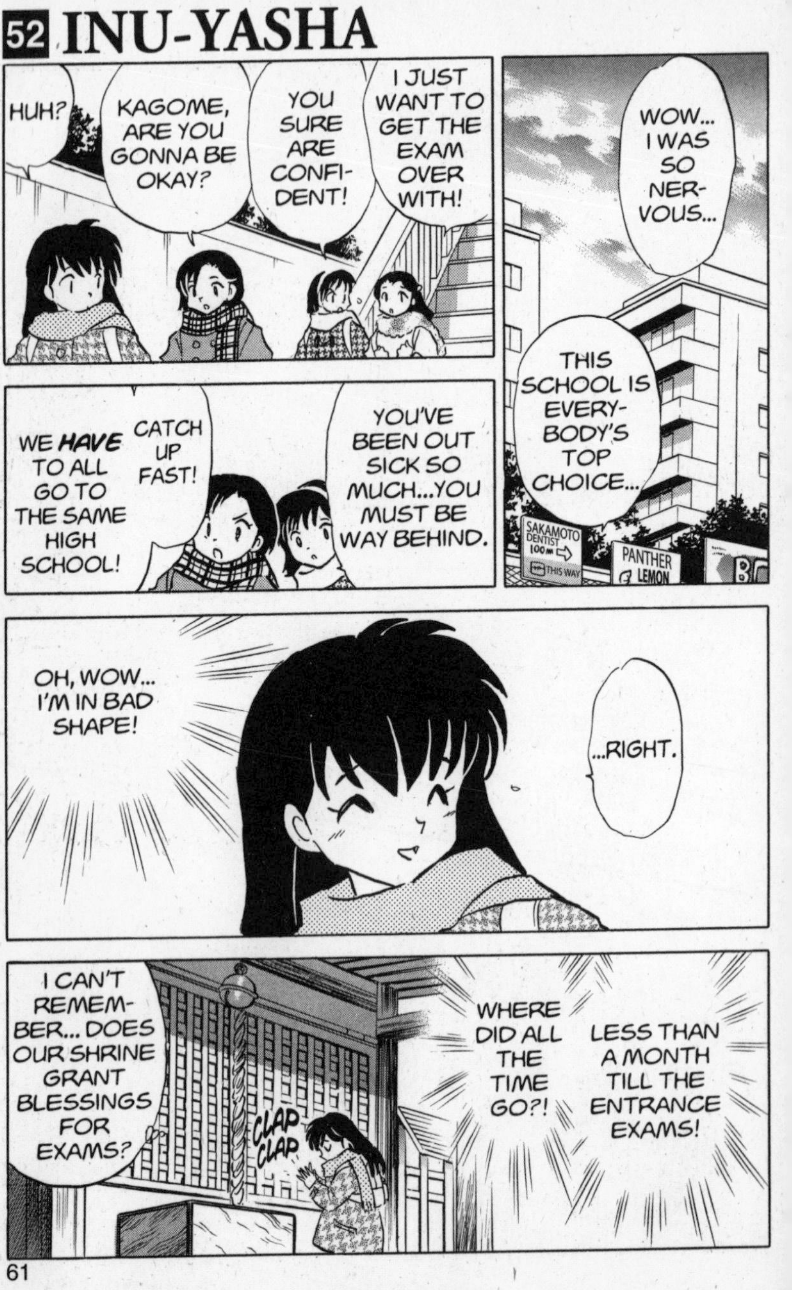
WOW... I WAS SO NER-VOUS...
THIS SCHOOL IS EVERY-BODY'S TOP CHOICE...
SAKAMOTO DENTIST 100m THIS WAY
PANTHER LEMON
I JUST WANT TO GET THE EXAM OVER WITH!
YOU SURE ARE CONFI-DENT!
KAGOME, ARE YOU GONNA BE OKAY?
HUH?
YOU'VE BEEN OUT SICK SO MUCH...YOU MUST BE WAY BEHIND.
CATCH UP FAST!
WE HAVE TO ALL GO TO THE SAME HIGH SCHOOL!
...RIGHT.
OH, WOW... I'M IN BAD SHAPE!
LESS THAN A MONTH TILL THE ENTRANCE EXAMS!
WHERE DID ALL THE TIME GO?!
CLAP CLAP
I CAN'T REMEM-BER... DOES OUR SHRINE GRANT BLESSINGS FOR EXAMS?

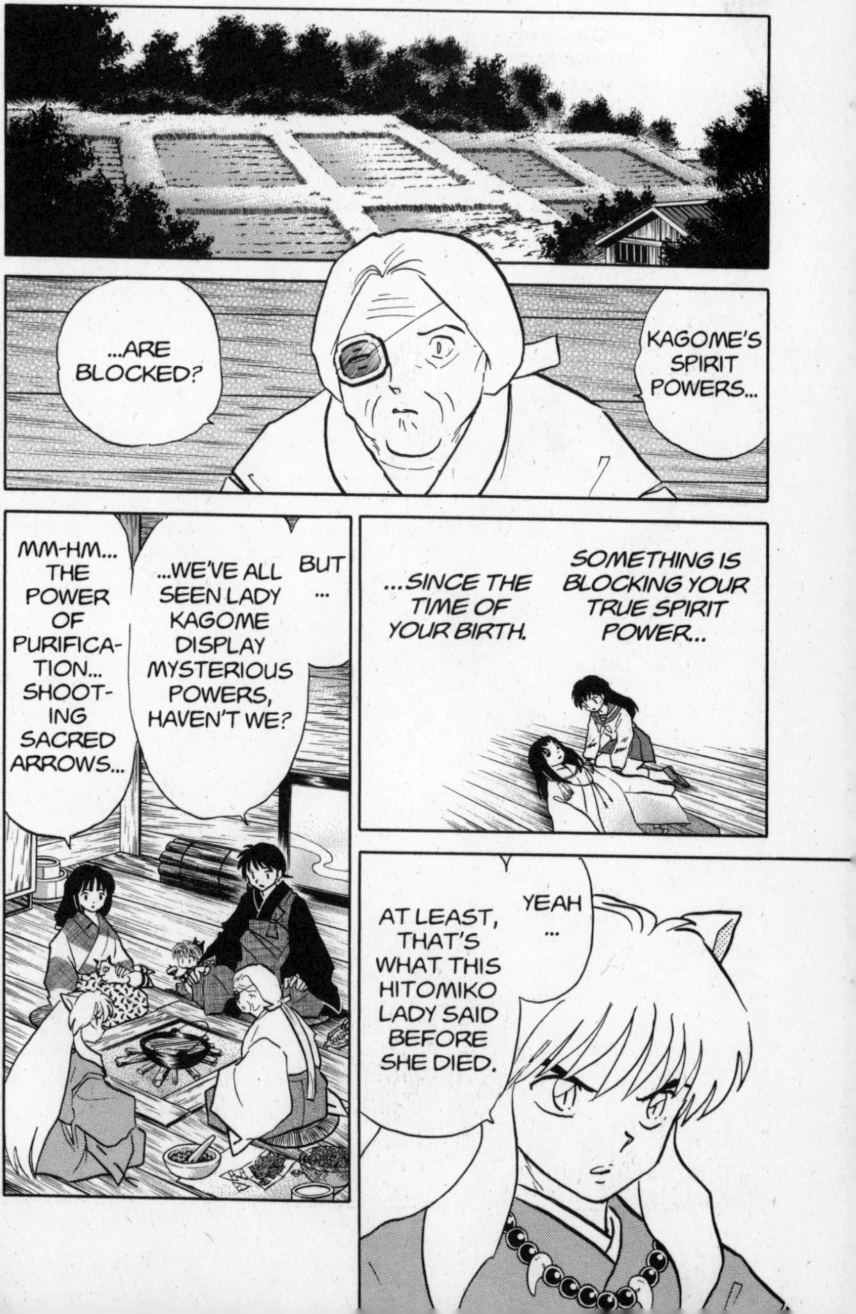
KAGOME'S SPIRIT POWERS...
...ARE BLOCKED?
SOMETHING IS BLOCKING YOUR TRUE SPIRIT POWER...
...SINCE THE TIME OF YOUR BIRTH.
YEAH ...
AT LEAST, THAT'S WHAT THIS HITOMIKO LADY SAID BEFORE SHE DIED.
BUT ...
...WE'VE ALL SEEN LADY KAGOME DISPLAY MYSTERIOUS POWERS, HAVEN'T WE?
MM-HM... THE POWER OF PURIFICATION... SHOOTING SACRED ARROWS...

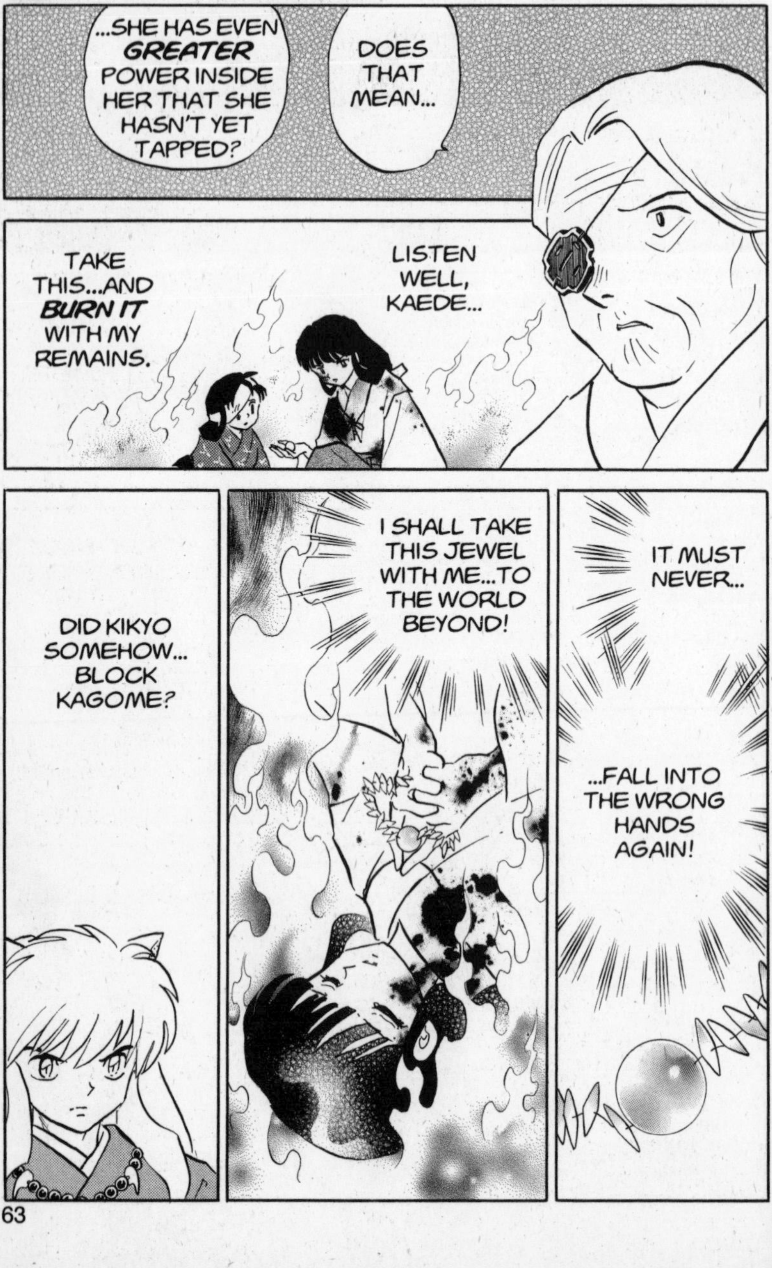
DOES THAT MEAN...
...SHE HAS EVEN GREATER POWER INSIDE HER THAT SHE HASN'T YET TAPPED?
LISTEN WELL, KAEDE...
TAKE THIS...AND BURN IT WITH MY REMAINS.
IT MUST NEVER...
...FALL INTO THE WRONG HANDS AGAIN!
I SHALL TAKE THIS JEWEL WITH ME...TO THE WORLD BEYOND!
DID KIKYO SOMEHOW... BLOCK KAGOME?

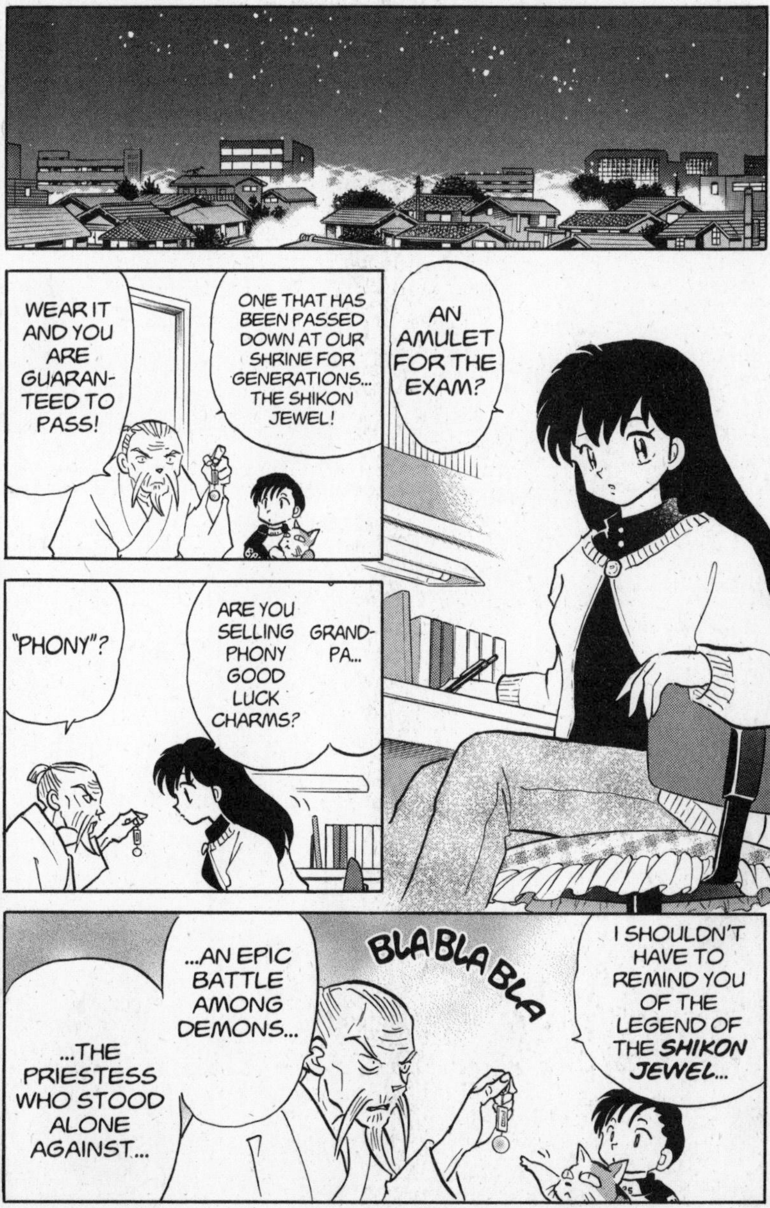
AN AMULET FOR THE EXAM?
ONE THAT HAS BEEN PASSED DOWN AT OUR SHRINE FOR GENERATIONS... THE SHIKON JEWEL!
WEAR IT AND YOU ARE GUARANTEED TO PASS!
GRANDPA...
ARE YOU SELLING PHONY GOOD LUCK CHARMS?
"PHONY"?
I SHOULDN'T HAVE TO REMIND YOU OF THE LEGEND OF THE *SHIKON JEWEL*...
BLA BLA BLA
...AN EPIC BATTLE AMONG DEMONS...
...THE PRIESTESS WHO STOOD ALONE AGAINST...

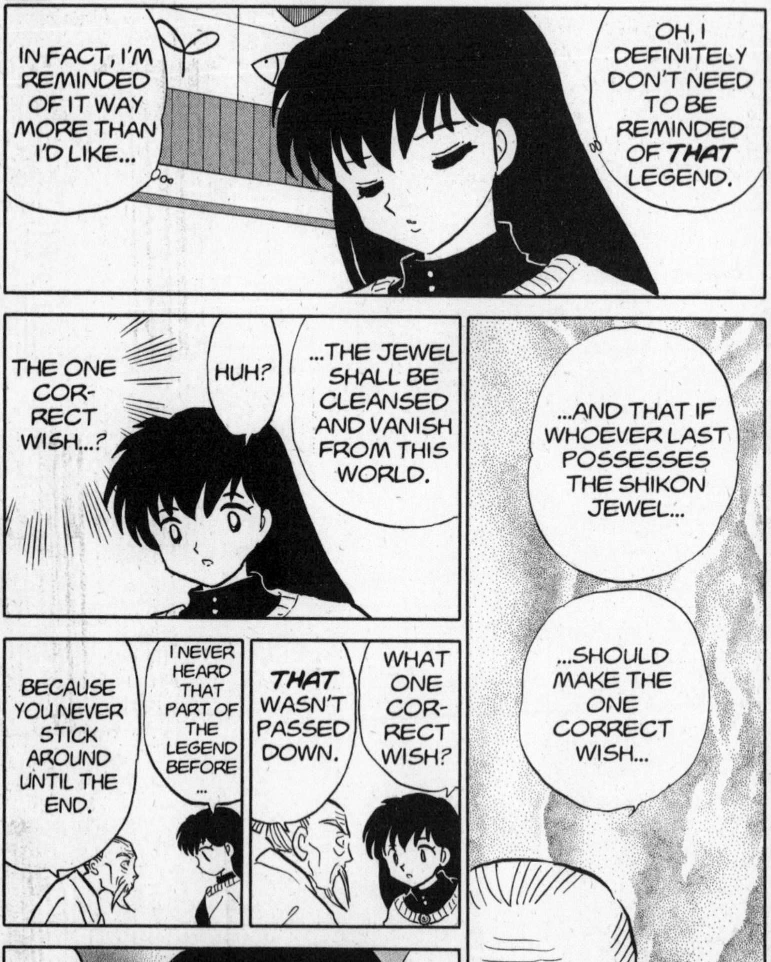
OH, I DEFINITELY DON'T NEED TO BE REMINDED OF *THAT* LEGEND.
IN FACT, I'M REMINDED OF IT WAY MORE THAN I'D LIKE...
...AND THAT IF WHOEVER LAST POSSESSES THE SHIKON JEWEL...
...SHOULD MAKE THE ONE CORRECT WISH...
...THE JEWEL SHALL BE CLEANSED AND VANISH FROM THIS WORLD.
HUH?
THE ONE COR-RECT WISH...?
WHAT ONE COR-RECT WISH?
THAT WASN'T PASSED DOWN.
I NEVER HEARD THAT PART OF THE LEGEND BEFORE...
BECAUSE YOU NEVER STICK AROUND UNTIL THE END.
GRAND-PA...
THIS STORY...

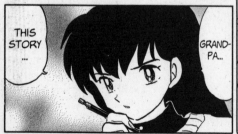

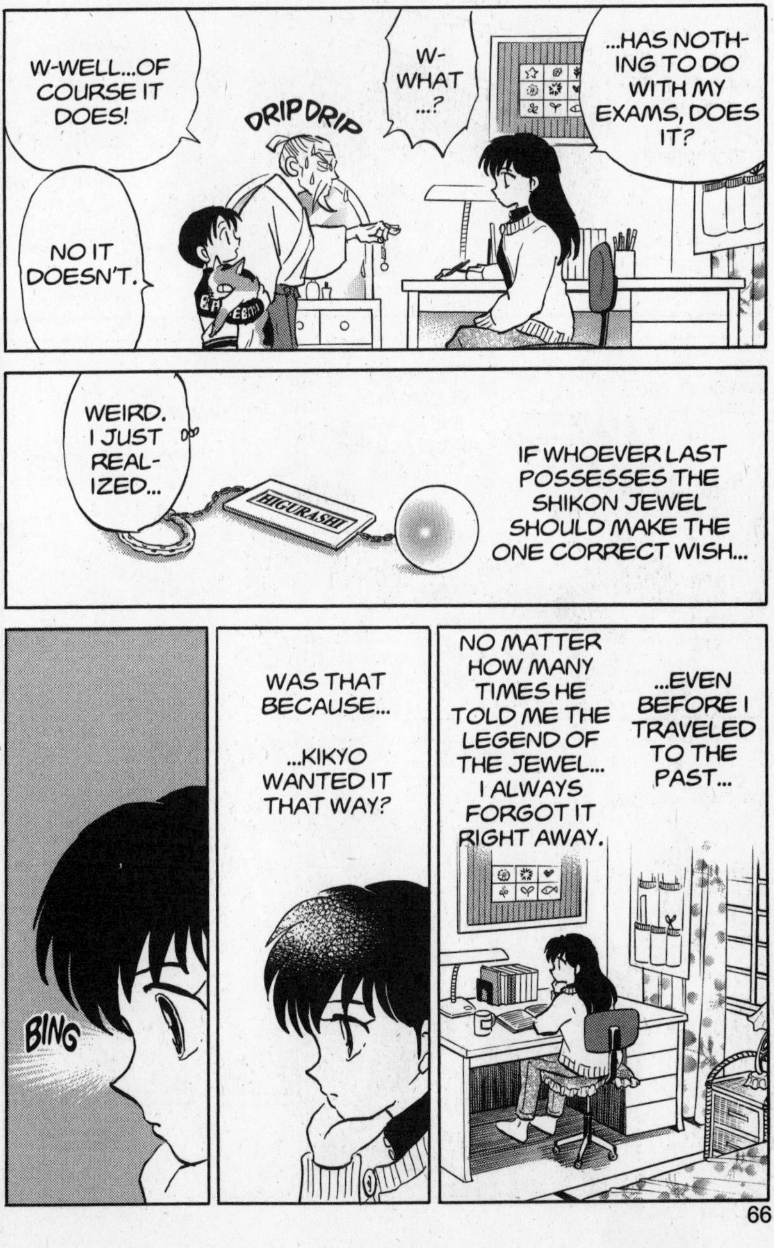
...HAS NOTHING TO DO WITH MY EXAMS, DOES IT?
W-WHAT...?
DRIP DRIP
W-WELL...OF COURSE IT DOES!
NO IT DOESN'T.
IF WHOEVER LAST POSSESSES THE SHIKON JEWEL SHOULD MAKE THE ONE CORRECT WISH...
WEIRD. I JUST REALIZED...
HIGURASHI
...EVEN BEFORE I TRAVELED TO THE PAST...
NO MATTER HOW MANY TIMES HE TOLD ME THE LEGEND OF THE JEWEL... I ALWAYS FORGOT IT RIGHT AWAY.
WAS THAT BECAUSE...
...KIKYO WANTED IT THAT WAY?
BING

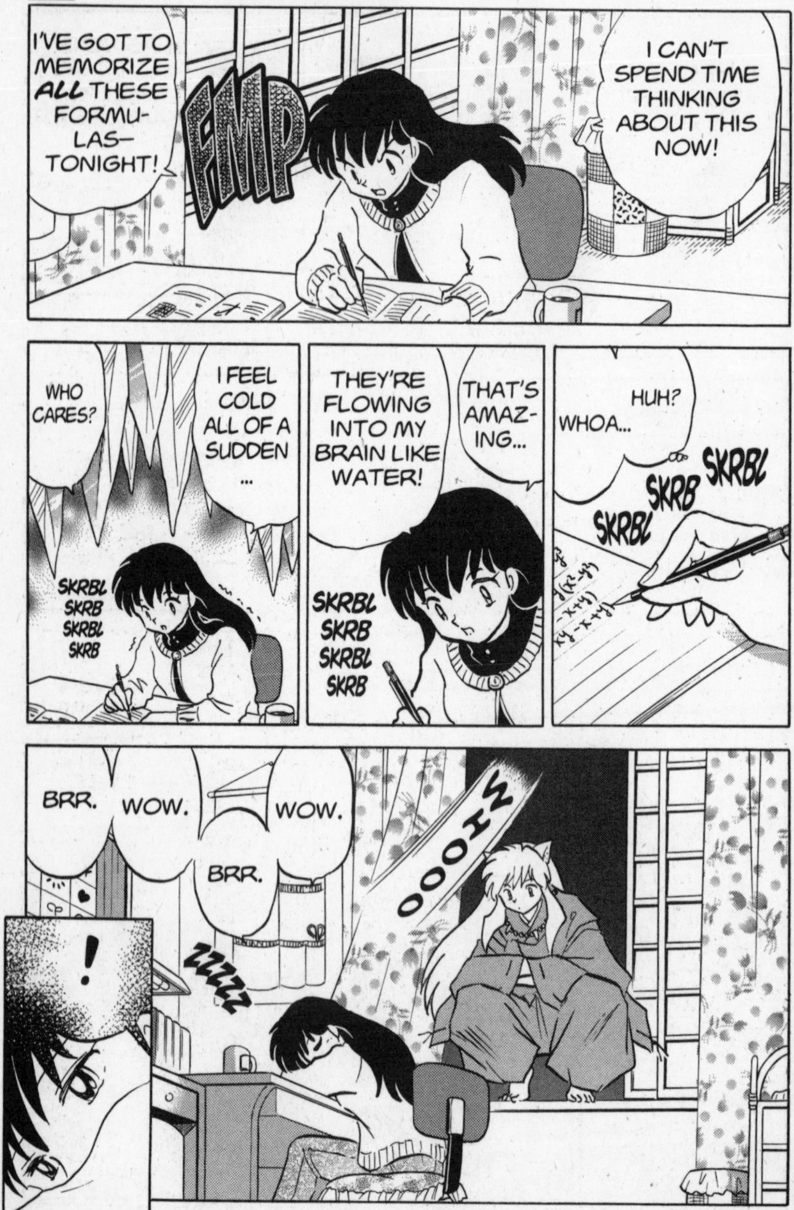
I CAN'T SPEND TIME THINKING ABOUT THIS NOW!
FMP
I'VE GOT TO MEMORIZE ALL THESE FORMULAS—TONIGHT!
HUH?
WHOA...
SKRBL
SKRB
SKRBL
THAT'S AMAZING...
THEY'RE FLOWING INTO MY BRAIN LIKE WATER!
SKRBL SKRB SKRBL SKRB
I FEEL COLD ALL OF A SUDDEN...
WHO CARES?
SKRBL SKRB SKRBL SKRB
WOW.
BRR.
WOW.
BRR.
WHOOOO
ZZZZZ
!

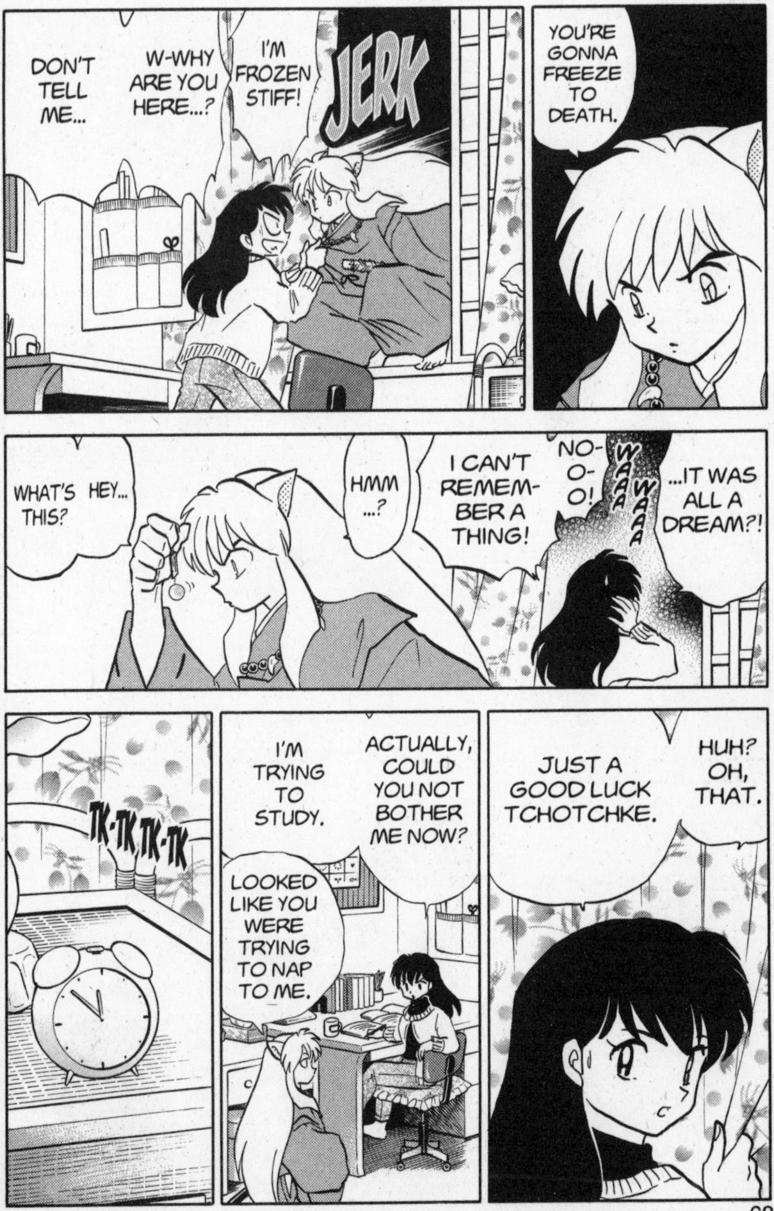
YOU'RE GONNA FREEZE TO DEATH.
JERK
I'M FROZEN STIFF!
W-WHY ARE YOU HERE...?
DON'T TELL ME...
...IT WAS ALL A DREAM?!
WAAAA WAAAA
NO-O-O!
I CAN'T REMEM-BER A THING!
HMM ...?
HEY...
WHAT'S THIS?
HUH? OH, THAT.
JUST A GOOD LUCK TCHOTCHKE.
ACTUALLY, COULD YOU NOT BOTHER ME NOW?
I'M TRYING TO STUDY.
LOOKED LIKE YOU WERE TRYING TO NAP TO ME.
TK-TK TK-TK

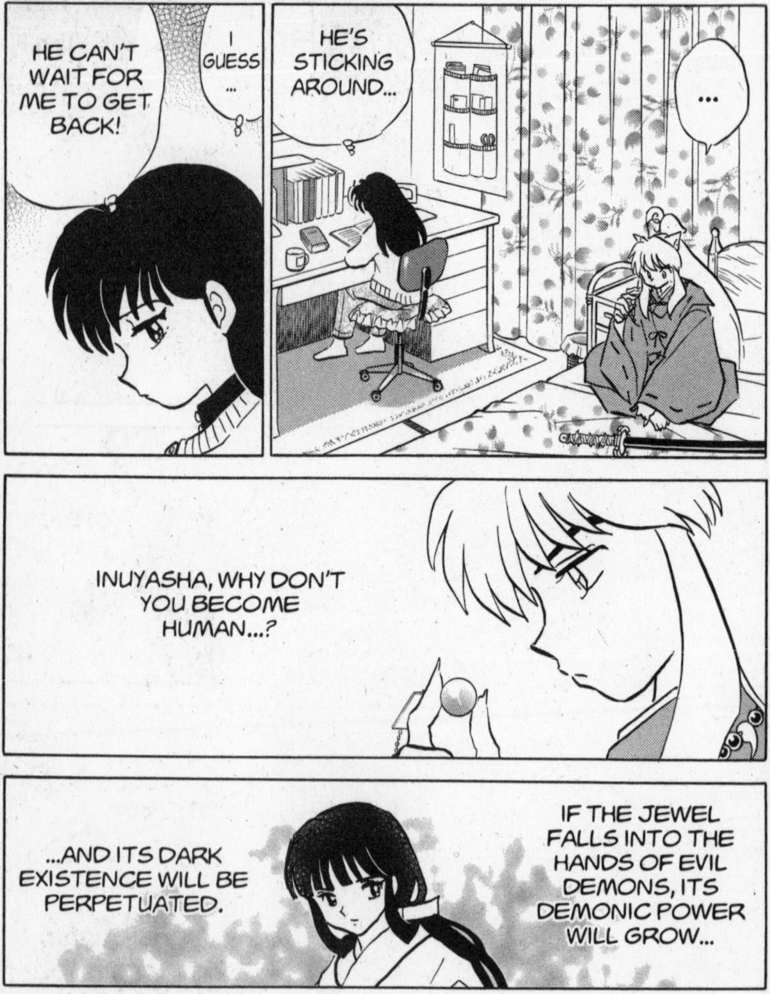
...
HE'S STICKING AROUND...
I GUESS ...
HE CAN'T WAIT FOR ME TO GET BACK!
INUYASHA, WHY DON'T YOU BECOME HUMAN...?
IF THE JEWEL FALLS INTO THE HANDS OF EVIL DEMONS, ITS DEMONIC POWER WILL GROW...
...AND ITS DARK EXISTENCE WILL BE PERPETUATED.
BUT IF YOU USE IT TO TURN HUMAN...
...THE JEWEL WILL BE CLEANSED...
...AND CEASE TO EXIST.

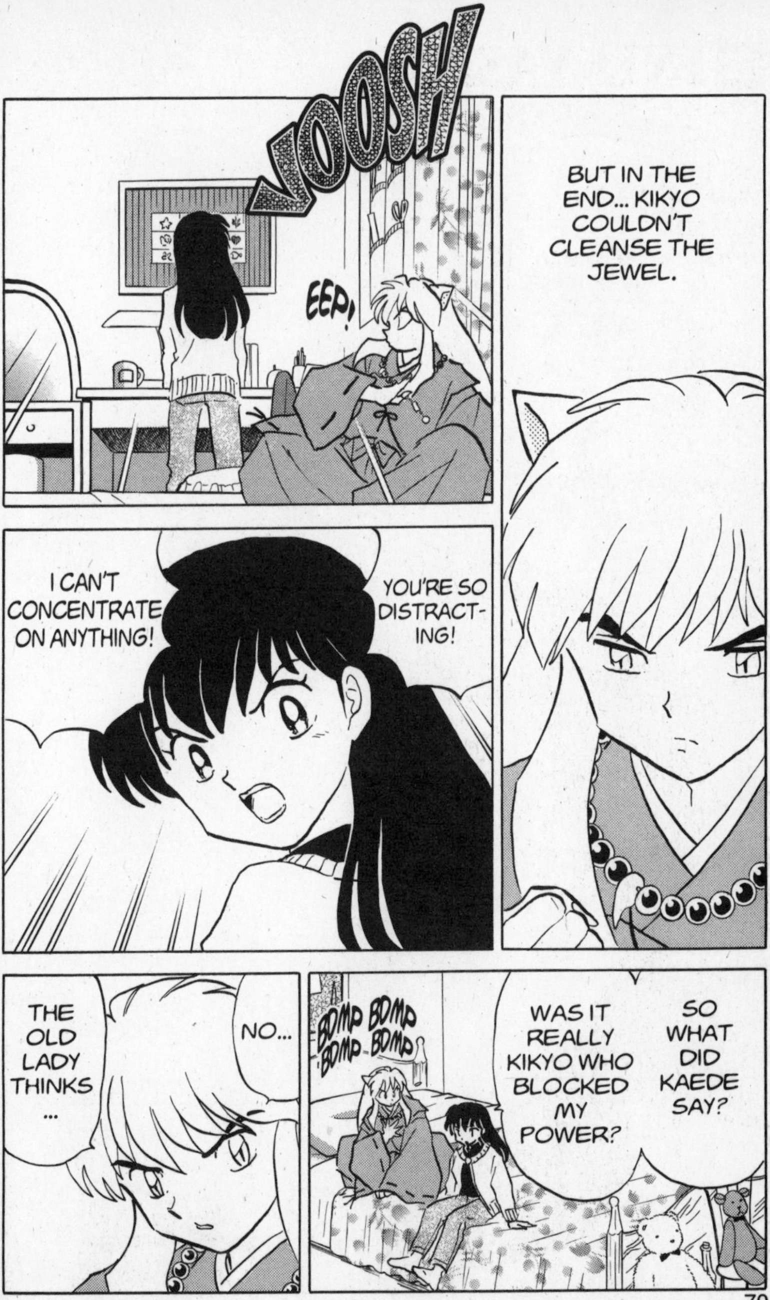
BUT IN THE END... KIKYO COULDN'T CLEANSE THE JEWEL.
VOOSH
EEP!
YOU'RE SO DISTRACT-ING!
I CAN'T CONCENTRATE ON ANYTHING!
SO WHAT DID KAEDE SAY?
WAS IT REALLY KIKYO WHO BLOCKED MY POWER?
BDMP BDMP BDMP BDMP
NO...
THE OLD LADY THINKS ...

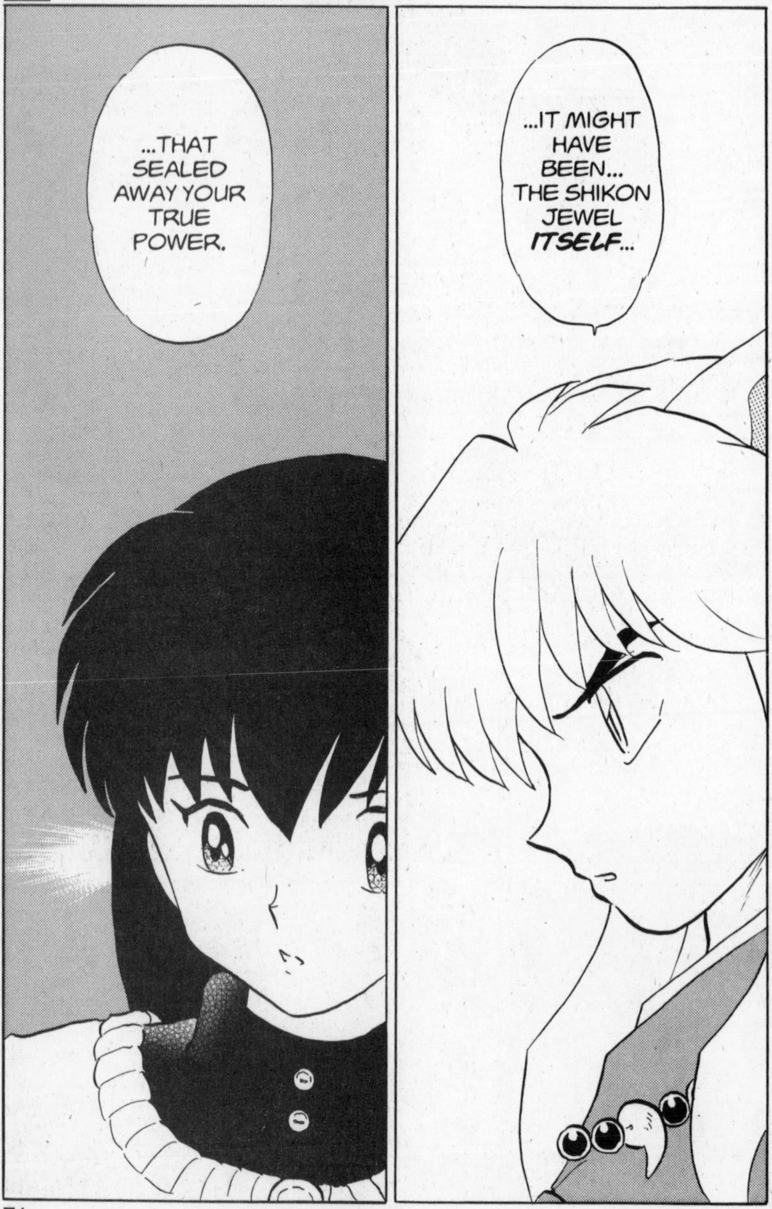
...IT MIGHT HAVE BEEN... THE SHIKON JEWEL *ITSELF*...
...THAT SEALED AWAY YOUR TRUE POWER.

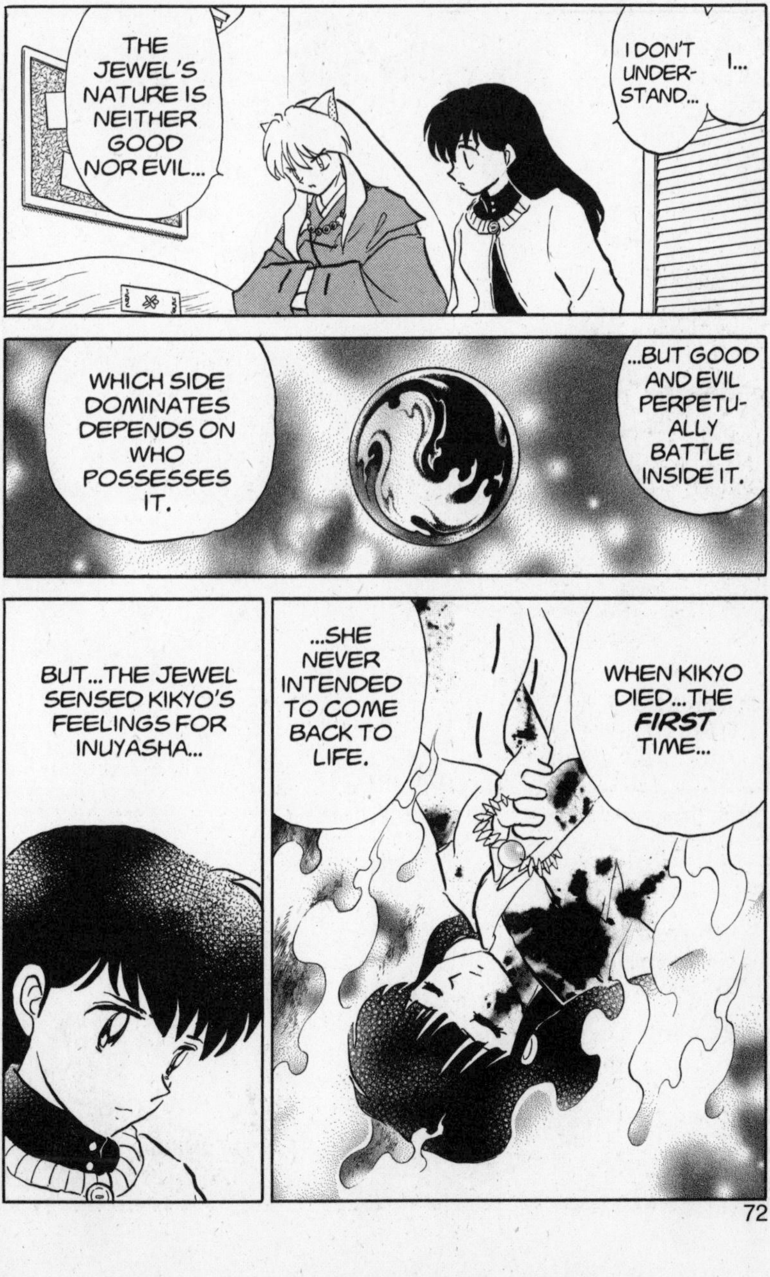
I...
I DON'T UNDER-STAND...
THE JEWEL'S NATURE IS NEITHER GOOD NOR EVIL...
...BUT GOOD AND EVIL PERPETU-ALLY BATTLE INSIDE IT.
WHICH SIDE DOMINATES DEPENDS ON WHO POSSESSES IT.
WHEN KIKYO DIED...THE *FIRST* TIME...
...SHE NEVER INTENDED TO COME BACK TO LIFE.
BUT...THE JEWEL SENSED KIKYO'S FEELINGS FOR INUYASHA...

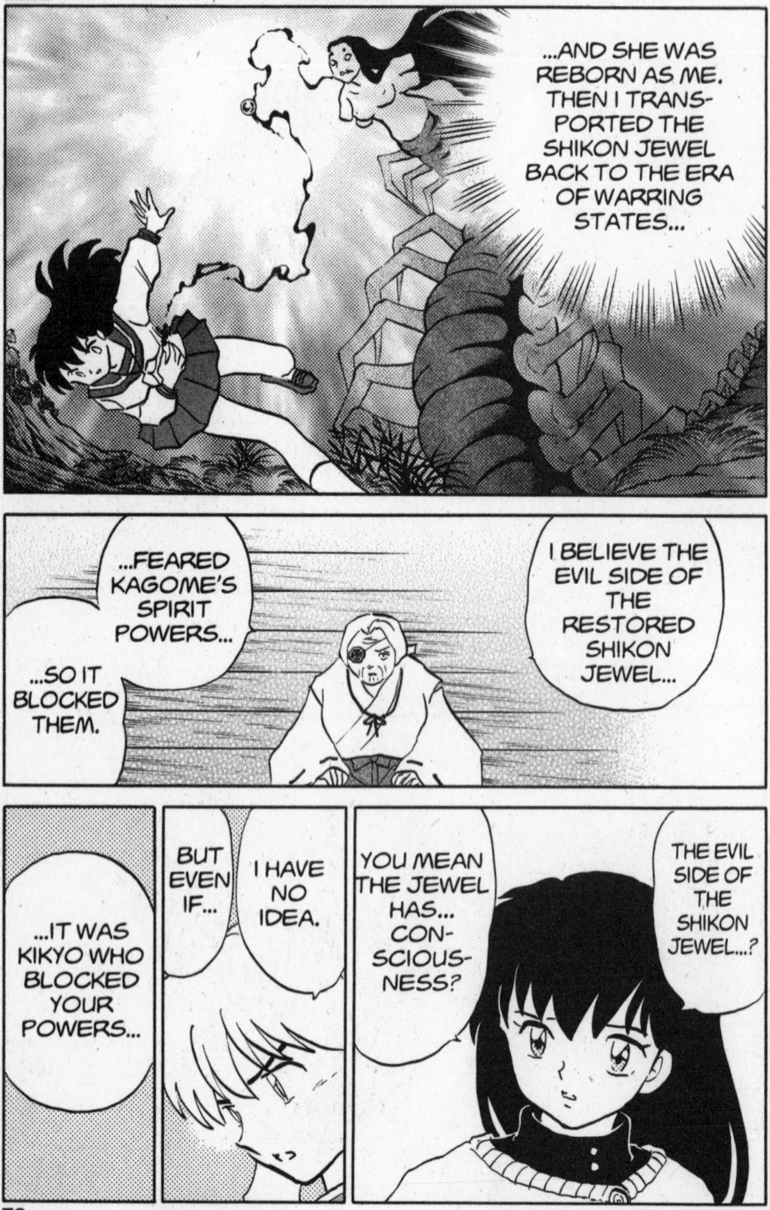
...AND SHE WAS REBORN AS ME. THEN I TRANSPORTED THE SHIKON JEWEL BACK TO THE ERA OF WARRING STATES...
I BELIEVE THE EVIL SIDE OF THE RESTORED SHIKON JEWEL...
...FEARED KAGOME'S SPIRIT POWERS...
...SO IT BLOCKED THEM.
THE EVIL SIDE OF THE SHIKON JEWEL...?
YOU MEAN THE JEWEL HAS... CONSCIOUSNESS?
I HAVE NO IDEA.
BUT EVEN IF...
...IT WAS KIKYO WHO BLOCKED YOUR POWERS...

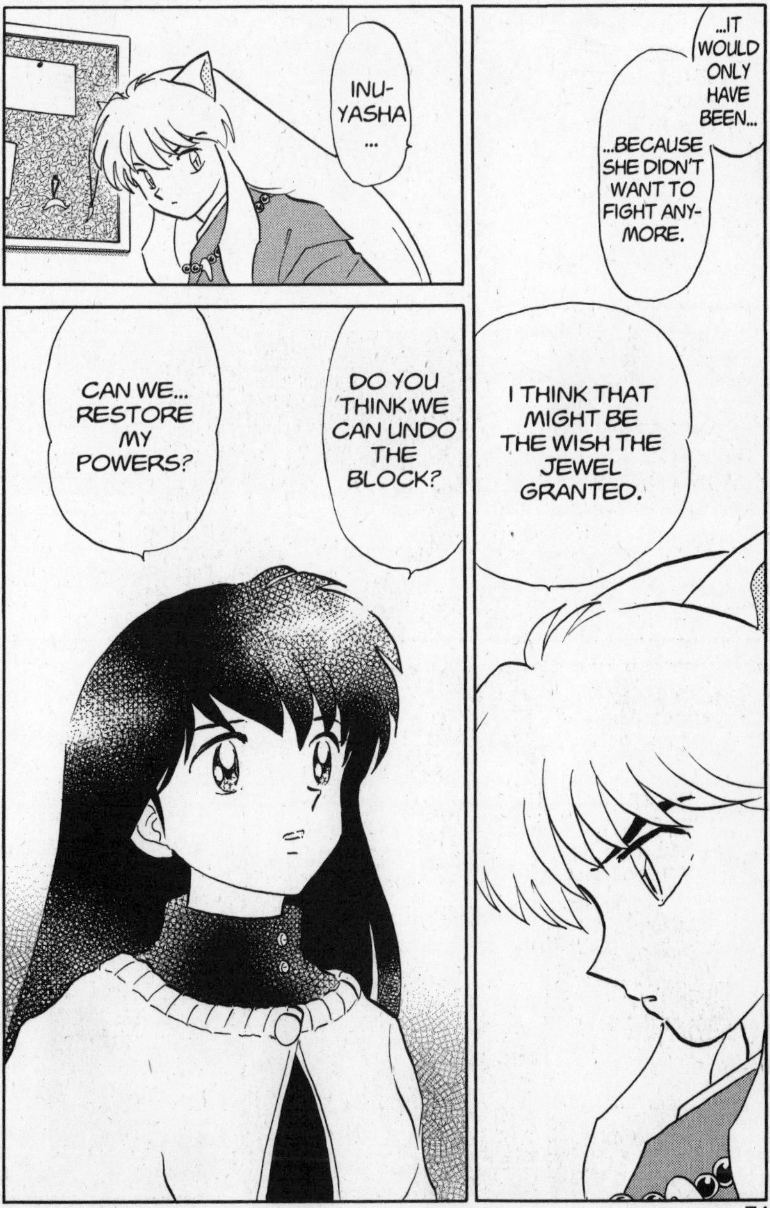
...IT WOULD ONLY HAVE BEEN...
...BECAUSE SHE DIDN'T WANT TO FIGHT ANY-MORE.
I THINK THAT MIGHT BE THE WISH THE JEWEL GRANTED.
INU-YASHA...
DO YOU THINK WE CAN UNDO THE BLOCK?
CAN WE... RESTORE MY POWERS?

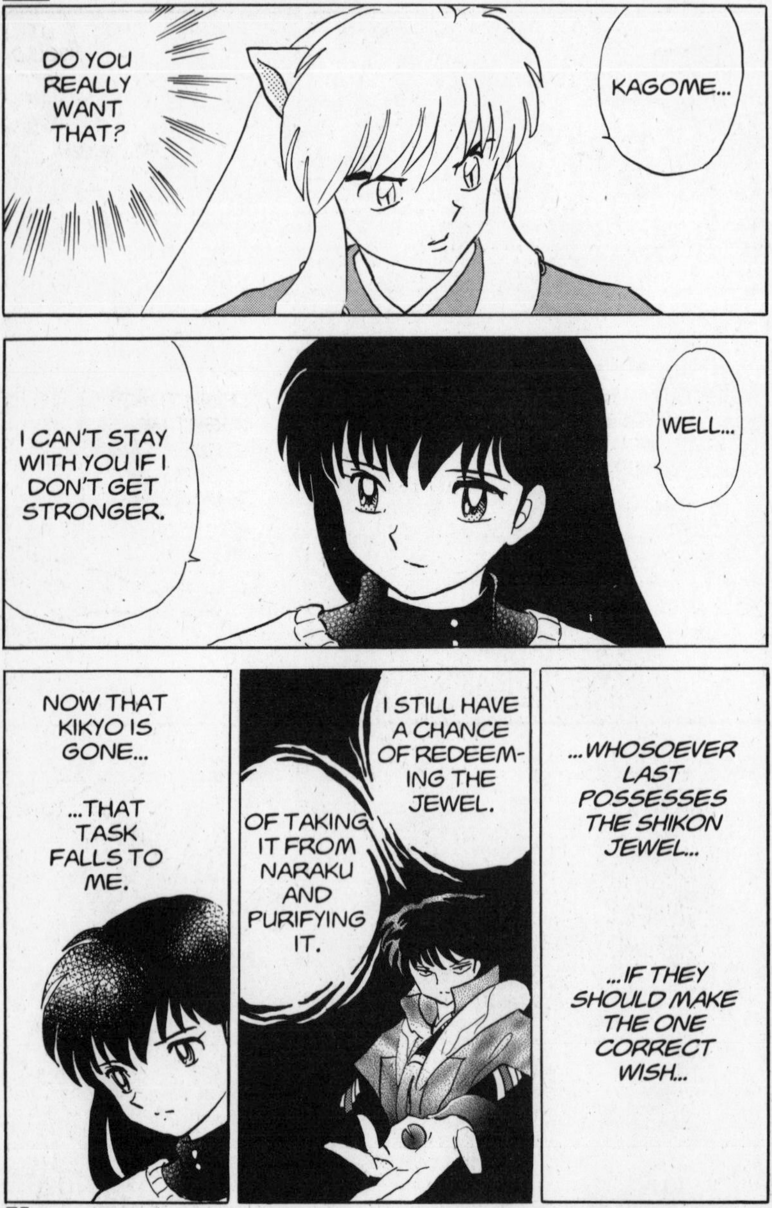
KAGOME...
DO YOU REALLY WANT THAT?
WELL...
I CAN'T STAY WITH YOU IF I DON'T GET STRONGER.
...WHOSOEVER LAST POSSESSES THE SHIKON JEWEL...
...IF THEY SHOULD MAKE THE ONE CORRECT WISH...
I STILL HAVE A CHANCE OF REDEEM-ING THE JEWEL.
OF TAKING IT FROM NARAKU AND PURIFYING IT.
NOW THAT KIKYO IS GONE...
...THAT TASK FALLS TO ME.

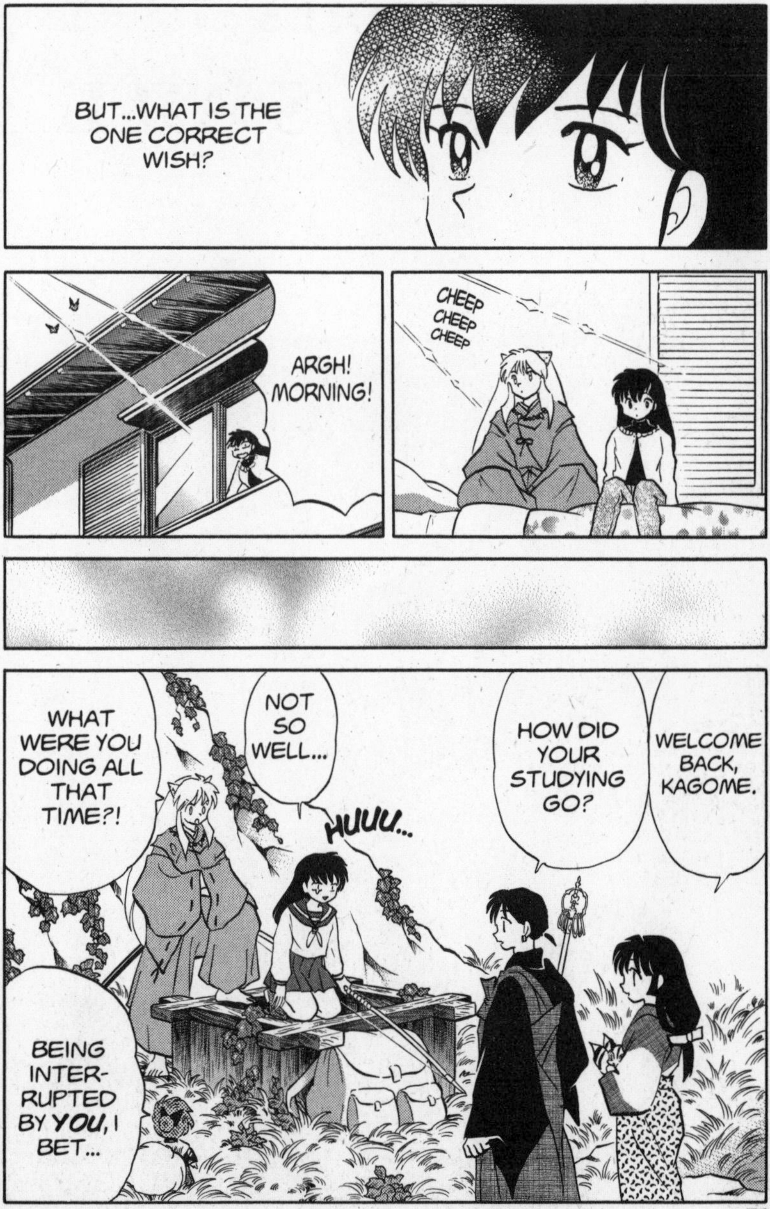
BUT...WHAT IS THE ONE CORRECT WISH?
CHEEP CHEEP CHEEP
ARGH! MORNING!
WELCOME BACK, KAGOME.
HOW DID YOUR STUDYING GO?
NOT SO WELL...
HUUU...
WHAT WERE YOU DOING ALL THAT TIME?!
BEING INTER-RUPTED BY **YOU**, I BET...

SCROLL 5

THE JEWEL'S WILL

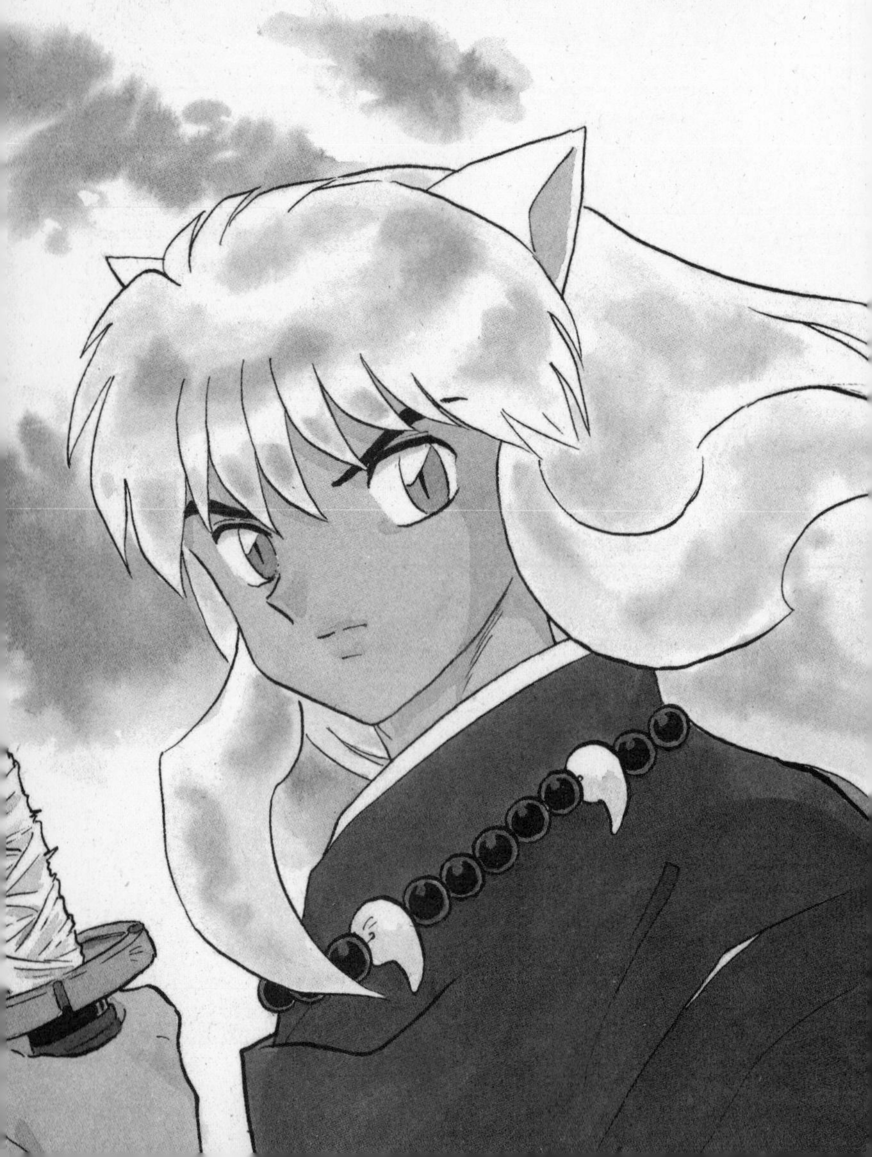

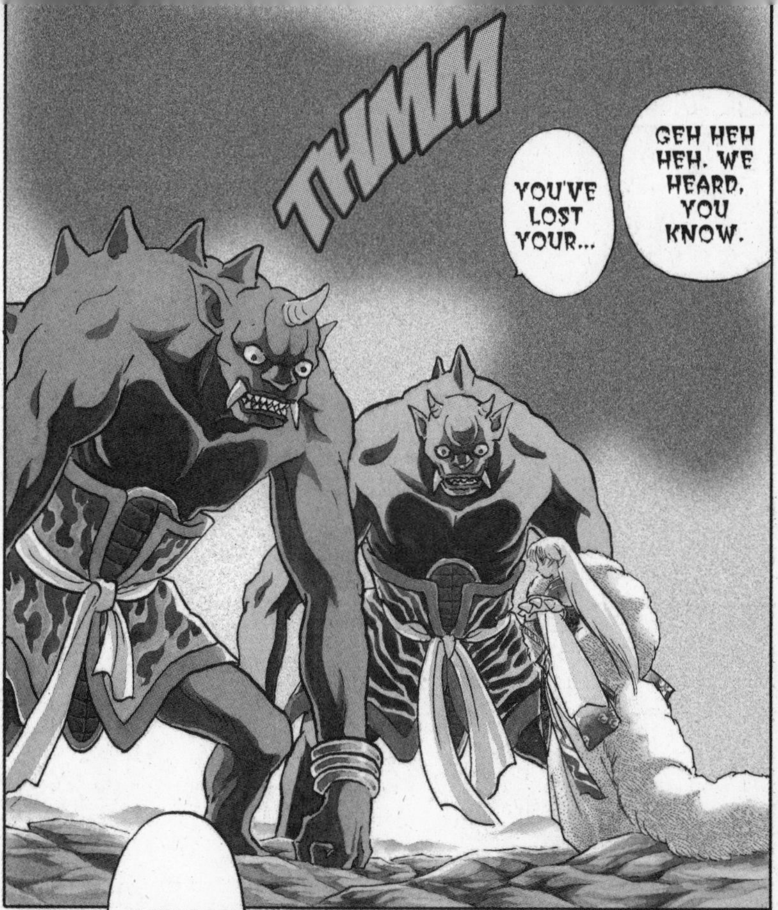
GEH HEH HEH. WE HEARD, YOU KNOW.
YOU'VE LOST YOUR...
THMM

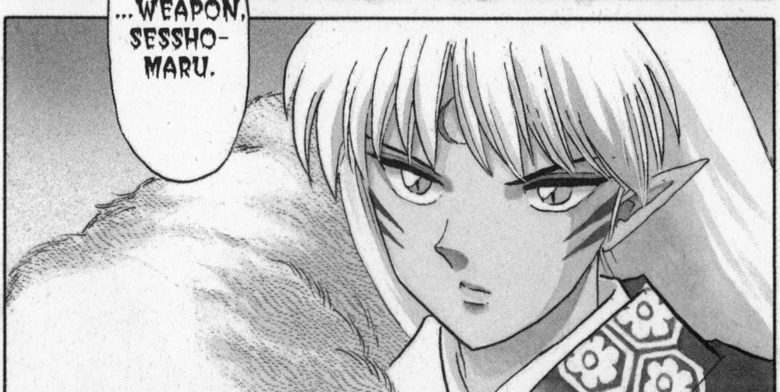
...WEAPON, SESSHO-MARU.

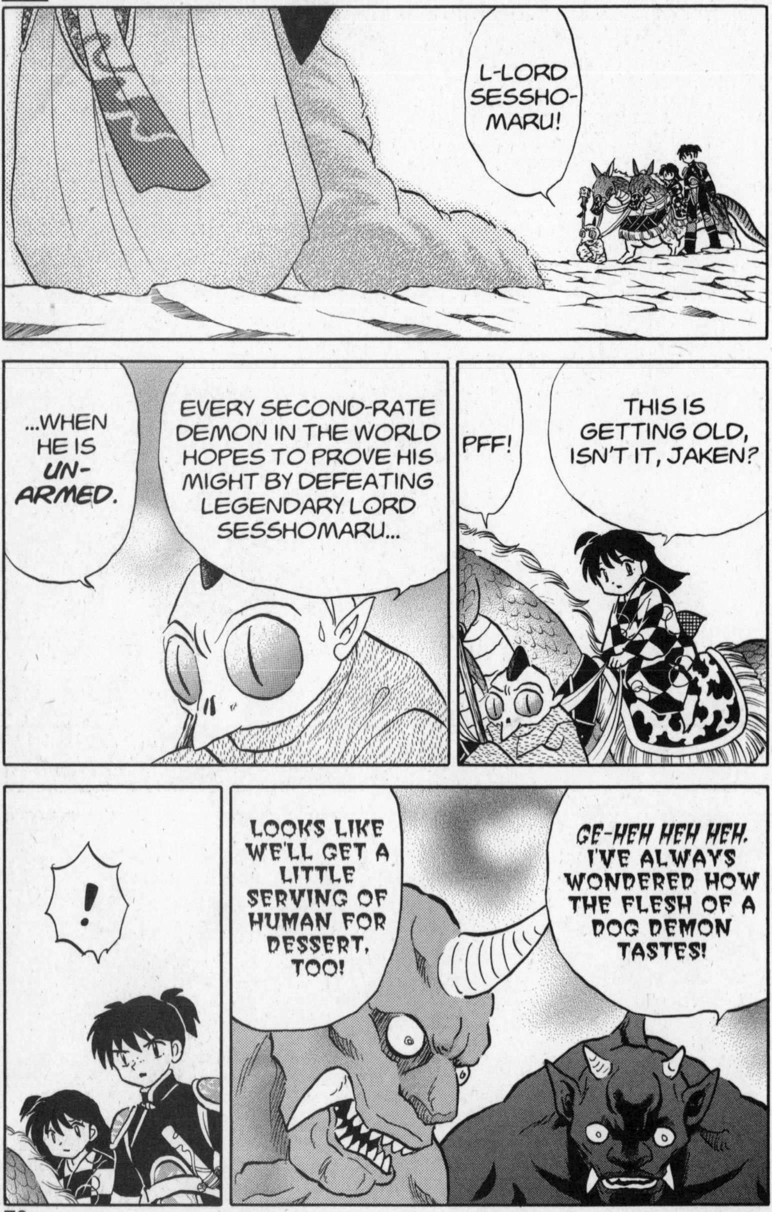
L-LORD SESSHO-MARU!
THIS IS GETTING OLD, ISN'T IT, JAKEN?
PFF!
EVERY SECOND-RATE DEMON IN THE WORLD HOPES TO PROVE HIS MIGHT BY DEFEATING LEGENDARY LORD SESSHOMARU...
...WHEN HE IS *UN-ARMED*.
GE-HEH HEH HEH. I'VE ALWAYS WONDERED HOW THE FLESH OF A DOG DEMON TASTES!
LOOKS LIKE WE'LL GET A LITTLE SERVING OF HUMAN FOR DESSERT, TOO!
!

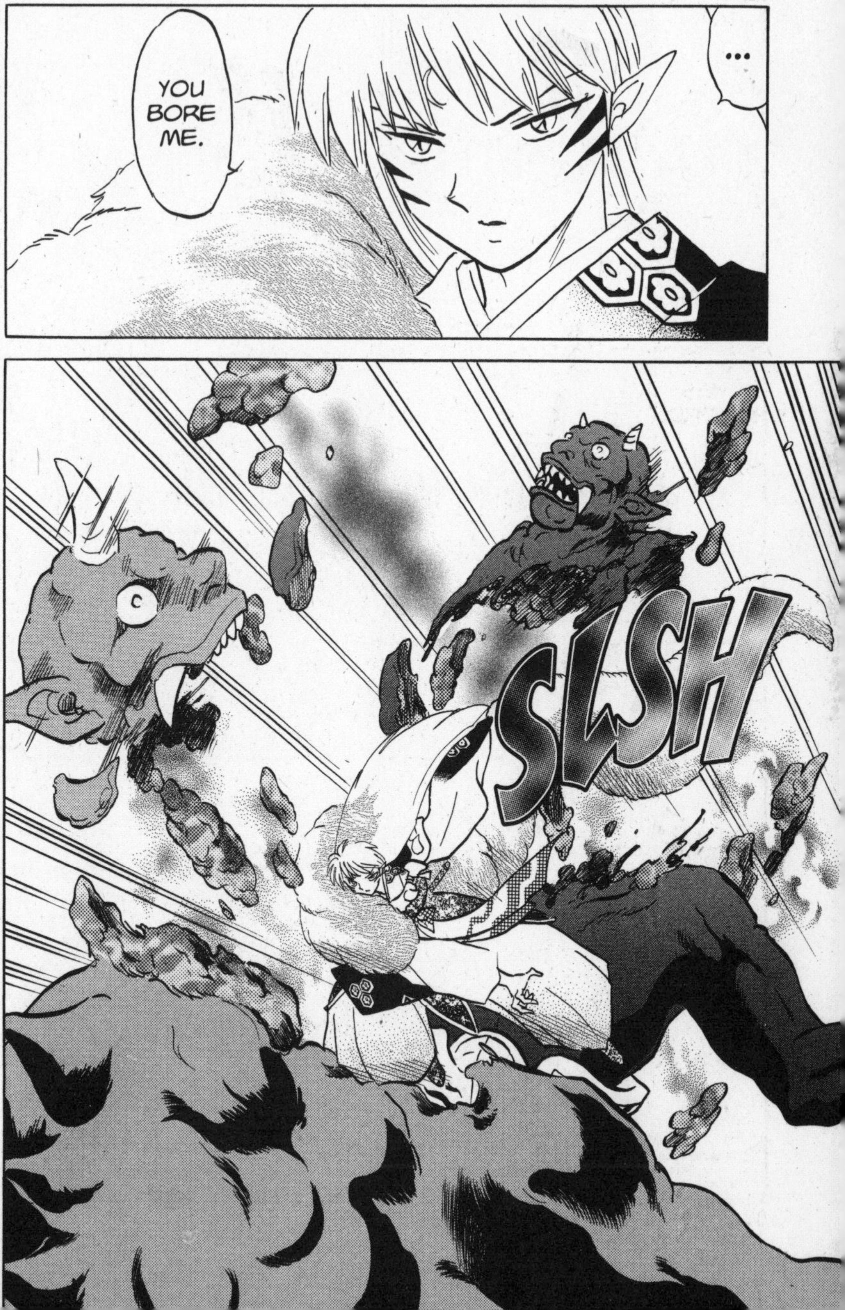
...
YOU BORE ME.
SLSH

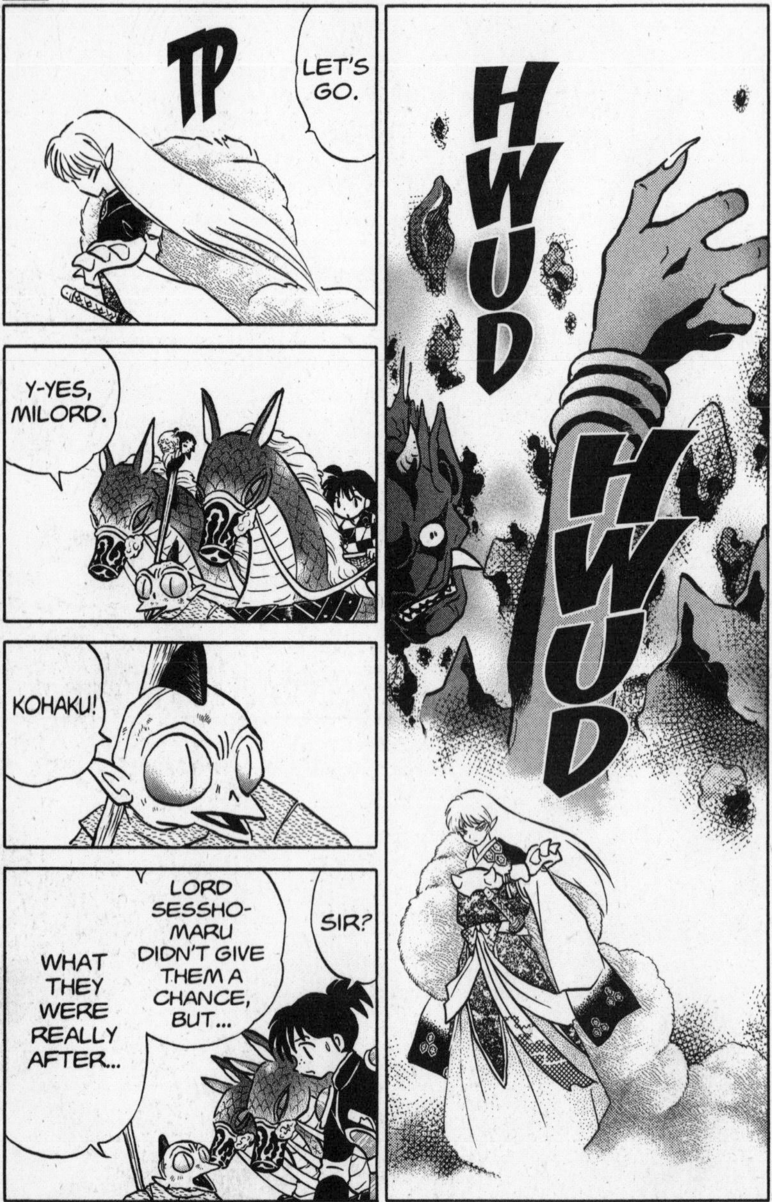
HWUD
HWUD
LET'S GO.
TP
Y-YES, MILORD.
KOHAKU!
SIR?
LORD SESSHO-MARU DIDN'T GIVE THEM A CHANCE, BUT...
WHAT THEY WERE REALLY AFTER...

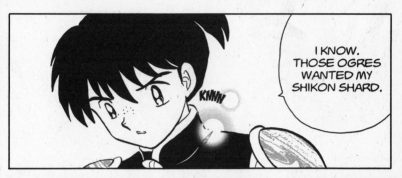

I KNOW. THOSE OGRES WANTED MY SHIKON SHARD.
KNNN
ONE OF THESE DAYS I'M GOING TO GET EATEN, THANKS TO YOU!
DON'T WORRY. YOU'RE TOO SMALL FOR AN OGRE TO BOTHER WITH.
...
WHHHH
HMM ...
IT'S TRUE... SESSHO-MARU DOESN'T WIELD HIS BLADE ANYMORE.
I HEARD THAT EVER SINCE HE LOST THAT MEIDO MOVE OF HIS...
...THE BLADE AT HIS SIDE IS JUST A FASHION ACCESSORY.

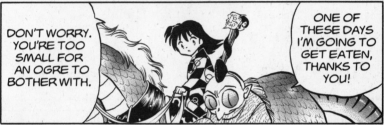

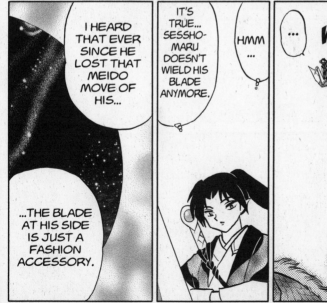

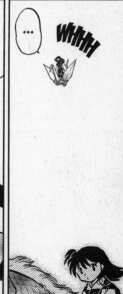

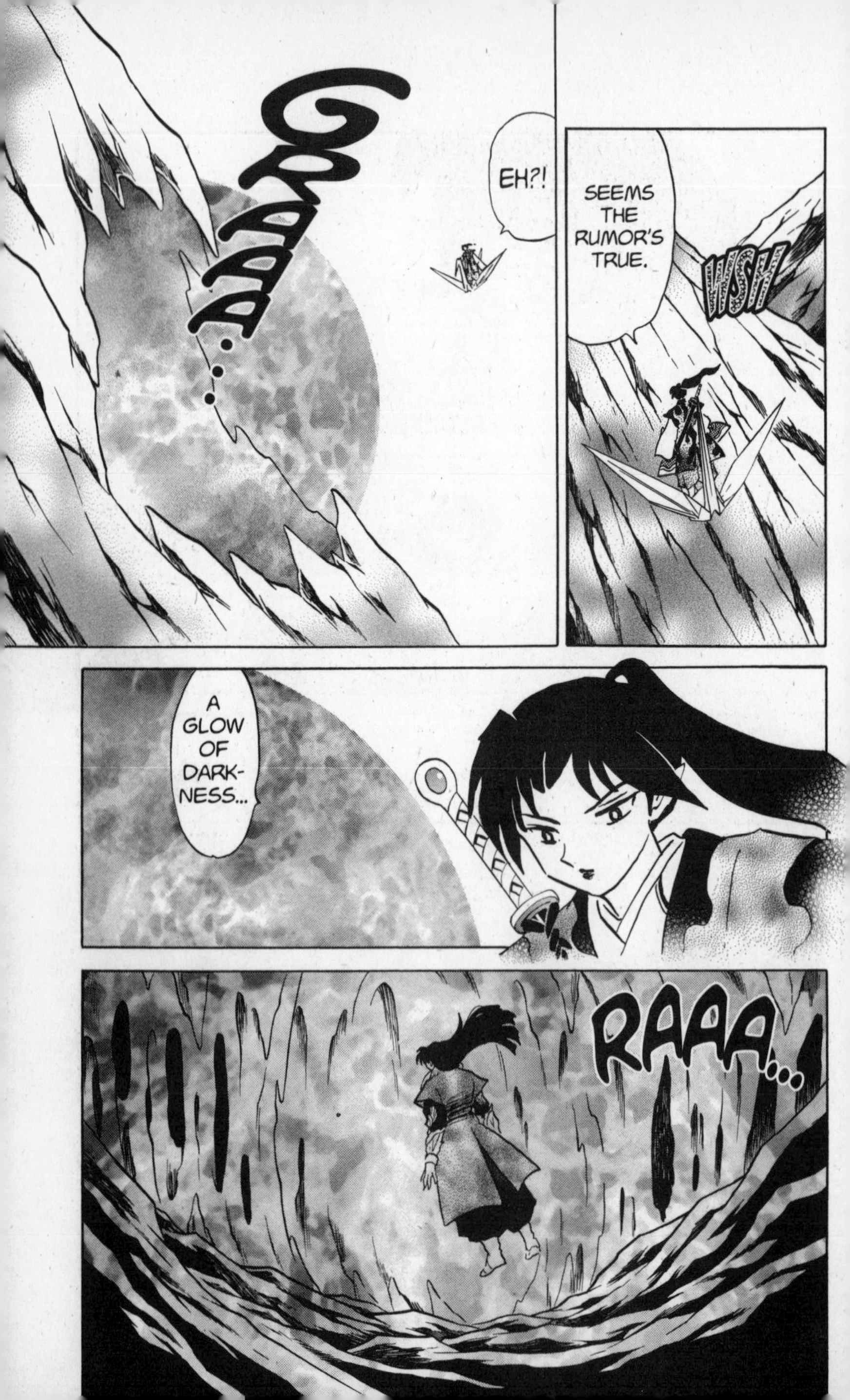
SEEMS THE RUMOR'S TRUE.
WSH
EH?!
GRAAA...
A GLOW OF DARK-NESS...
RAAA...

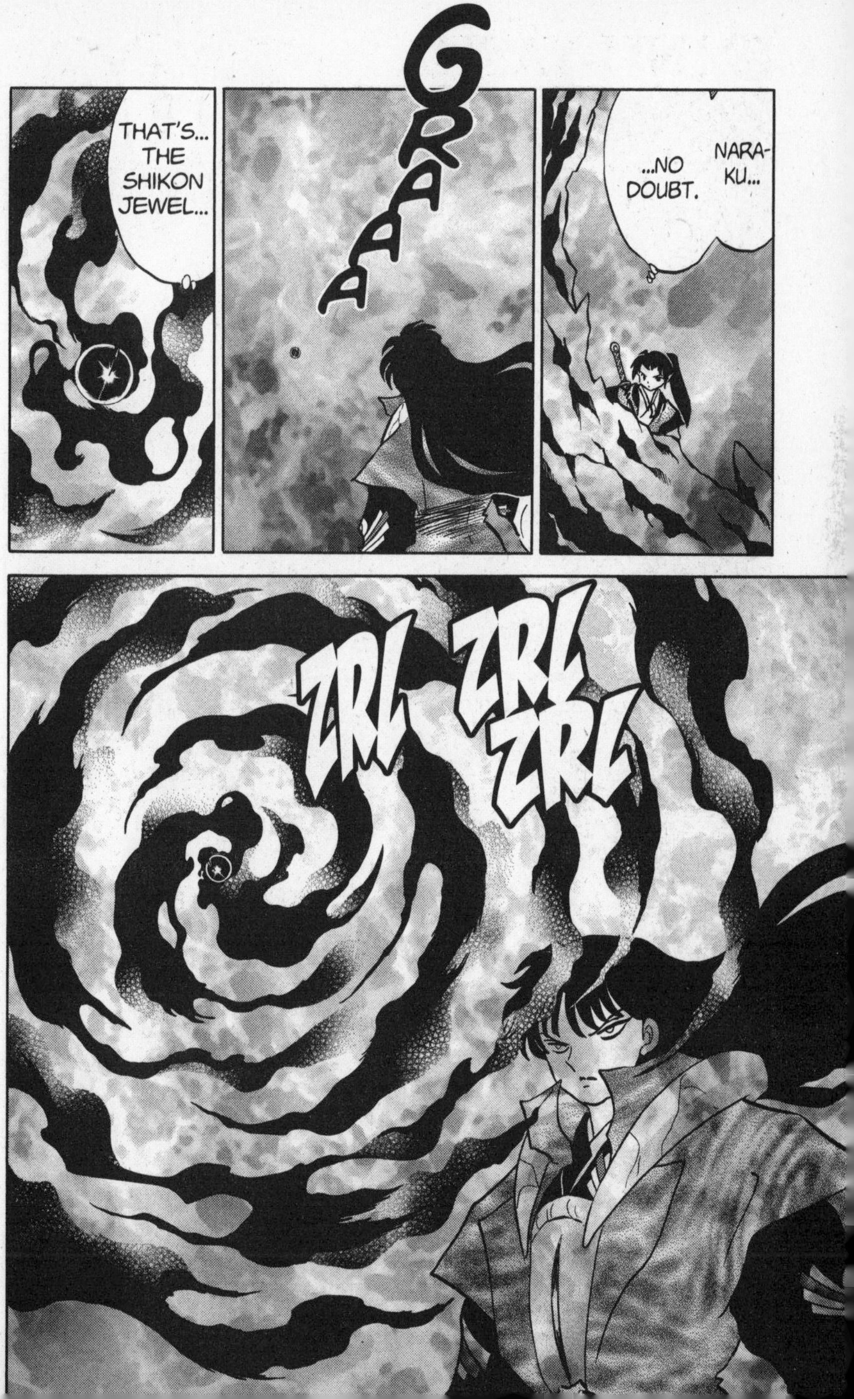
NARA-KU...
...NO DOUBT.
GRAAAA
THAT'S... THE SHIKON JEWEL...
ZRL ZRL ZRL ZRL

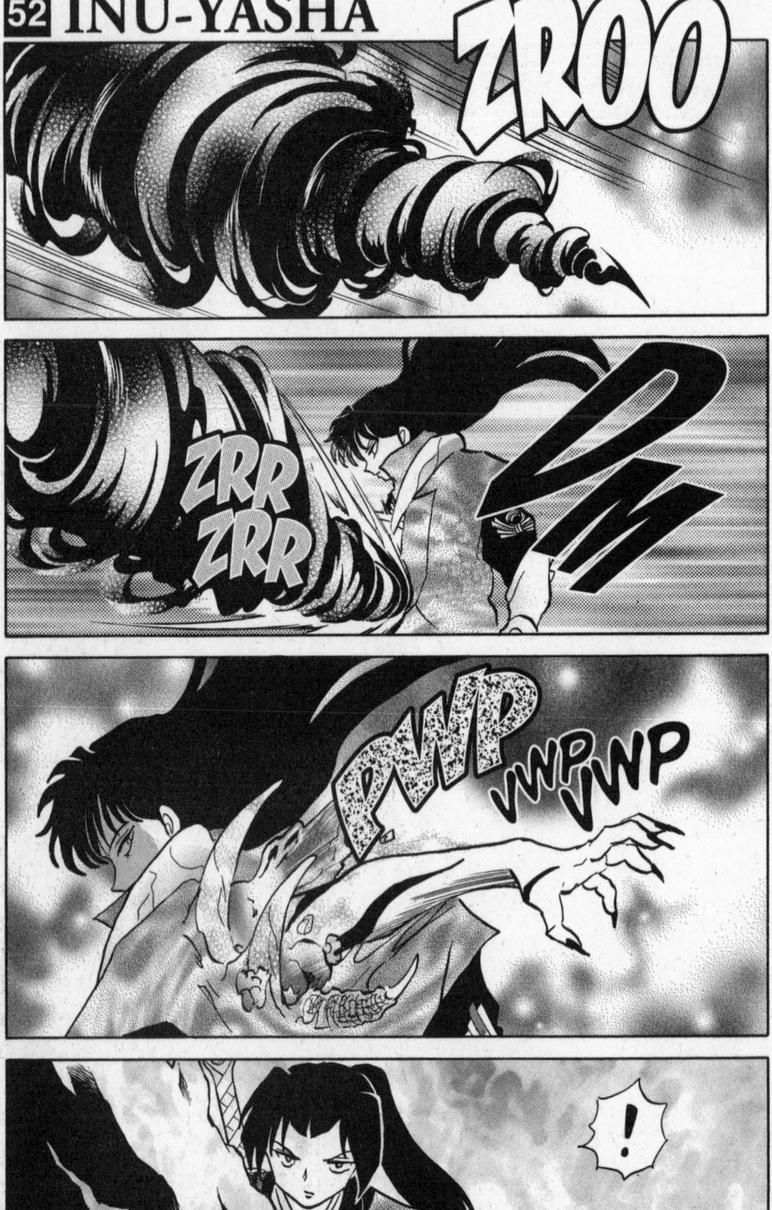
ZROO
DM
ZRR ZRR
VWP VWP
DWP
!

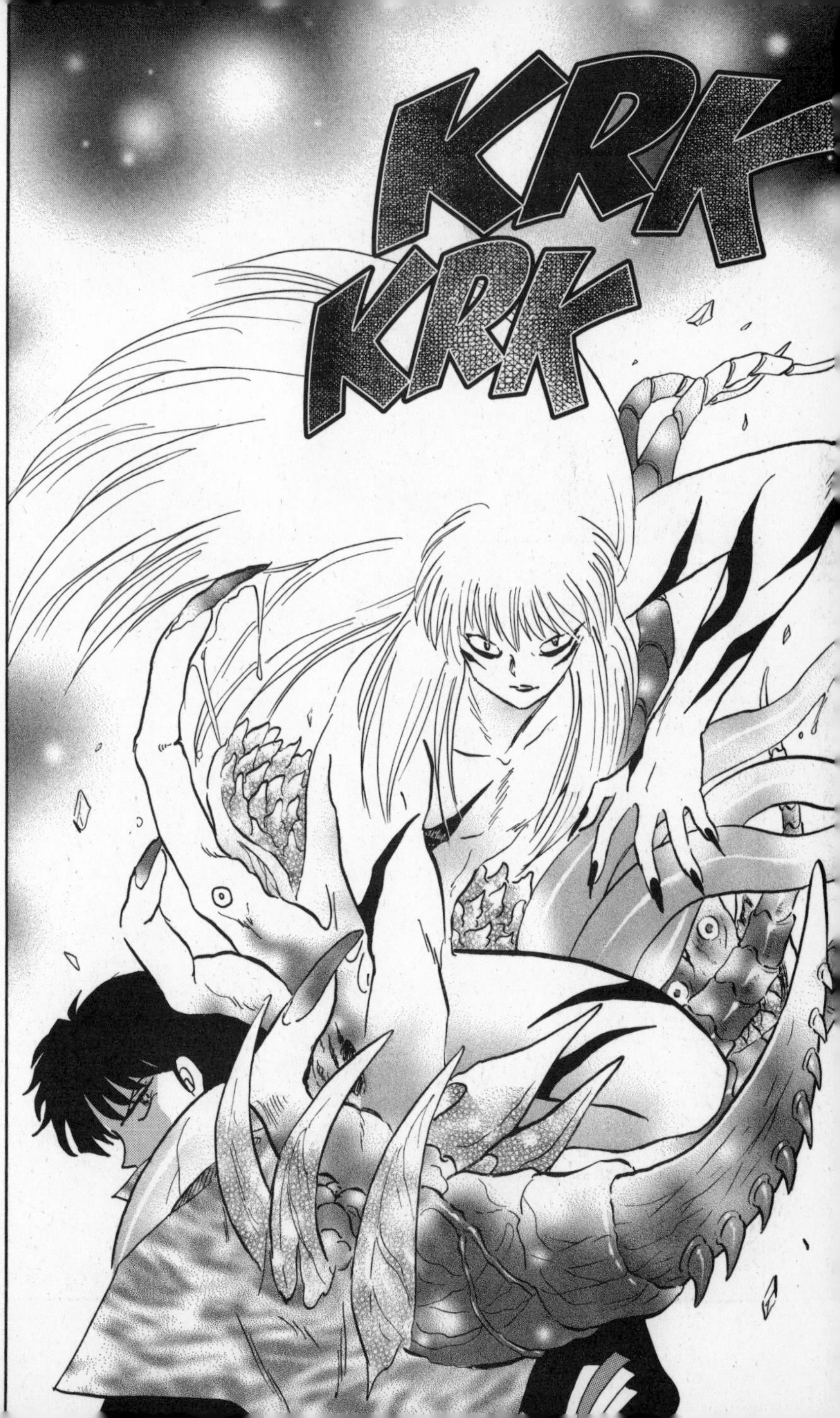
KRK
KRK

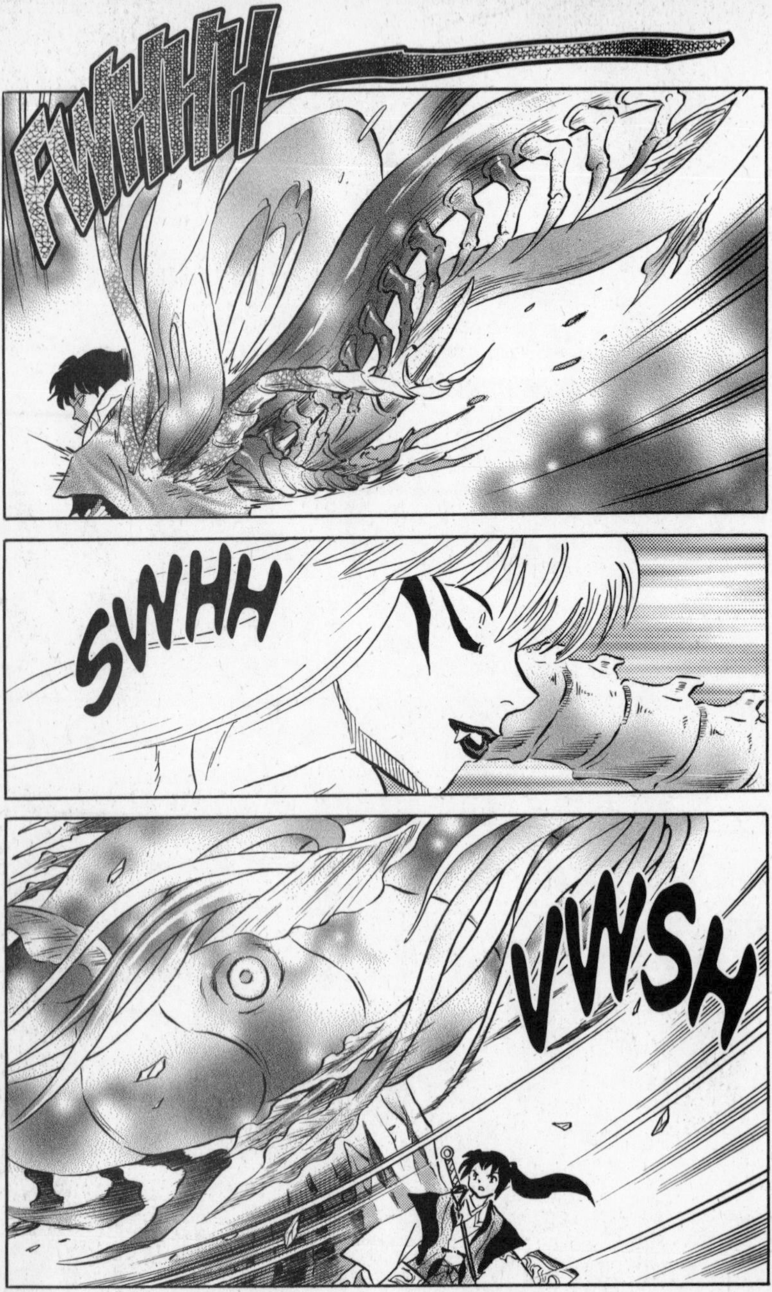
FWHHH
SWHH
VWSH

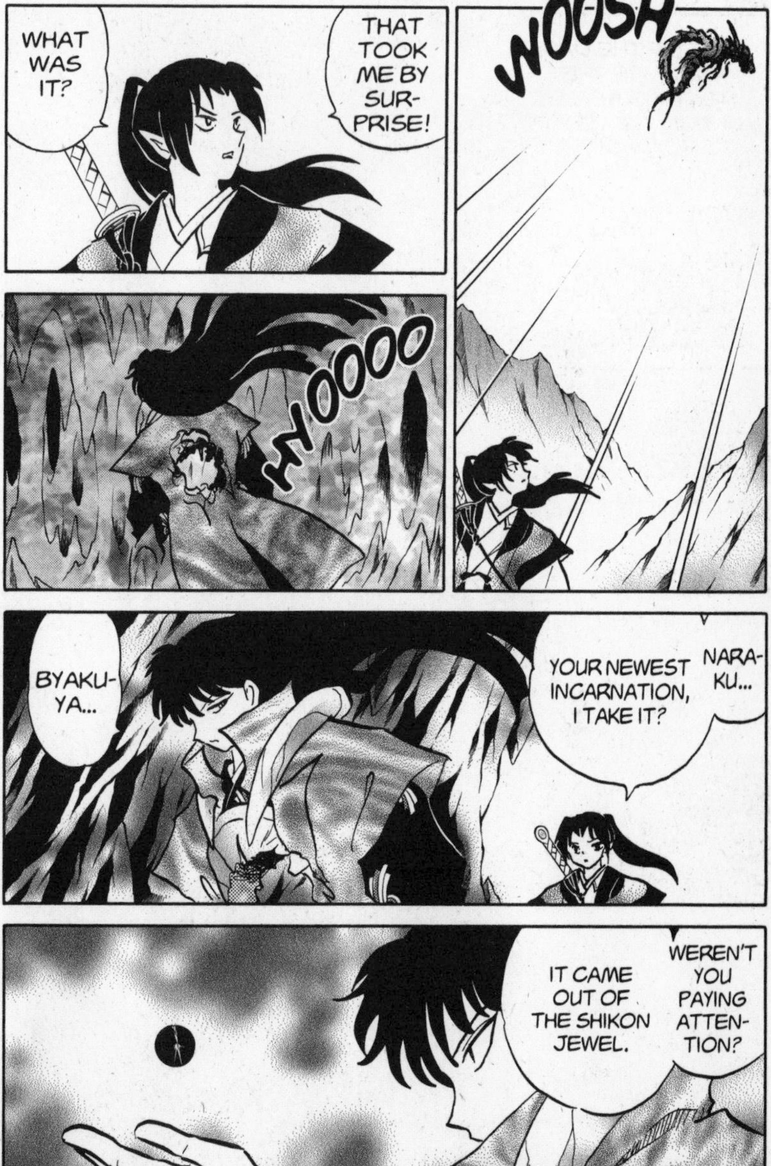
WOOSH
THAT TOOK ME BY SURPRISE!
WHAT WAS IT?
WHOOOO
NARAKU...
YOUR NEWEST INCARNATION, I TAKE IT?
BYAKUYA...
WEREN'T YOU PAYING ATTENTION?
IT CAME OUT OF THE SHIKON JEWEL.

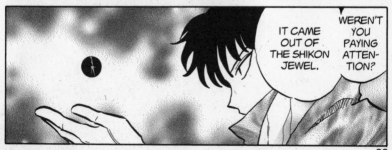

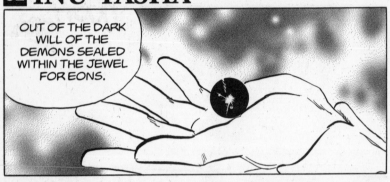

OUT OF THE DARK WILL OF THE DEMONS SEALED WITHIN THE JEWEL FOR EONS.

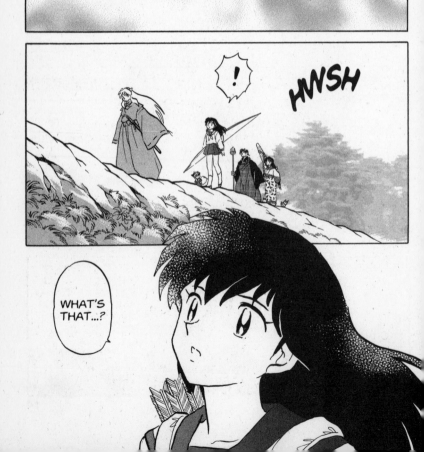

!

HWSH

WHAT'S THAT...?

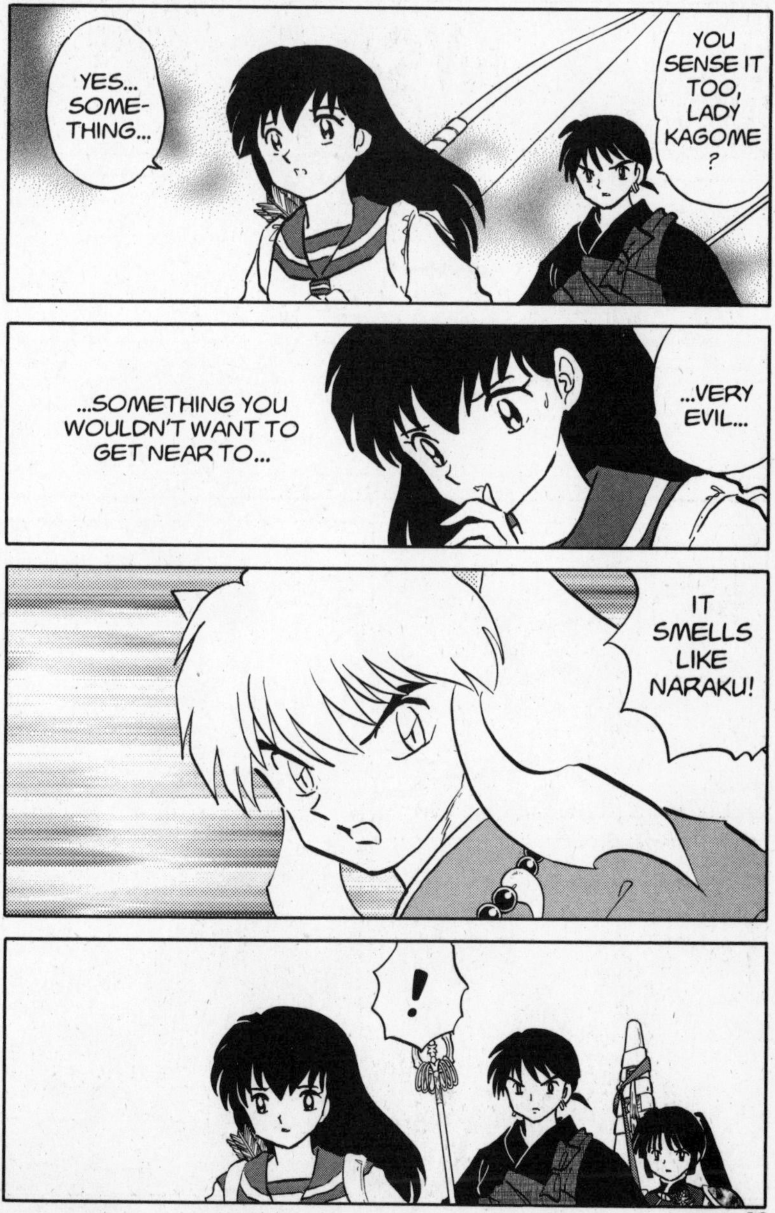
YOU SENSE IT TOO, LADY KAGOME?
YES... SOME-THING...
...VERY EVIL...
...SOMETHING YOU WOULDN'T WANT TO GET NEAR TO...
IT SMELLS LIKE NARAKU!
!

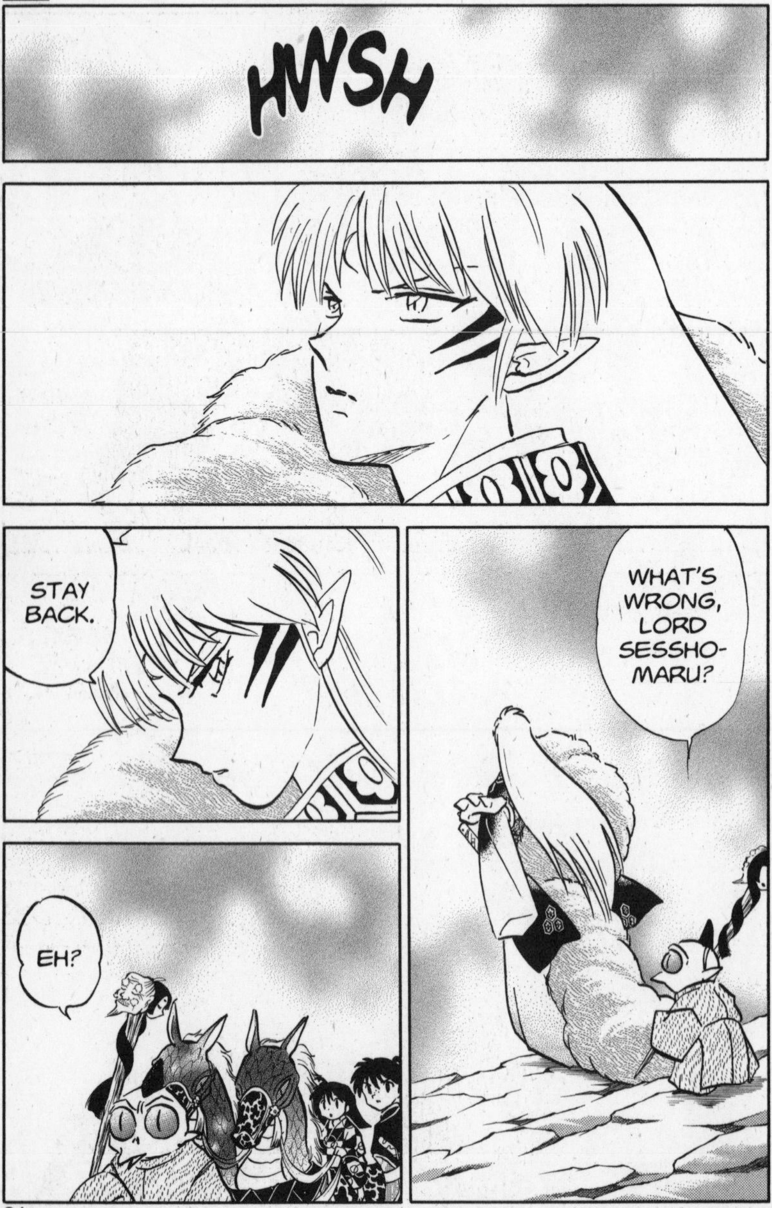
HWSH
WHAT'S WRONG, LORD SESSHO-MARU?
STAY BACK.
EH?

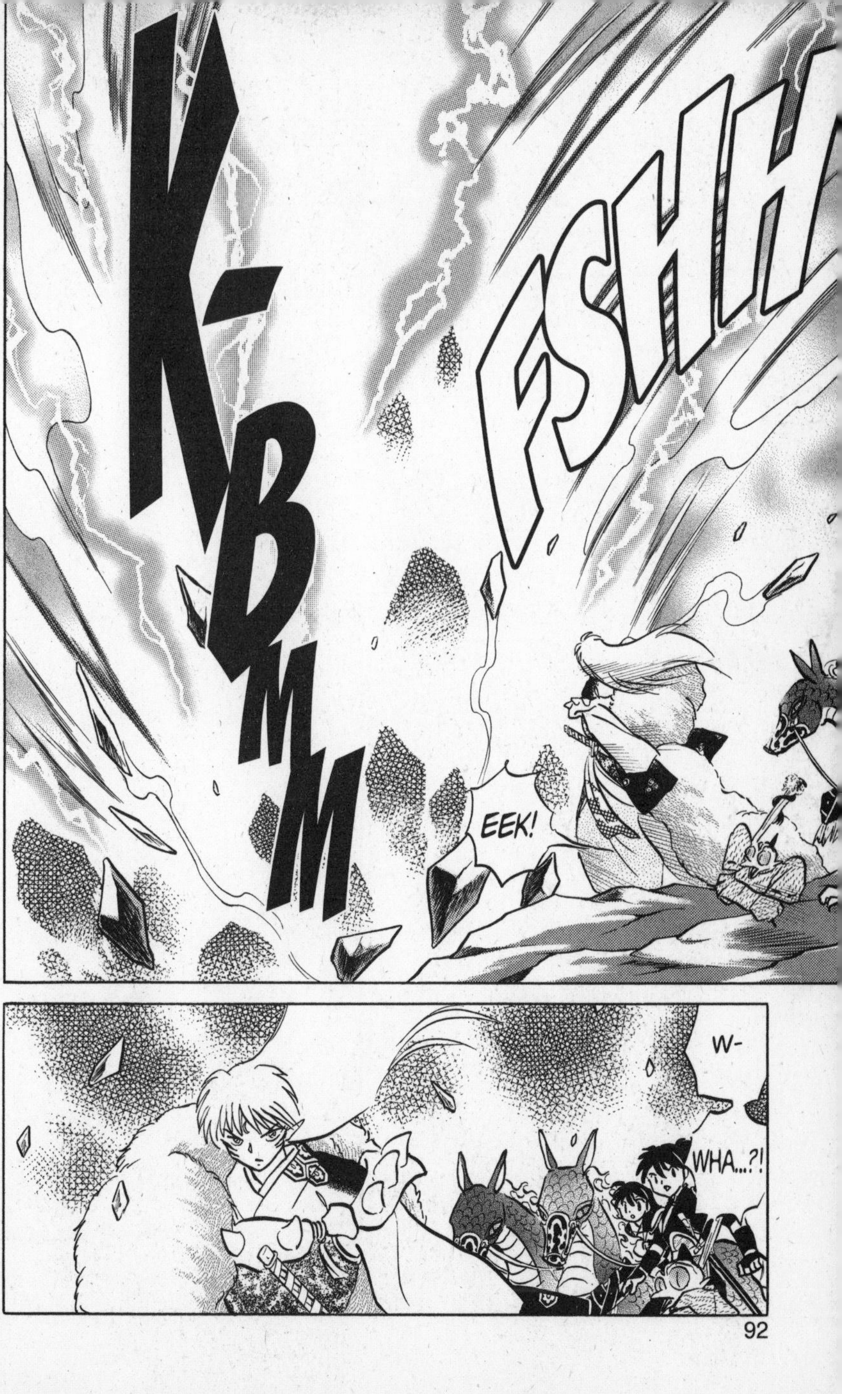
FSHH
K-BMMM
EEK!
W-
WHA...?!

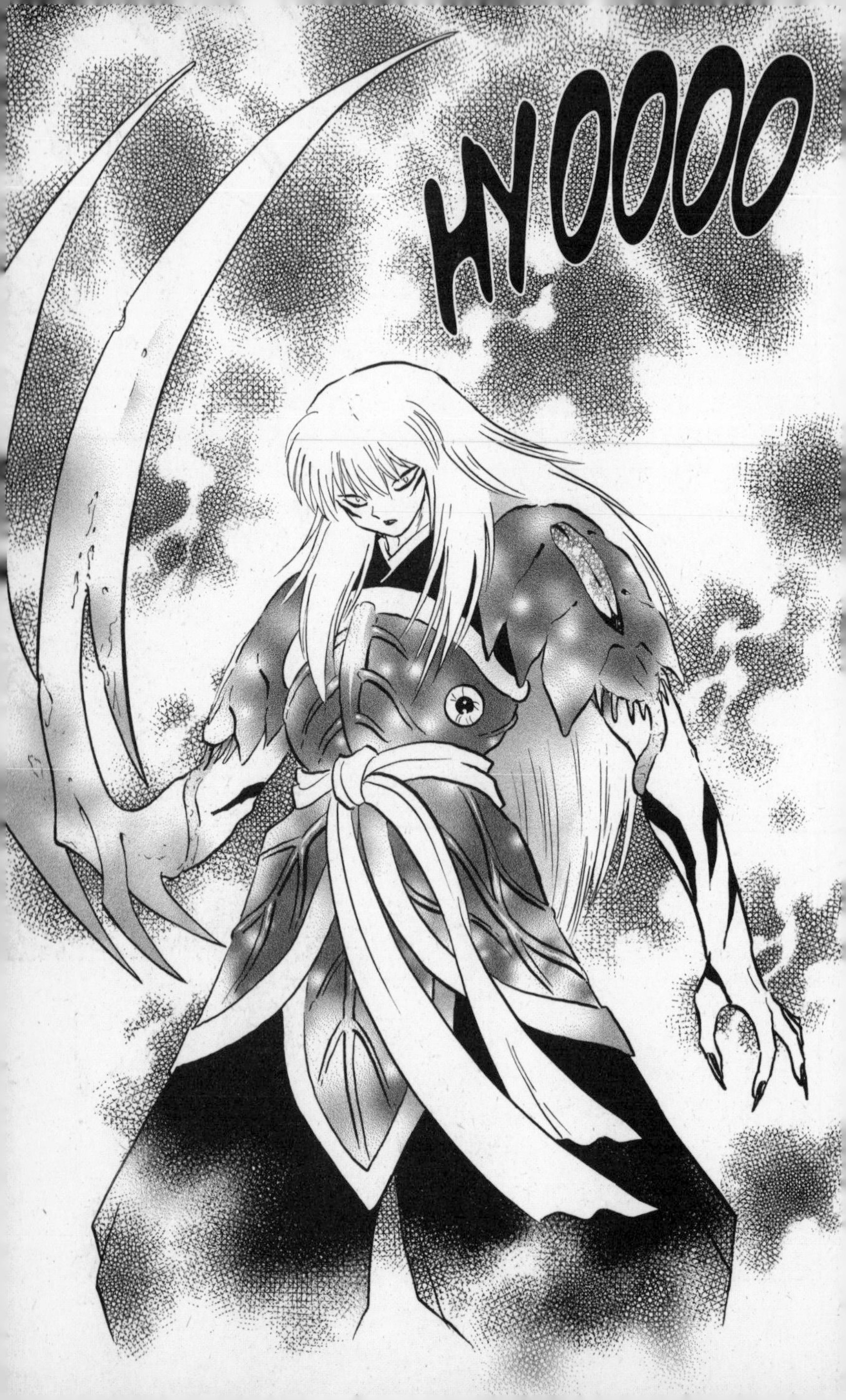
HYOOOO

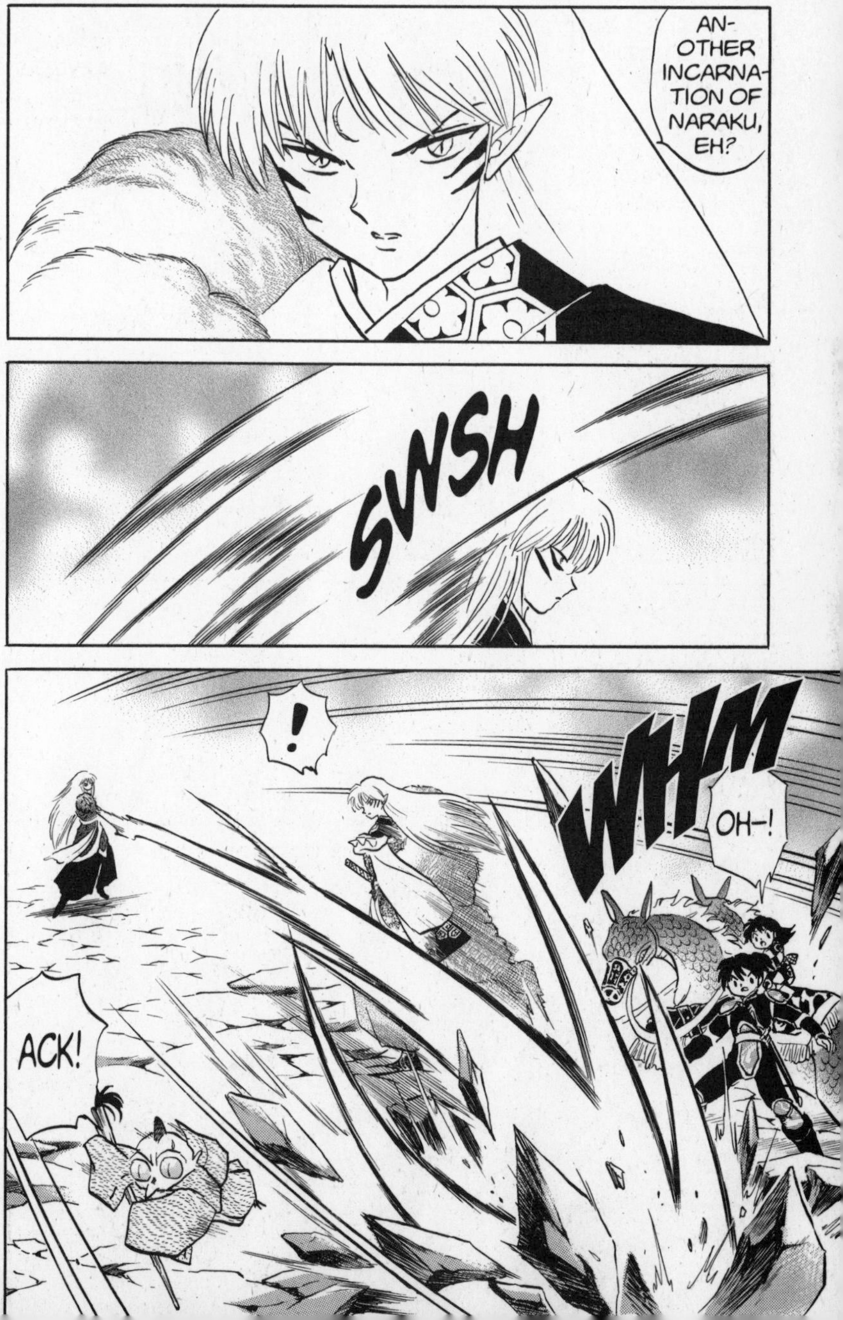
AN-OTHER INCARNATION OF NARAKU, EH?
SWSH
WHM
OH—!
!
ACK!

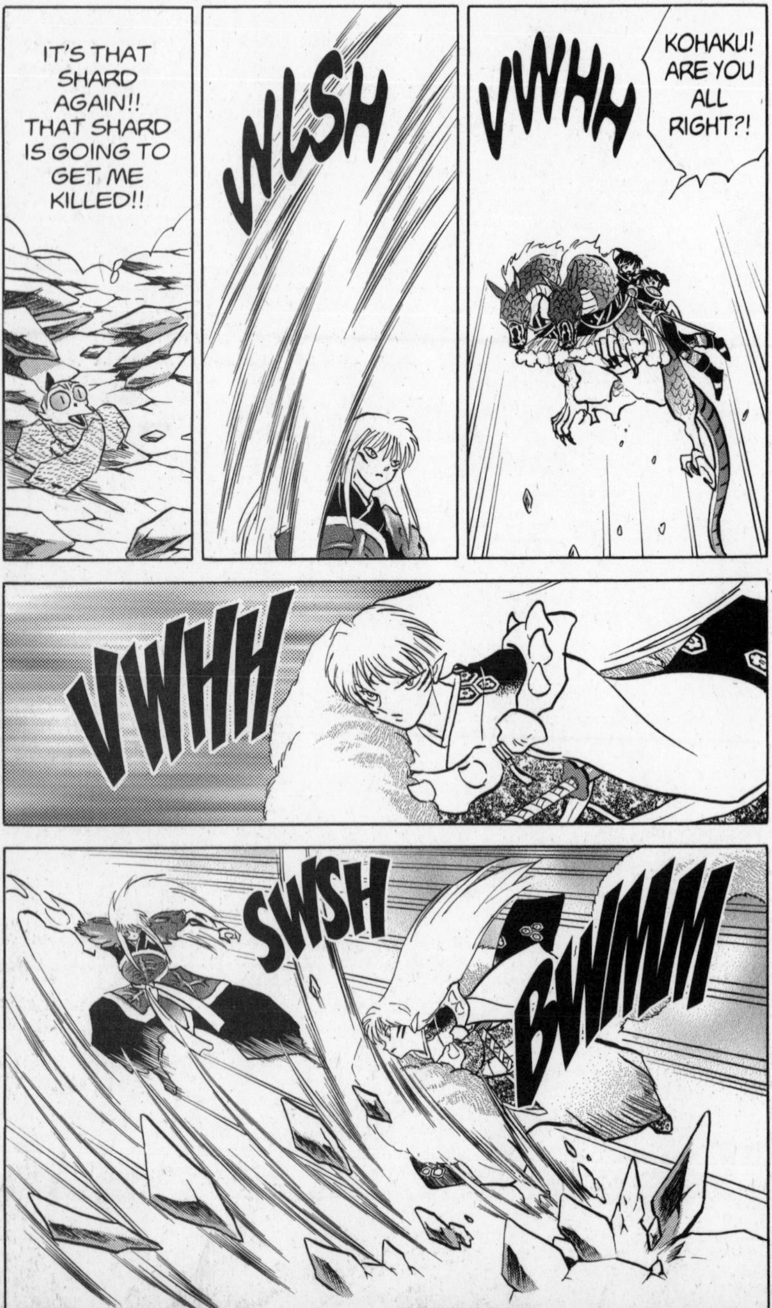
KOHAKU! ARE YOU ALL RIGHT?!
VWHH
WLSH
IT'S THAT SHARD AGAIN!! THAT SHARD IS GOING TO GET ME KILLED!!
VWHH
BWMM
SWSH

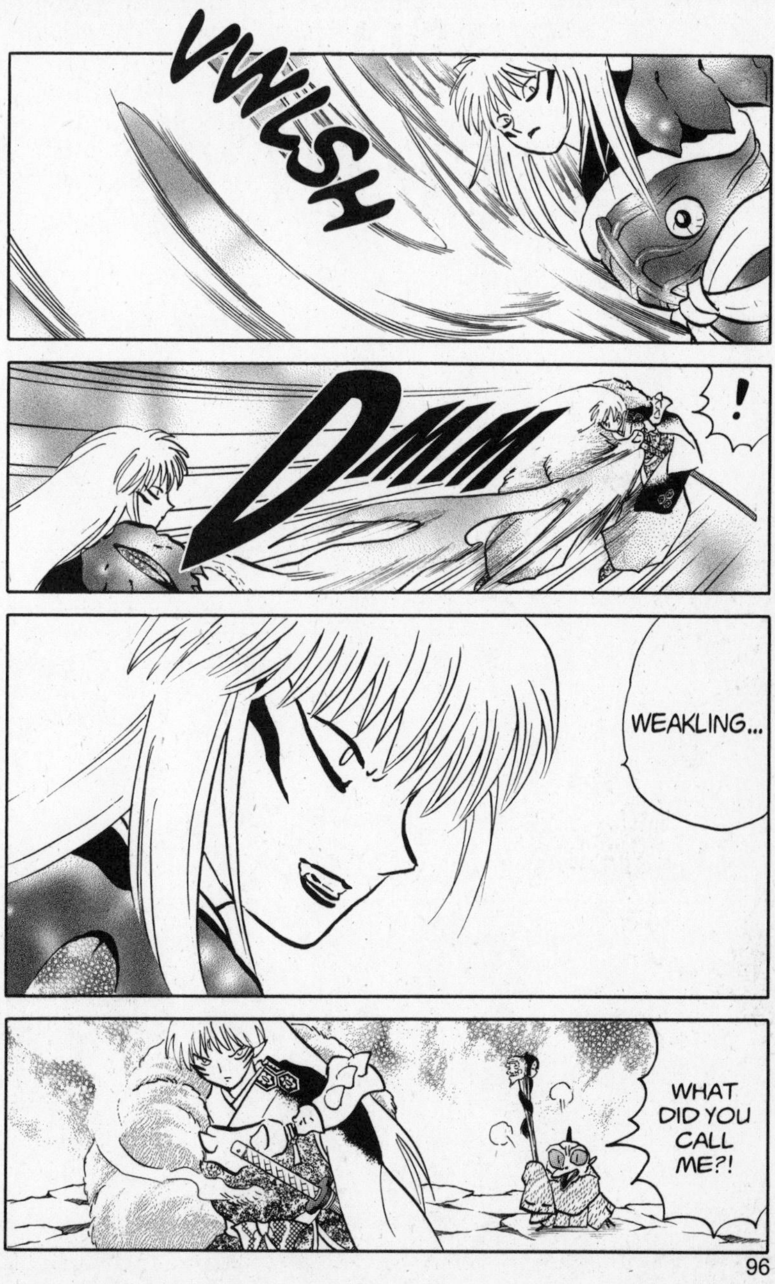
VWISH
!
DMM
WEAKLING...
WHAT DID YOU CALL ME?!

SCROLL 6

PERIL

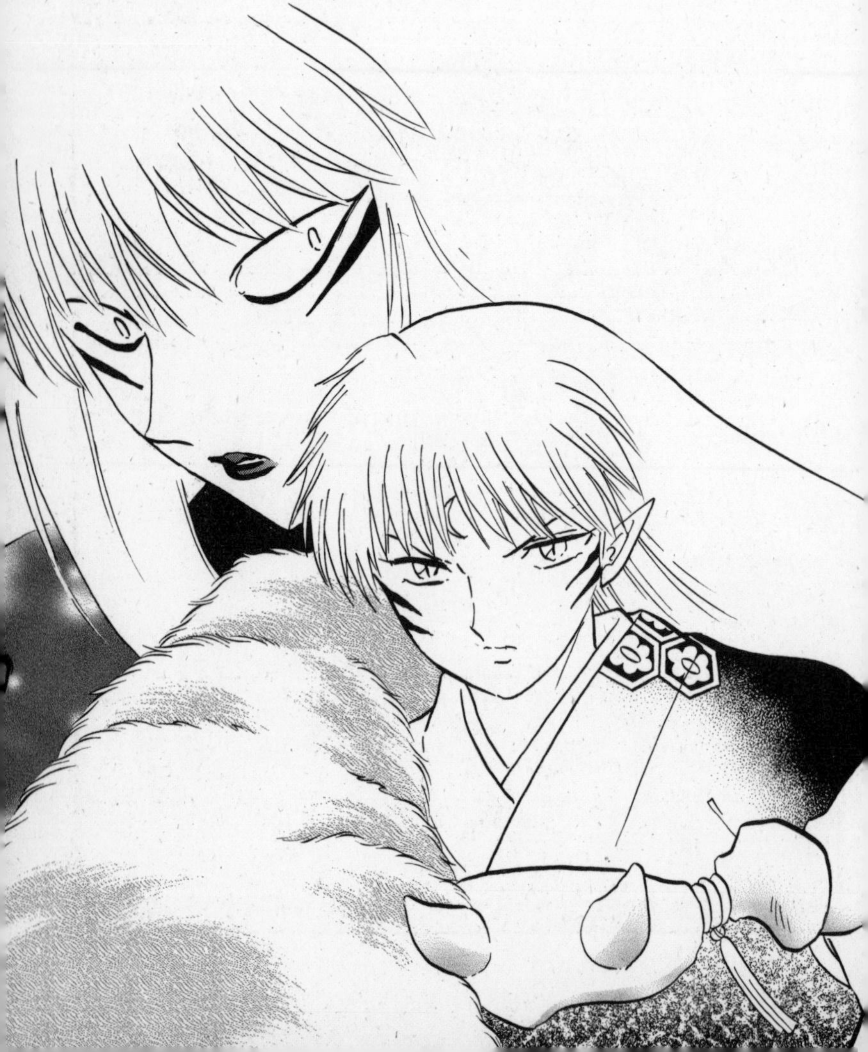

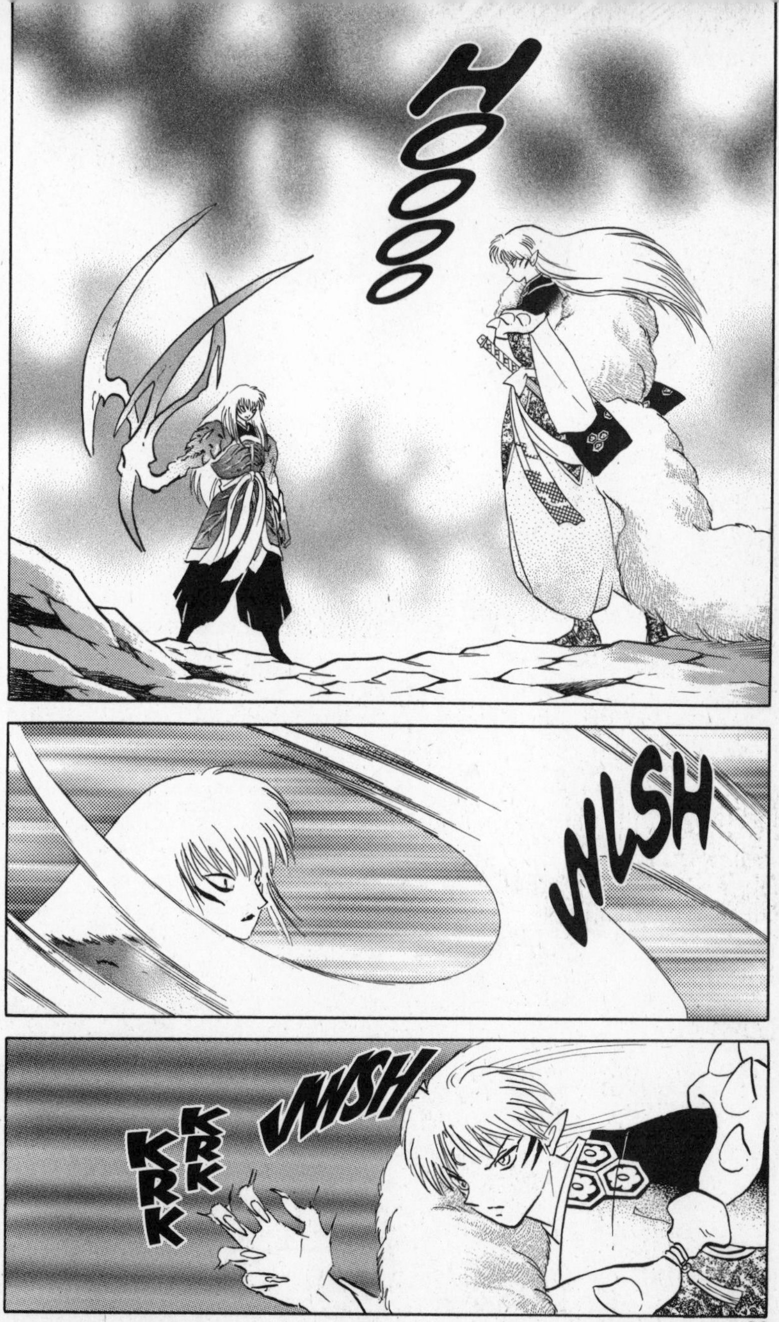
HOOOOO
WUSH
WUSH
KRK
KRK

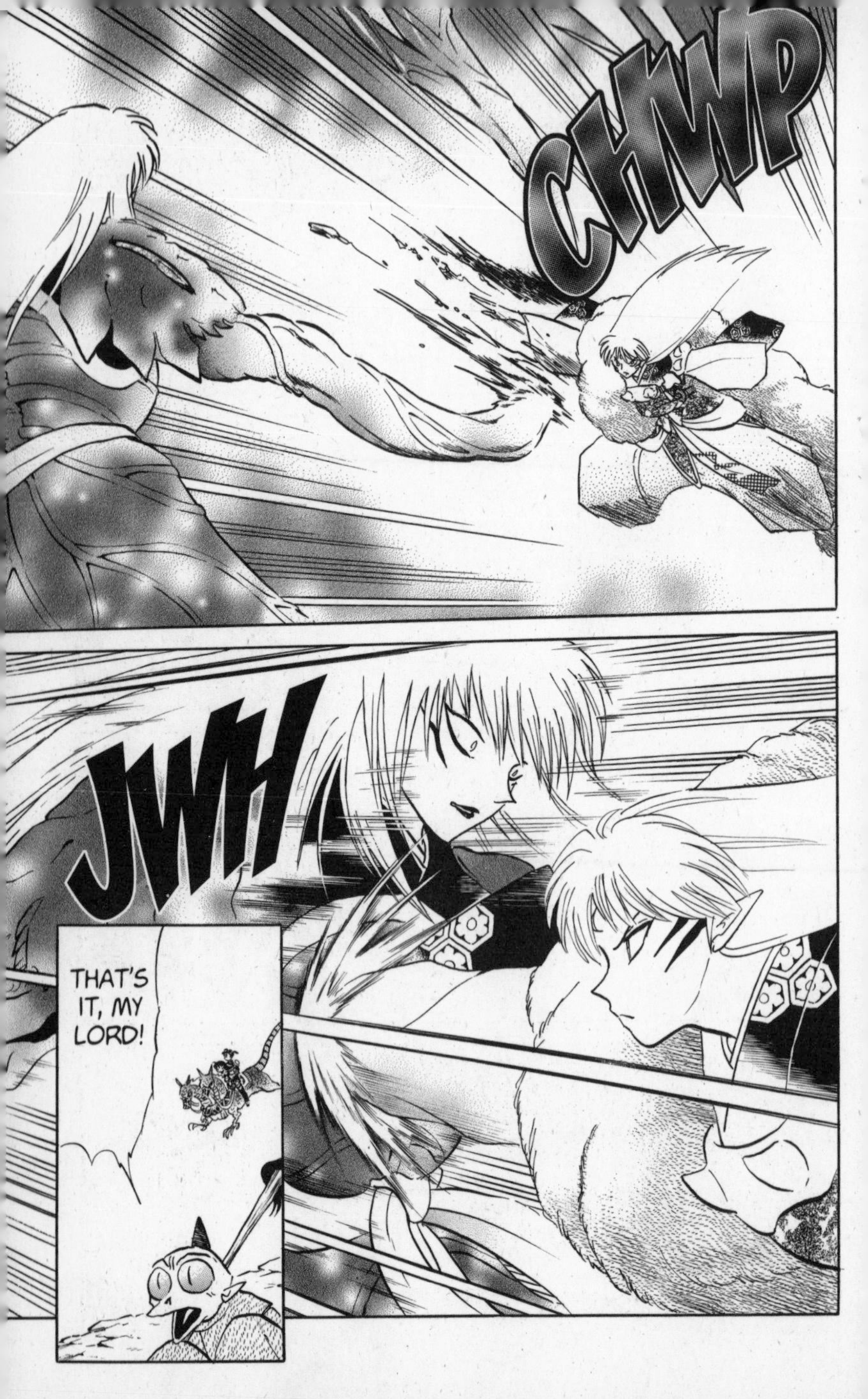
CHWP
JWH
THAT'S IT, MY LORD!

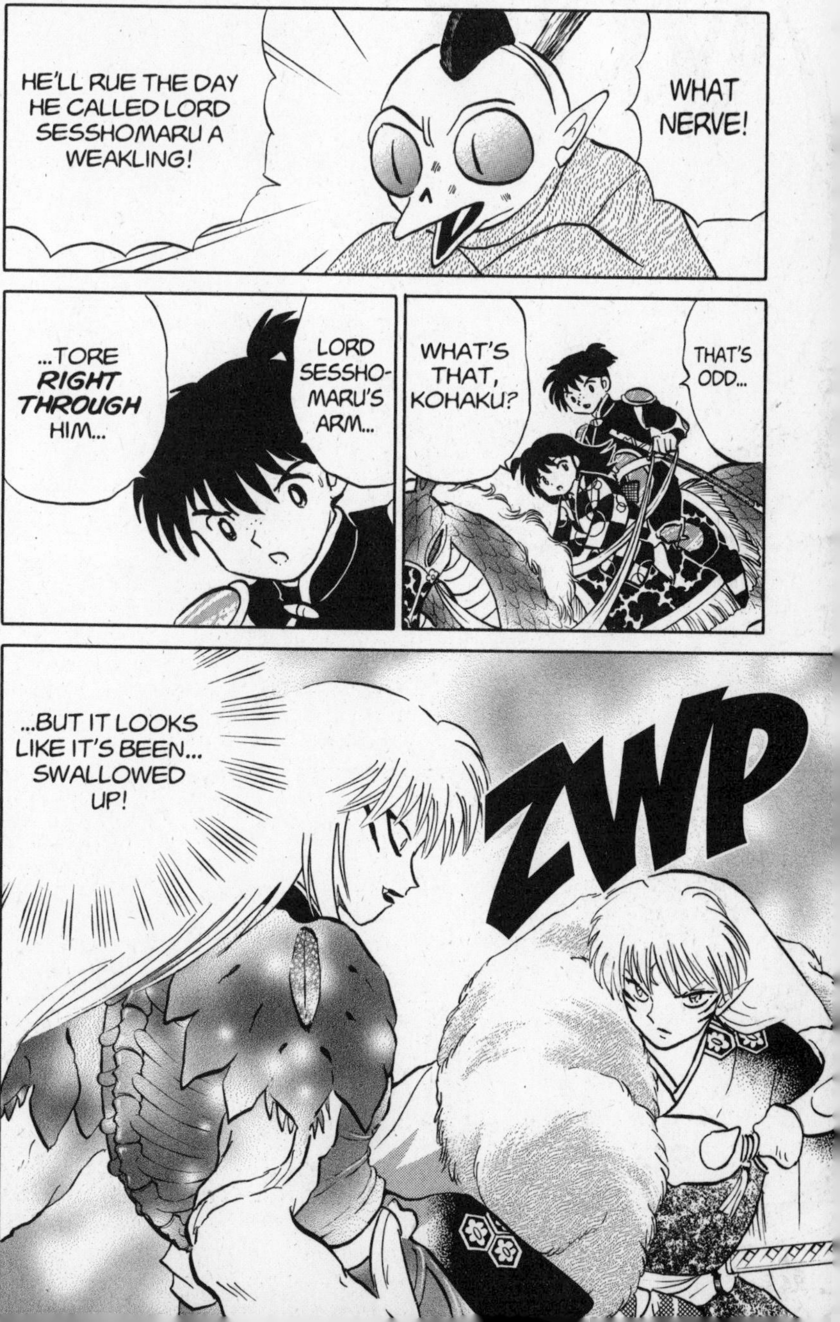
WHAT NERVE!
HE'LL RUE THE DAY HE CALLED LORD SESSHOMARU A WEAKLING!
THAT'S ODD...
WHAT'S THAT, KOHAKU?
LORD SESSHOMARU'S ARM...
...TORE **RIGHT THROUGH** HIM...
...BUT IT LOOKS LIKE IT'S BEEN... SWALLOWED UP!
ZWP

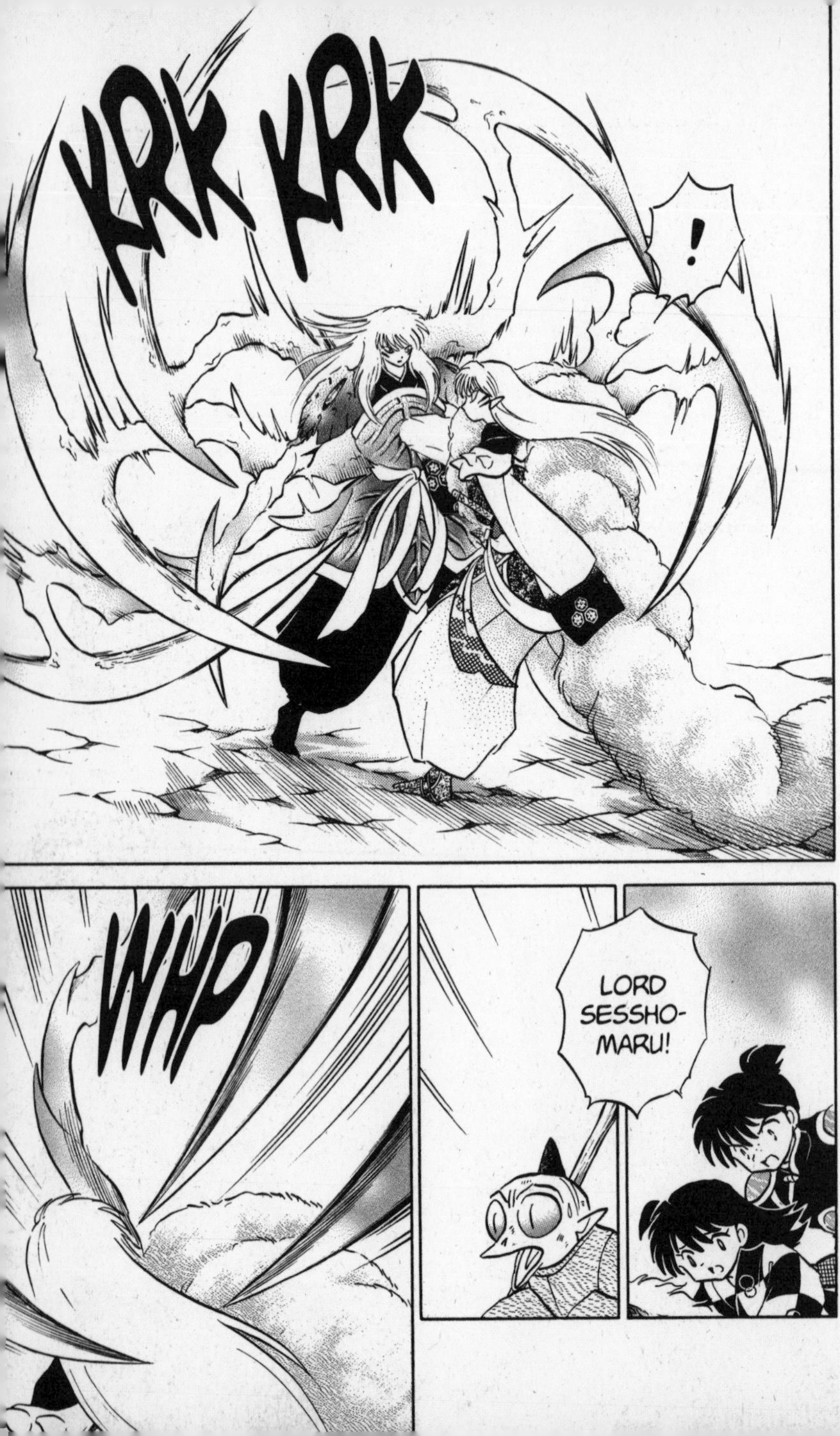
!
KRK KRK
LORD SESSHO-MARU!
WHP

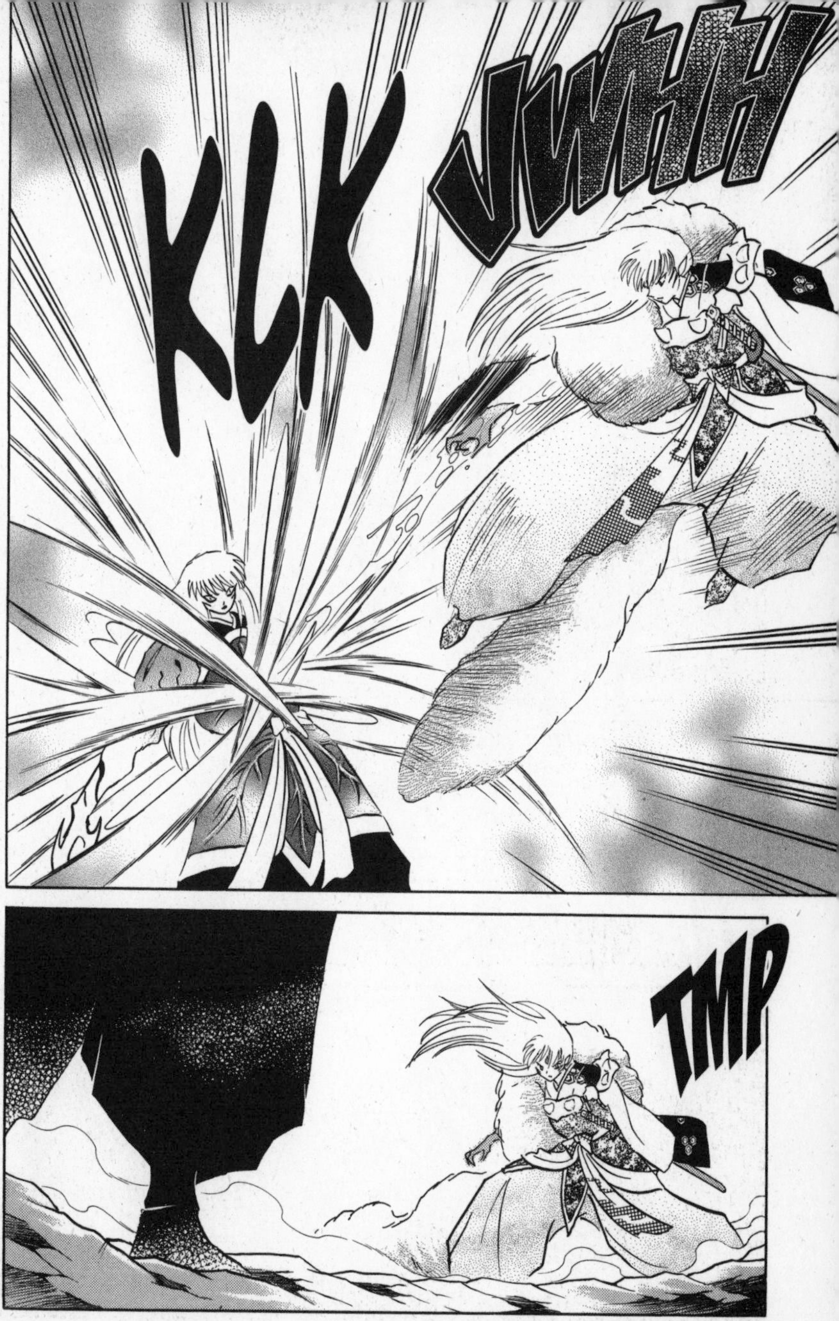
JWHH
KLK
TMP

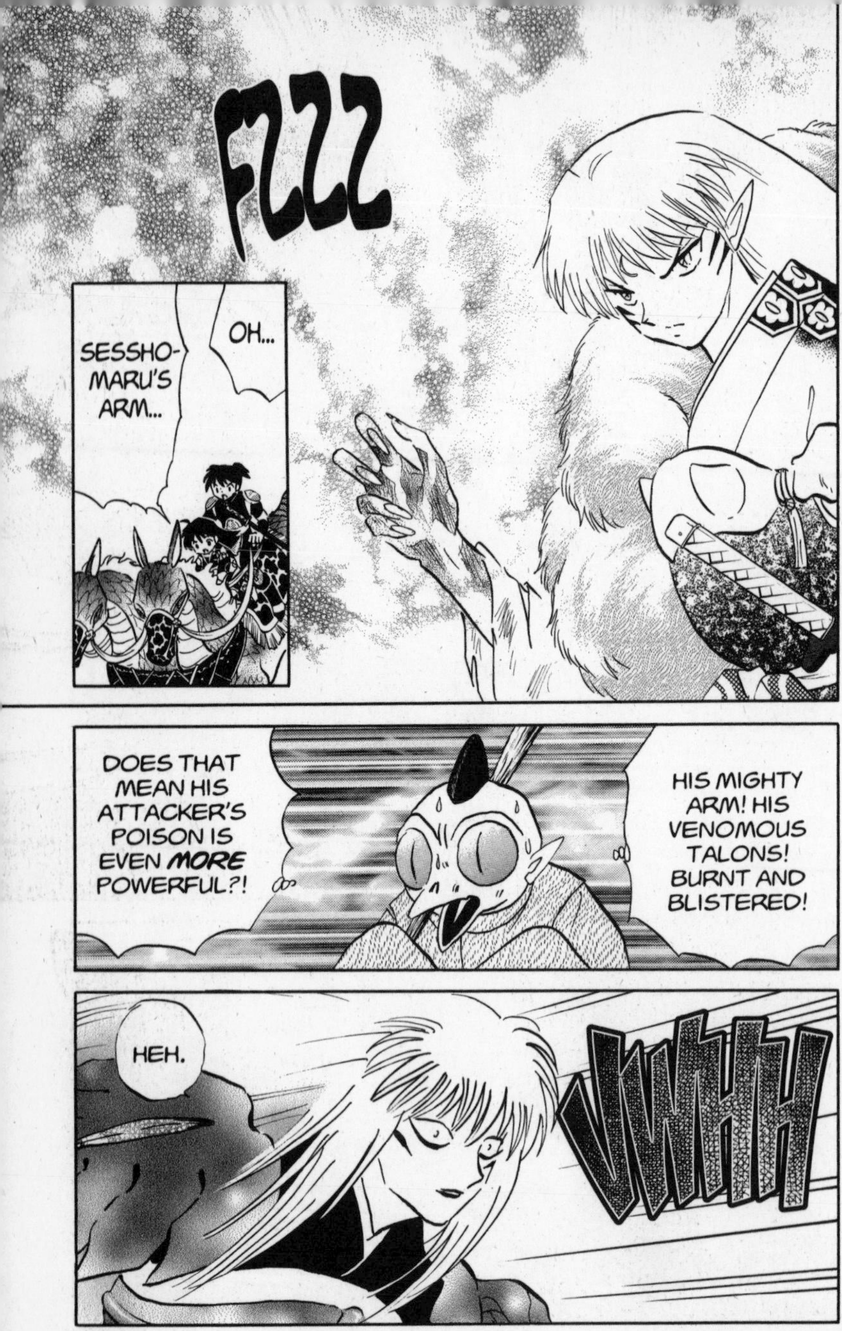
FZZZ
OH...
SESSHO-MARU'S ARM...
HIS MIGHTY ARM! HIS VENOMOUS TALONS! BURNT AND BLISTERED!
DOES THAT MEAN HIS ATTACKER'S POISON IS EVEN MORE POWERFUL?!
VWHH
HEH.

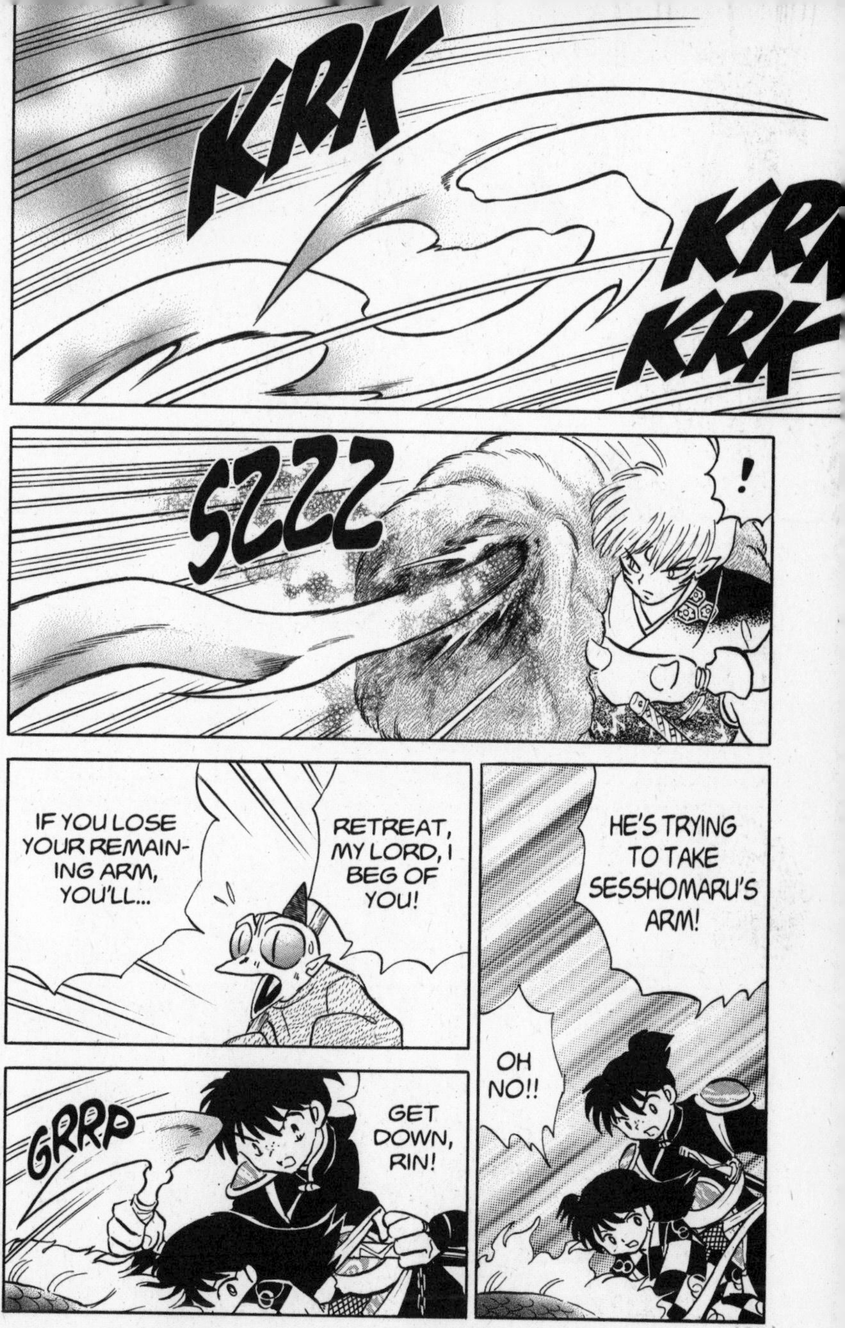
KR
KRK
KRK
!
SZZZ
HE'S TRYING TO TAKE SESSHOMARU'S ARM!
OH NO!!
RETREAT, MY LORD, I BEG OF YOU!
IF YOU LOSE YOUR REMAIN-ING ARM, YOU'LL...
GET DOWN, RIN!
GRRP

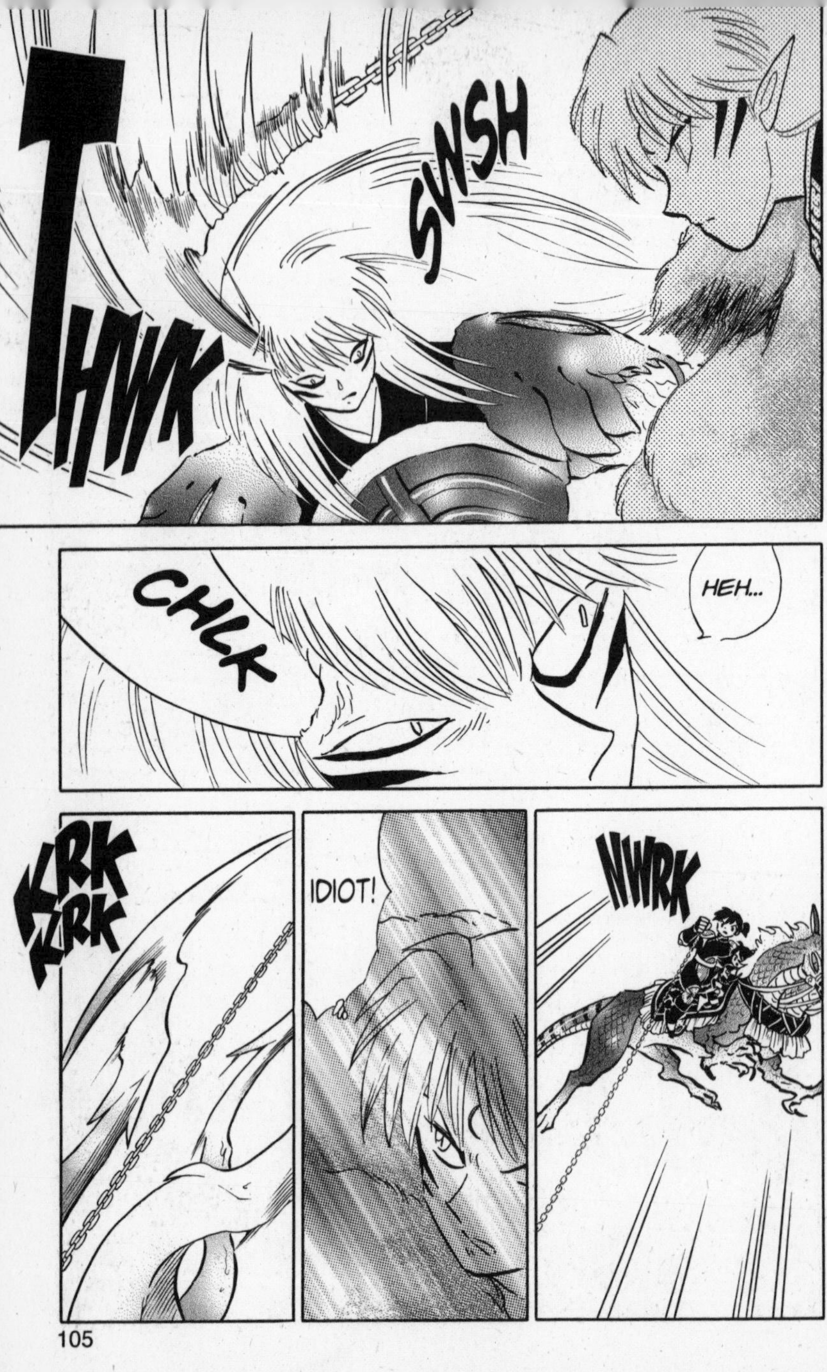
SWSH
THWK
HEH...
CHLK
NWRK
IDIOT!
KRK KRK

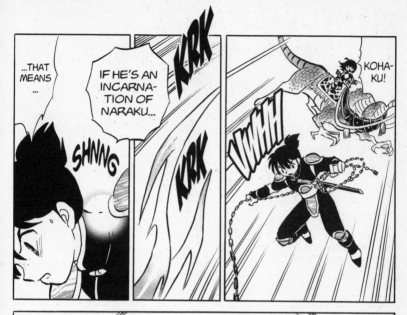

KOHA-KU!
VWHH
KRK
IF HE'S AN INCARNATION OF NARAKU...
KRK
...THAT MEANS ...
SHNNG
...THANKS TO LADY KIKYO'S CLEANSING SPELL...
...HE WON'T BE ABLE TO TOUCH MY SHIKON SHARD!
KRK KRK
JWH

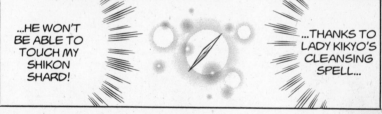

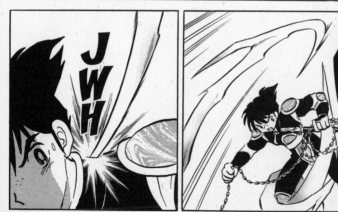

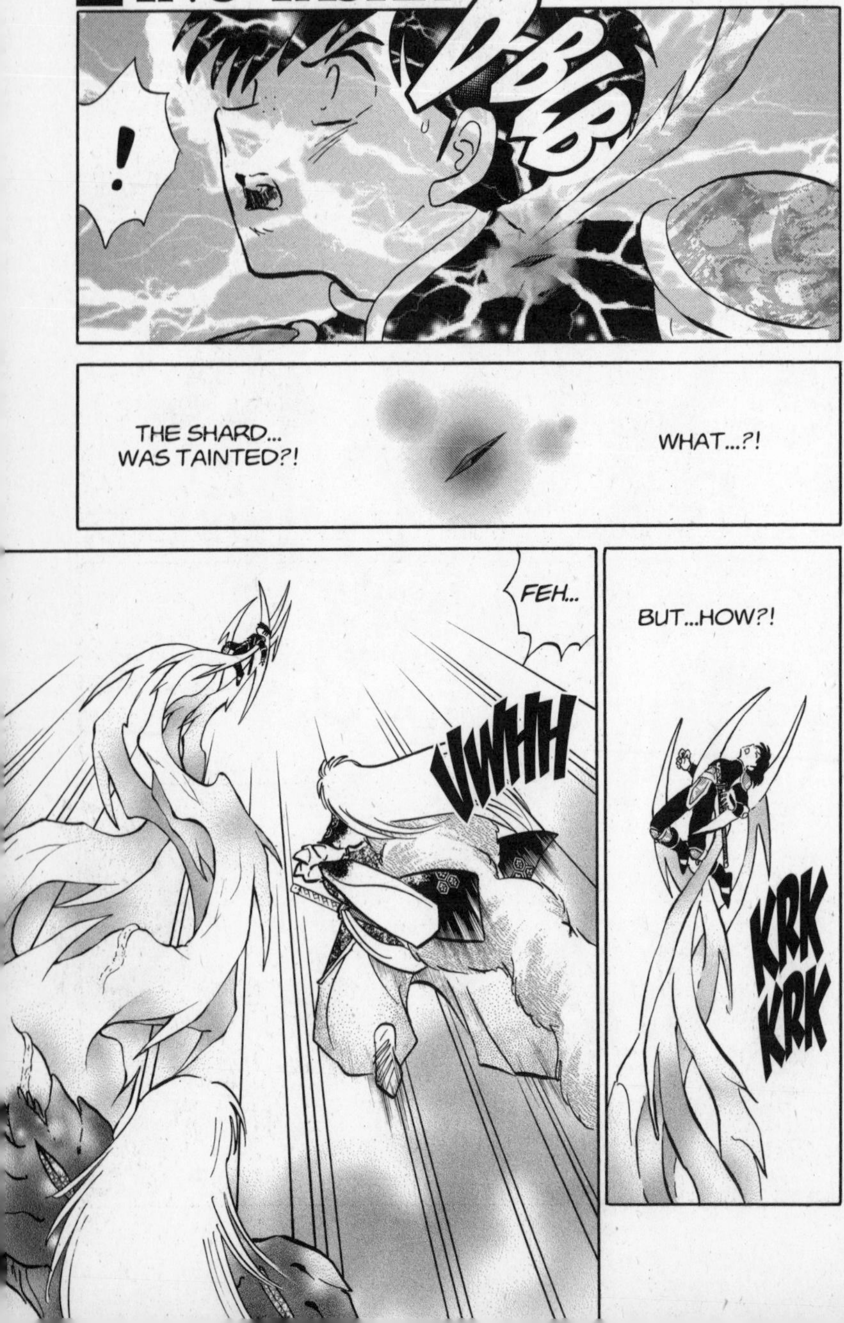
BBIB
!
WHAT...?!
THE SHARD... WAS TAINTED?!
BUT...HOW?!
KRK KRK
FEH...
VWHH

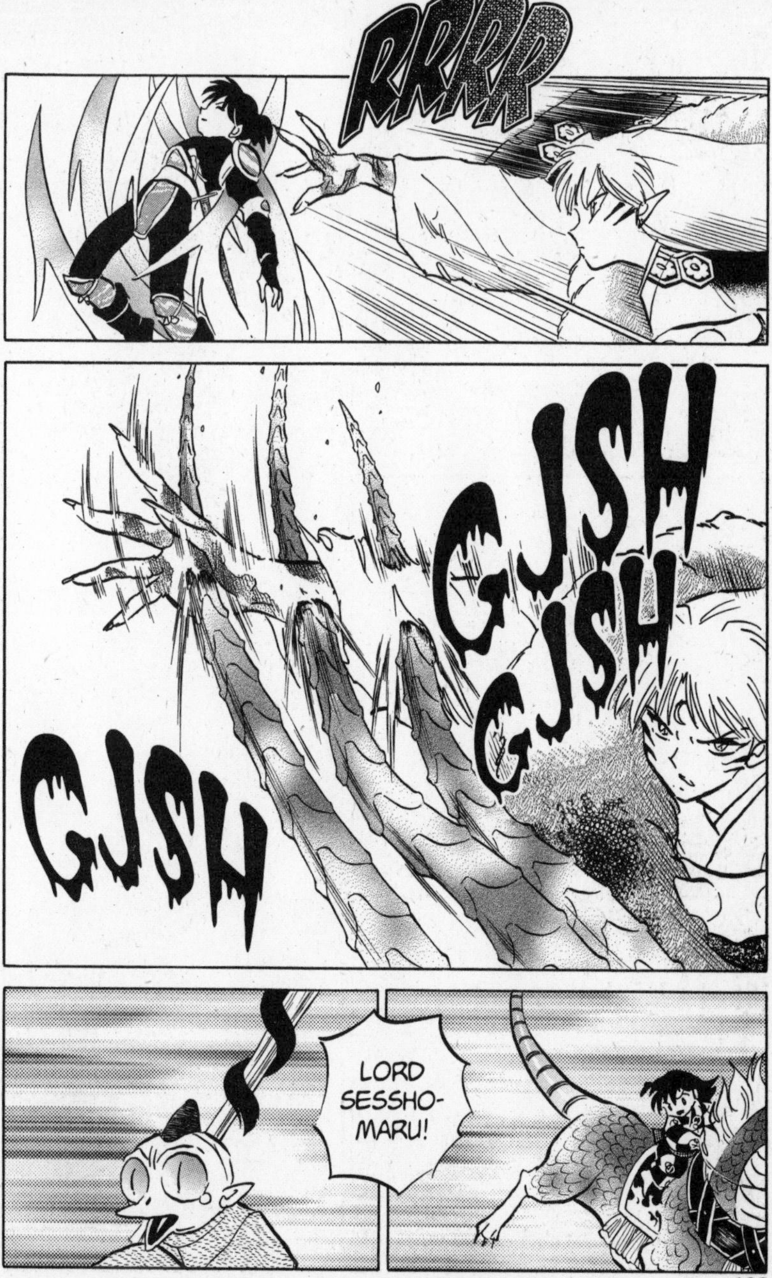
RRRR
GJSH
GJSH
GJSH
LORD SESSHO-MARU!

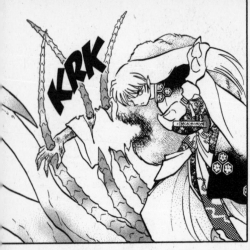

KRK

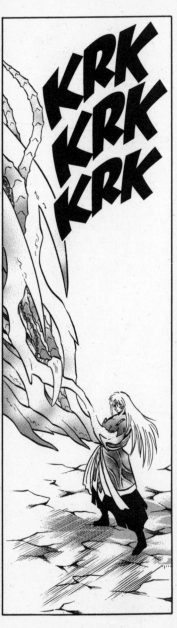

KRK
KRK
KRK

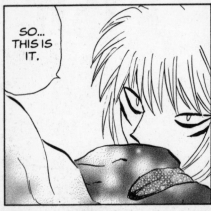

SO... THIS IS IT.

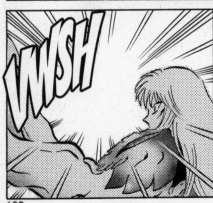

VWSH

109

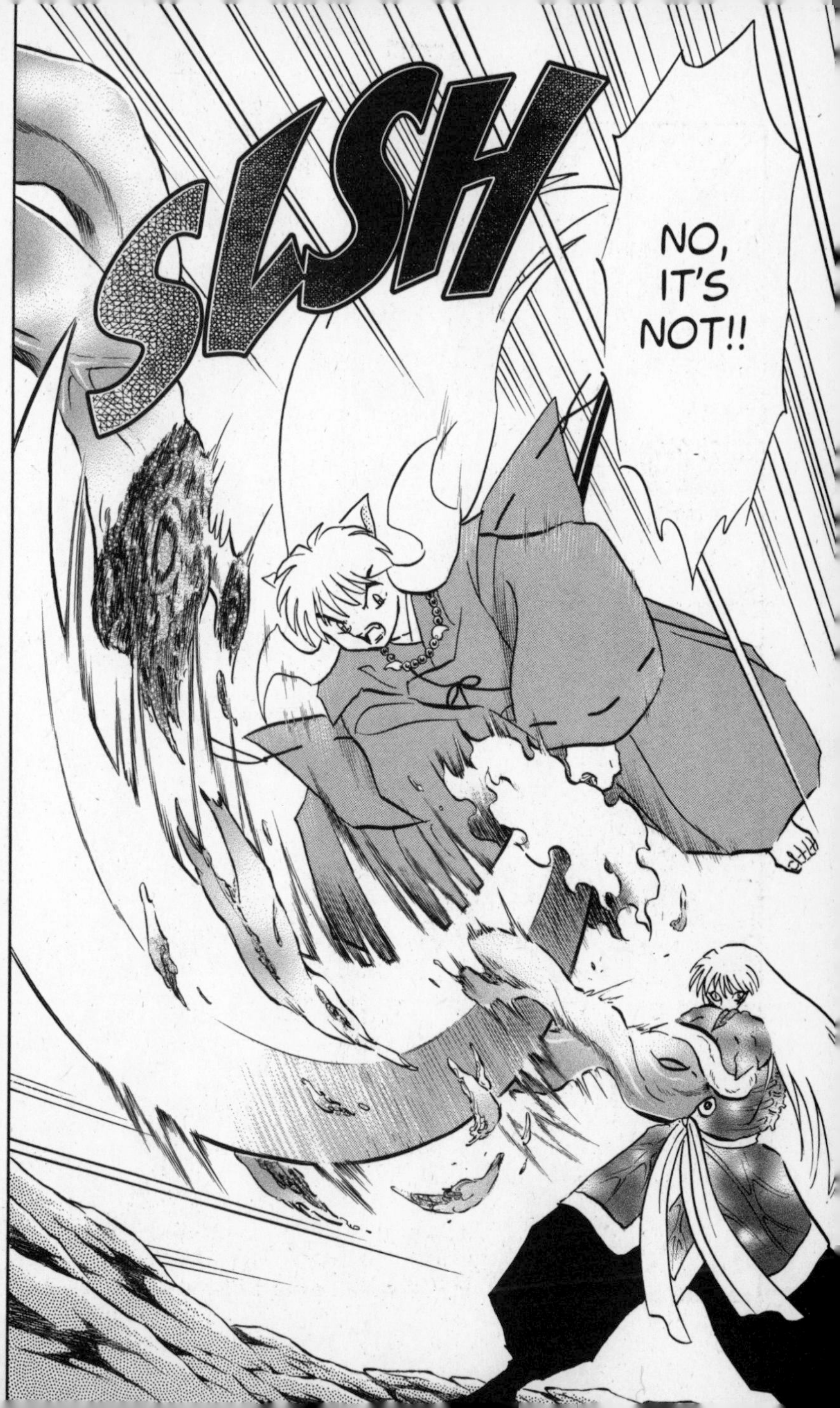
NO, IT'S NOT!!
SLSH

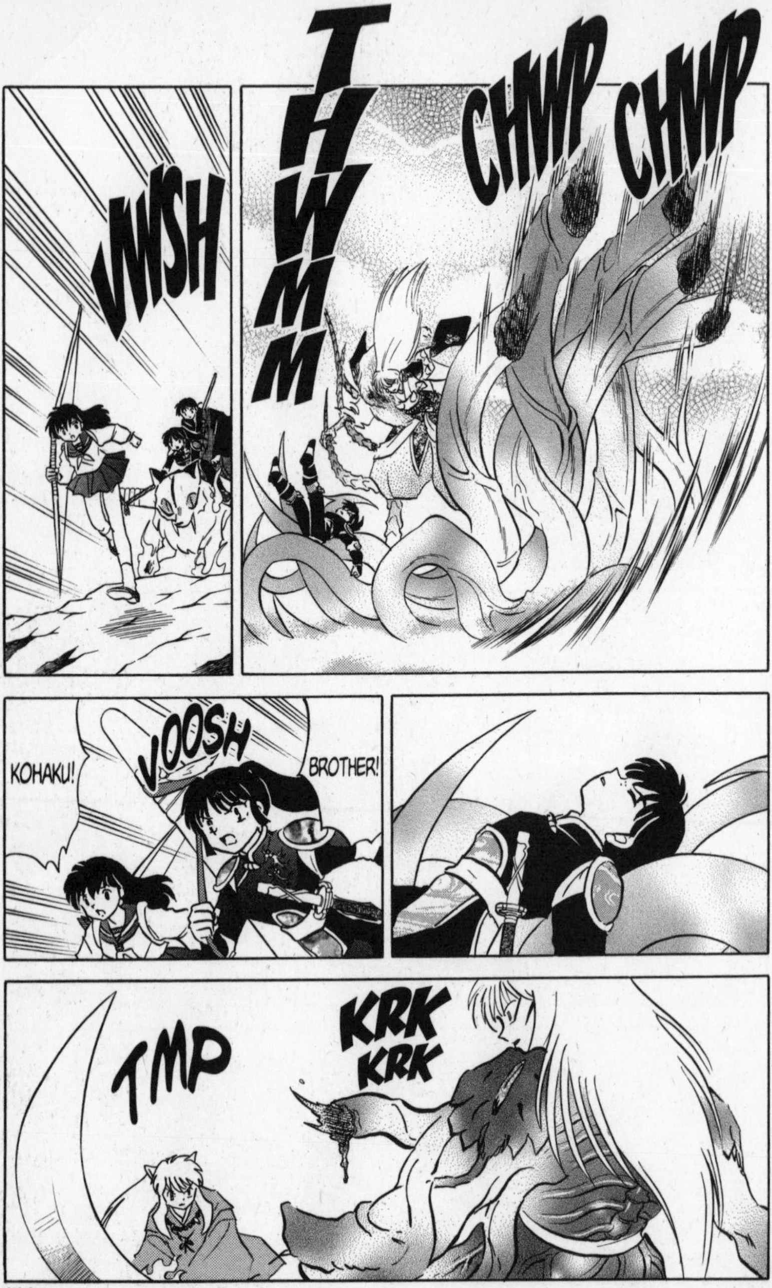
CHWP CHWP
THWMM
VWISH
BROTHER!
VOOSH
KOHAKU!
KRK KRK
TMP

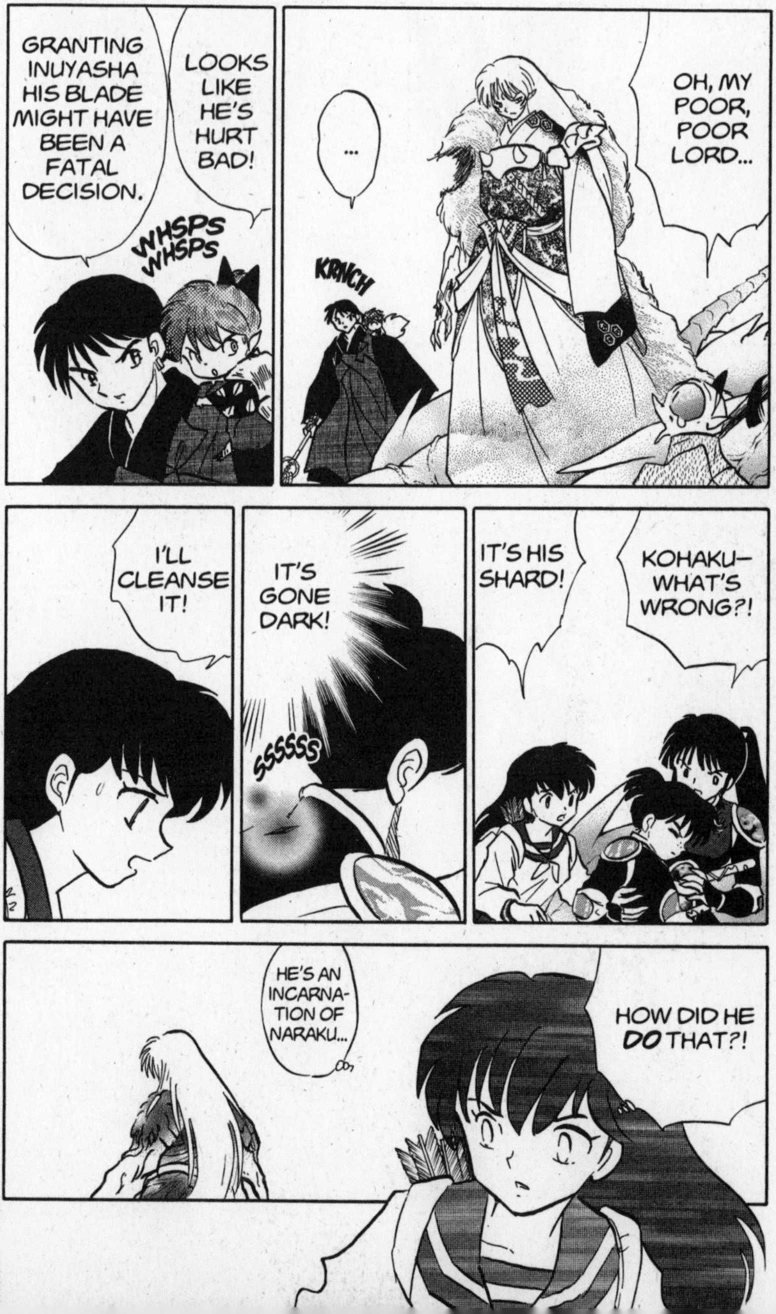
OH, MY POOR, POOR LORD...
...
KRNCH
LOOKS LIKE HE'S HURT BAD!
GRANTING INUYASHA HIS BLADE MIGHT HAVE BEEN A FATAL DECISION.
WHSPS WHSPS
KOHAKU—WHAT'S WRONG?!
IT'S HIS SHARD!
IT'S GONE DARK!
SSSSSS
I'LL CLEANSE IT!
HOW DID HE DO THAT?!
HE'S AN INCARNATION OF NARAKU...

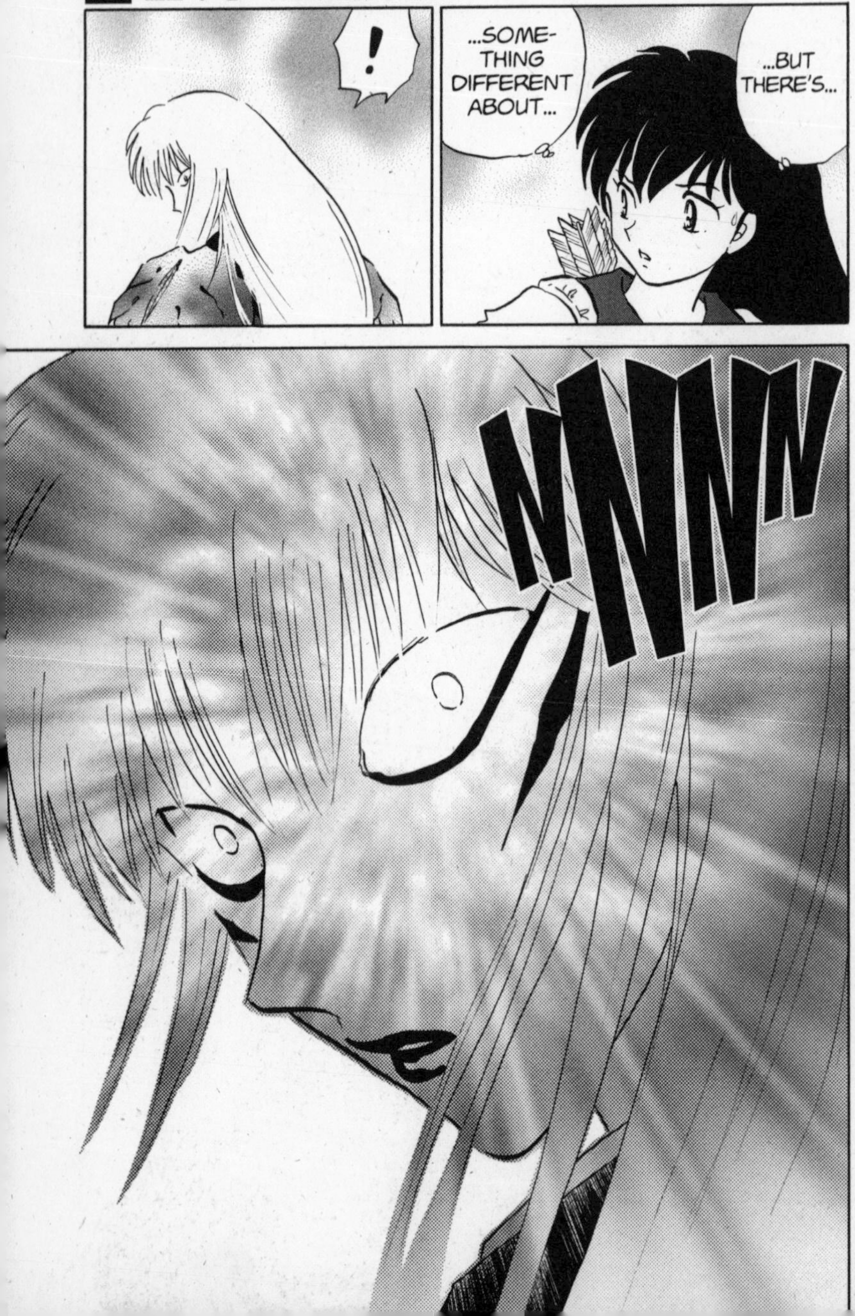
...BUT THERE'S...
...SOME-THING DIFFERENT ABOUT...
!
NNNN

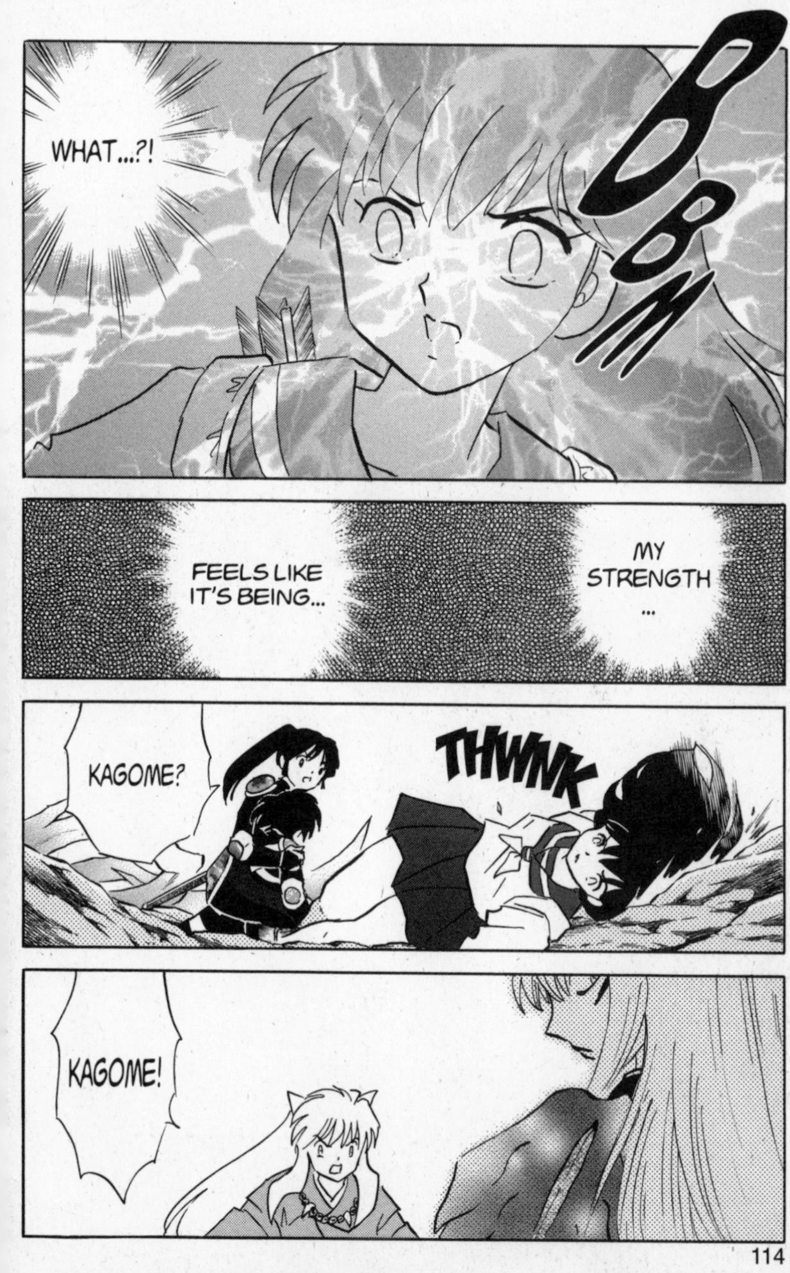
WHAT...?!
MY STRENGTH ...
FEELS LIKE IT'S BEING...
THWNK
KAGOME?
KAGOME!

SCROLL 7
THE BORROWED BODY

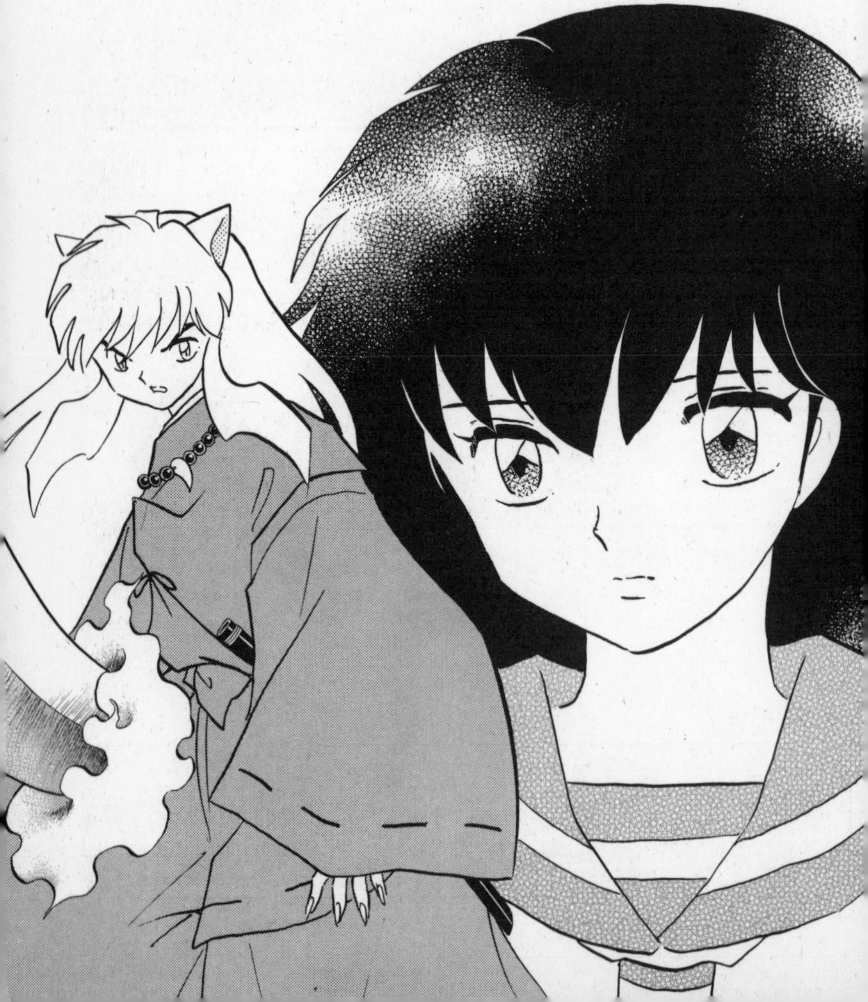

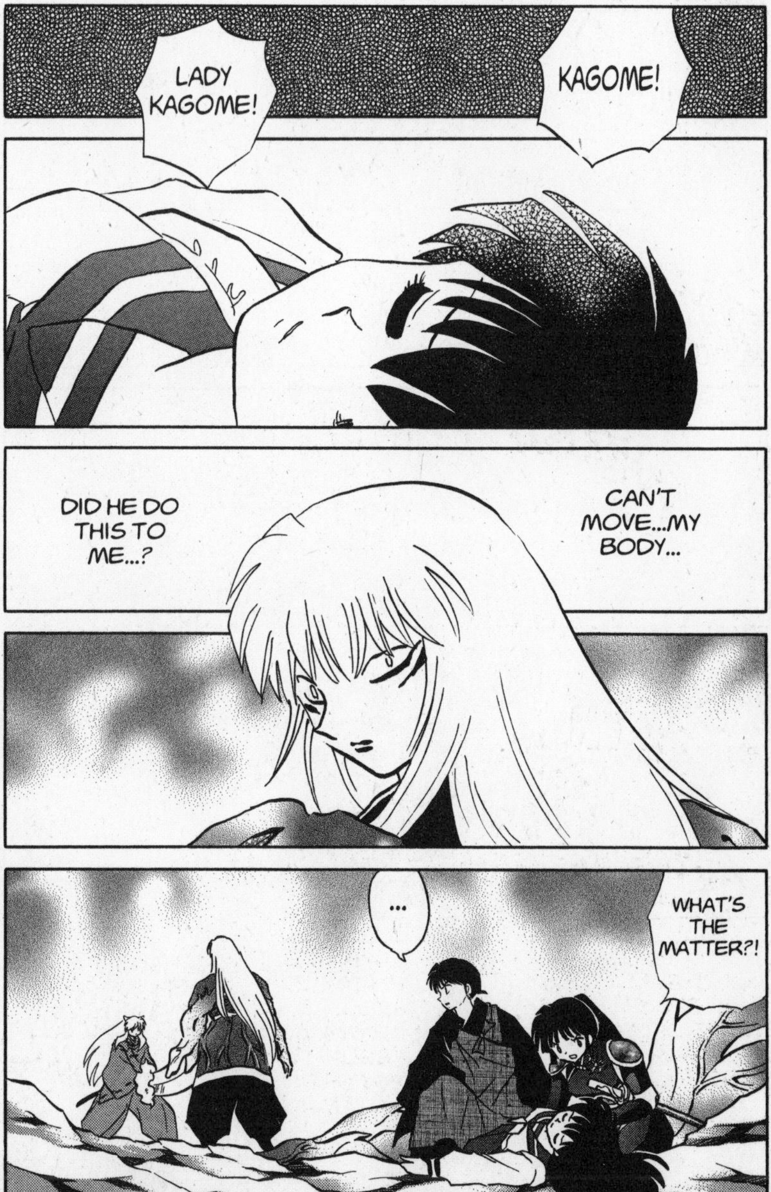
KAGOME!
LADY KAGOME!
CAN'T MOVE...MY BODY...
DID HE DO THIS TO ME...?
WHAT'S THE MATTER?!
...

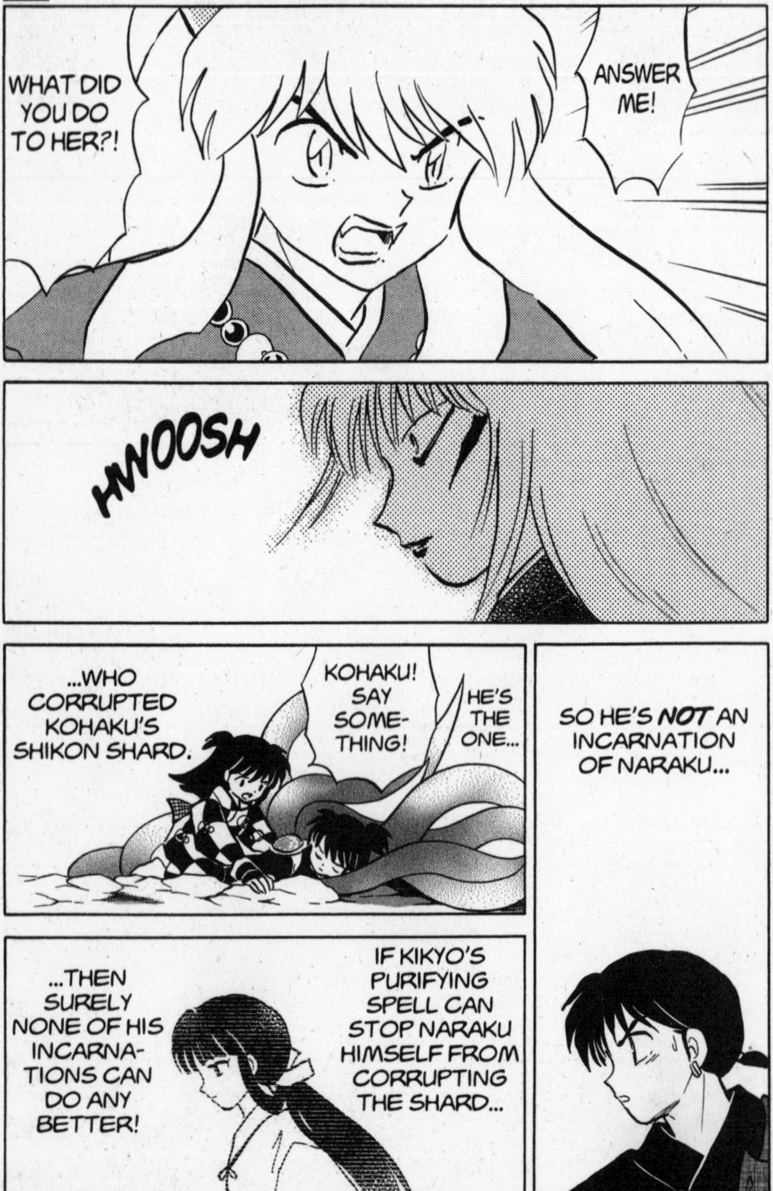
ANSWER ME!
WHAT DID YOU DO TO HER?!
HWOOSH
SO HE'S **NOT** AN INCARNATION OF NARAKU...
HE'S THE ONE...
KOHAKU! SAY SOME-THING!
...WHO CORRUPTED KOHAKU'S SHIKON SHARD.
IF KIKYO'S PURIFYING SPELL CAN STOP NARAKU HIMSELF FROM CORRUPTING THE SHARD...
...THEN SURELY NONE OF HIS INCARNA-TIONS CAN DO ANY BETTER!

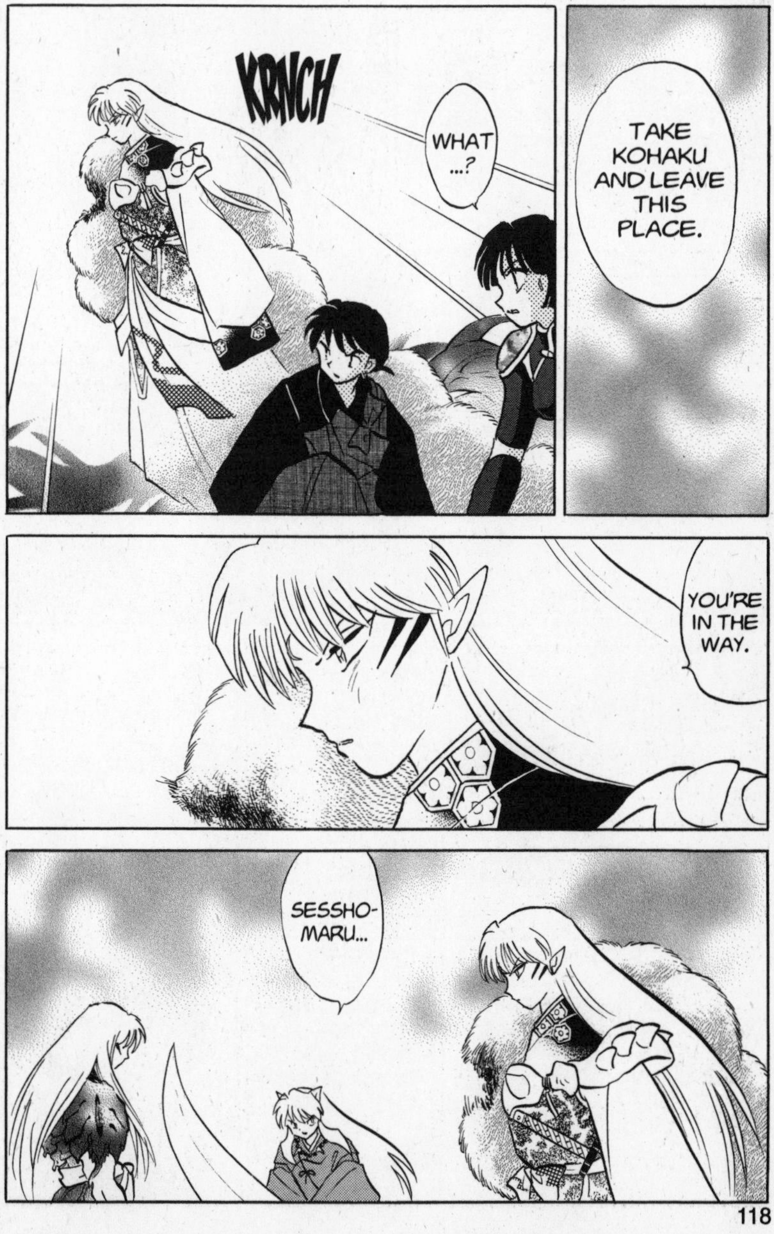
TAKE KOHAKU AND LEAVE THIS PLACE.
KRNCH
WHAT ...?
YOU'RE IN THE WAY.
SESSHO-MARU...

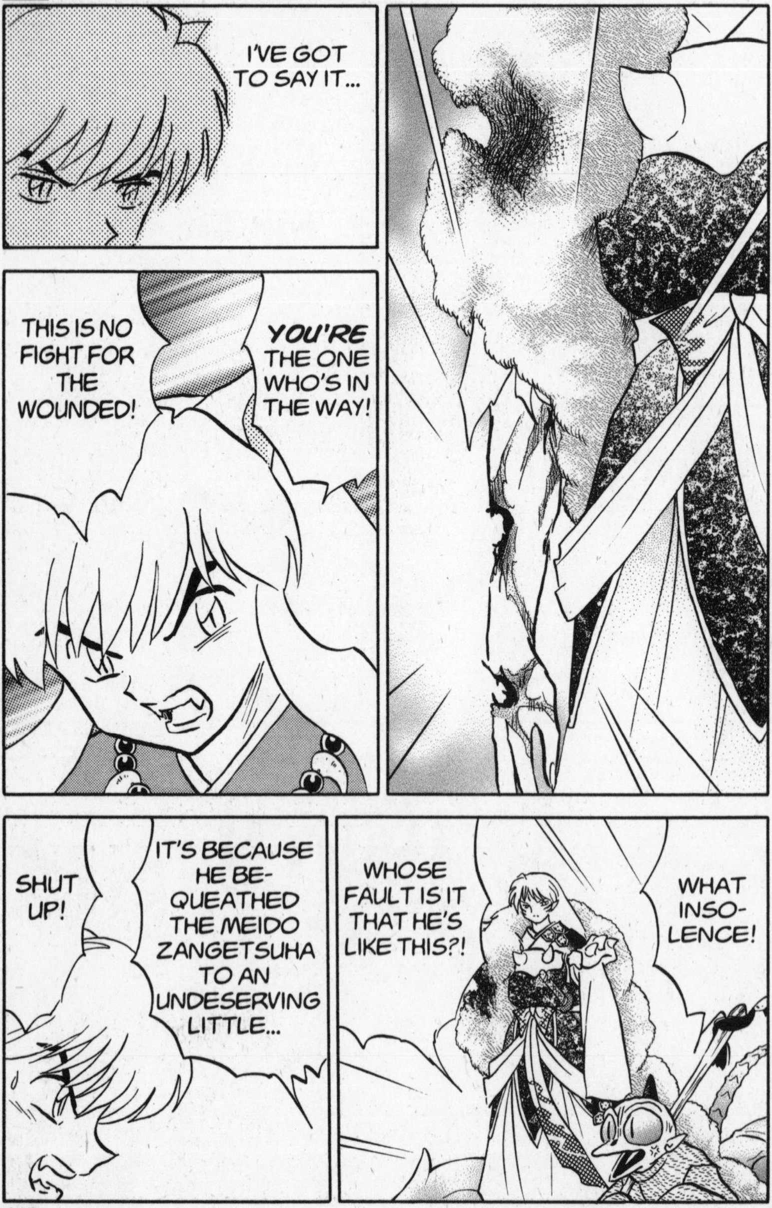
I'VE GOT TO SAY IT...
YOU'RE THE ONE WHO'S IN THE WAY!
THIS IS NO FIGHT FOR THE WOUNDED!
WHAT INSO-LENCE!
WHOSE FAULT IS IT THAT HE'S LIKE THIS?!
IT'S BECAUSE HE BE-QUEATHED THE MEIDO ZANGETSUHA TO AN UNDESERVING LITTLE...
SHUT UP!

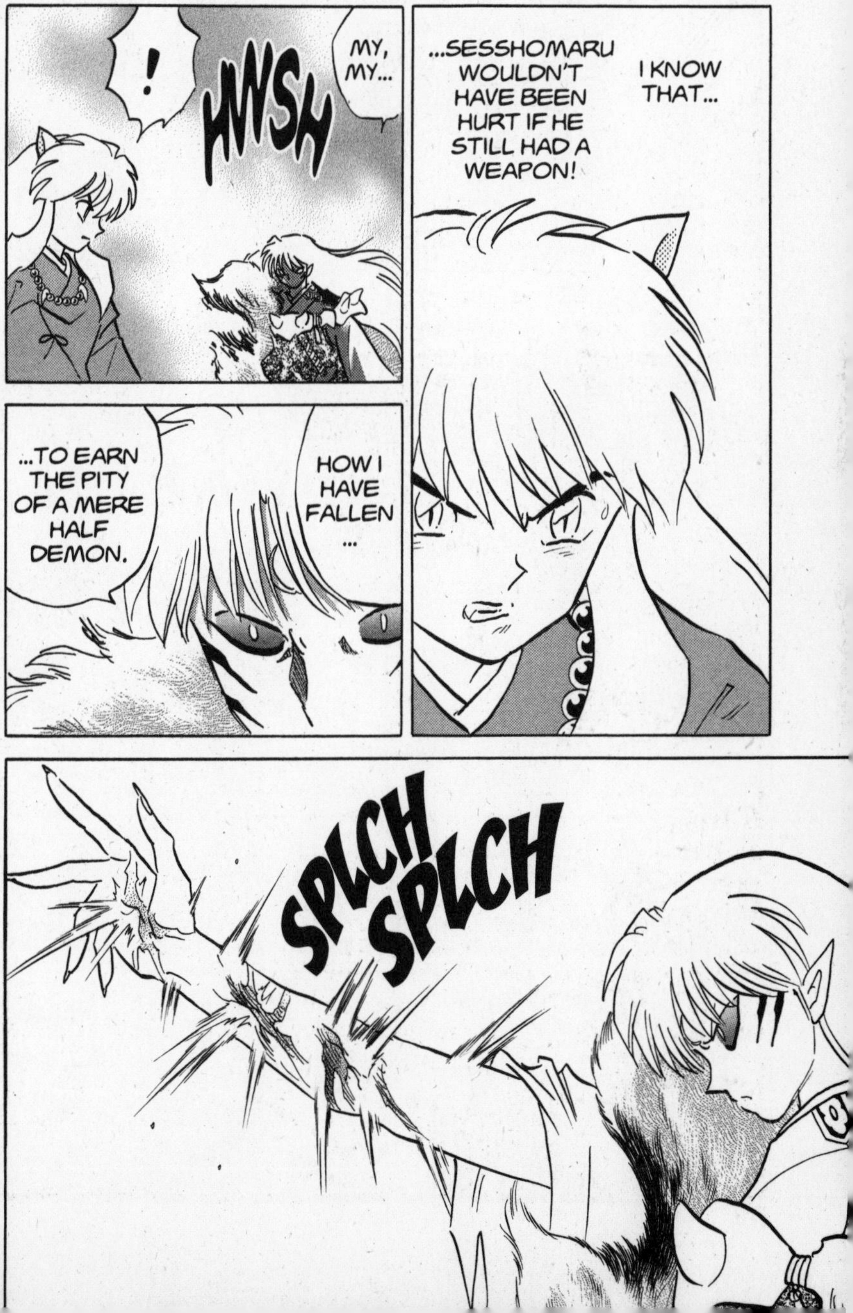
I KNOW THAT...
...SESSHOMARU WOULDN'T HAVE BEEN HURT IF HE STILL HAD A WEAPON!
MY, MY...
HNNSH
!
HOW I HAVE FALLEN ...
...TO EARN THE PITY OF A MERE HALF DEMON.
SPLCH SPLCH

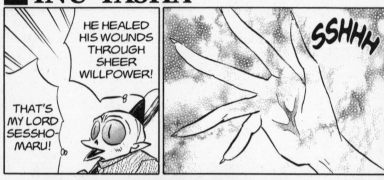

HE HEALED HIS WOUNDS THROUGH SHEER WILLPOWER!

THAT'S MY LORD SESSHO-MARU!

SSHH

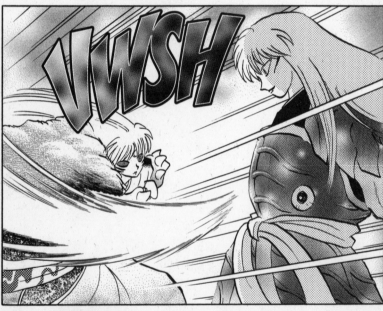

VWSH

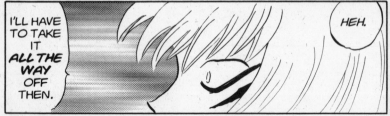

I'LL HAVE TO TAKE IT *ALL THE WAY* OFF THEN.

HEH.

121

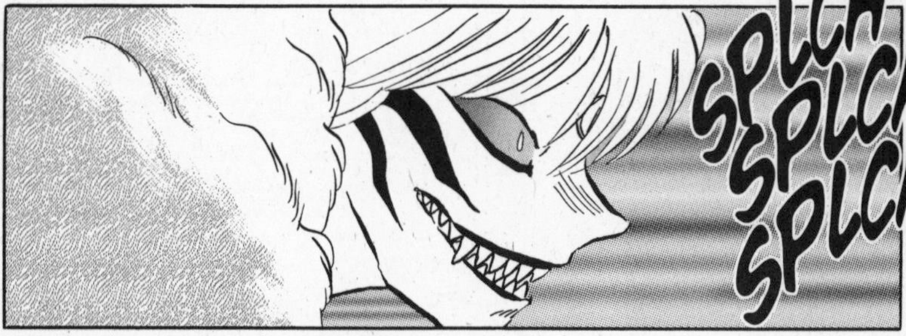
SPLCH
SPLCH
SPLCH

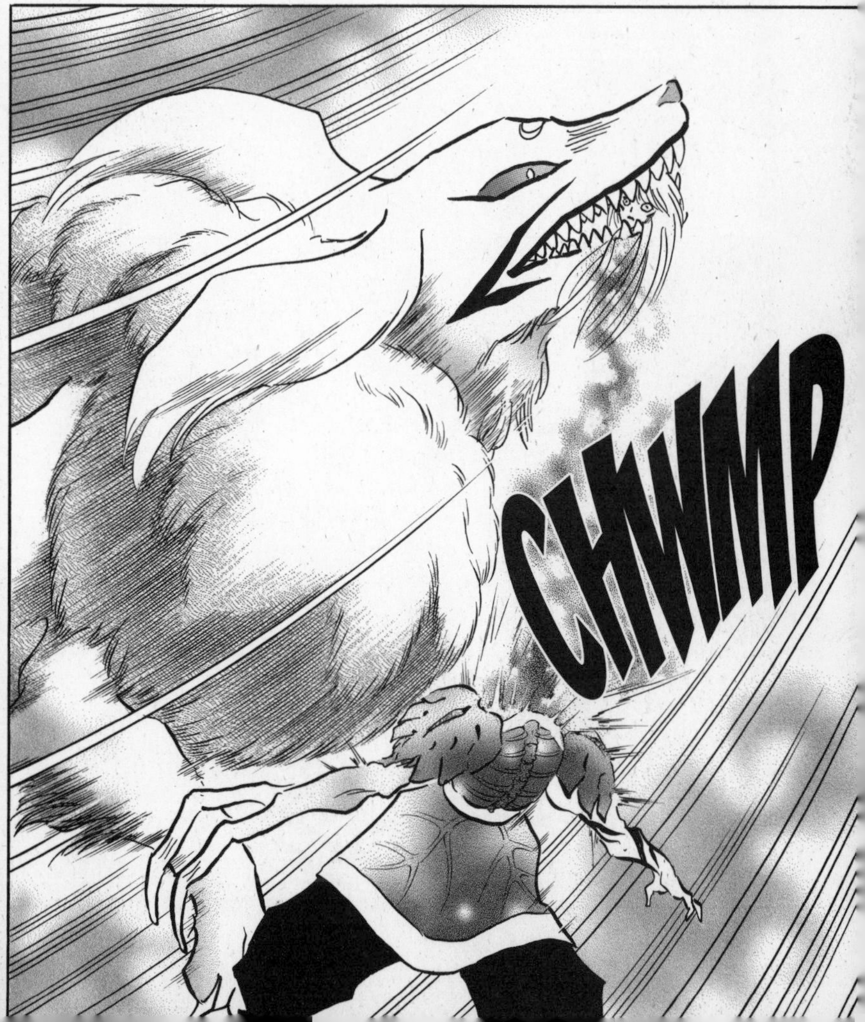
CHWMP

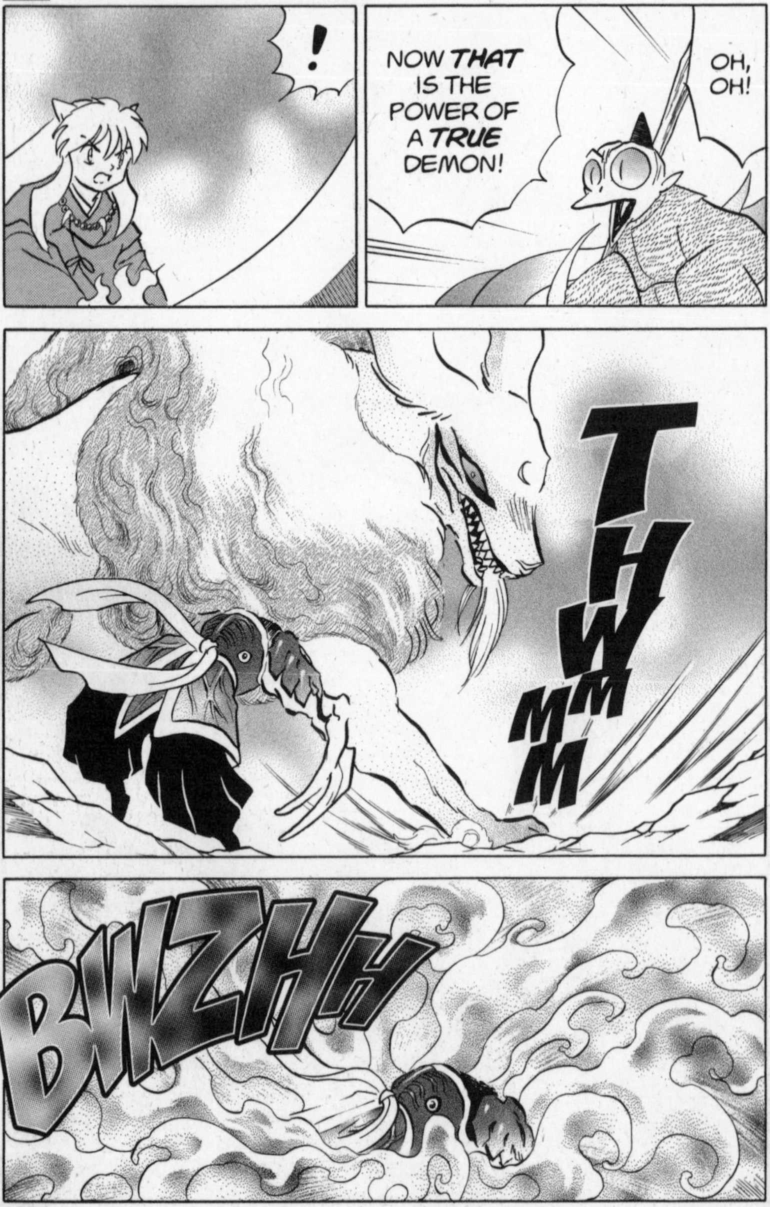
OH, OH!
NOW *THAT* IS THE POWER OF A *TRUE* DEMON!
!
THWMMM
BWZHH

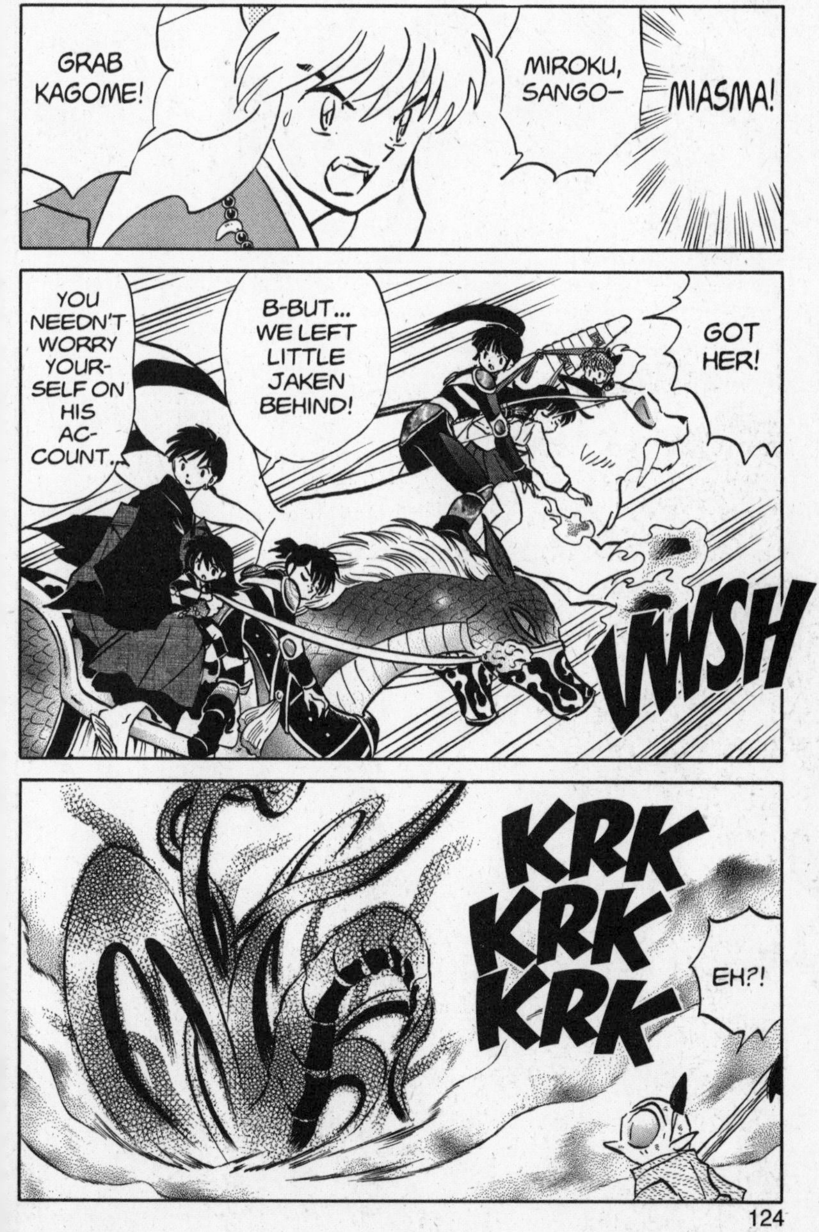
MIASMA!
MIROKU, SANGO–
GRAB KAGOME!
GOT HER!
B-BUT... WE LEFT LITTLE JAKEN BEHIND!
YOU NEEDN'T WORRY YOURSELF ON HIS ACCOUNT...
VWSH
KRK KRK KRK
EH?!

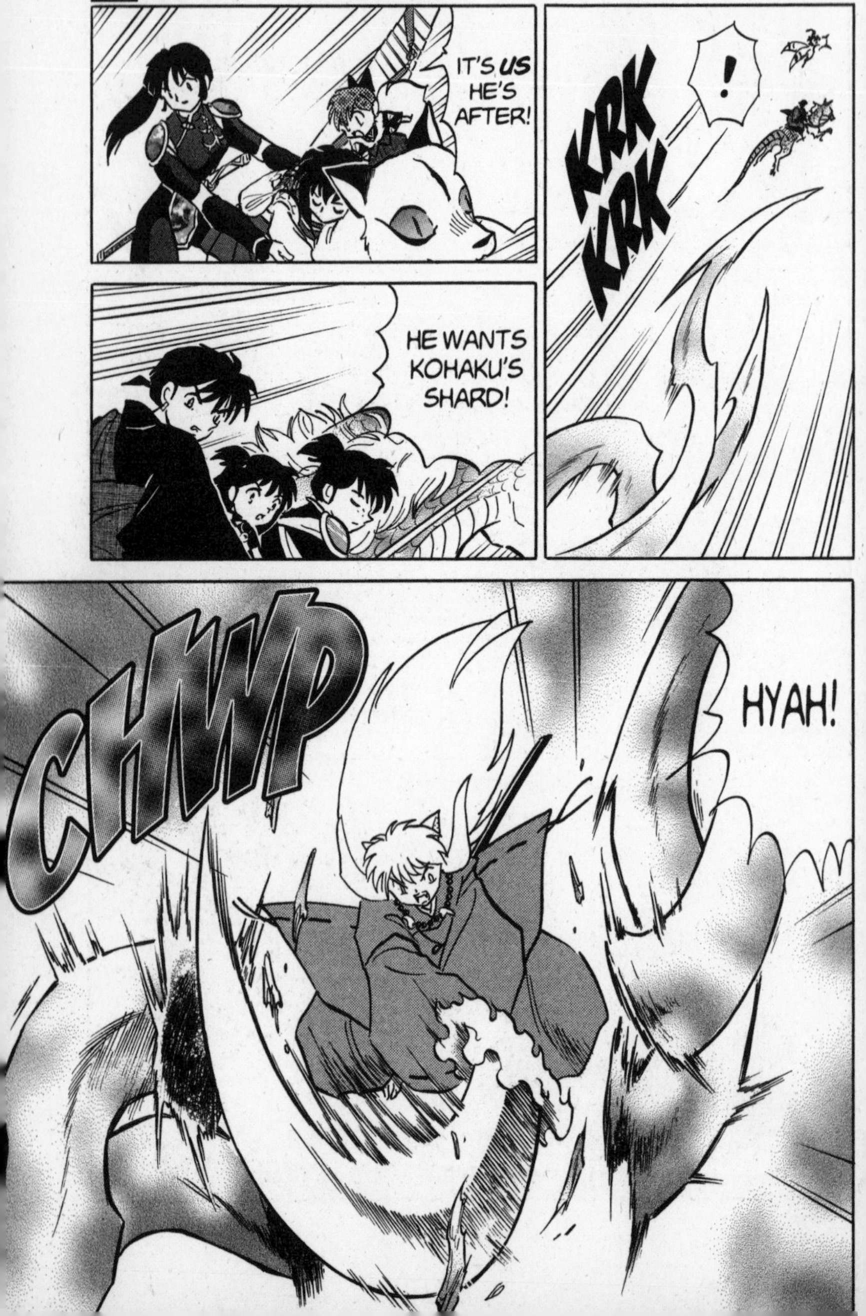
KRK KRK
!
IT'S US HE'S AFTER!
HE WANTS KOHAKU'S SHARD!
HYAH!
CHMP

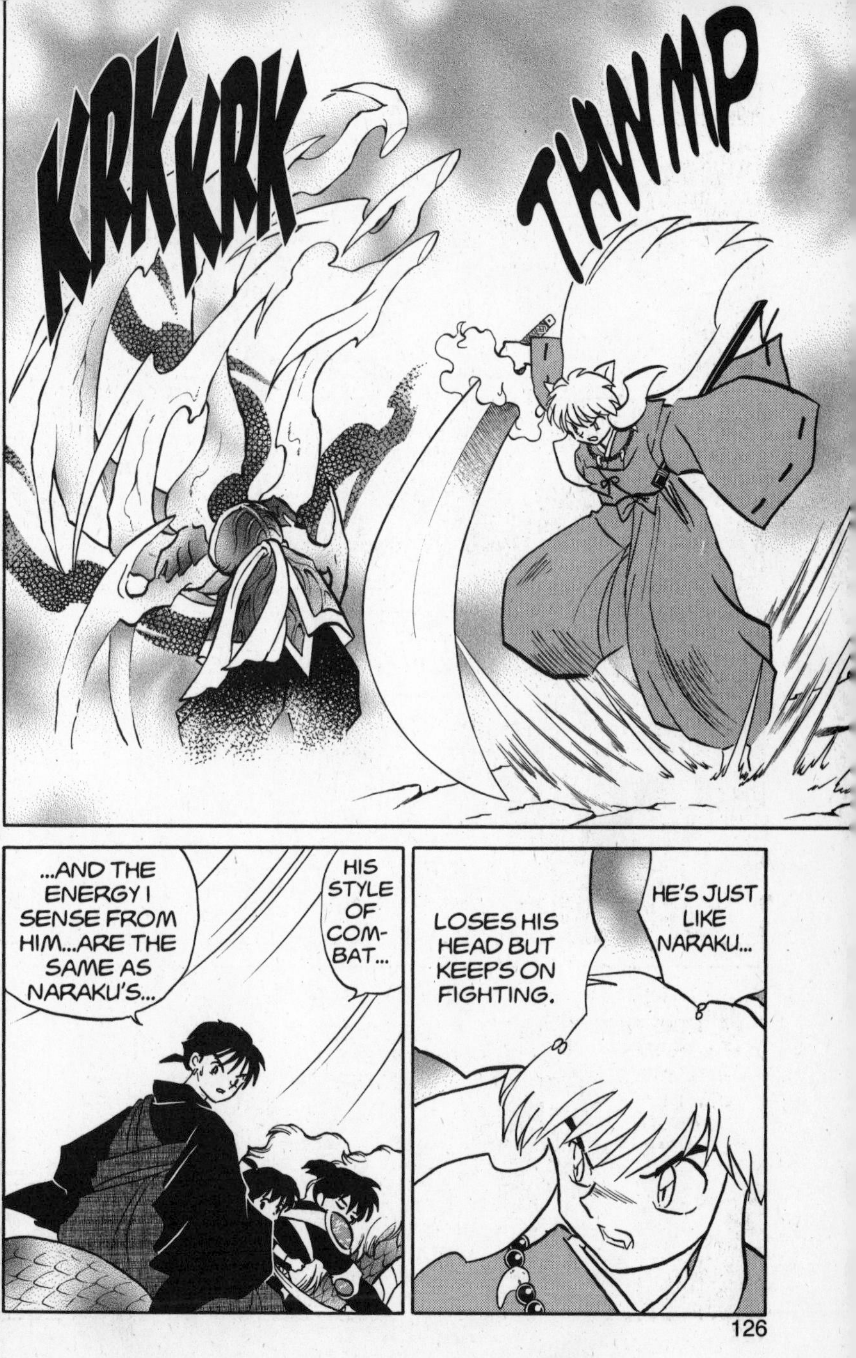
THWMP
KRKKRK
HE'S JUST LIKE NARAKU...
LOSES HIS HEAD BUT KEEPS ON FIGHTING.
HIS STYLE OF COM-BAT...
...AND THE ENERGY I SENSE FROM HIM...ARE THE SAME AS NARAKU'S...

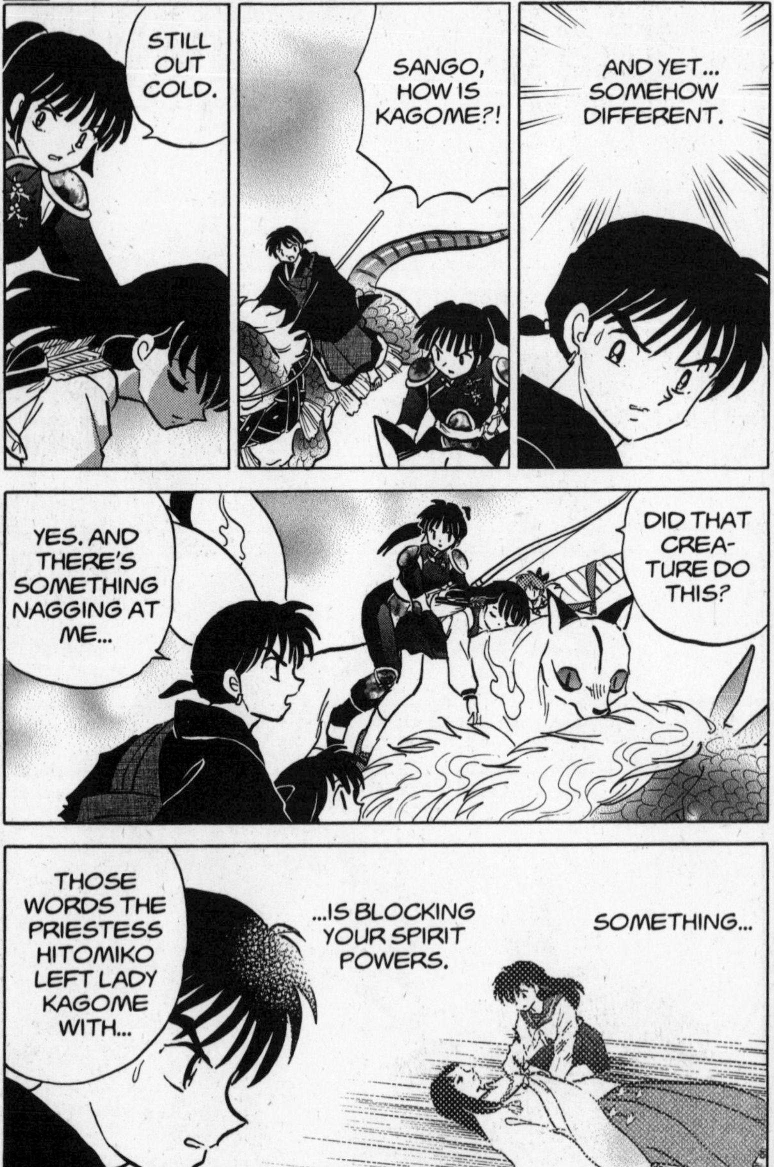
AND YET... SOMEHOW DIFFERENT.
SANGO, HOW IS KAGOME?!
STILL OUT COLD.
DID THAT CREA-TURE DO THIS?
YES. AND THERE'S SOMETHING NAGGING AT ME...
SOMETHING...
...IS BLOCKING YOUR SPIRIT POWERS.
THOSE WORDS THE PRIESTESS HITOMIKO LEFT LADY KAGOME WITH...

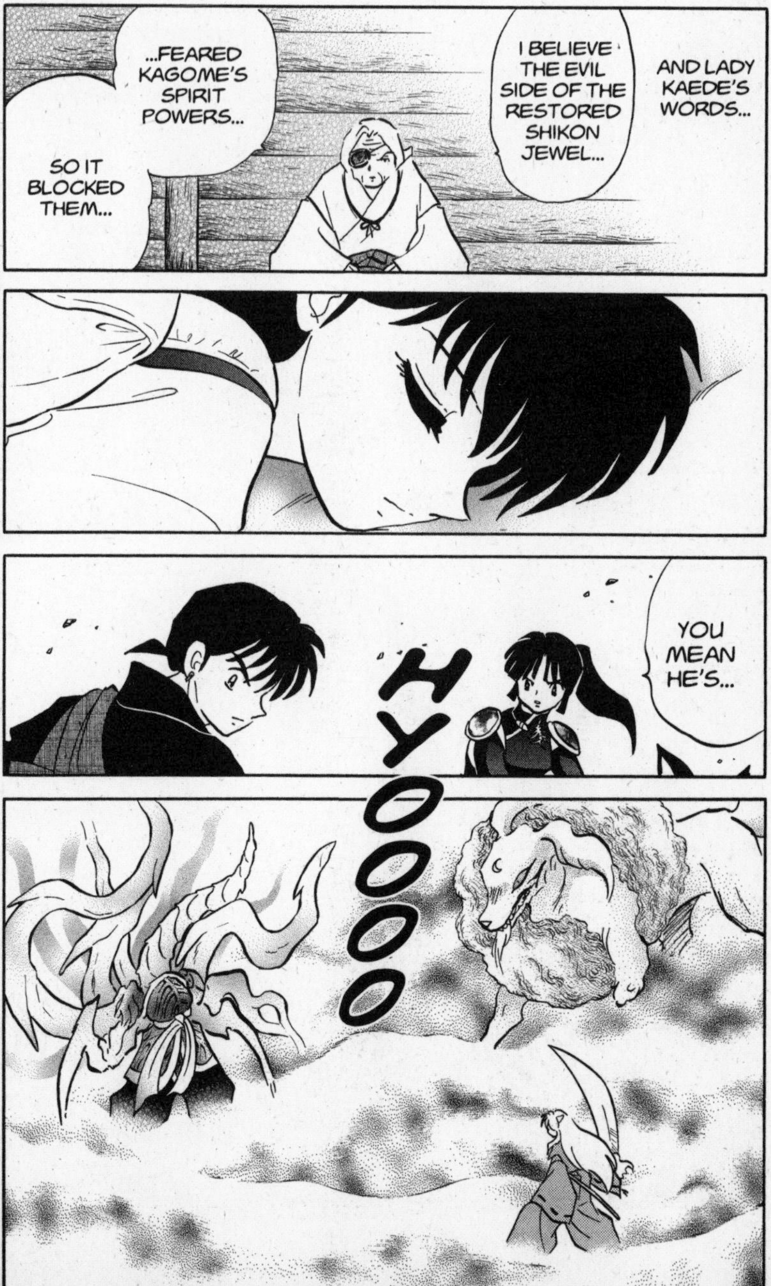
AND LADY KAEDE'S WORDS...
I BELIEVE THE EVIL SIDE OF THE RESTORED SHIKON JEWEL...
...FEARED KAGOME'S SPIRIT POWERS...
SO IT BLOCKED THEM...
YOU MEAN HE'S...
HYOOOOO

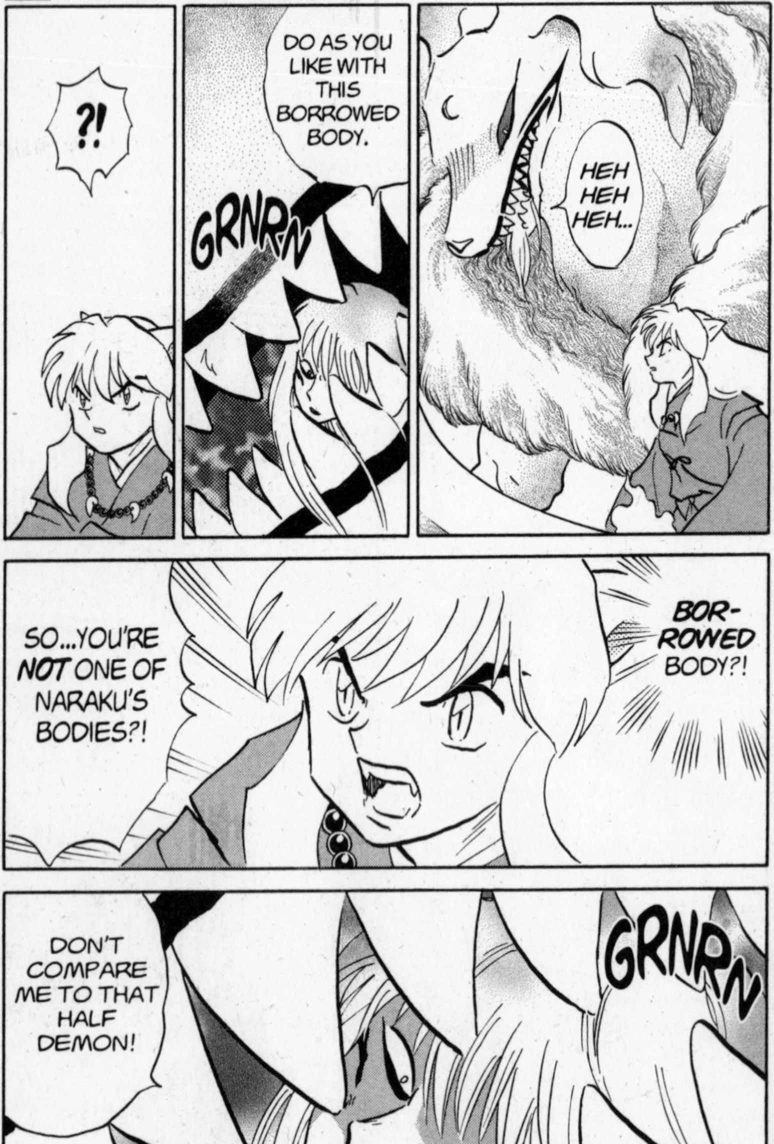
HEH HEH HEH...
DO AS YOU LIKE WITH THIS BORROWED BODY.
GRNRN
?!
BOR-ROWED BODY?!
SO...YOU'RE **NOT** ONE OF NARAKU'S BODIES?!
GRNRN
DON'T COMPARE ME TO THAT HALF DEMON!

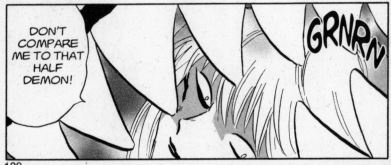

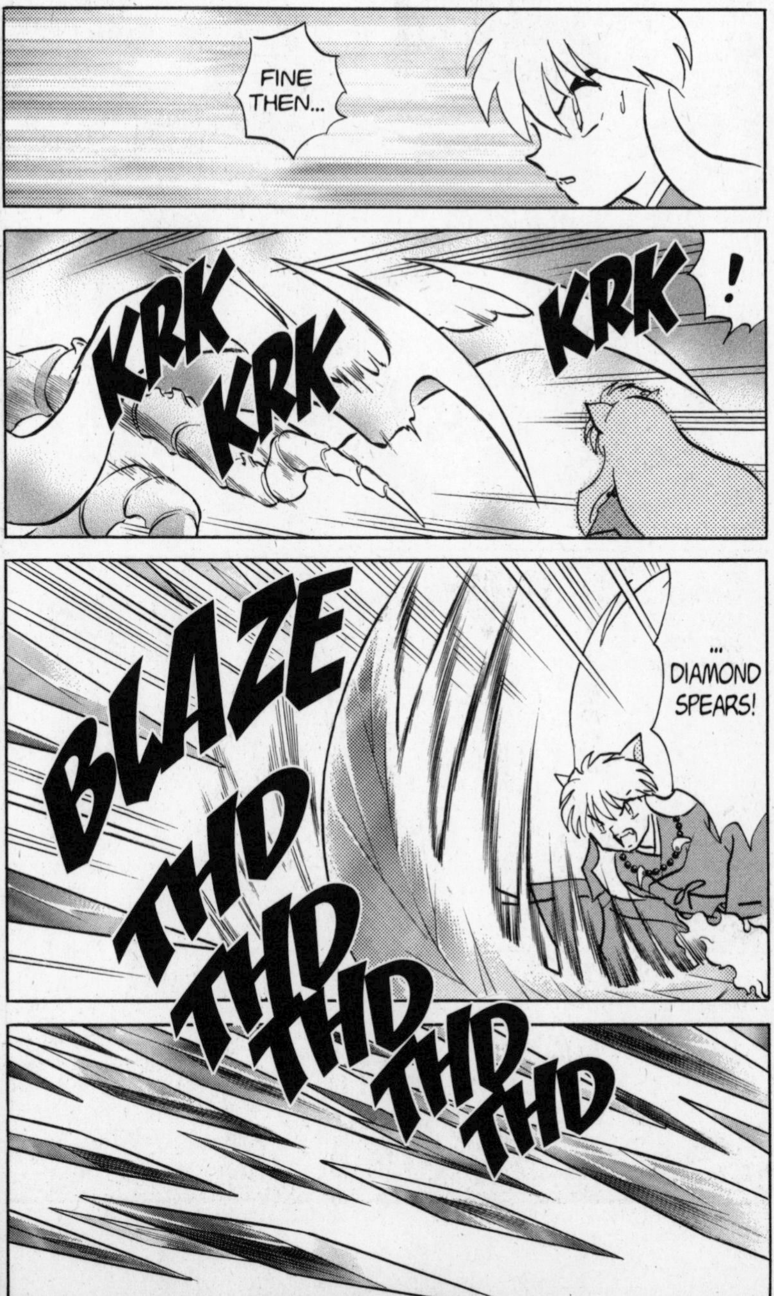
FINE THEN...
KRK KRK
KRK!
...DIAMOND SPEARS!
BLAZE
THD THD THD THD THD

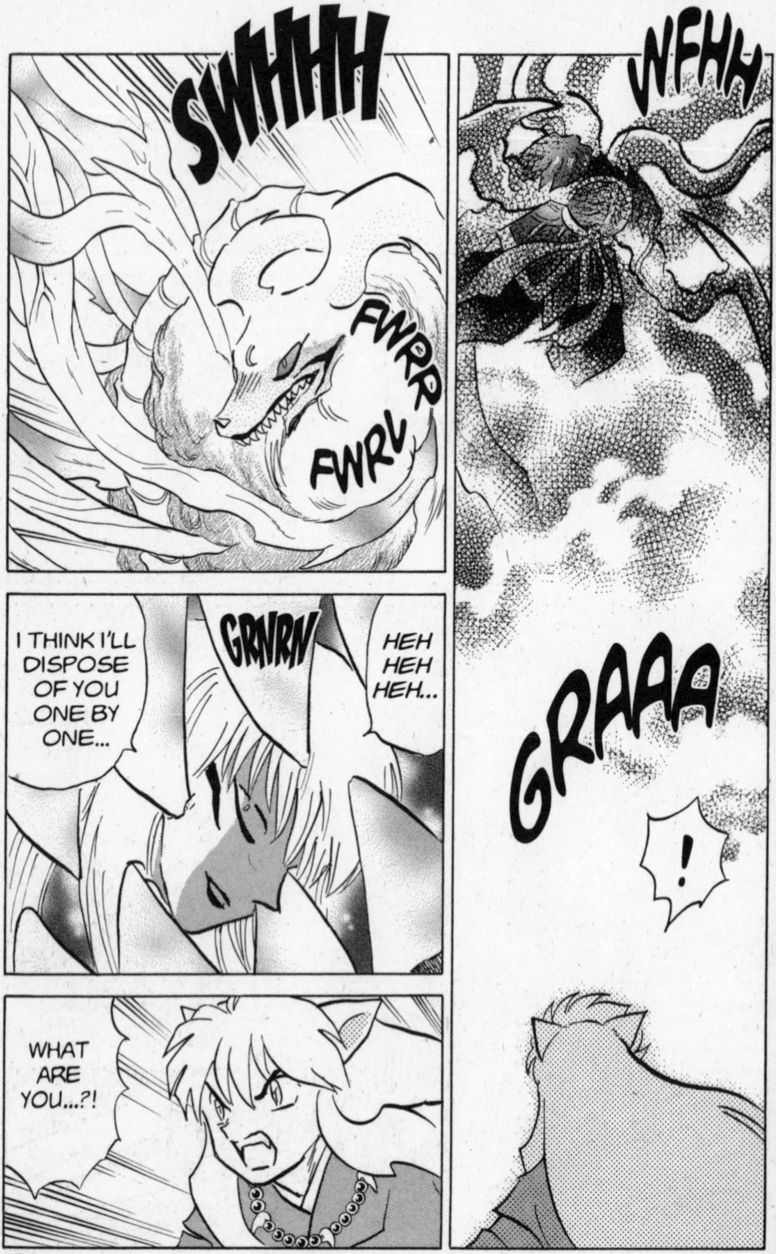
WFHH
GRAAA
!
SWHHH
FWRR
FWRL
HEH HEH HEH...
GRNRN
I THINK I'LL DISPOSE OF YOU ONE BY ONE...
WHAT ARE YOU...?!

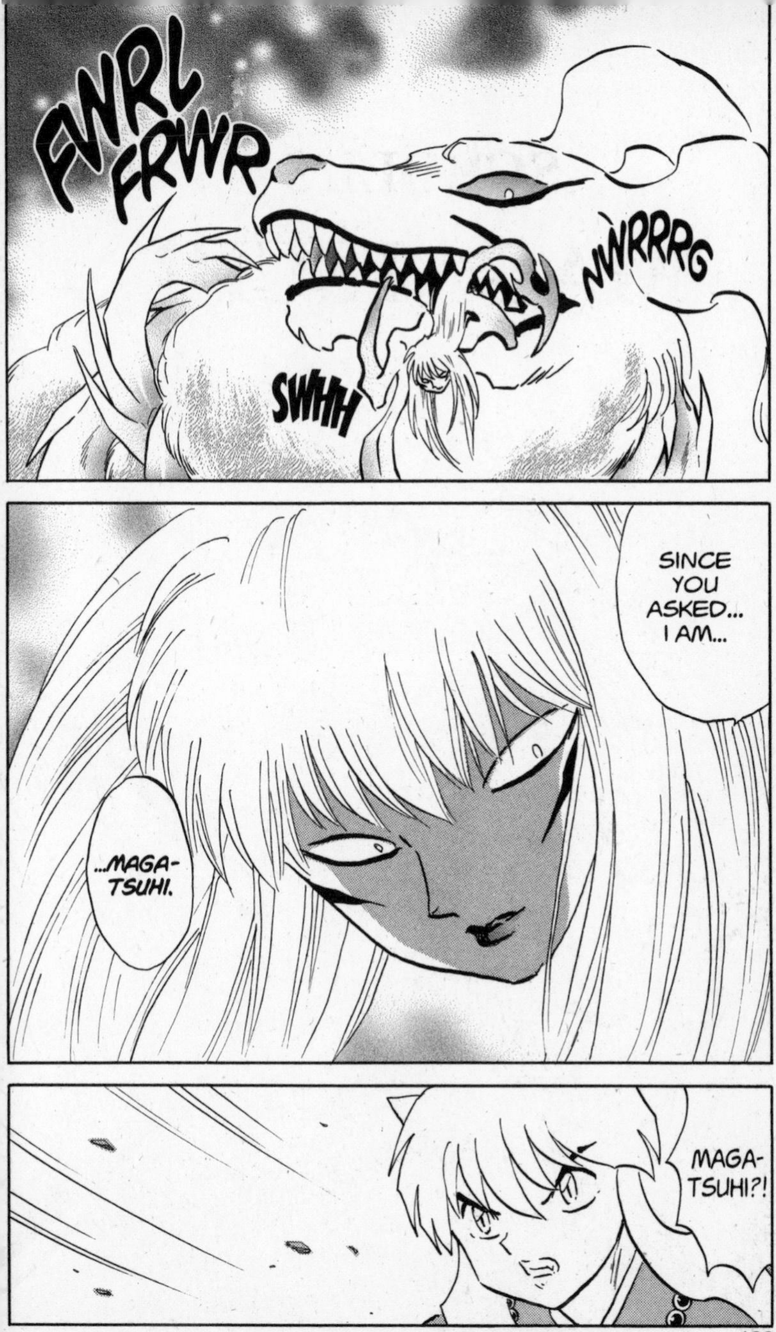
FWRL FRWR
NWRRRG
SWHH
SINCE YOU ASKED... I AM...
...MAGA-TSUHI.
MAGA-TSUHI?!

SCROLL 8
MAGATSUHI

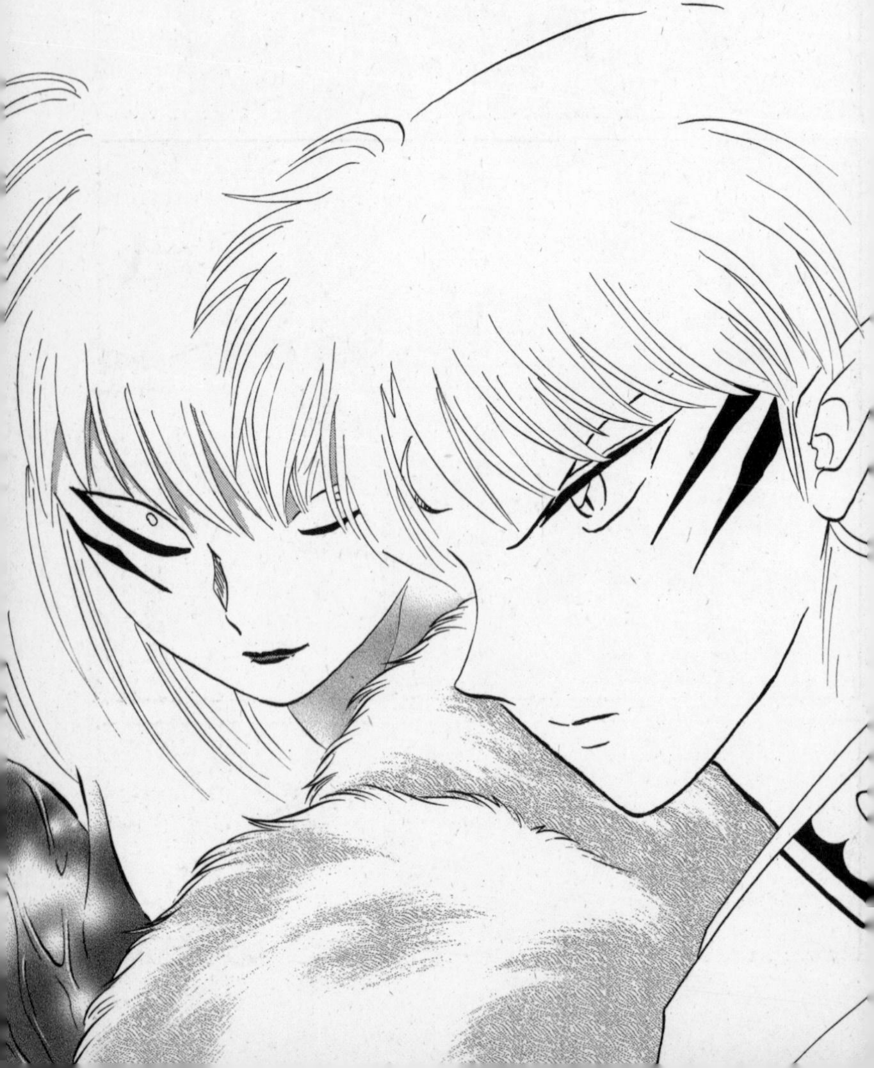

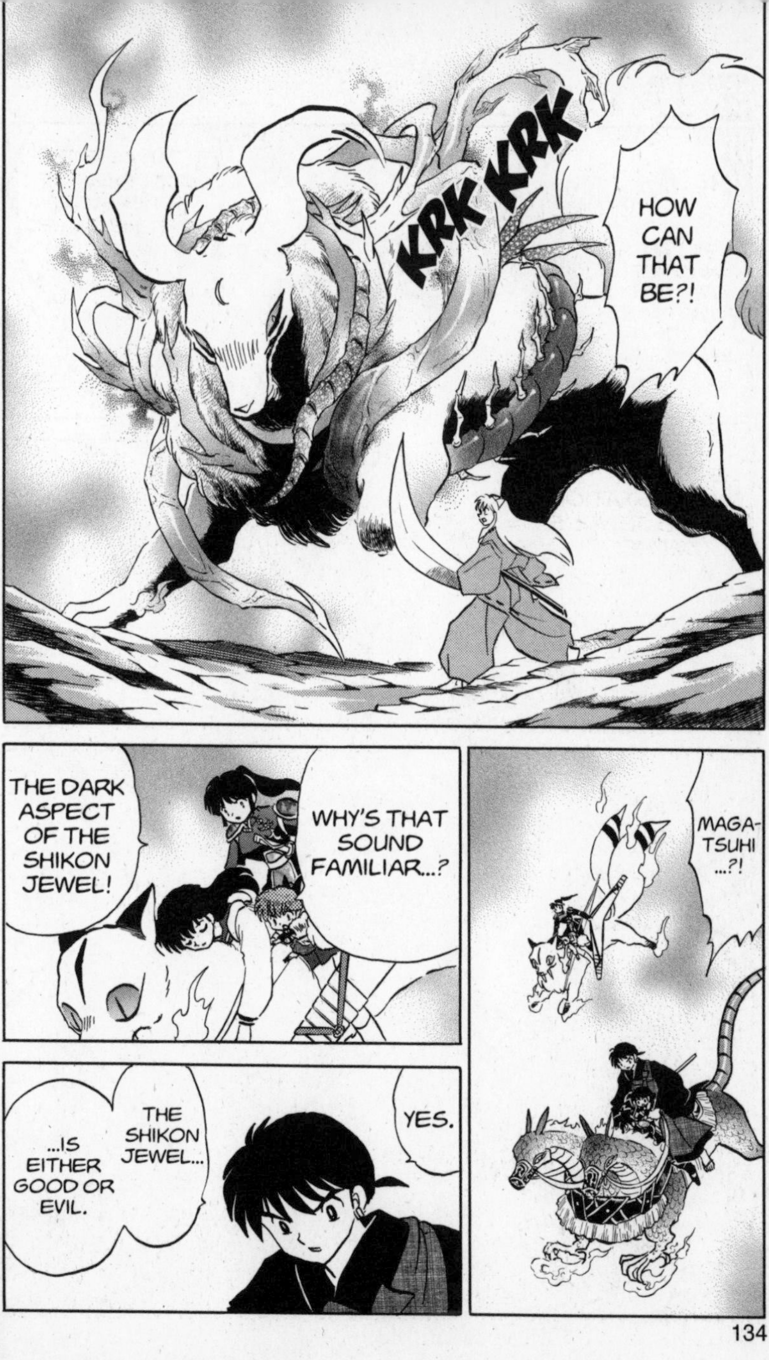
HOW CAN THAT BE?!
KRK KRK
MAGA-TSUHI ...?!
WHY'S THAT SOUND FAMILIAR...?
THE DARK ASPECT OF THE SHIKON JEWEL!
YES.
THE SHIKON JEWEL...
...IS EITHER GOOD OR EVIL.

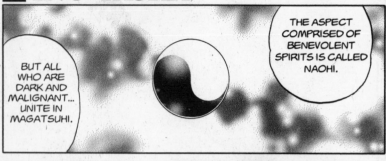

THE ASPECT COMPRISED OF BENEVOLENT SPIRITS IS CALLED NAOHI.
BUT ALL WHO ARE DARK AND MALIGNANT... UNITE IN MAGATSUHI.
HE'S THE LIVING MANIFESTATION OF THE JEWEL'S DARKEST SOULS!
KRK KRK
LISTEN...
...MAGA-TSUHI— OR WHOEVER YOU ARE.
IN THE END, YOU'RE JUST ANOTHER STEW OF NARAKU'S PIECES!
AND THAT MEANS ...
I'M *CUTTING YOU DOWN!*

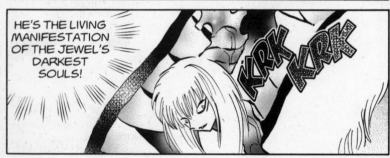

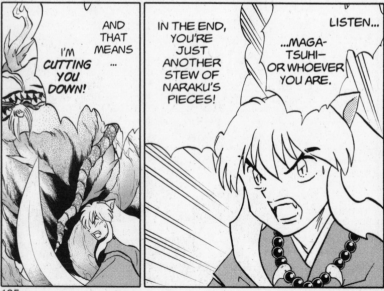

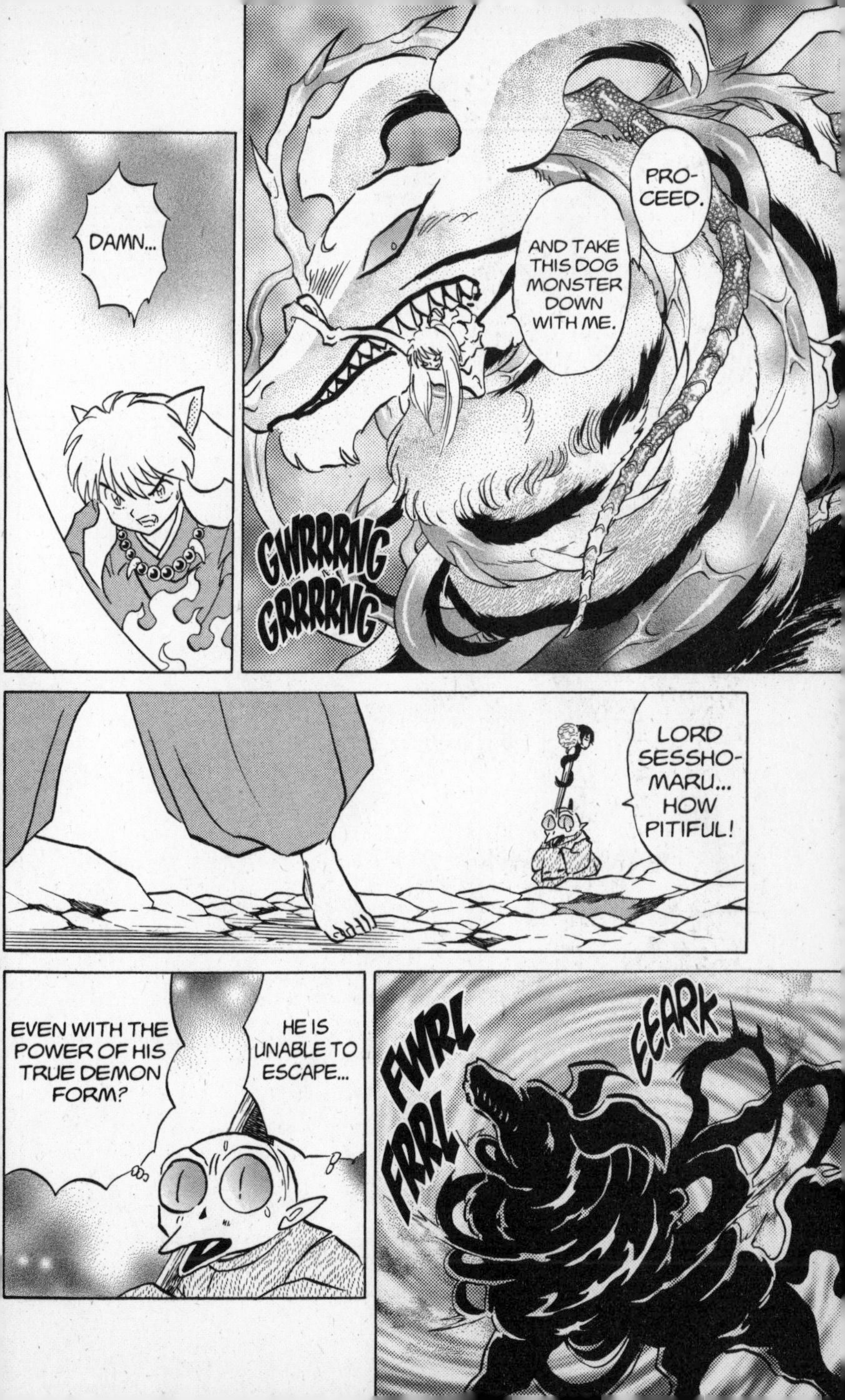
PRO-CEED.
AND TAKE THIS DOG MONSTER DOWN WITH ME.
GWRRRNG GRRRRNG
DAMN...
LORD SESSHO-MARU... HOW PITIFUL!
EEARK
FWRL FRRL
HE IS UNABLE TO ESCAPE...
EVEN WITH THE POWER OF HIS TRUE DEMON FORM?

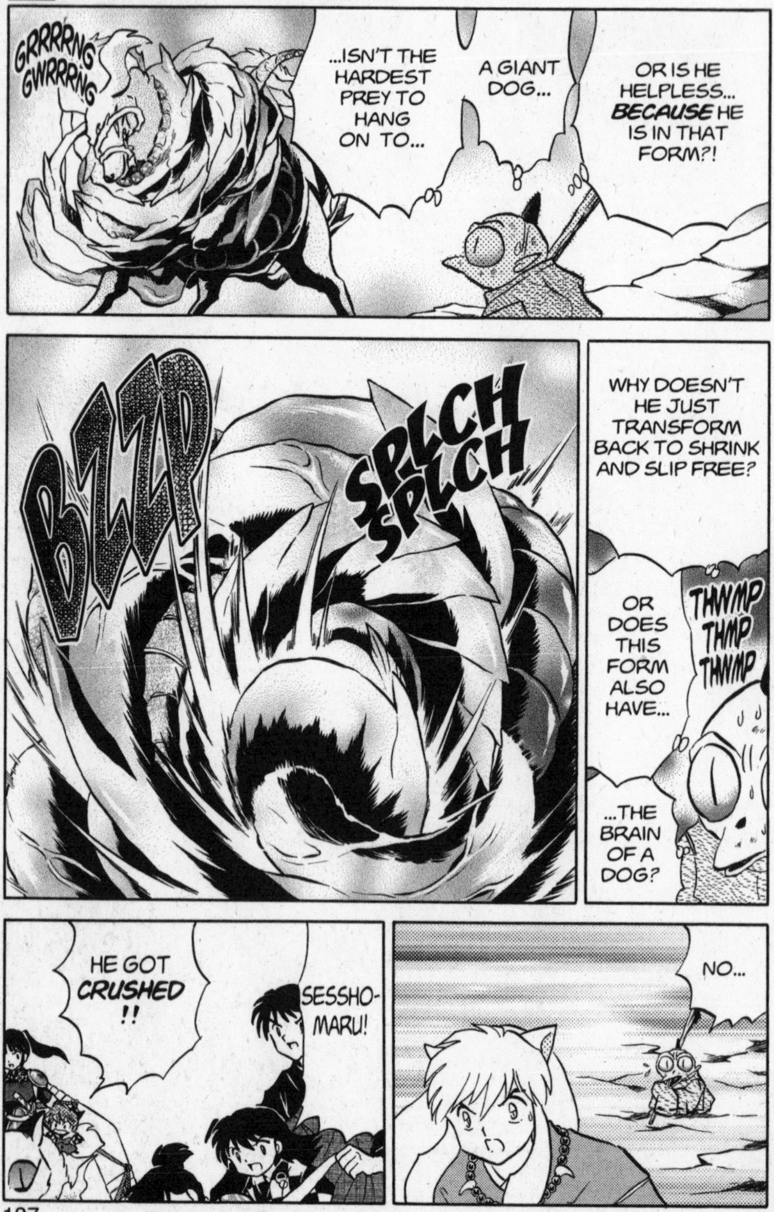
GRRRRNG GWRRRNG
...ISN'T THE HARDEST PREY TO HANG ON TO...
A GIANT DOG...
OR IS HE HELPLESS... BECAUSE HE IS IN THAT FORM?!
BZZP
SPLCH SPLCH
WHY DOESN'T HE JUST TRANSFORM BACK TO SHRINK AND SLIP FREE?
OR DOES THIS FORM ALSO HAVE...
THWMP THMP THWMP
...THE BRAIN OF A DOG?
HE GOT CRUSHED !!
SESSHO-MARU!
NO...

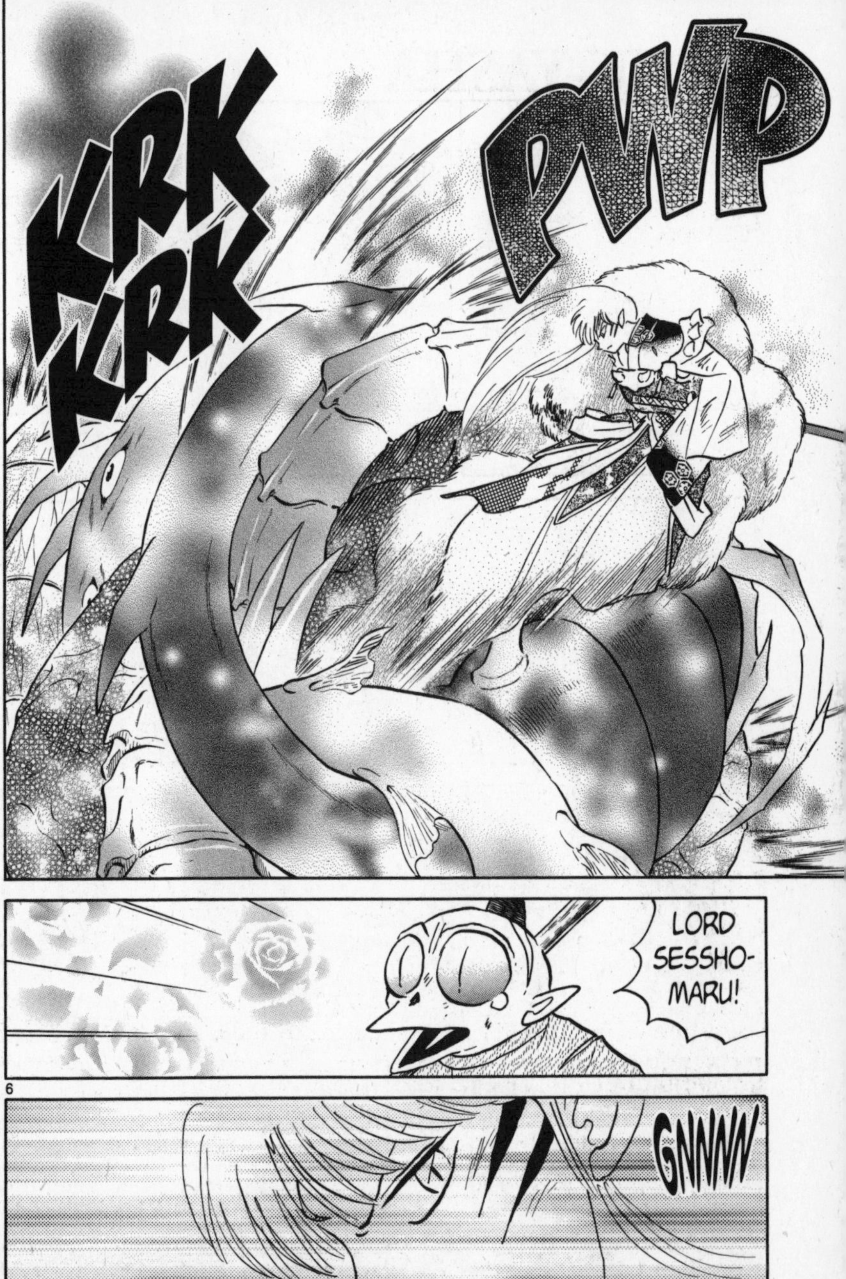
PWP
KIRK KIRK
LORD SESSHO-MARU!
GNNNN

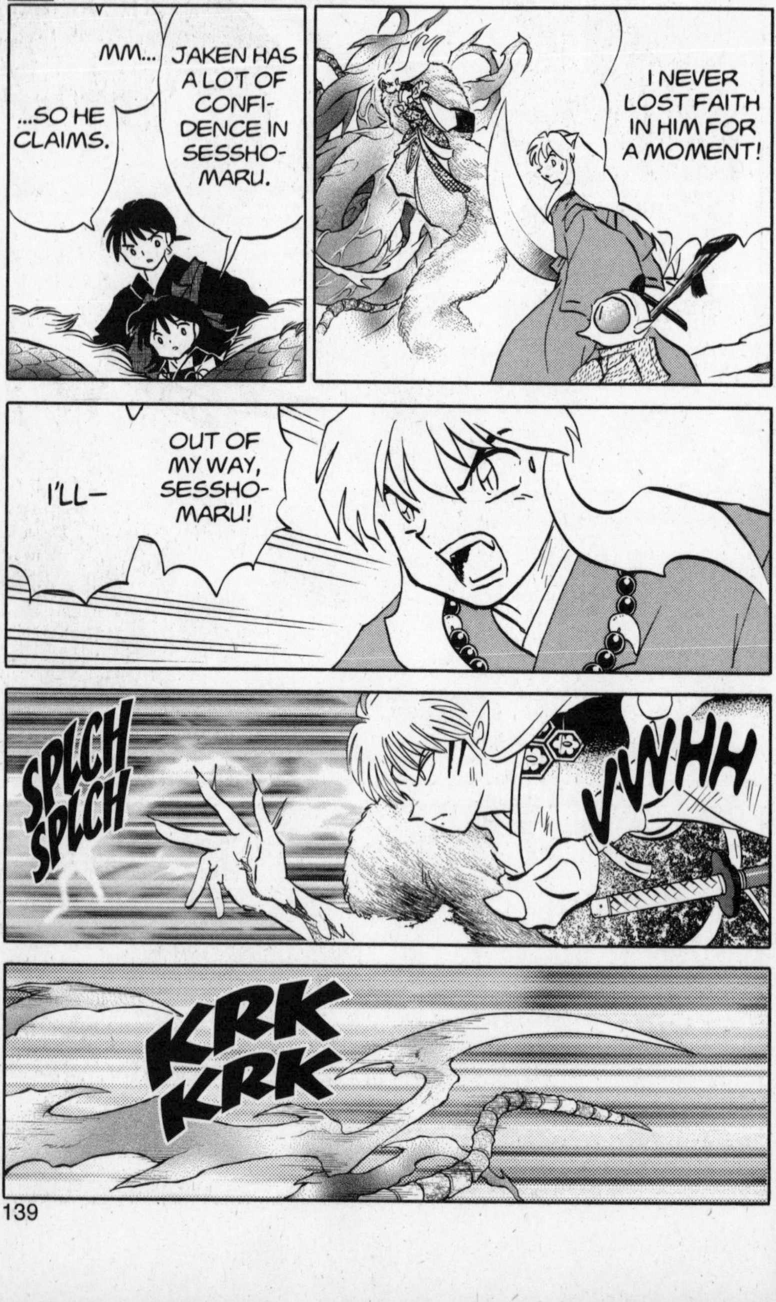
I NEVER LOST FAITH IN HIM FOR A MOMENT!
JAKEN HAS A LOT OF CONFI- DENCE IN SESSHO- MARU.
MM...
...SO HE CLAIMS.
OUT OF MY WAY, SESSHO- MARU!
I'LL—
VWHH
SPLCH SPLCH
KRK KRK

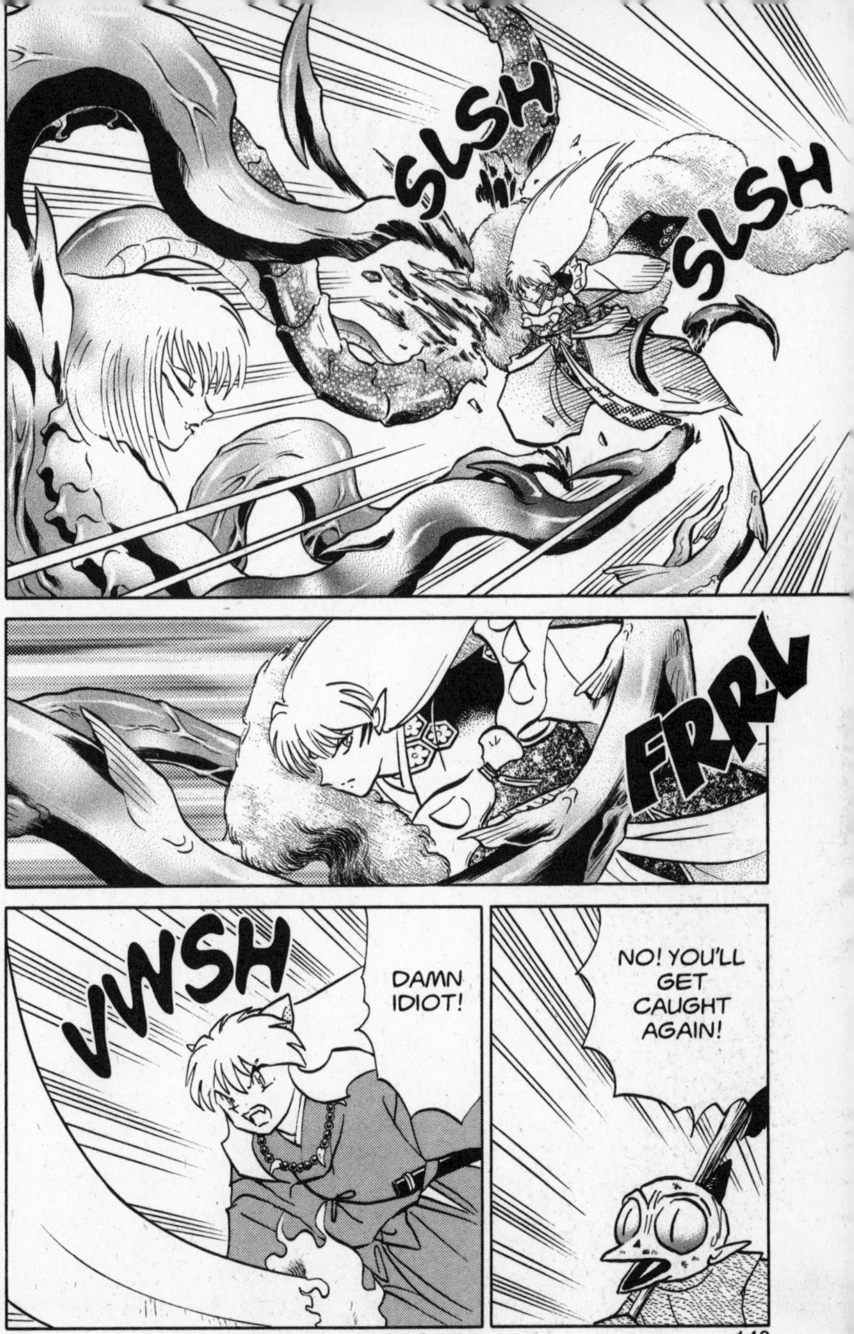
SLSH
SLSH
FRRL
NO! YOU'LL GET CAUGHT AGAIN!
VWSH
DAMN IDIOT!

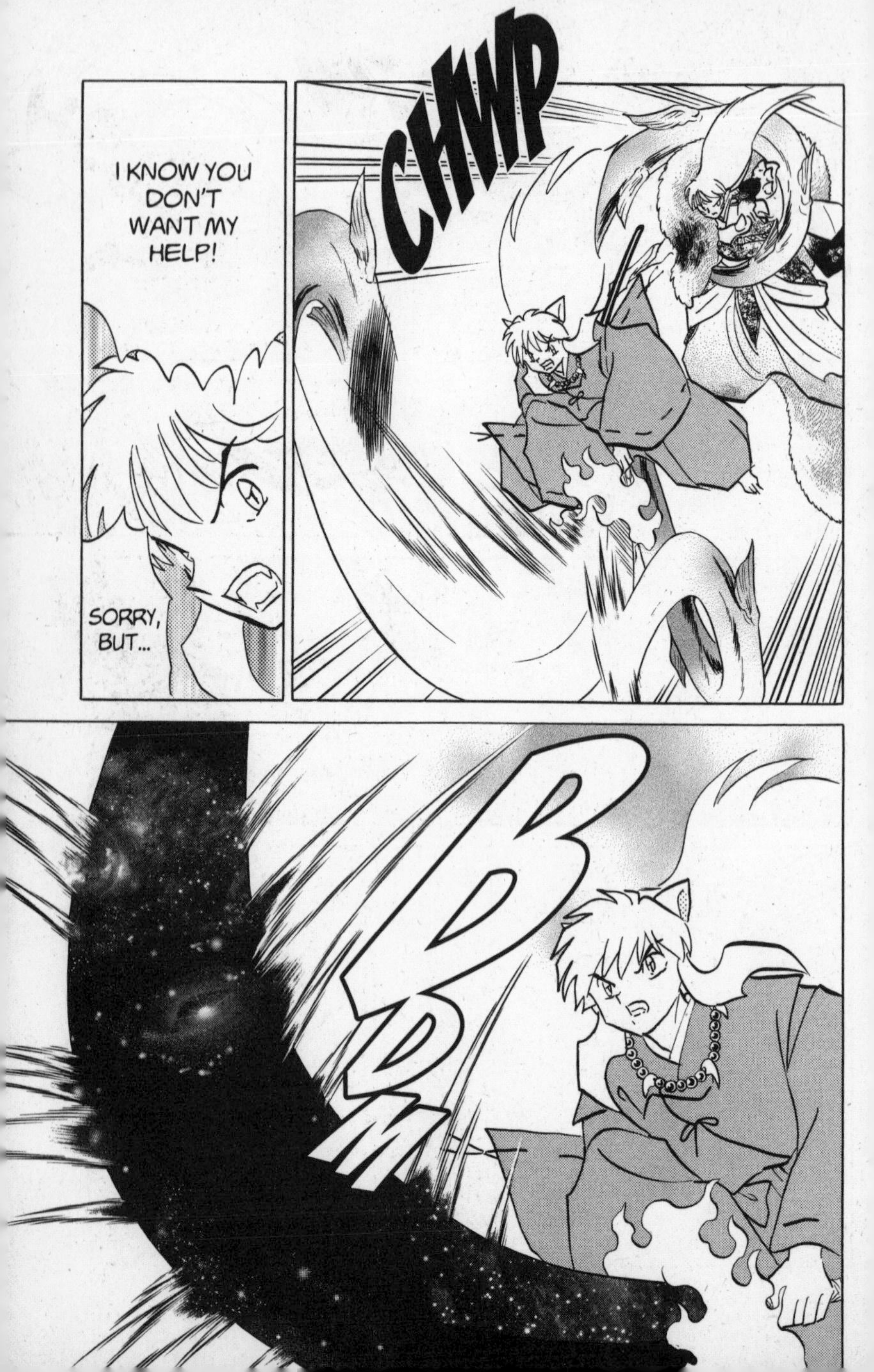
CHWP
I KNOW YOU DON'T WANT MY HELP!
SORRY, BUT...

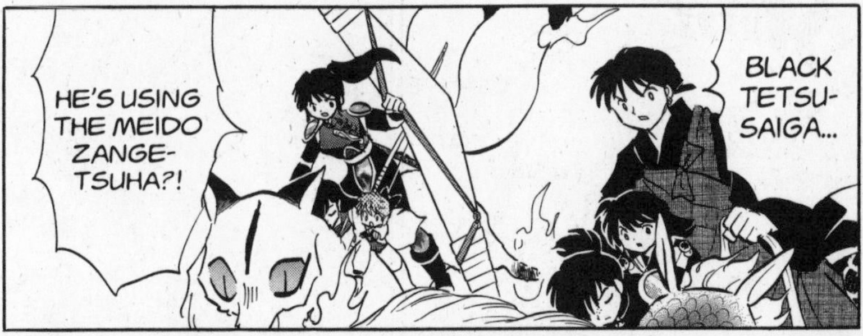
BLACK TETSU-SAIGA...
HE'S USING THE MEIDO ZANGE-TSUHA?!

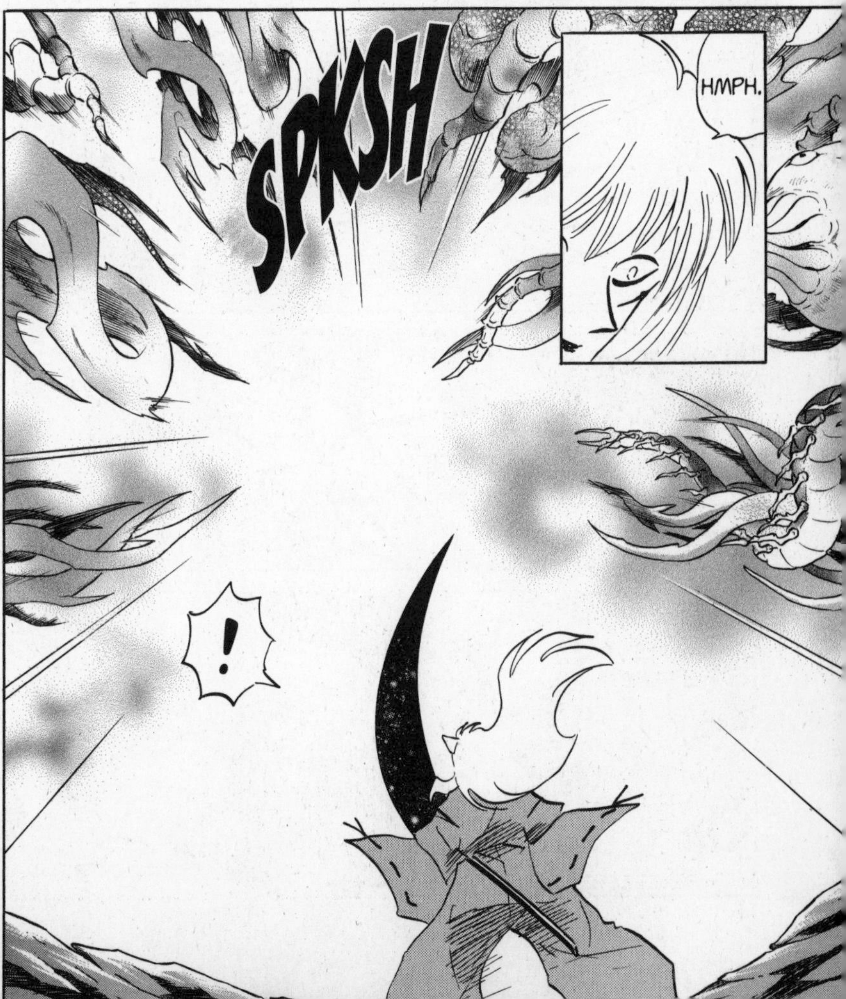
HMPH.
SPKSH
!

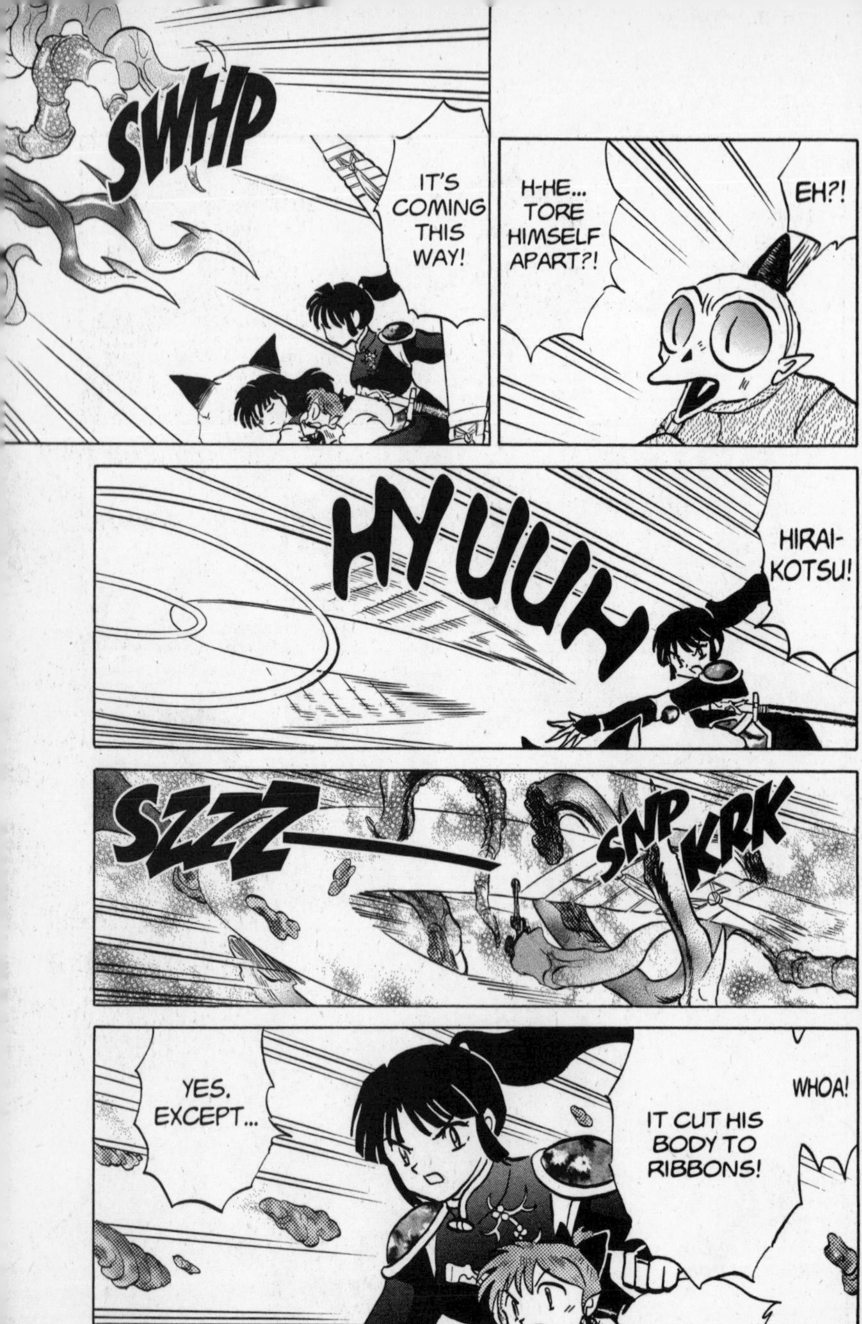
EH?!
H-HE... TORE HIMSELF APART?!
IT'S COMING THIS WAY!
SWHP
HIRAI-KOTSU!
HYUUH
KRK
SNP
SZZZ
WHOA!
IT CUT HIS BODY TO RIBBONS!
YES. EXCEPT...

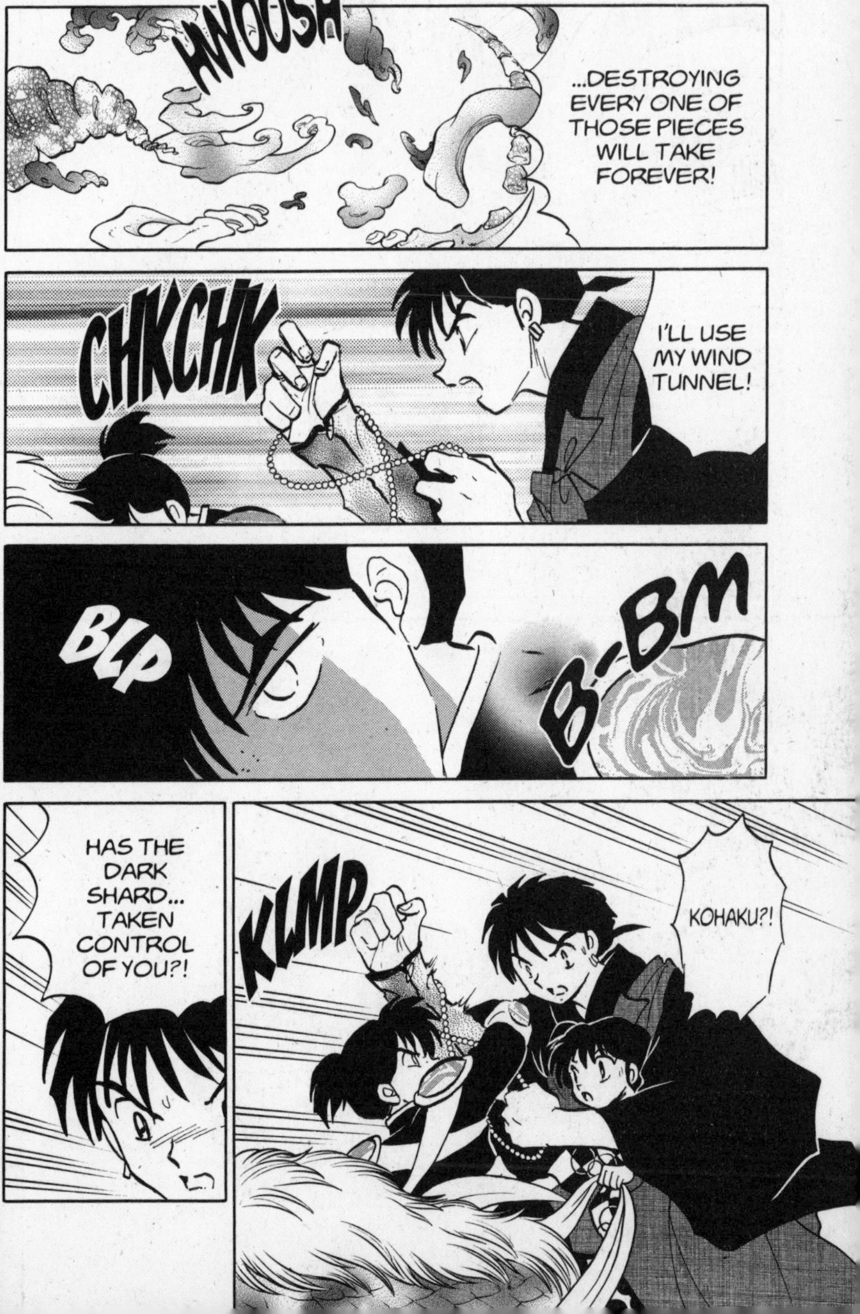
HWOOSH
...DESTROYING EVERY ONE OF THOSE PIECES WILL TAKE FOREVER!
I'LL USE MY WIND TUNNEL!
CHKCHK
B-BM
BLP
KOHAKU?!
KLMP
HAS THE DARK SHARD... TAKEN CONTROL OF YOU?!

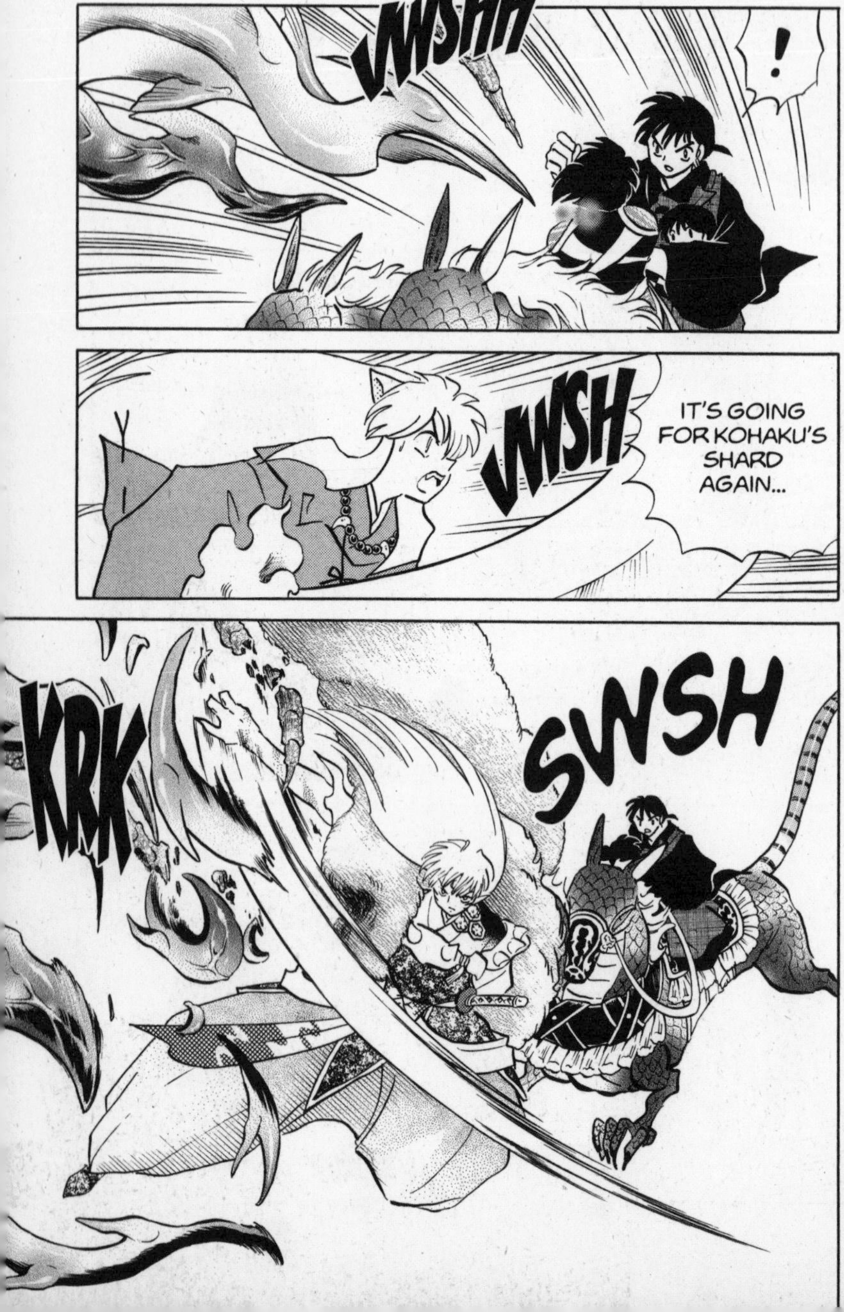
!
VWSHH
IT'S GOING FOR KOHAKU'S SHARD AGAIN...
VWSH
SWSH
KRK

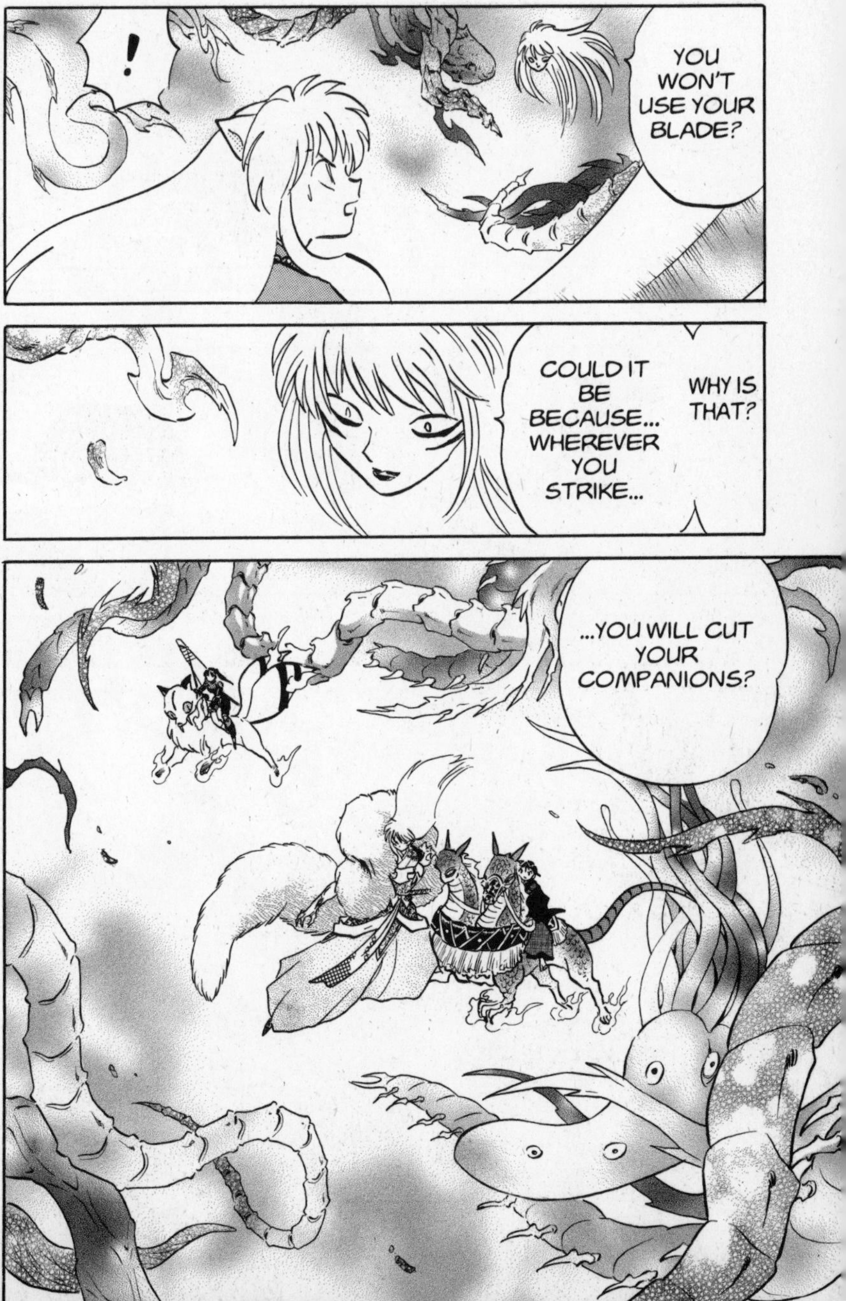
!
YOU WON'T USE YOUR BLADE?
WHY IS THAT?
COULD IT BE BECAUSE... WHEREVER YOU STRIKE...
...YOU WILL CUT YOUR COMPANIONS?

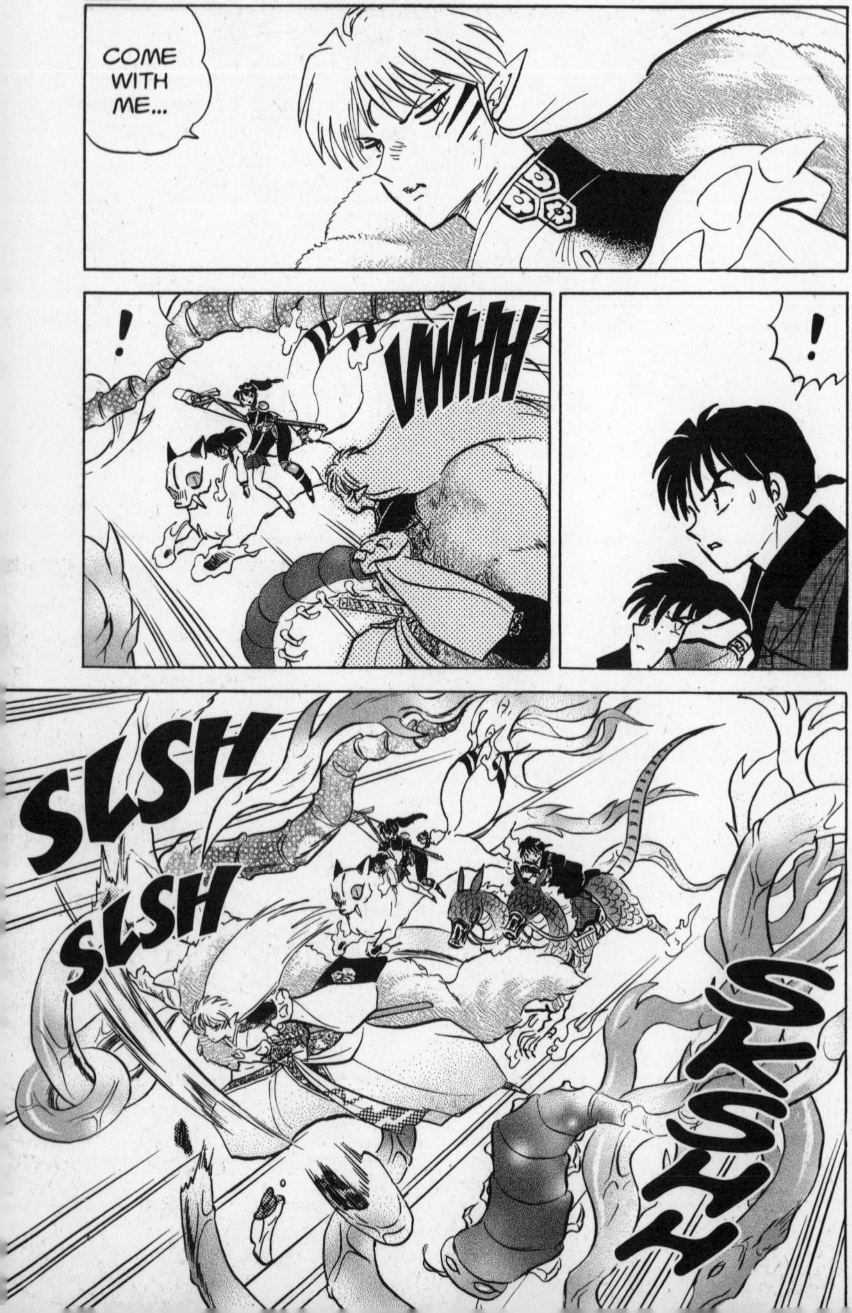
COME WITH ME...
!
!
VWHH
SLSH
SLSH
SHSH

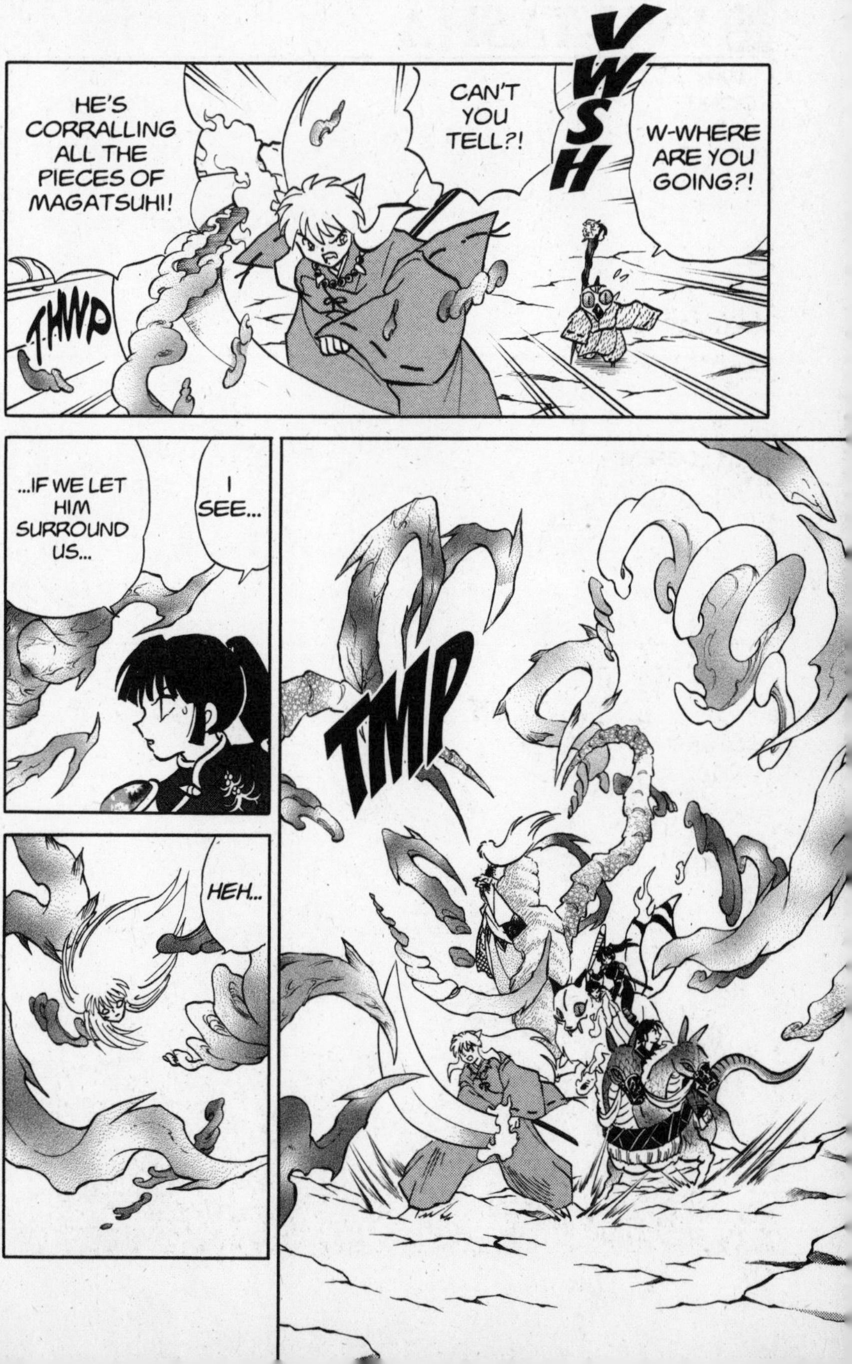
VWSH
W-WHERE ARE YOU GOING?!
CAN'T YOU TELL?!
HE'S CORRALLING ALL THE PIECES OF MAGATSUHI!
THWP
TMP
I SEE...
...IF WE LET HIM SURROUND US...
HEH...

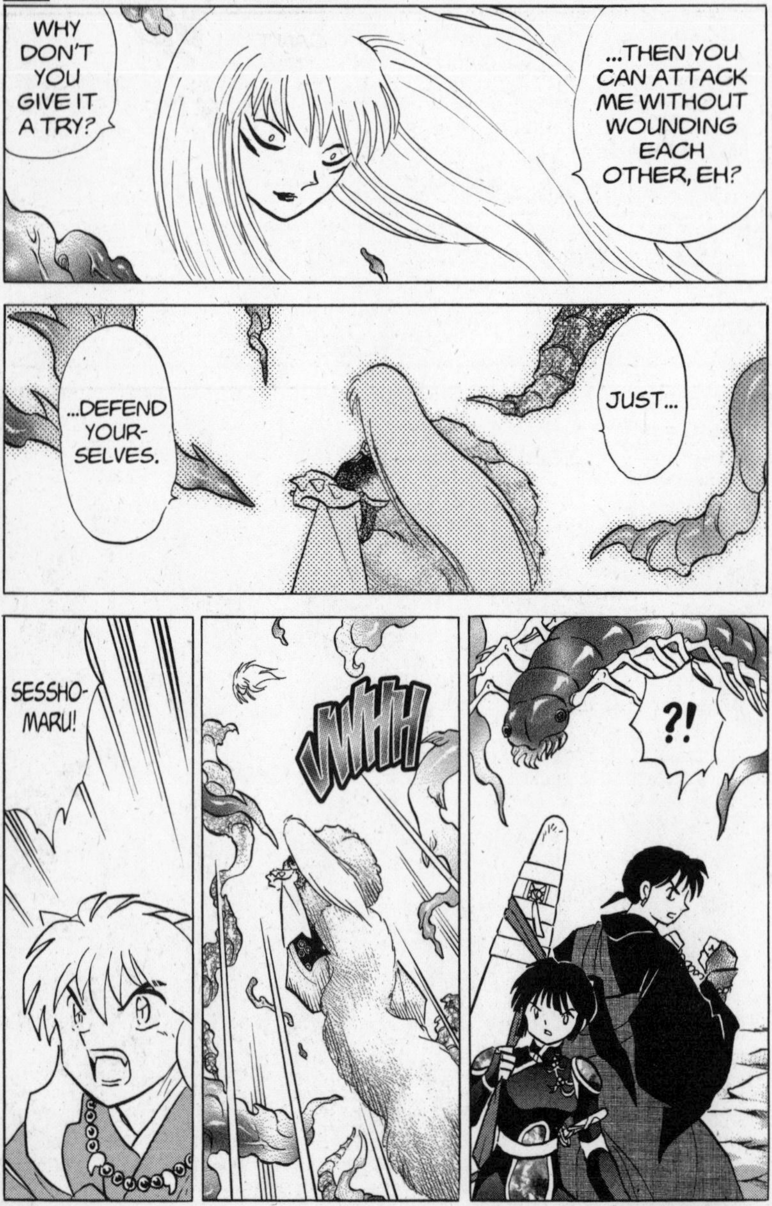
...THEN YOU CAN ATTACK ME WITHOUT WOUNDING EACH OTHER, EH?
WHY DON'T YOU GIVE IT A TRY?
JUST...
...DEFEND YOUR-SELVES.
?!
VWHH
SESSHO-MARU!

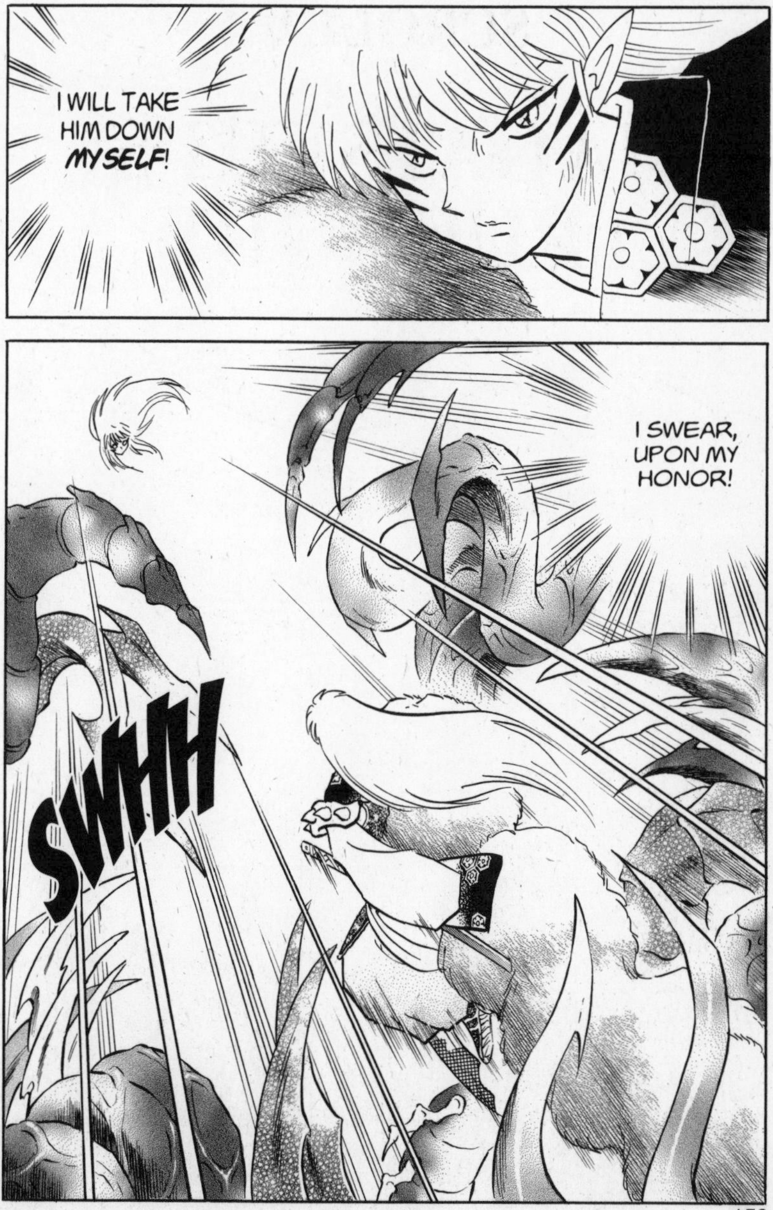
I WILL TAKE HIM DOWN MYSELF!
I SWEAR, UPON MY HONOR!
SWHH

SCROLL 9

MAGATSUHI'S TRUE BODY

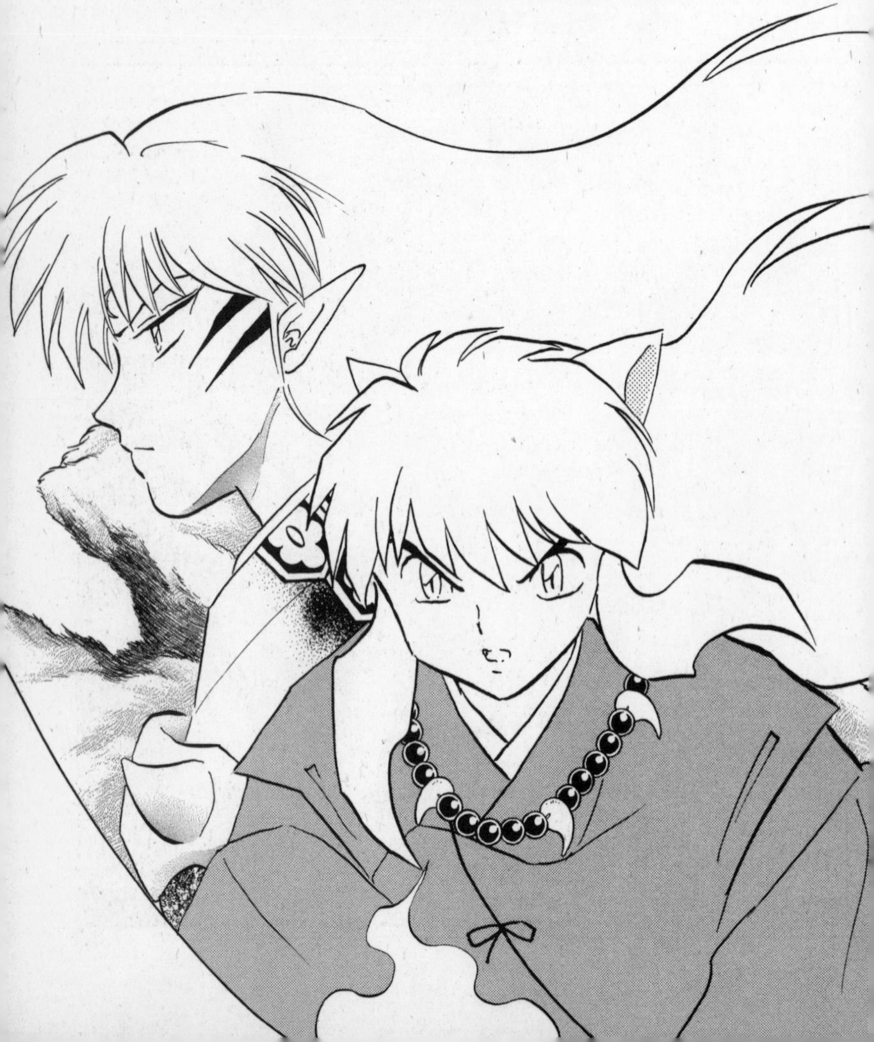

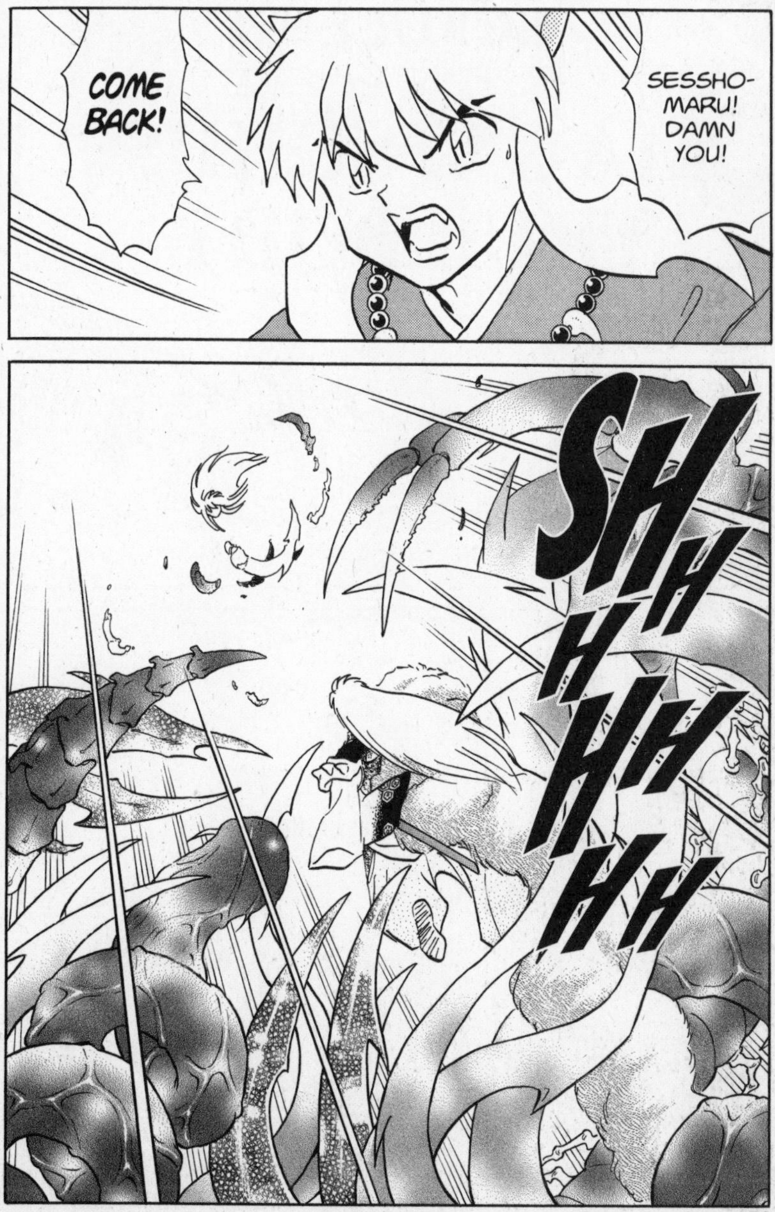
SESSHO-MARU! DAMN YOU!
COME BACK!
SHHHHHHHH

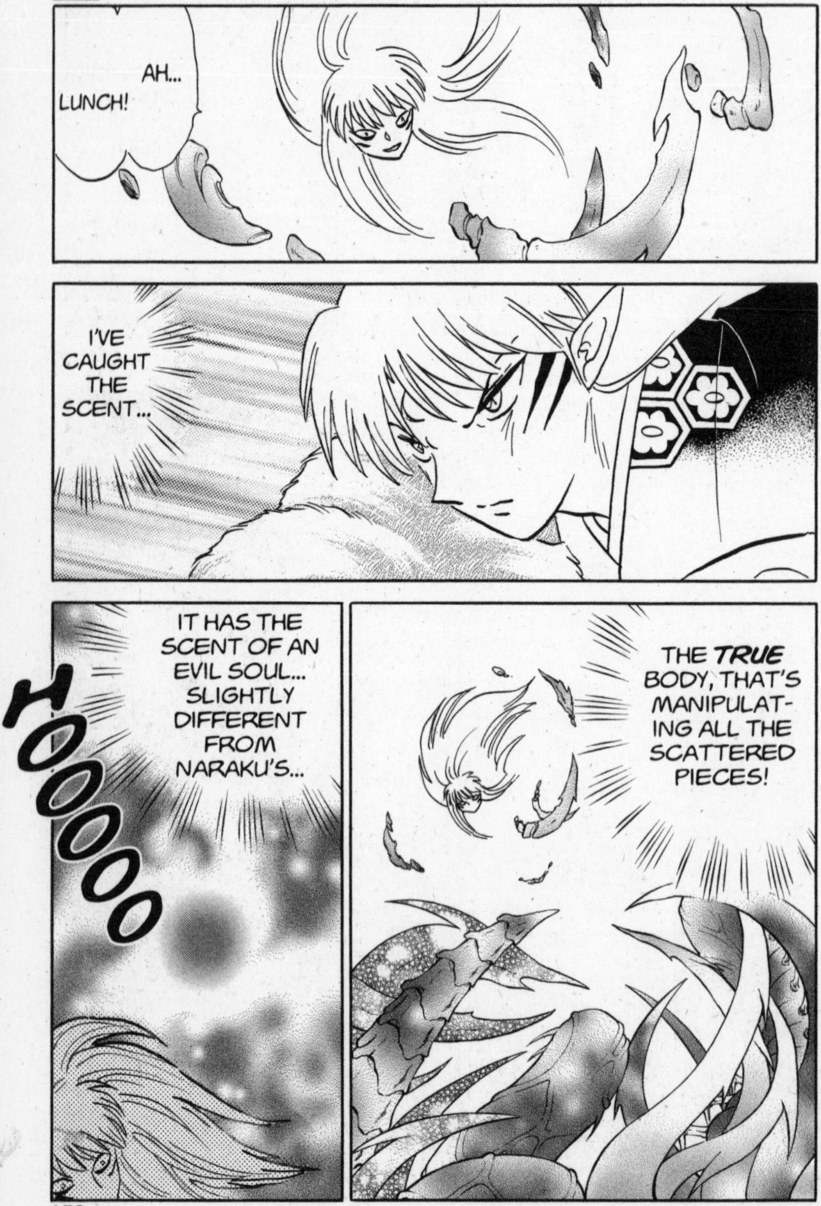
AH... LUNCH!
I'VE CAUGHT THE SCENT...
THE **TRUE** BODY, THAT'S MANIPULATING ALL THE SCATTERED PIECES!
IT HAS THE SCENT OF AN EVIL SOUL... SLIGHTLY DIFFERENT FROM NARAKU'S...
HOOOOO

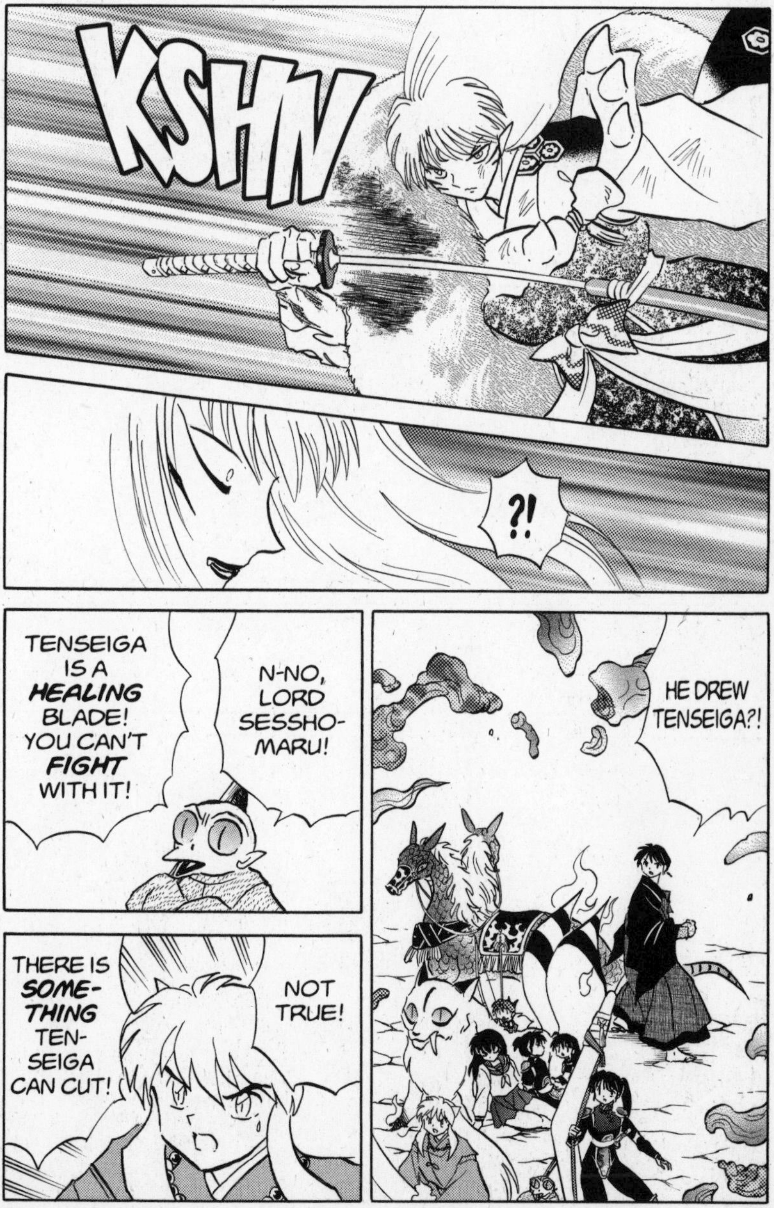
KSHN
?!
HE DREW TENSEIGA?!
N-NO, LORD SESSHOMARU!
TENSEIGA IS A HEALING BLADE! YOU CAN'T FIGHT WITH IT!
NOT TRUE!
THERE IS SOMETHING TENSEIGA CAN CUT!

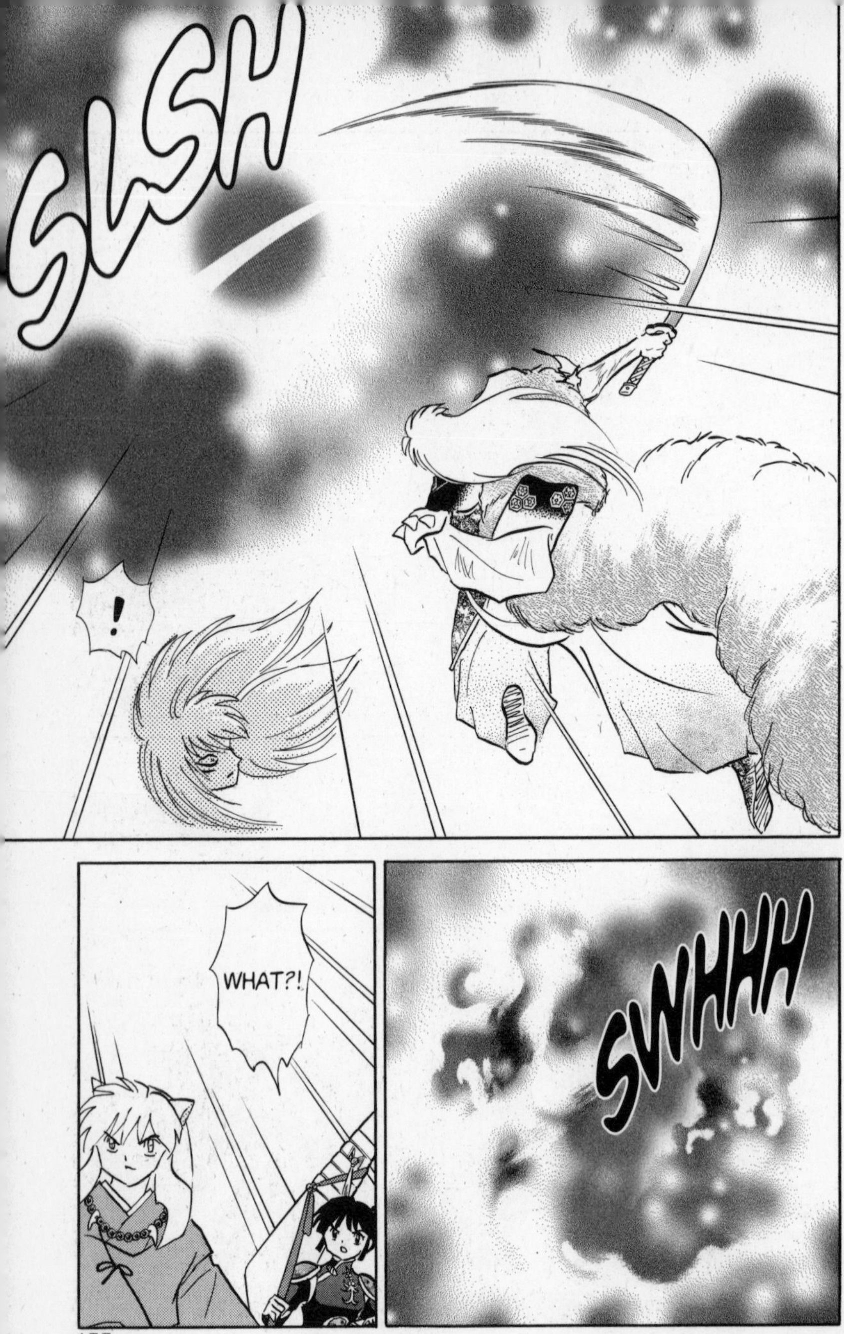
SLSH
!
SWHHH
WHAT?!

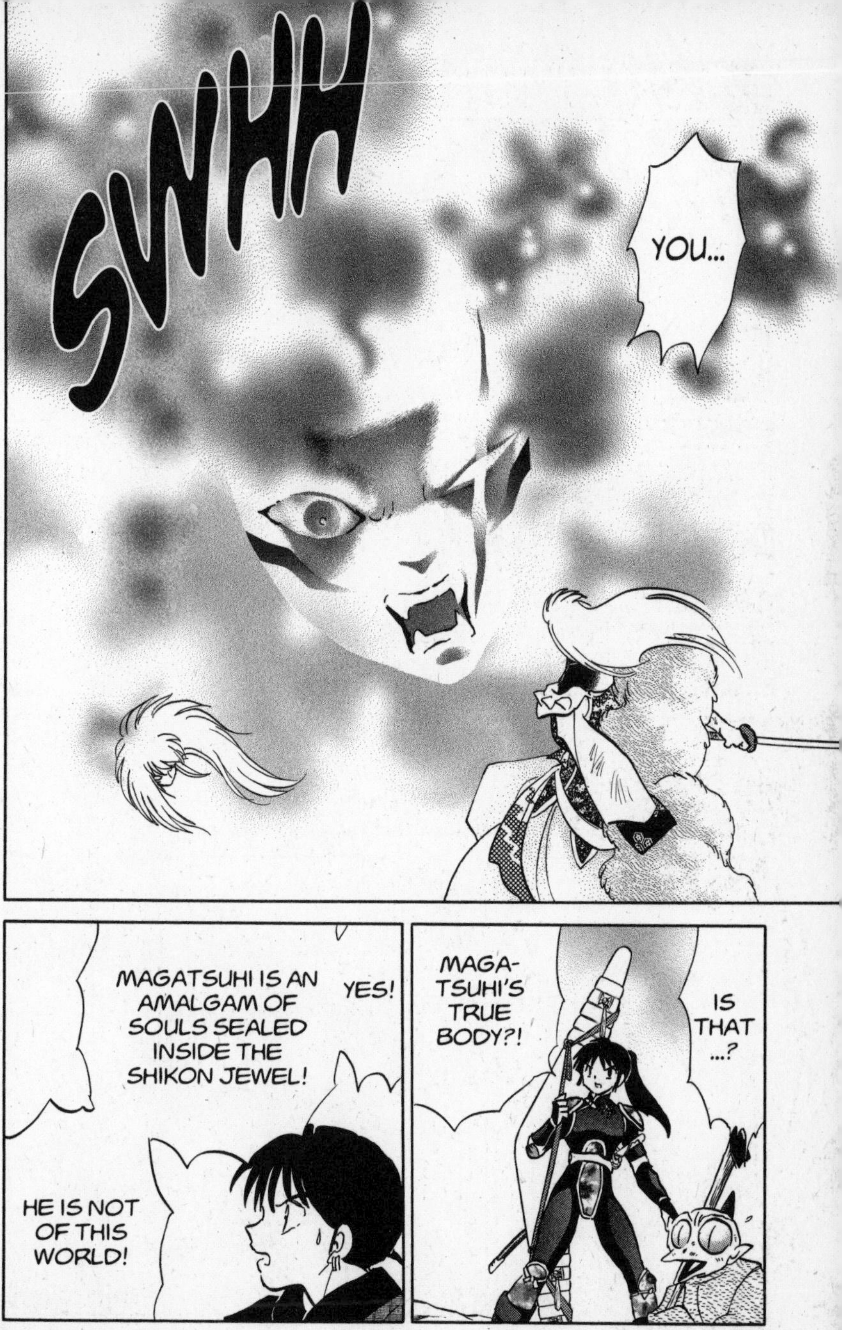
SWHH
YOU...
IS THAT ...?
MAGA-TSUHI'S TRUE BODY?!
YES!
MAGATSUHI IS AN AMALGAM OF SOULS SEALED INSIDE THE SHIKON JEWEL!
HE IS NOT OF THIS WORLD!

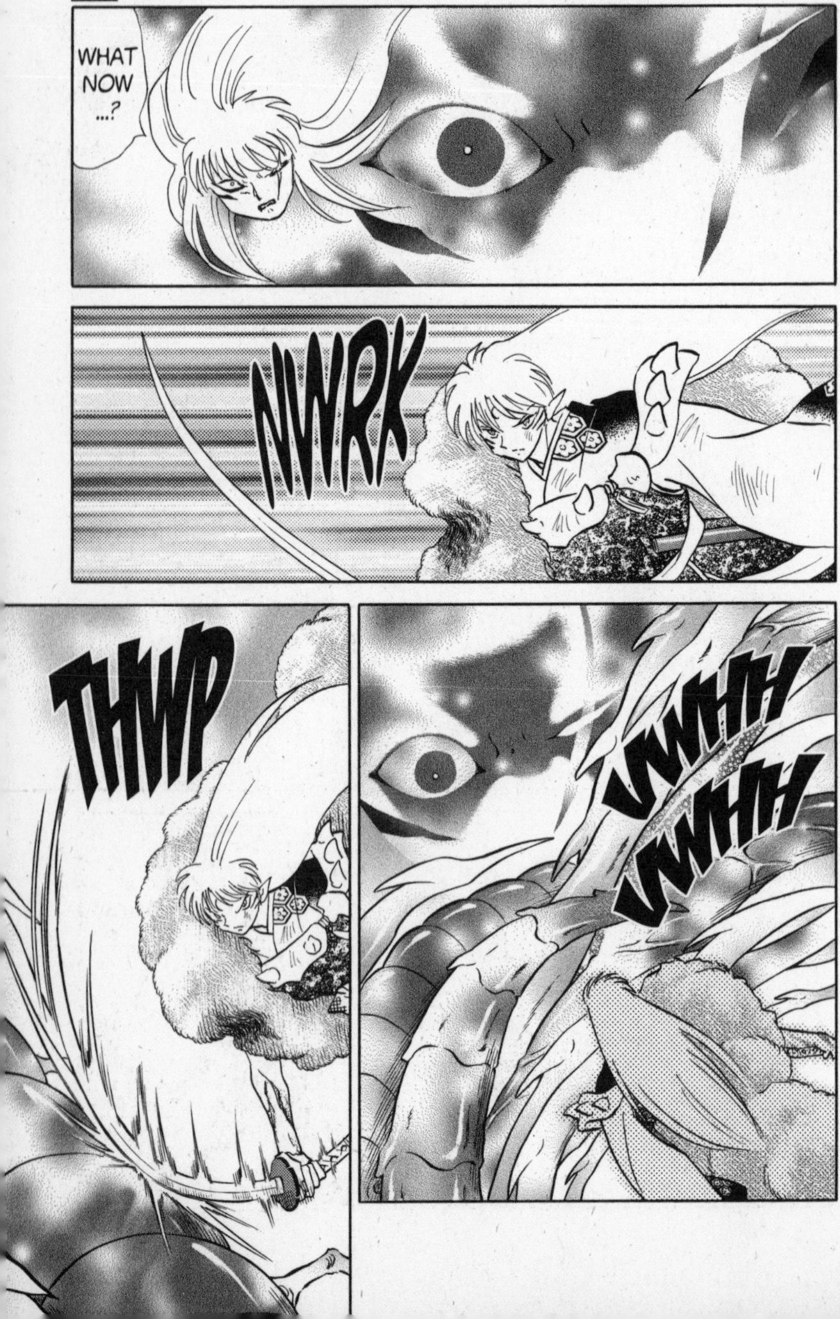
WHAT NOW ...?
NWRK
VWHH
VWHH
THWP

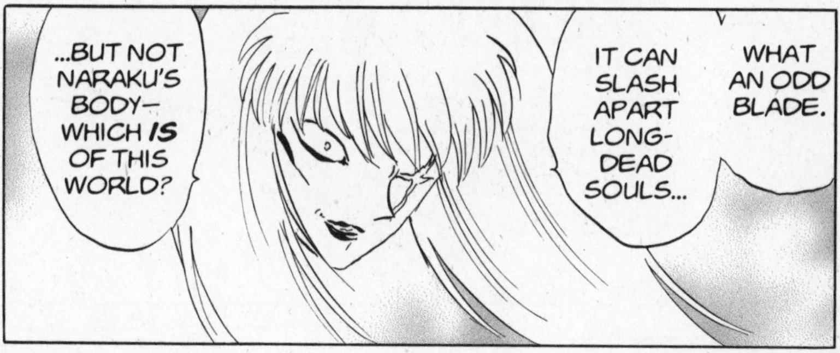
WHAT AN ODD BLADE.
IT CAN SLASH APART LONG-DEAD SOULS...
...BUT NOT NARAKU'S BODY—WHICH *IS* OF THIS WORLD?
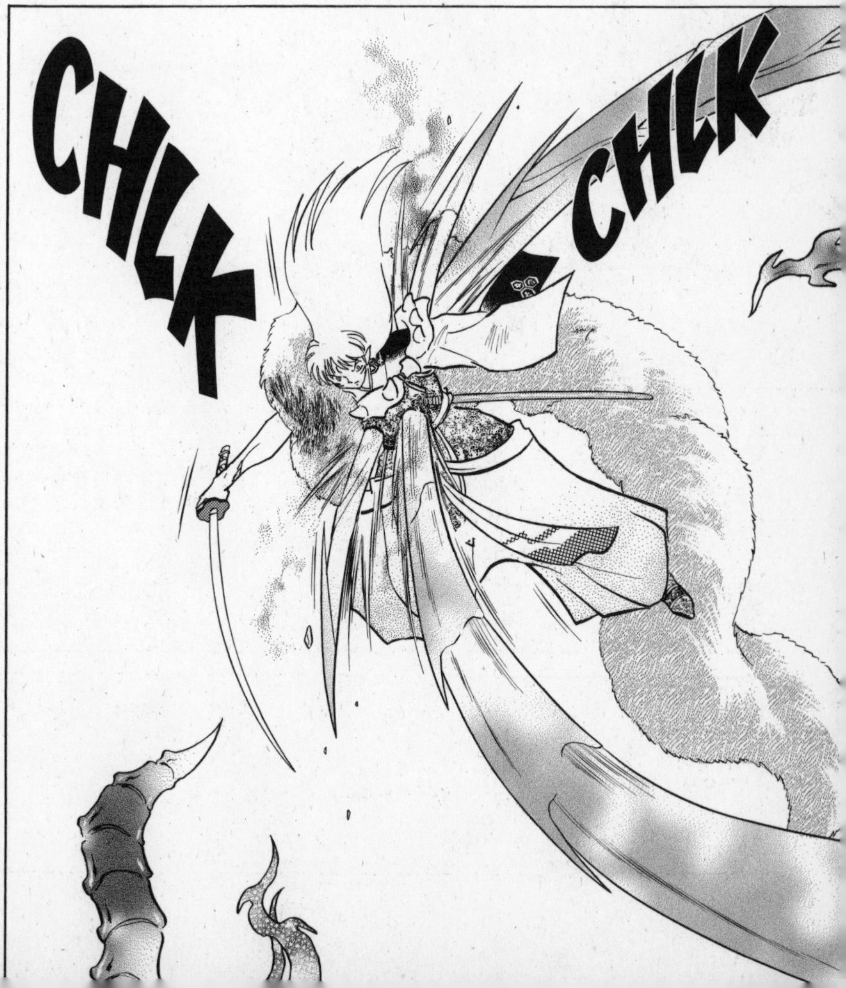
CHLK
CHLK

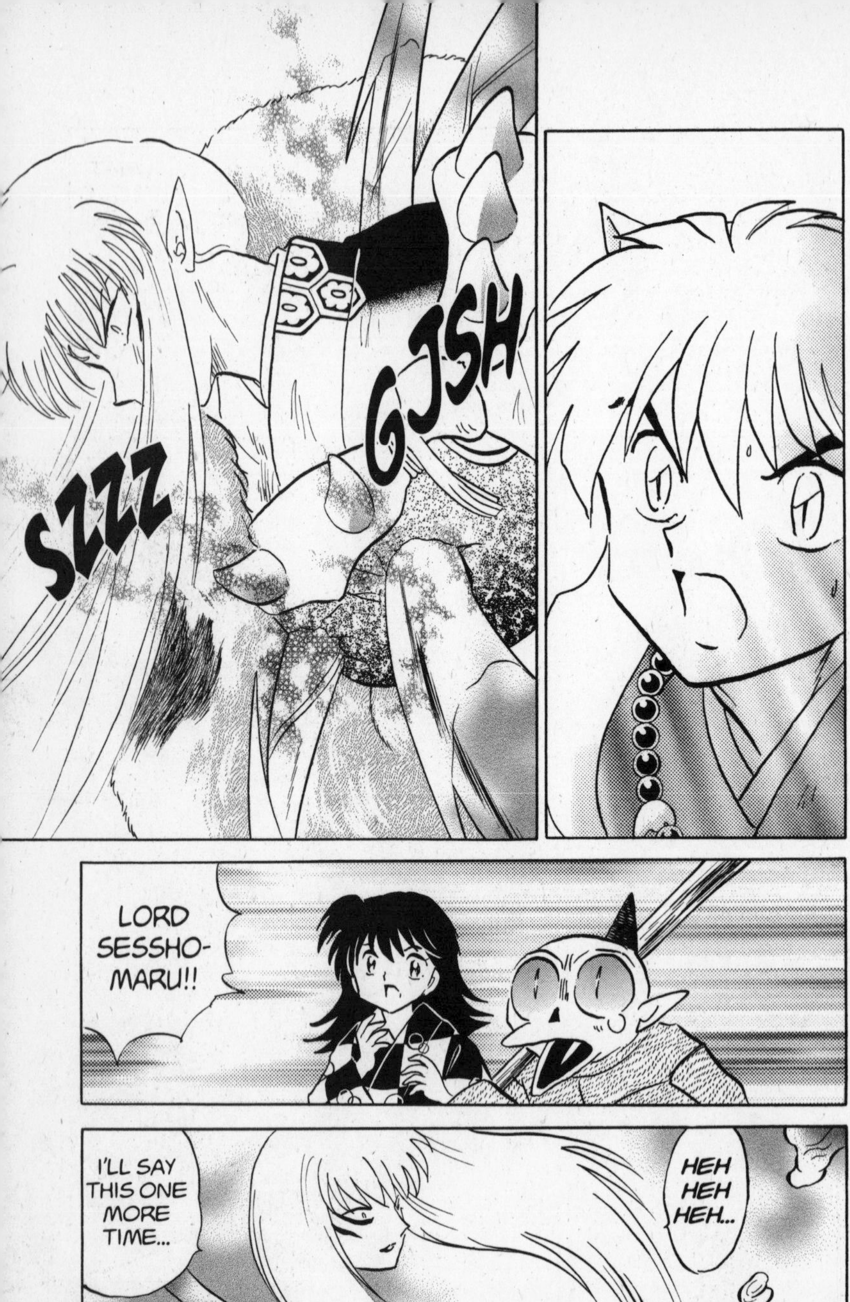
GJSH
SZZZ
LORD SESSHO-MARU!!
HEH HEH HEH...
I'LL SAY THIS ONE MORE TIME...

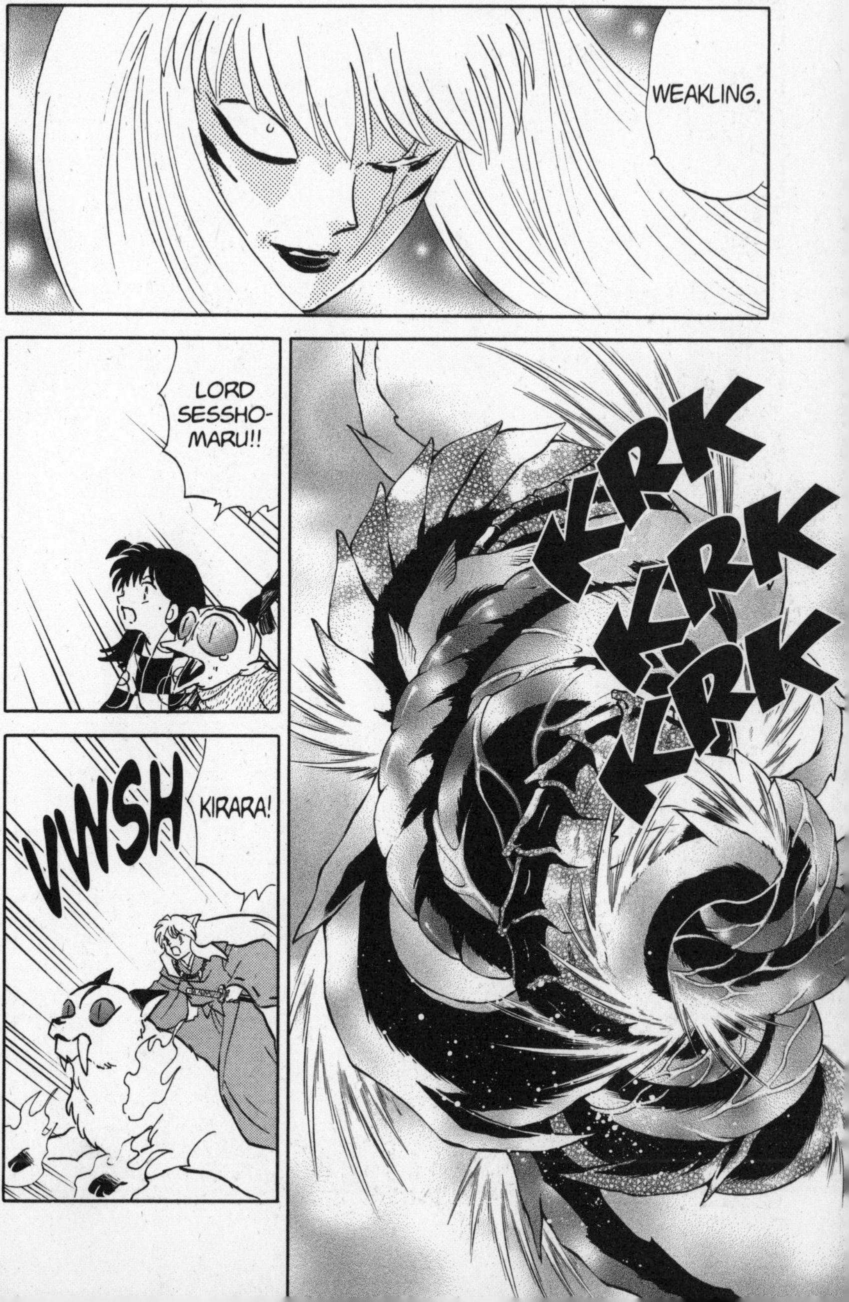
WEAKLING.
KRK KRK KRK
LORD SESSHOMARU!!
VWSH
KIRARA!

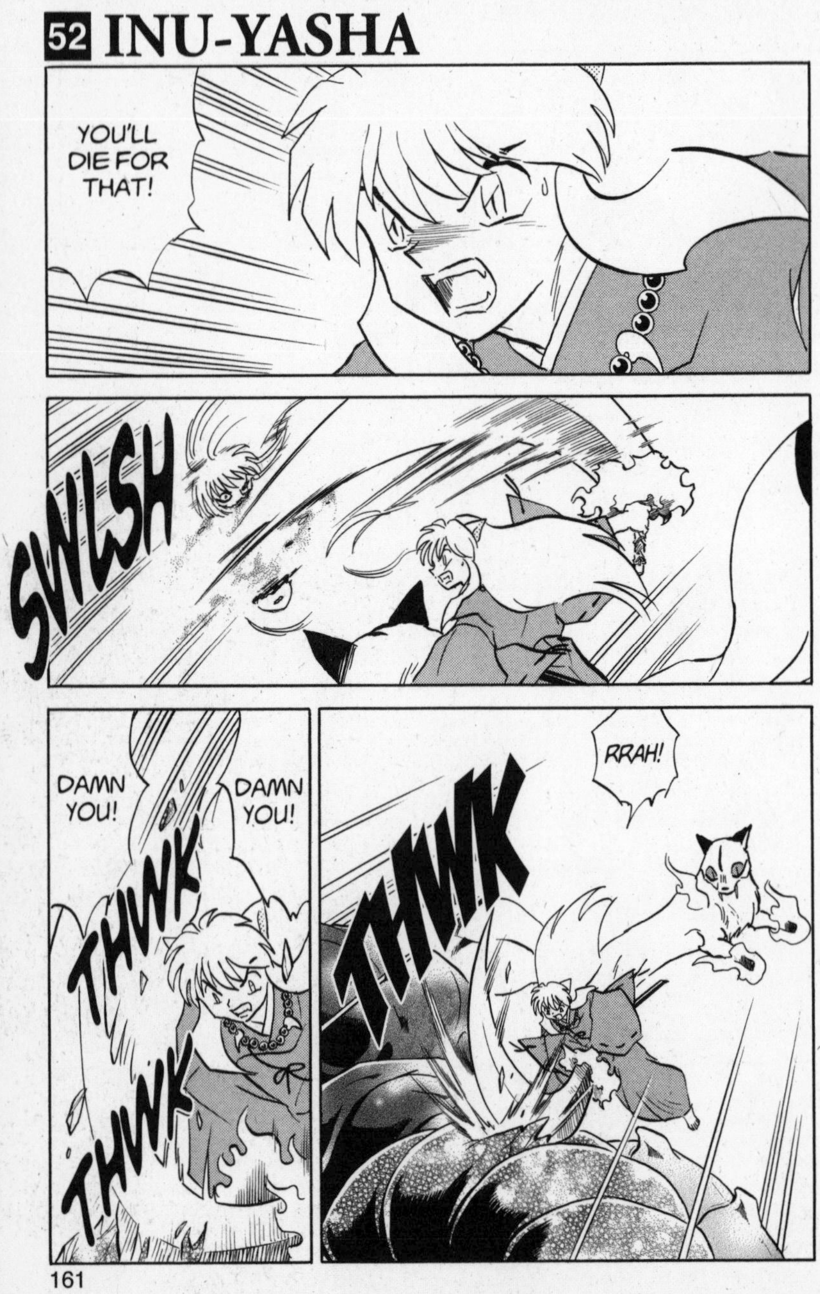
YOU'LL DIE FOR THAT!
SWISH
RRAH!
THWK
DAMN YOU!
DAMN YOU!
THWK
THWK

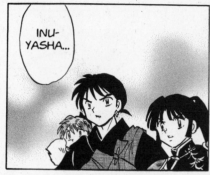

INU-YASHA...

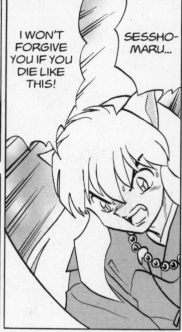

I WON'T FORGIVE YOU IF YOU DIE LIKE THIS!

SESSHO-MARU...

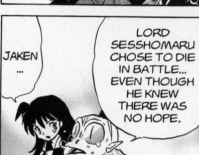

JAKEN ...

LORD SESSHOMARU CHOSE TO DIE IN BATTLE... EVEN THOUGH HE KNEW THERE WAS NO HOPE.

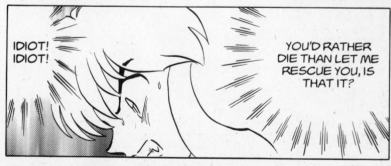

IDIOT! IDIOT!

YOU'D RATHER DIE THAN LET ME RESCUE YOU, IS THAT IT?

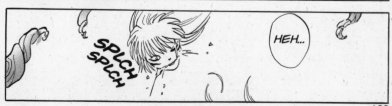

SPLCH SPLCH

HEH...

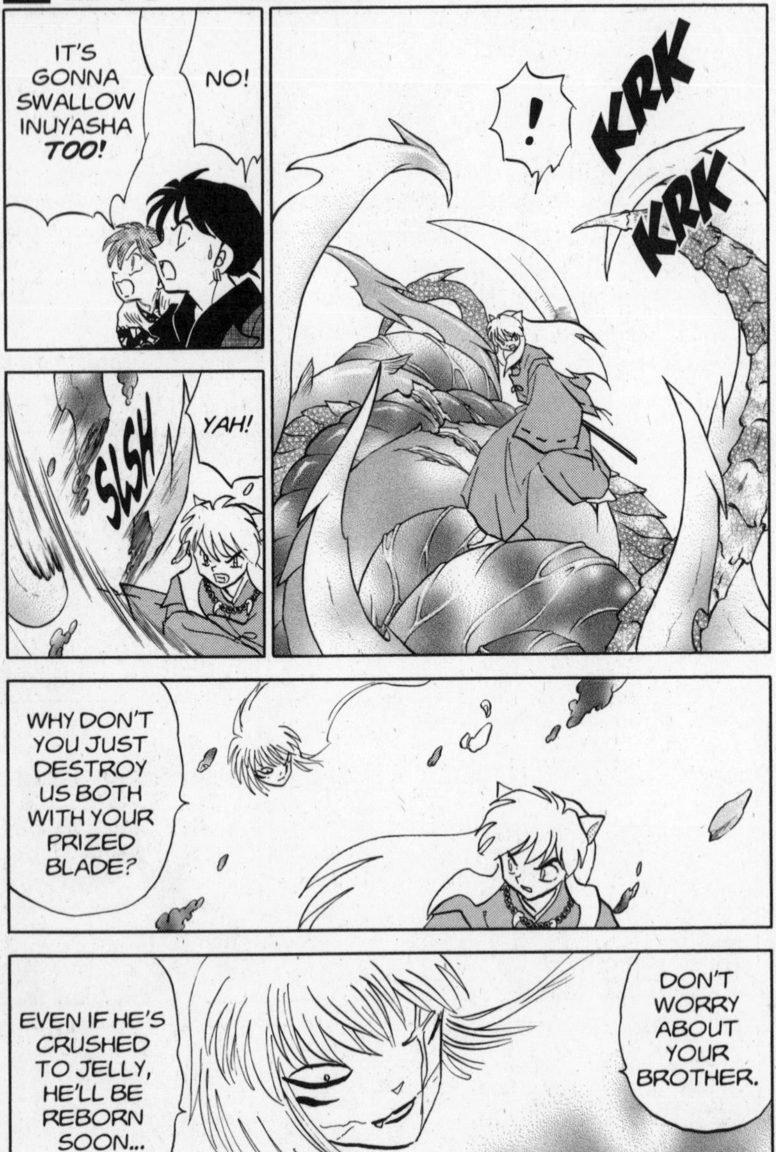
KRK
KRK
!
NO!
IT'S GONNA SWALLOW INUYASHA TOO!
YAH!
SLSH
WHY DON'T YOU JUST DESTROY US BOTH WITH YOUR PRIZED BLADE?
DON'T WORRY ABOUT YOUR BROTHER.
EVEN IF HE'S CRUSHED TO JELLY, HE'LL BE REBORN SOON...

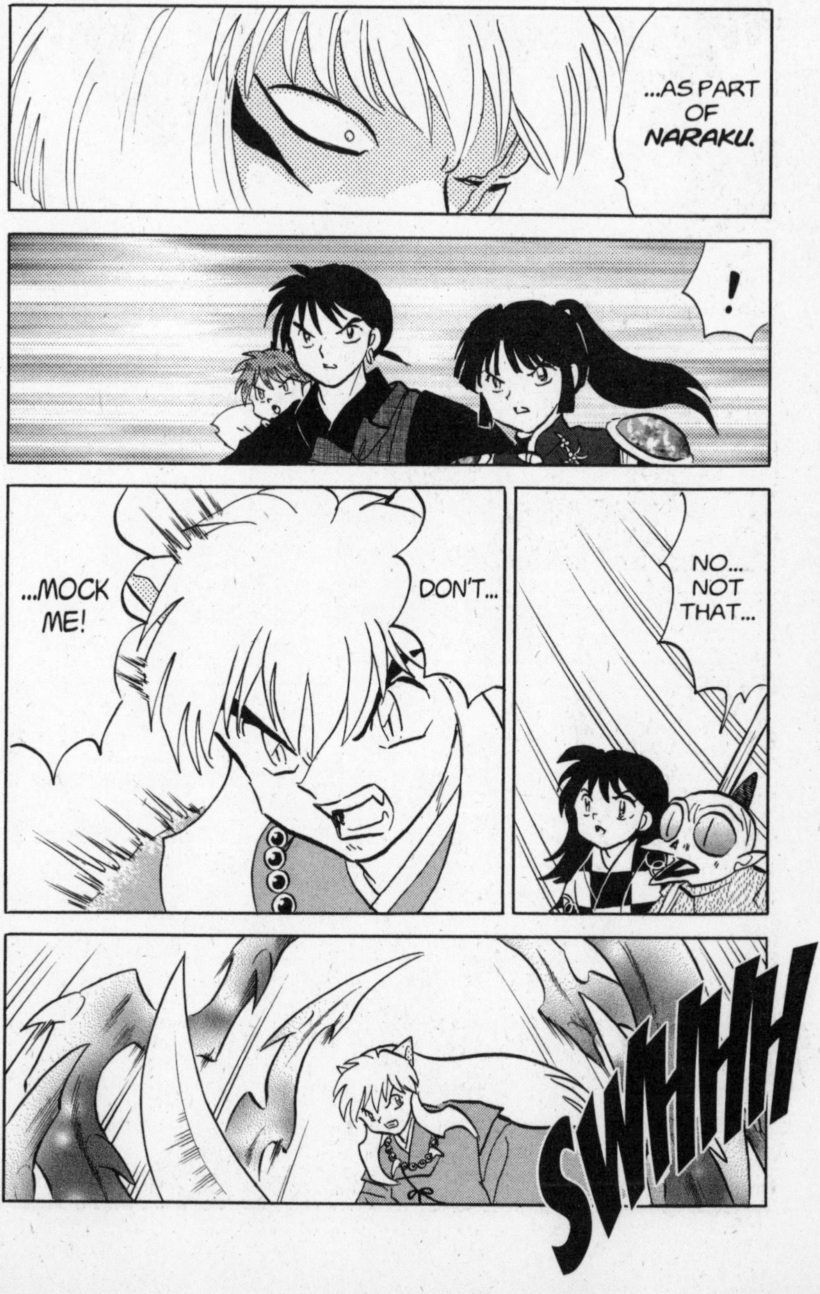
...AS PART OF NARAKU.
!
NO... NOT THAT...
DON'T...
...MOCK ME!
SWHHH

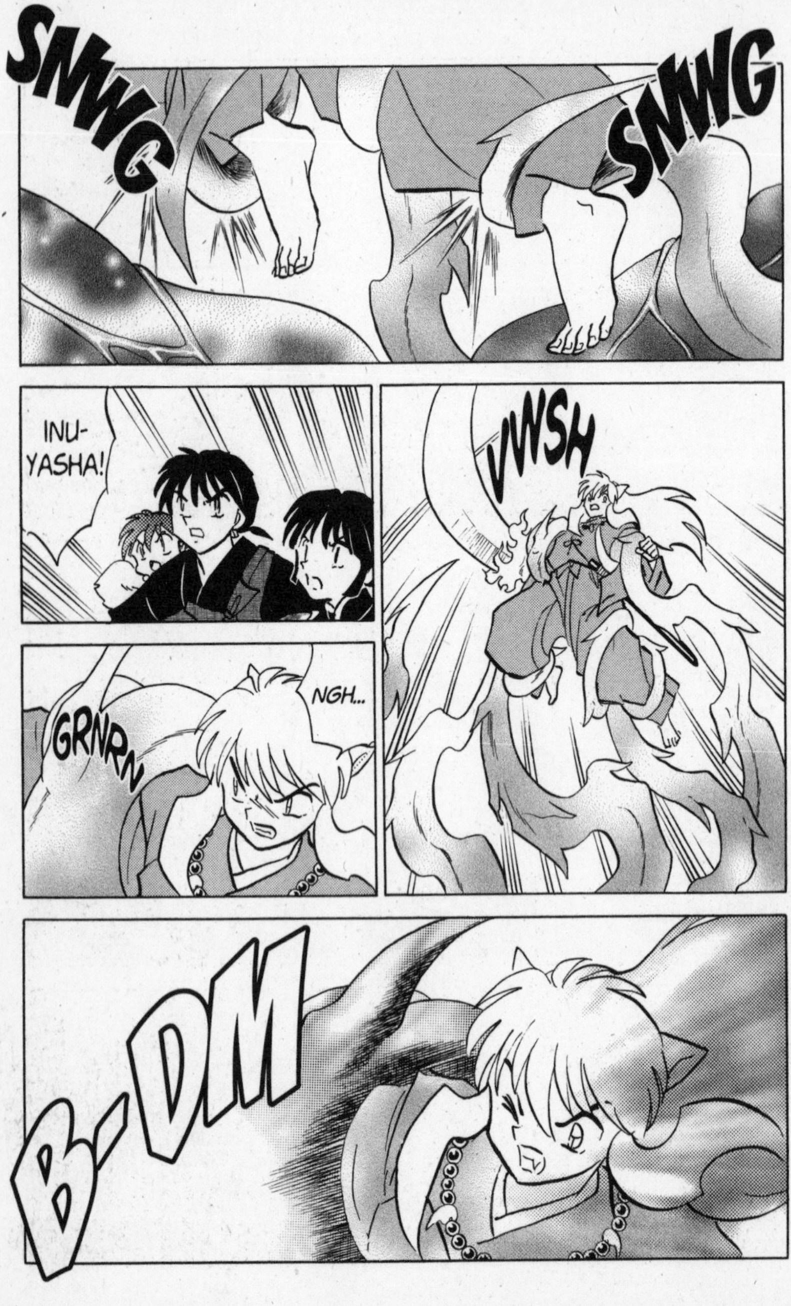
SNWG
SNWG
VWSH
INU-YASHA!
NGH...
GRNRN
B-DM

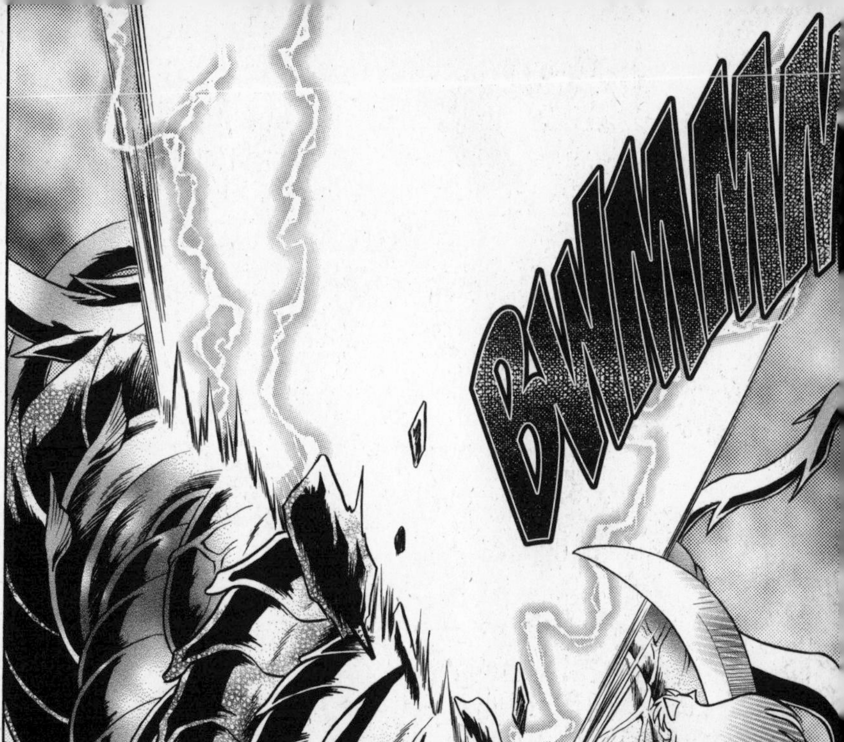
BWMMMMN
!

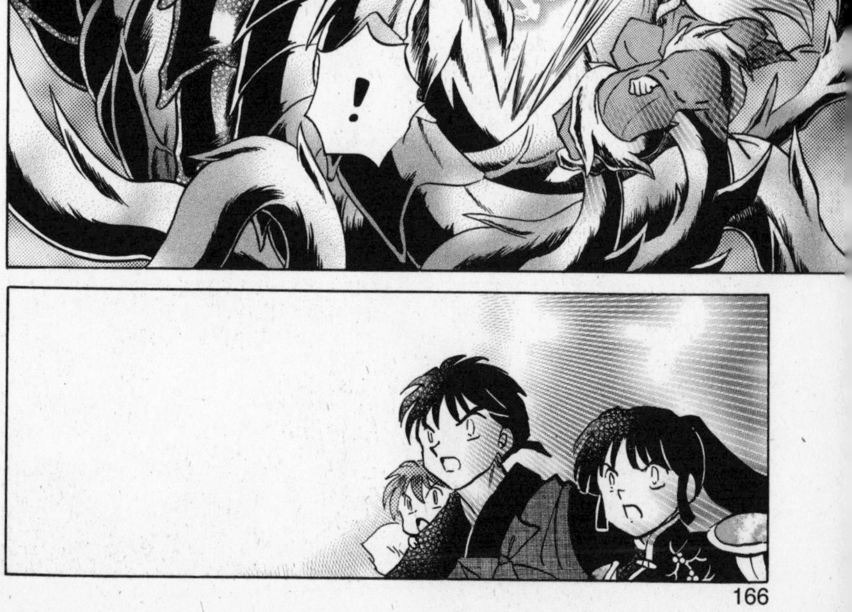

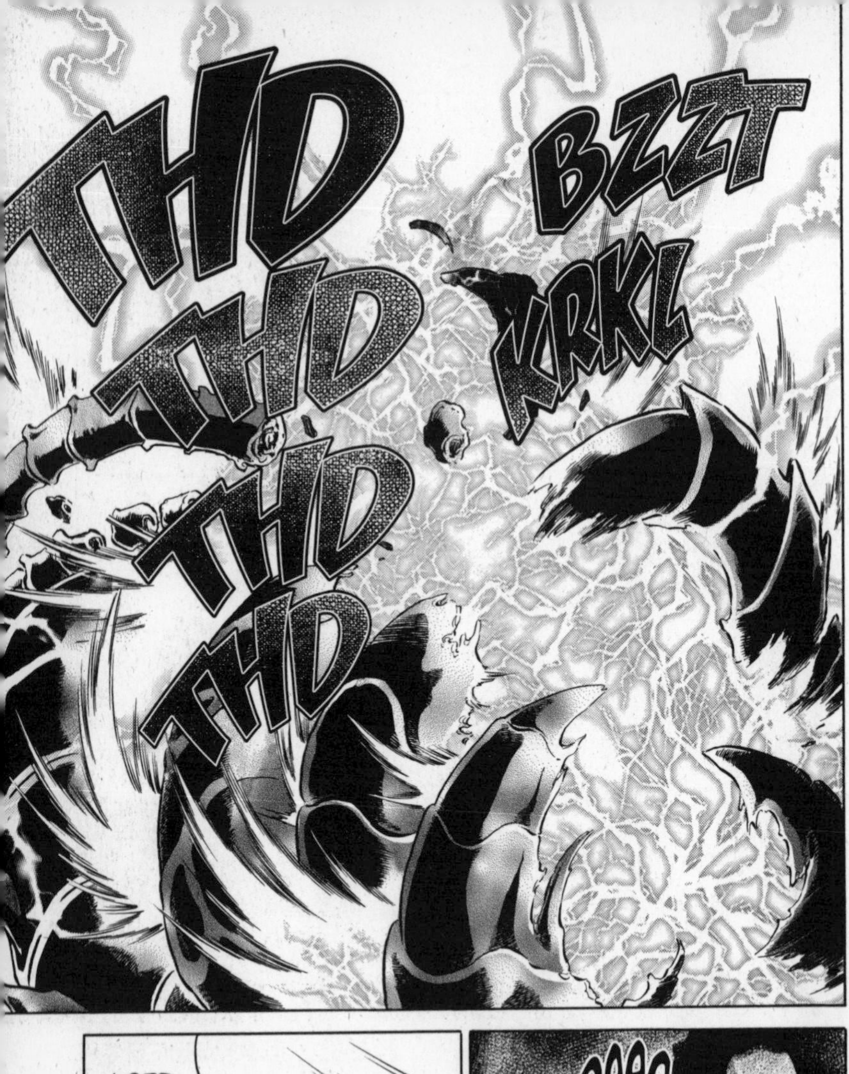
BZZT
KRKL
THD
THD
THD
THD
GRAAA
LORD SESSHO-MARU!

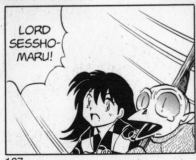

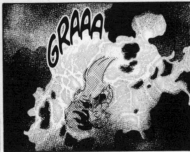

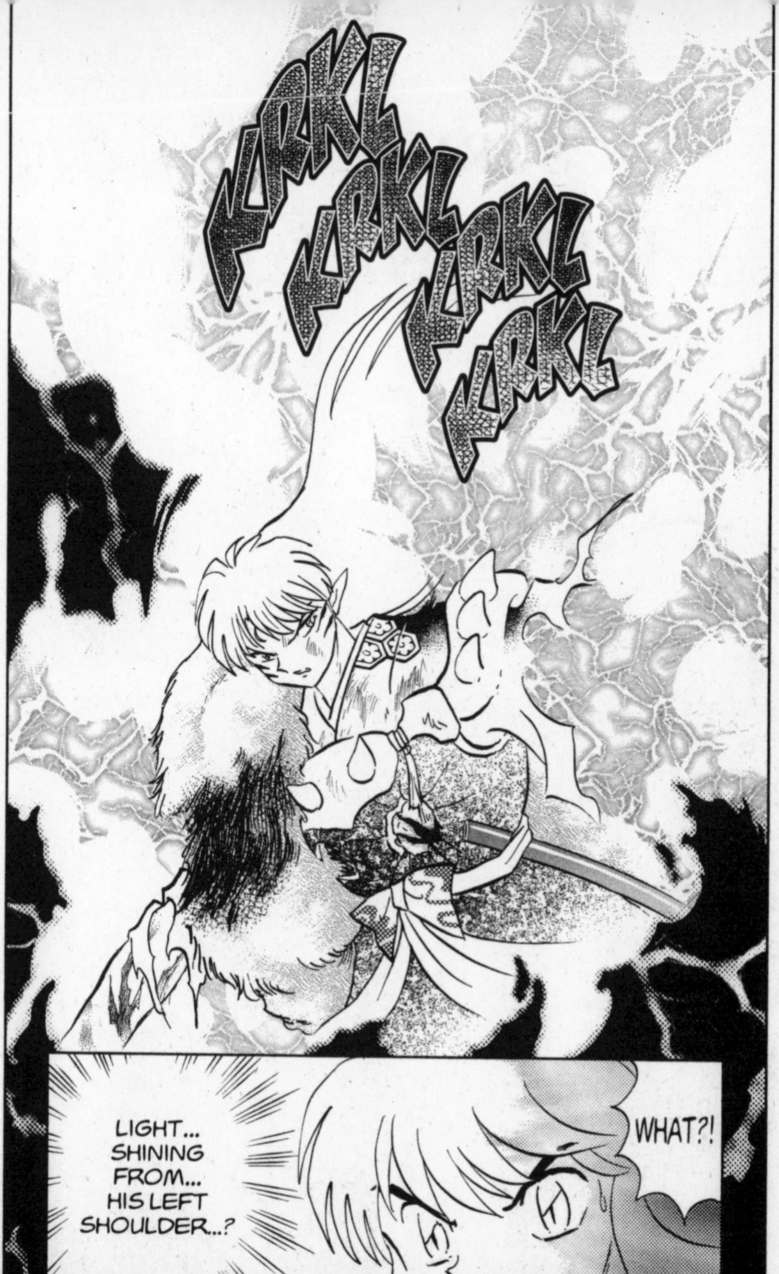
KIRKL KIRKL KIRKL KIRKL
WHAT?!
LIGHT... SHINING FROM... HIS LEFT SHOULDER...?

SCROLL 10
BAKUSAIGA

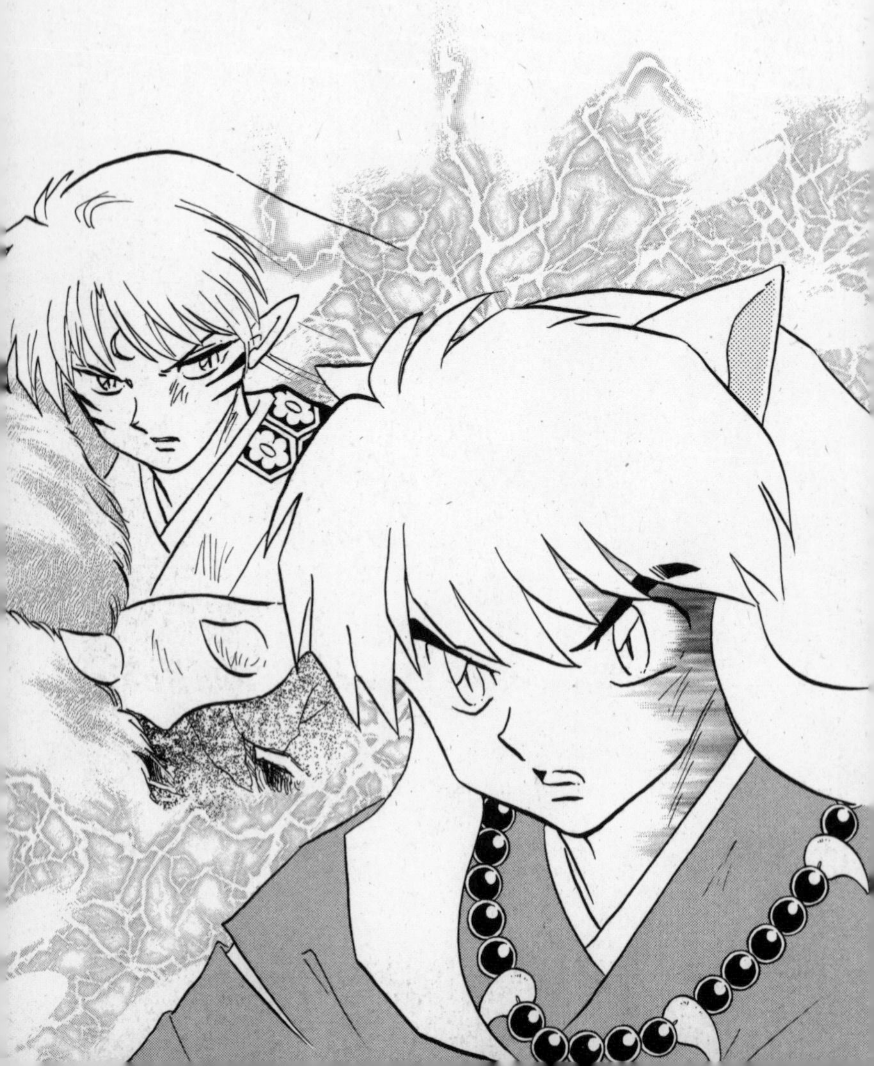

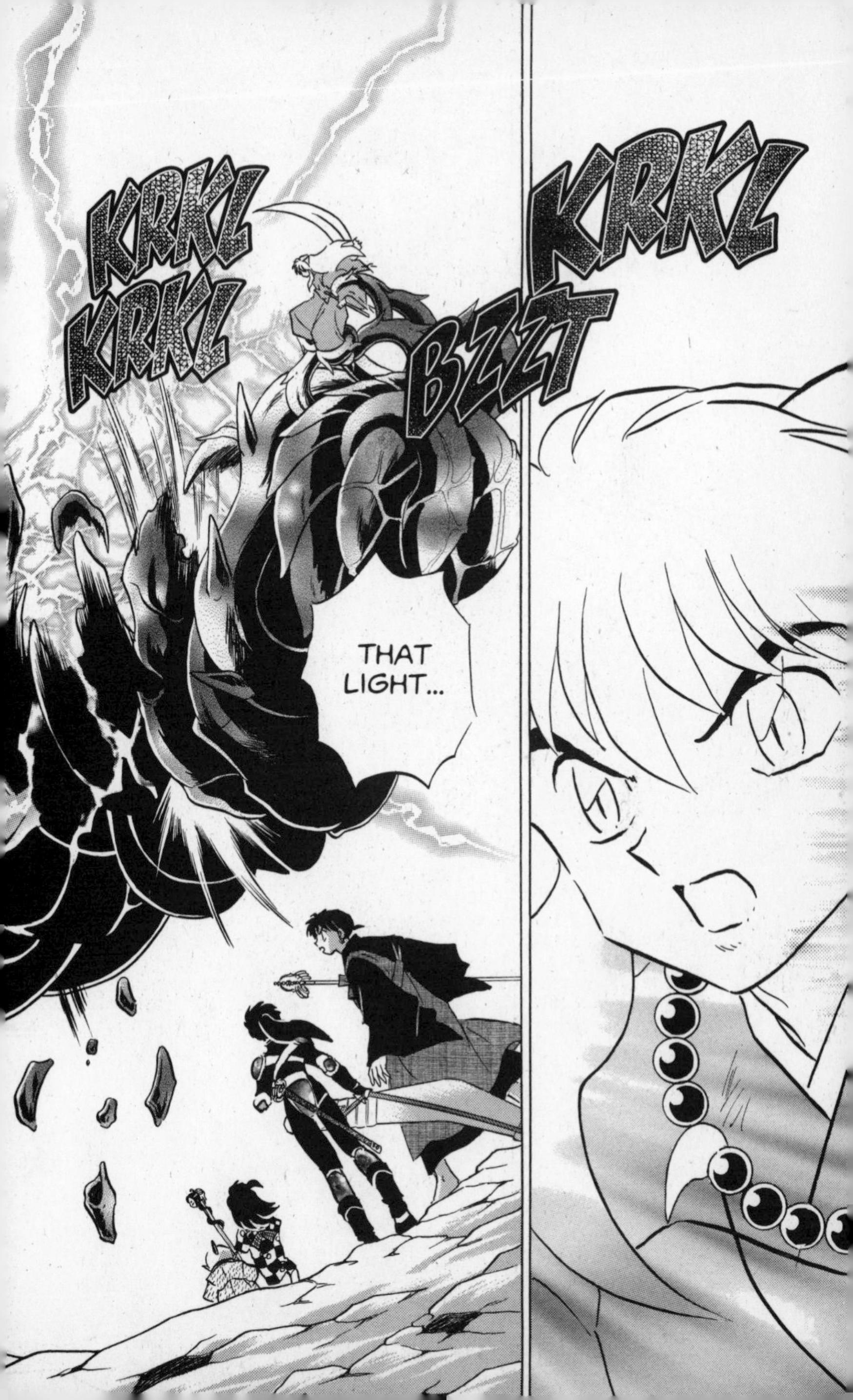
KRKL
BZZT
KRKL
KRKL
THAT LIGHT...

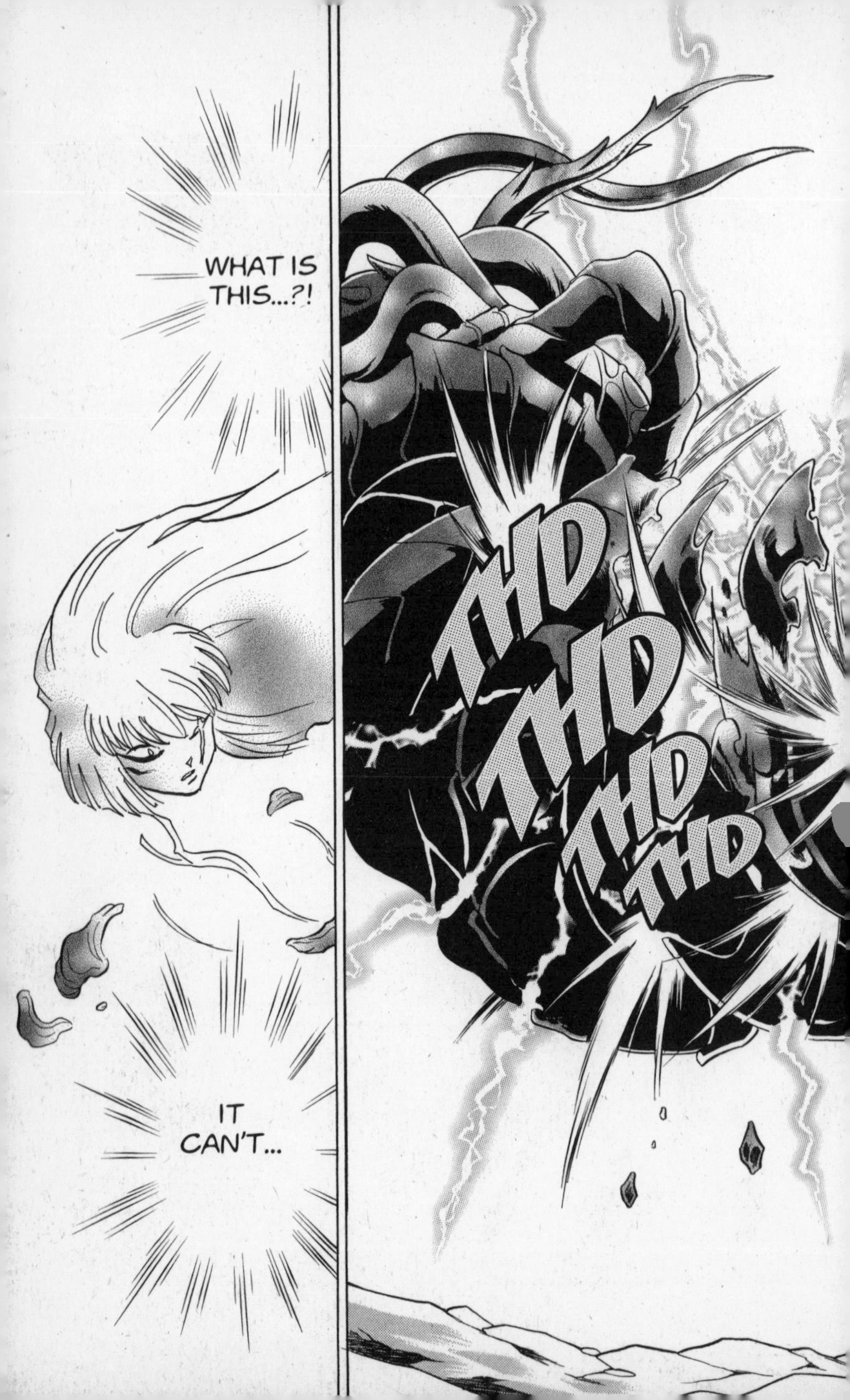
THD
THD
THD
THD
WHAT IS THIS...?!
IT CAN'T...

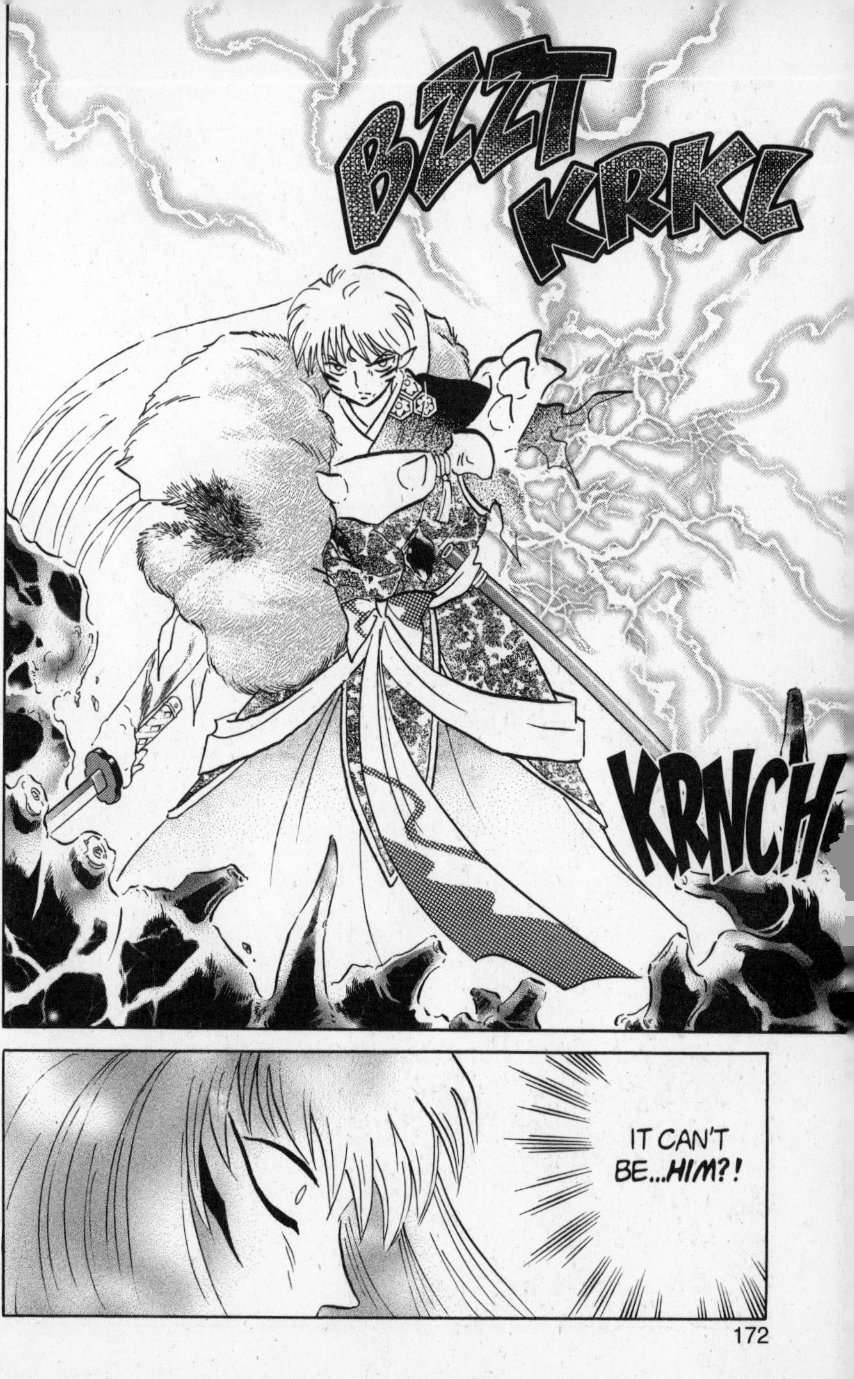
BZZT KRKL
KRNCH
IT CAN'T BE...*HIM?!*

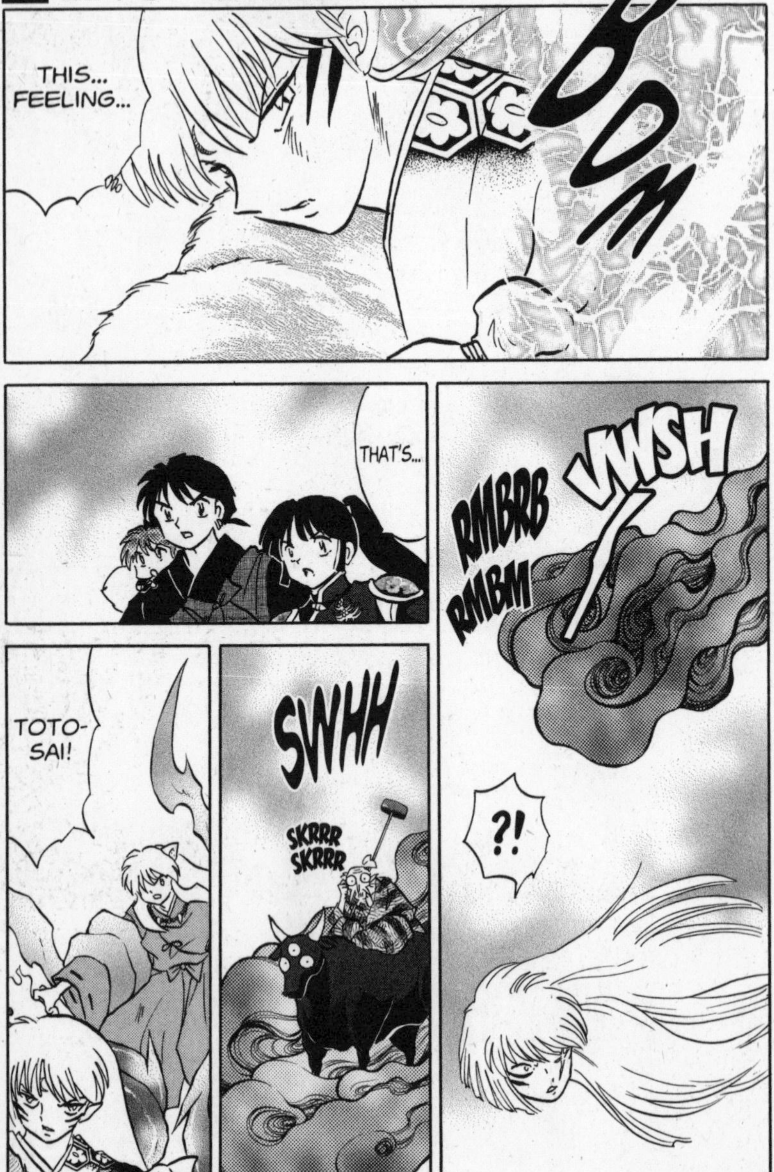
THIS... FEELING...
BOOM
VWSH
RMBRB RMBM
?!
THAT'S...
SWHH
SKRRR SKRRR
TOTO-SAI!

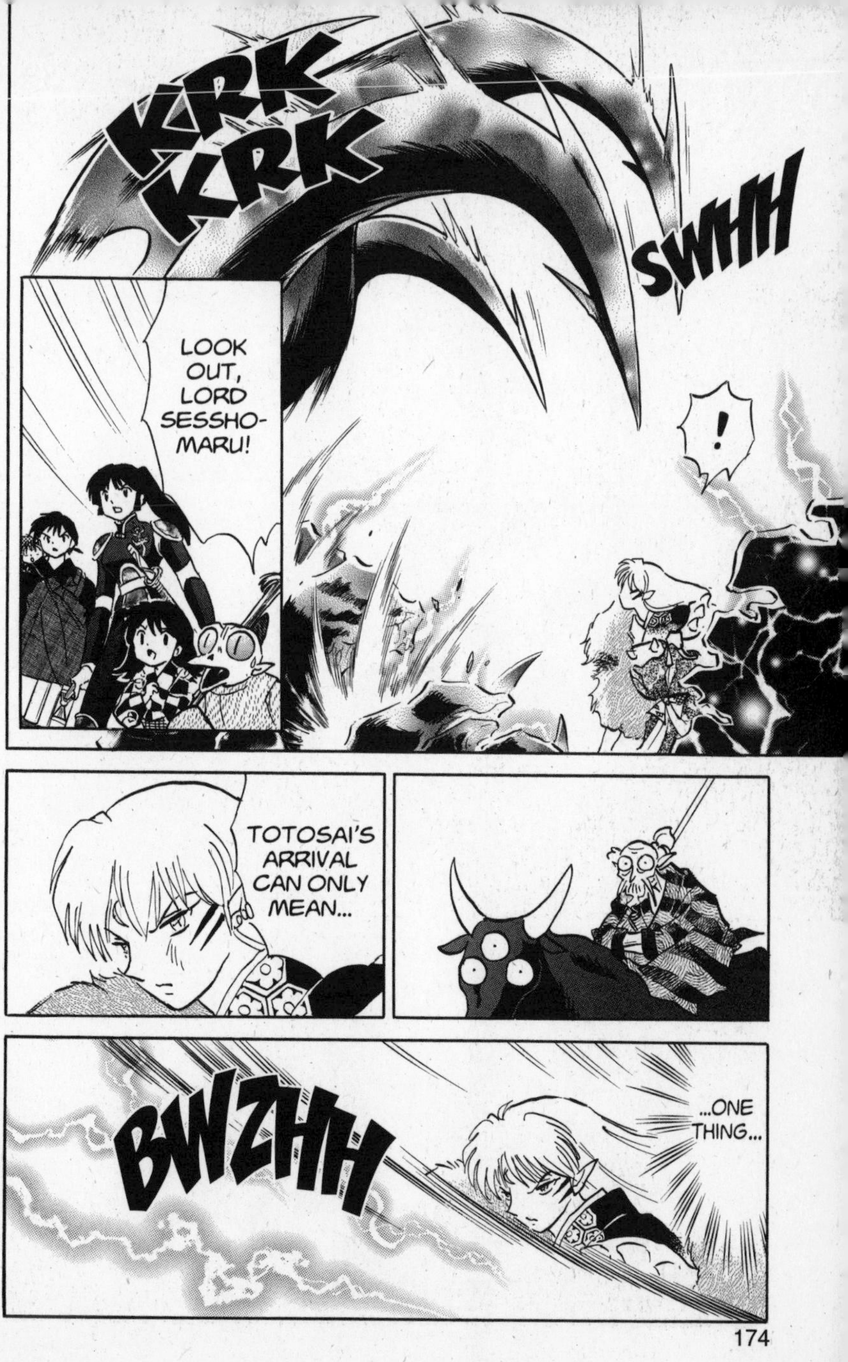
KRK KRK
SWHH
!
LOOK OUT, LORD SESSHO-MARU!
TOTOSAI'S ARRIVAL CAN ONLY MEAN...
...ONE THING...
BWZHH

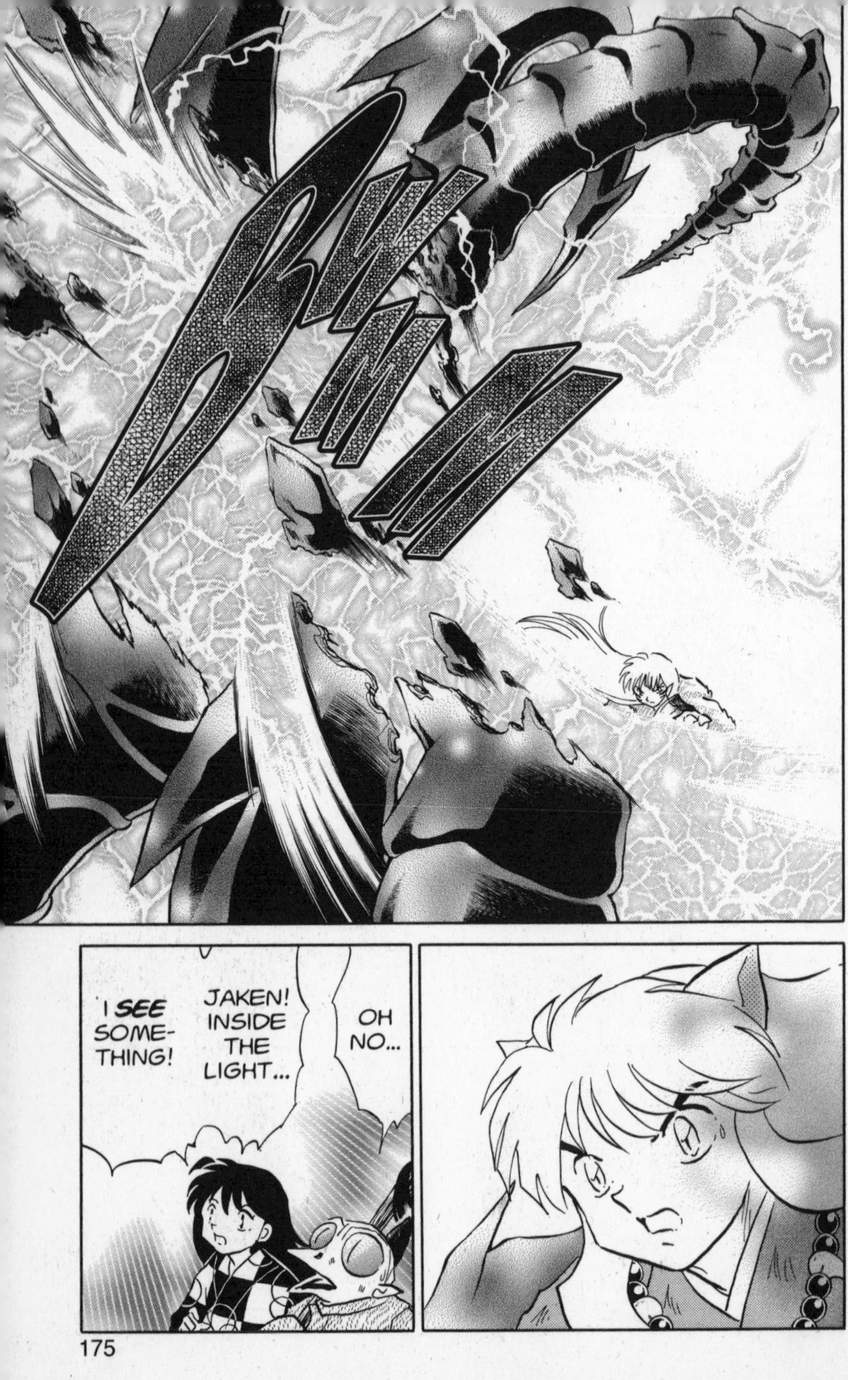
OH NO...
JAKEN! INSIDE THE LIGHT...
I SEE SOMETHING!

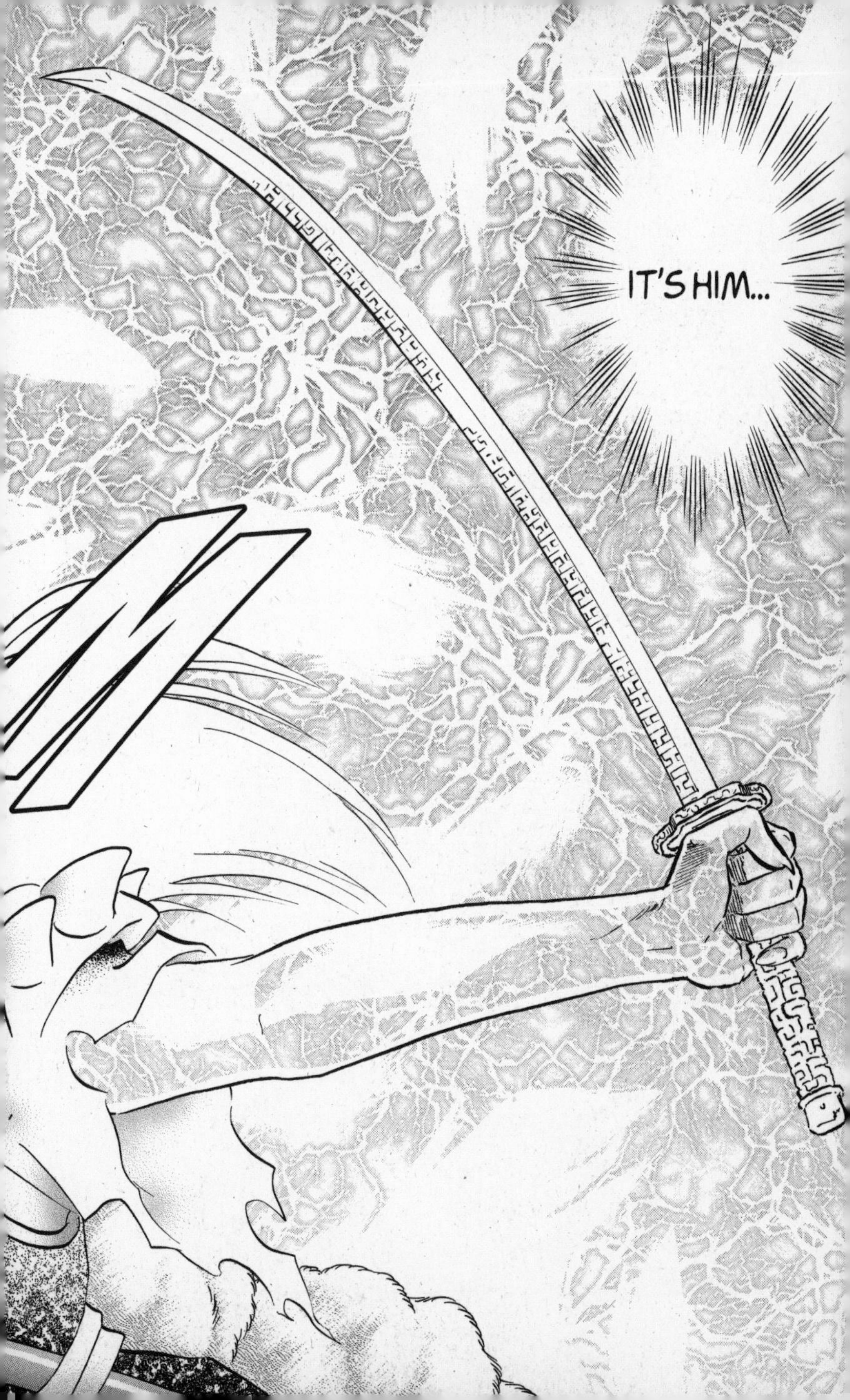
IT'S HIM...

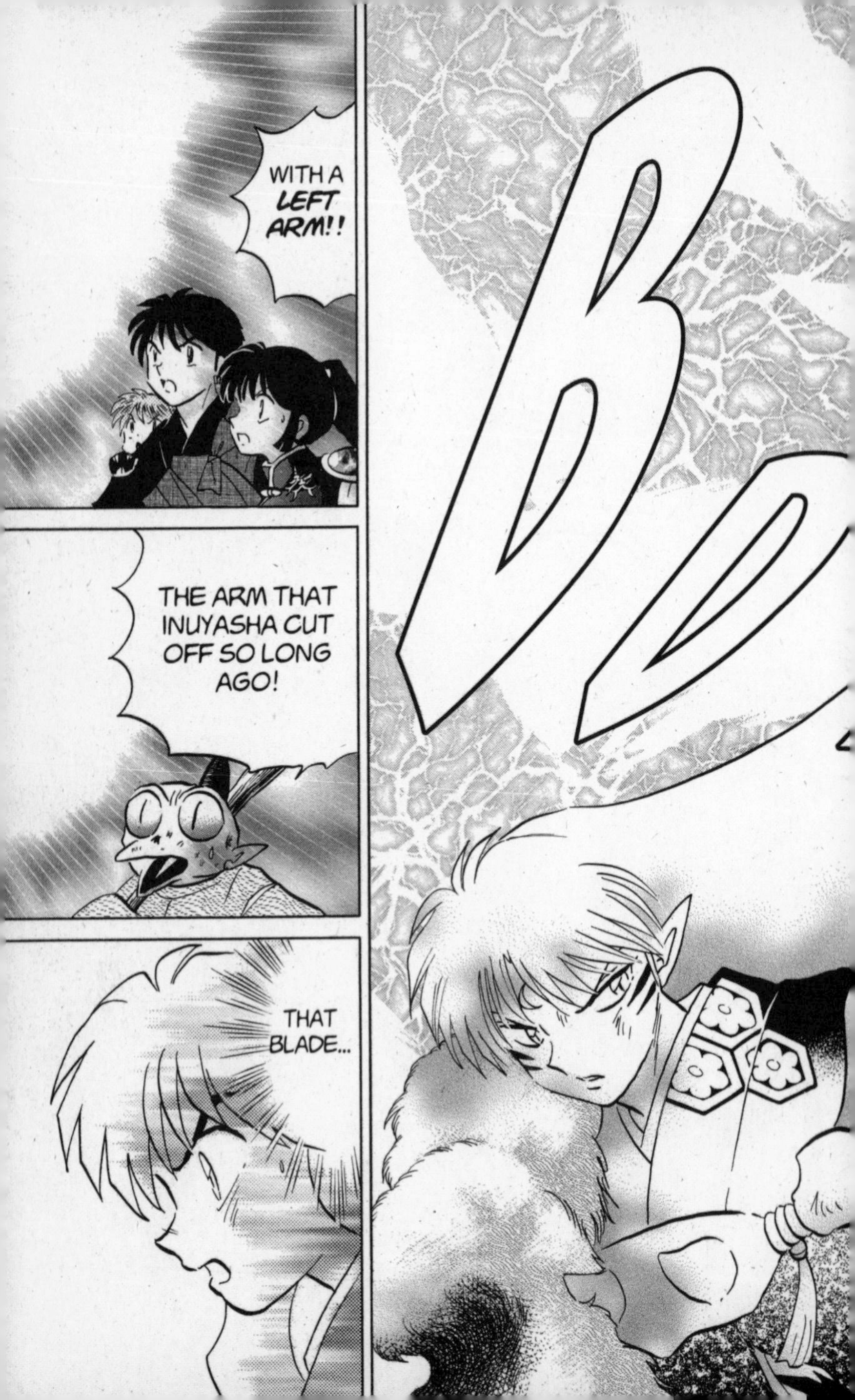
WITH A LEFT ARM!!
THE ARM THAT INUYASHA CUT OFF SO LONG AGO!
THAT BLADE...

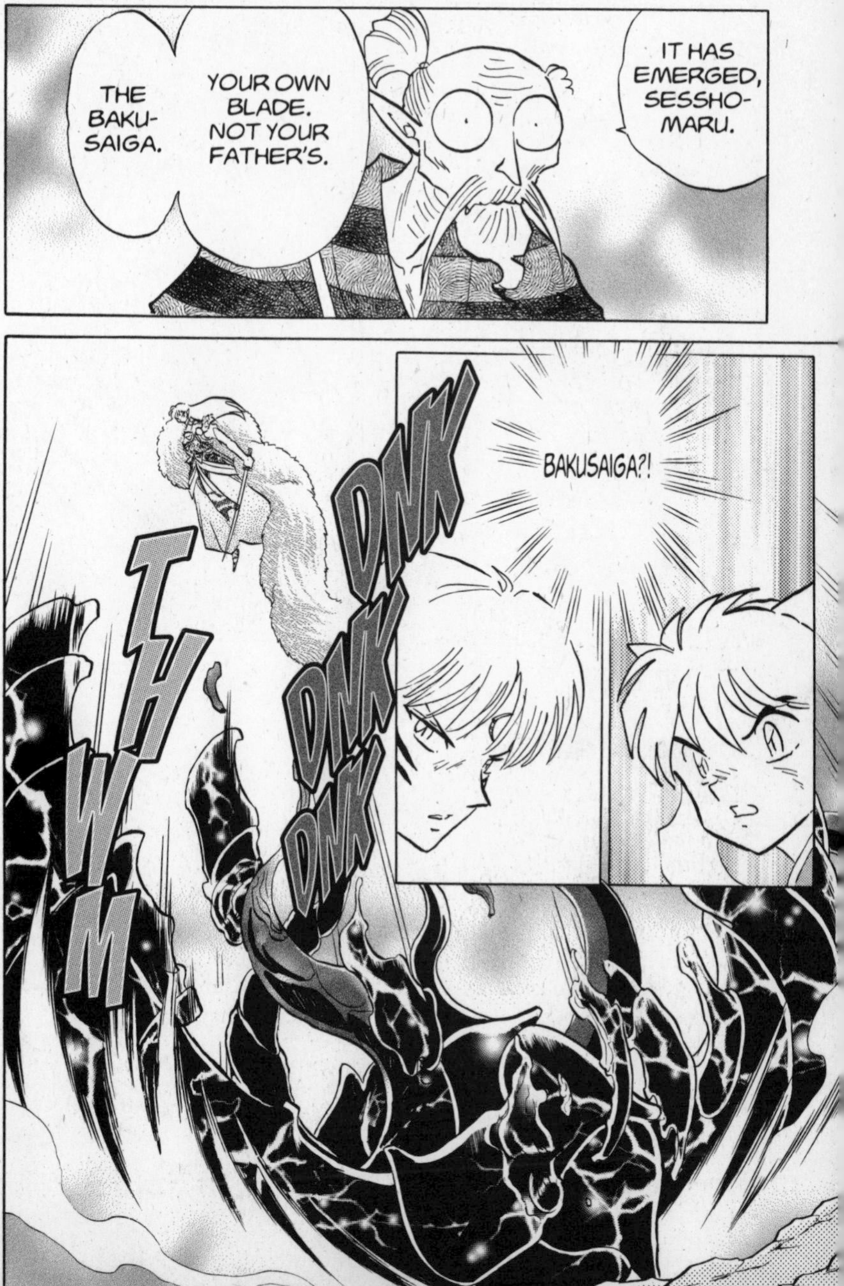
IT HAS EMERGED, SESSHOMARU.
YOUR OWN BLADE. NOT YOUR FATHER'S.
THE BAKUSAIGA.
BAKUSAIGA?!
DONK DONK DONK
THWM

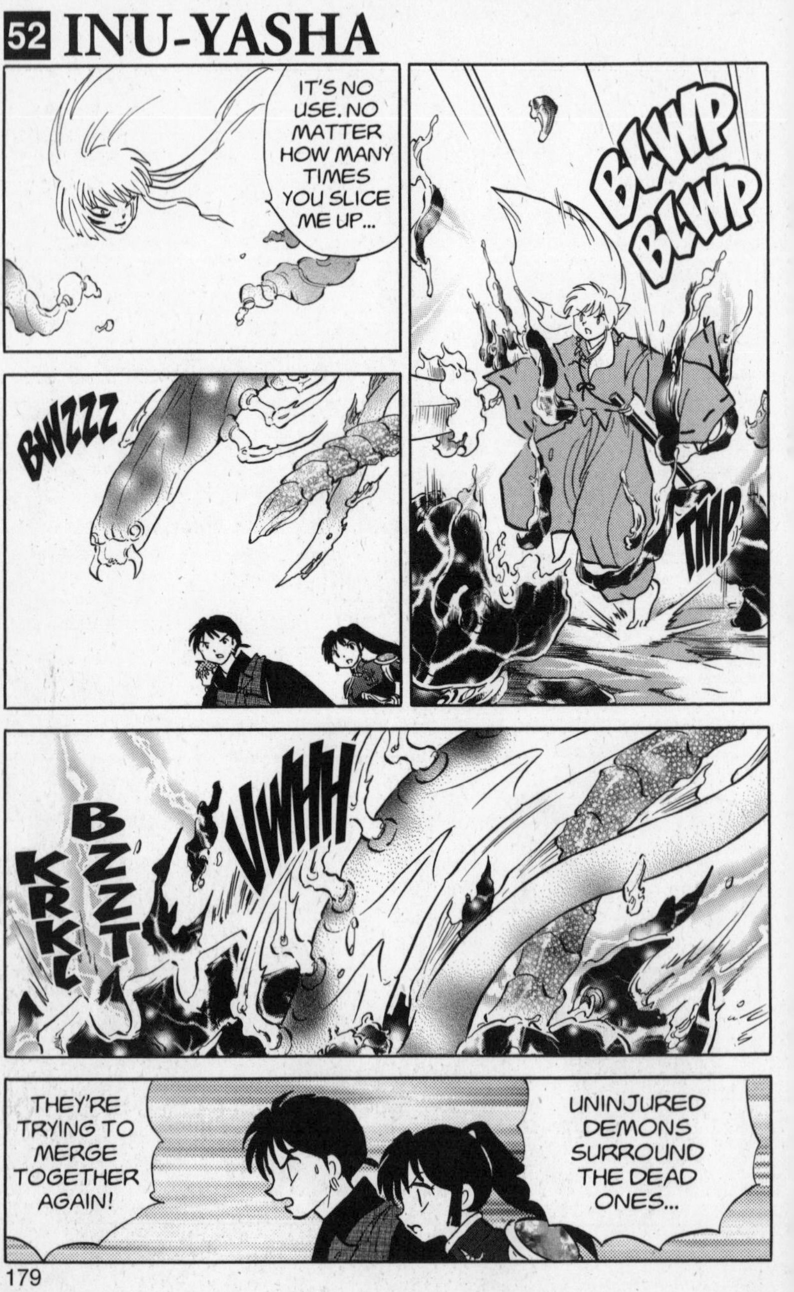
BLWP
BLWP
TMP
IT'S NO USE. NO MATTER HOW MANY TIMES YOU SLICE ME UP...
BWZZZ
VWHH
BZZZT
KRKL
UNINJURED DEMONS SURROUND THE DEAD ONES...
THEY'RE TRYING TO MERGE TOGETHER AGAIN!

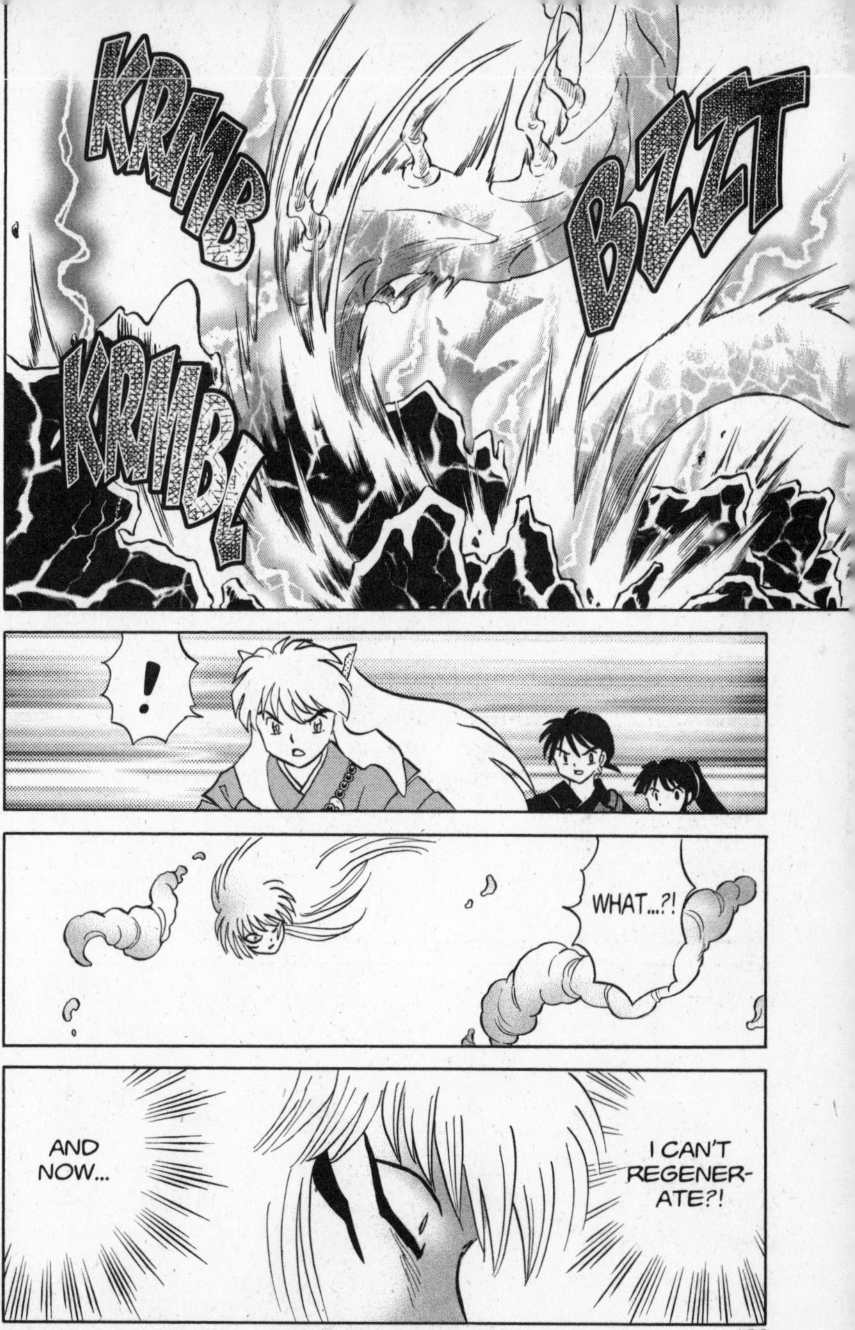
BZZT
KRMB
KRMBL
!
WHAT...?!
I CAN'T REGENER-ATE?!
AND NOW...

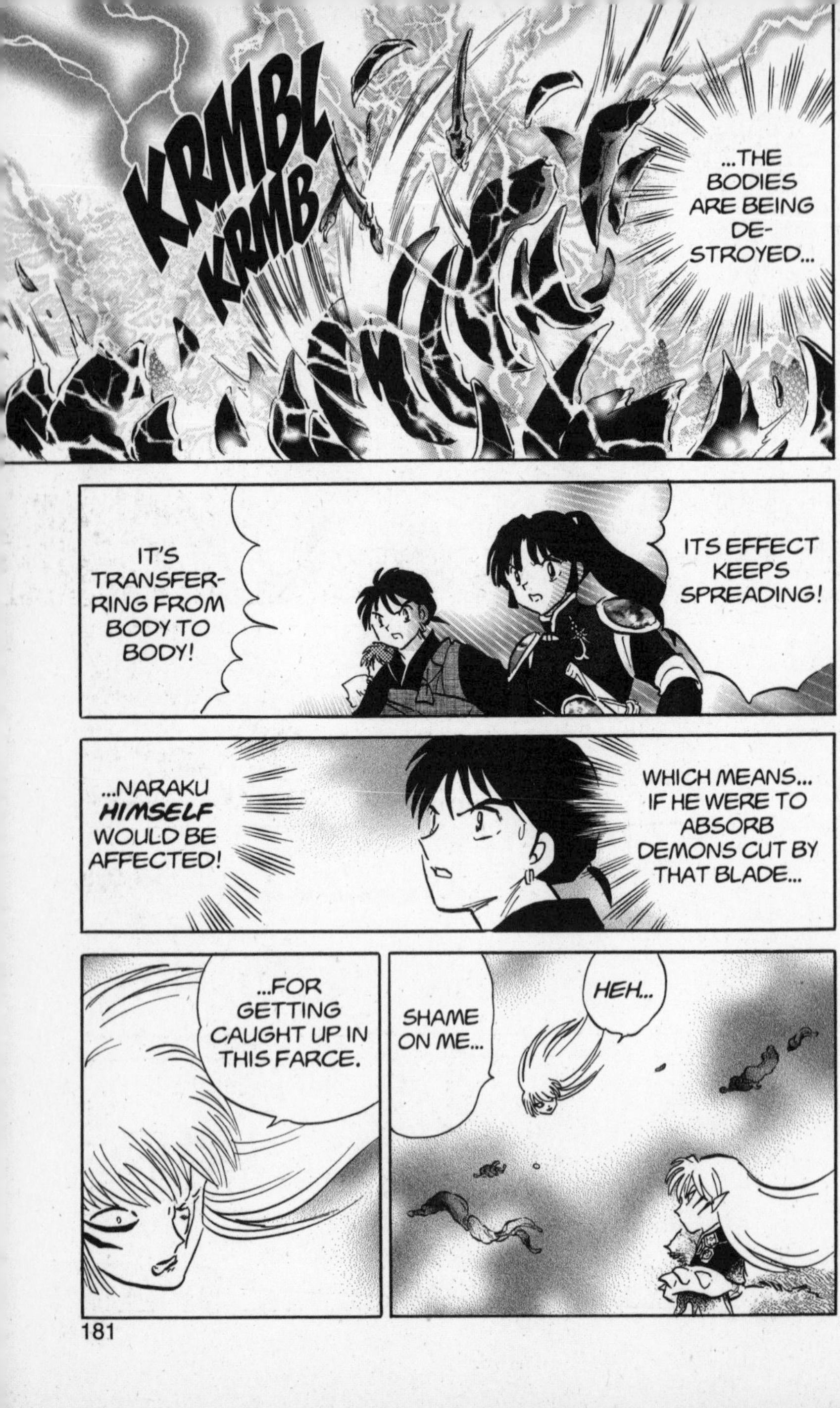
...THE BODIES ARE BEING DE-STROYED...
KRMBL KRMB
ITS EFFECT KEEPS SPREADING!
IT'S TRANSFER-RING FROM BODY TO BODY!
WHICH MEANS... IF HE WERE TO ABSORB DEMONS CUT BY THAT BLADE...
...NARAKU HIMSELF WOULD BE AFFECTED!
HEH...
SHAME ON ME...
...FOR GETTING CAUGHT UP IN THIS FARCE.

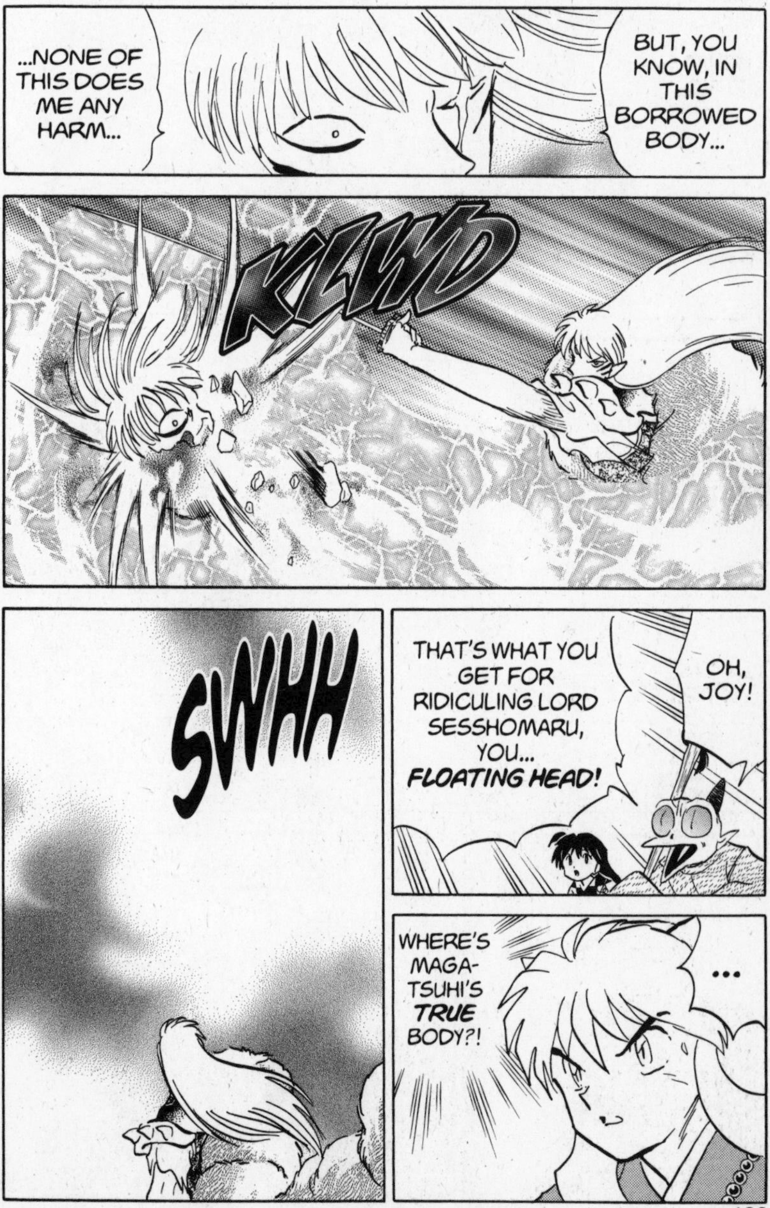
BUT, YOU KNOW, IN THIS BORROWED BODY...
...NONE OF THIS DOES ME ANY HARM...
KLWD
OH, JOY!
THAT'S WHAT YOU GET FOR RIDICULING LORD SESSHOMARU, YOU... **FLOATING HEAD!**
...
WHERE'S MAGA-TSUHI'S **TRUE** BODY?!
SWHH

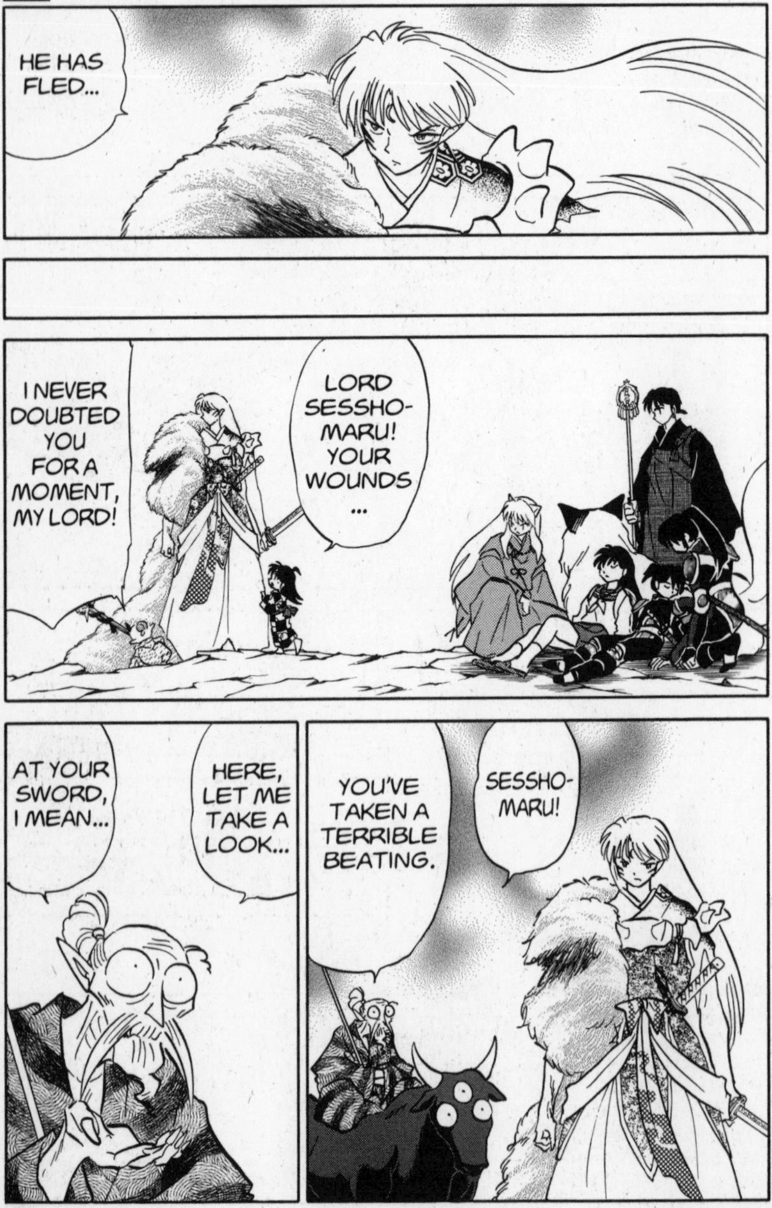
HE HAS FLED...
LORD SESSHOMARU! YOUR WOUNDS...
I NEVER DOUBTED YOU FOR A MOMENT, MY LORD!
SESSHOMARU!
YOU'VE TAKEN A TERRIBLE BEATING.
HERE, LET ME TAKE A LOOK...
AT YOUR SWORD, I MEAN...

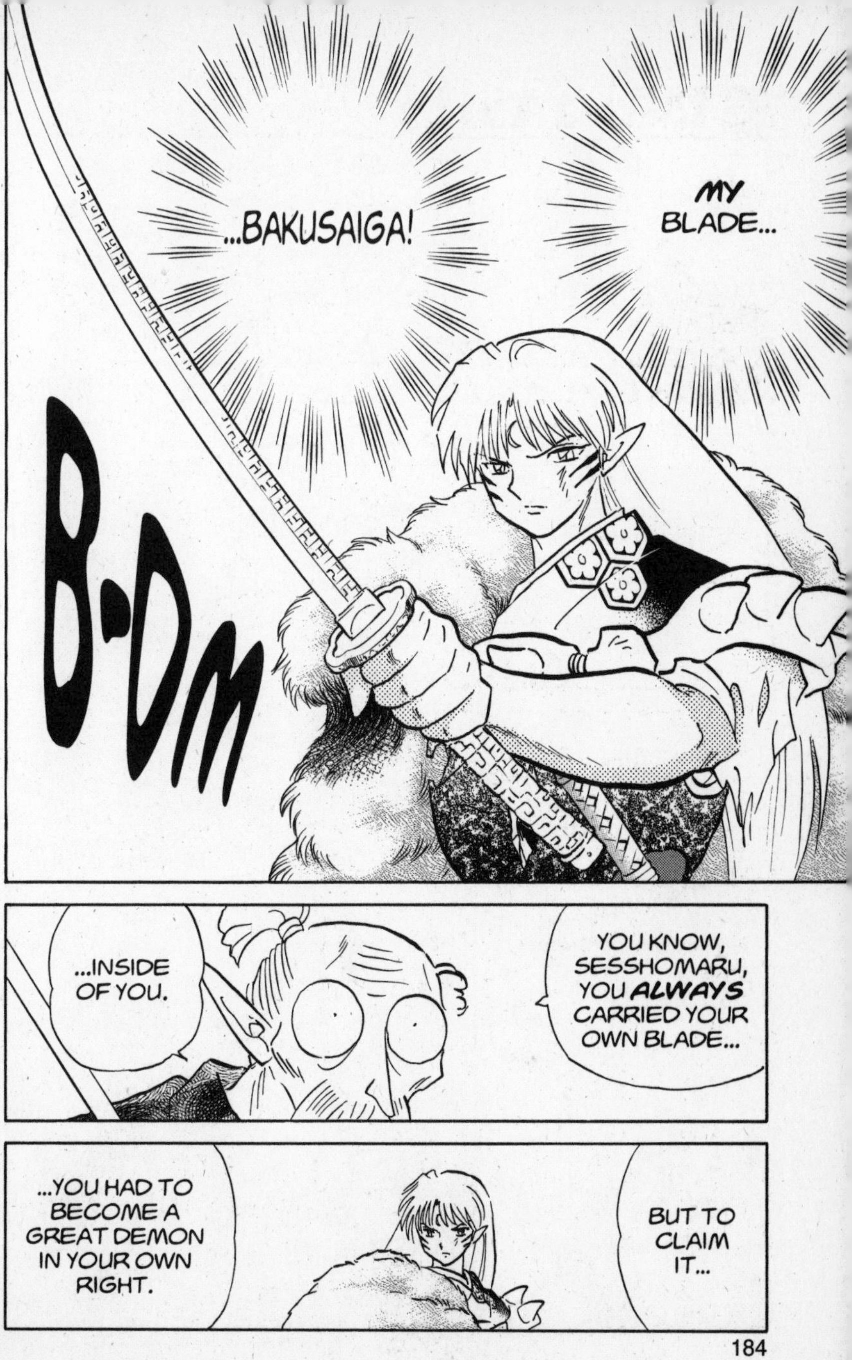
MY BLADE...
...BAKUSAIGA!
B-DM
YOU KNOW, SESSHOMARU, YOU ALWAYS CARRIED YOUR OWN BLADE...
...INSIDE OF YOU.
BUT TO CLAIM IT...
...YOU HAD TO BECOME A GREAT DEMON IN YOUR OWN RIGHT.

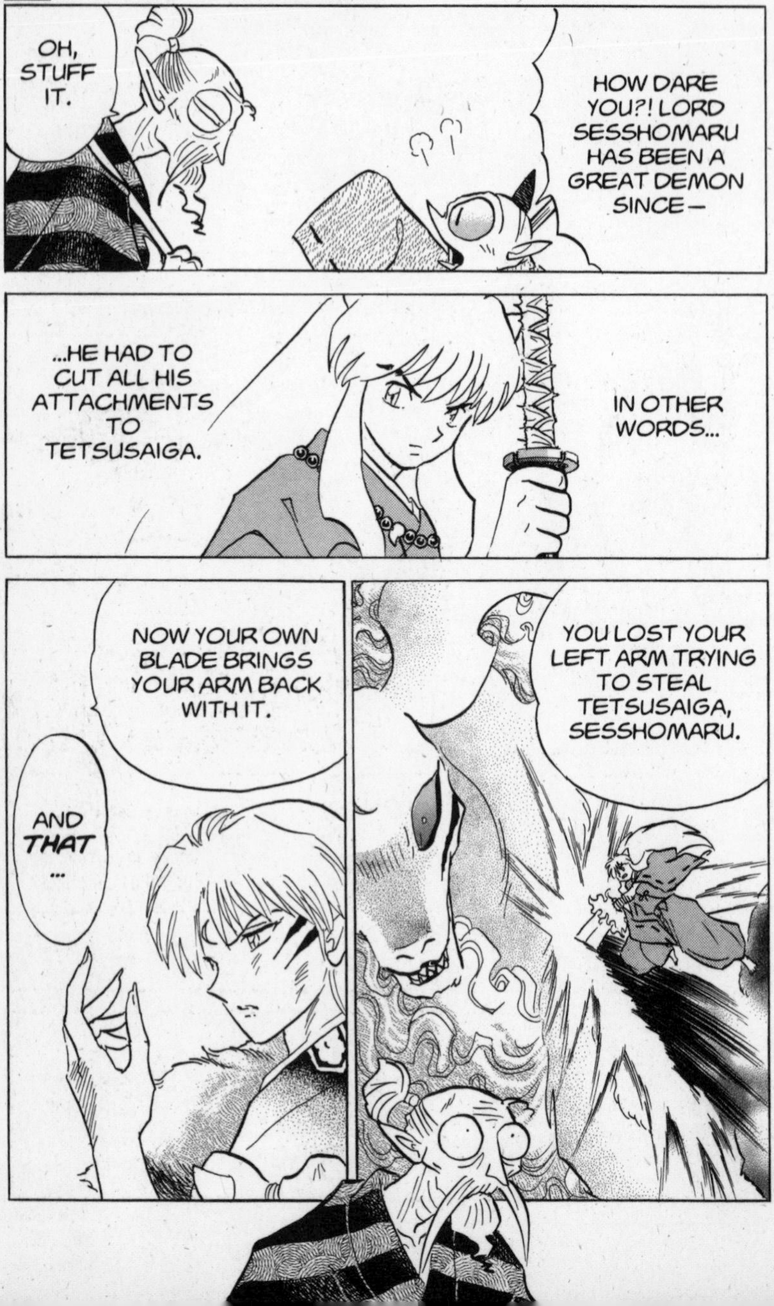
HOW DARE YOU?! LORD SESSHOMARU HAS BEEN A GREAT DEMON SINCE—
OH, STUFF IT.
IN OTHER WORDS...
...HE HAD TO CUT ALL HIS ATTACHMENTS TO TETSUSAIGA.
YOU LOST YOUR LEFT ARM TRYING TO STEAL TETSUSAIGA, SESSHOMARU.
NOW YOUR OWN BLADE BRINGS YOUR ARM BACK WITH IT.
AND *THAT* ...

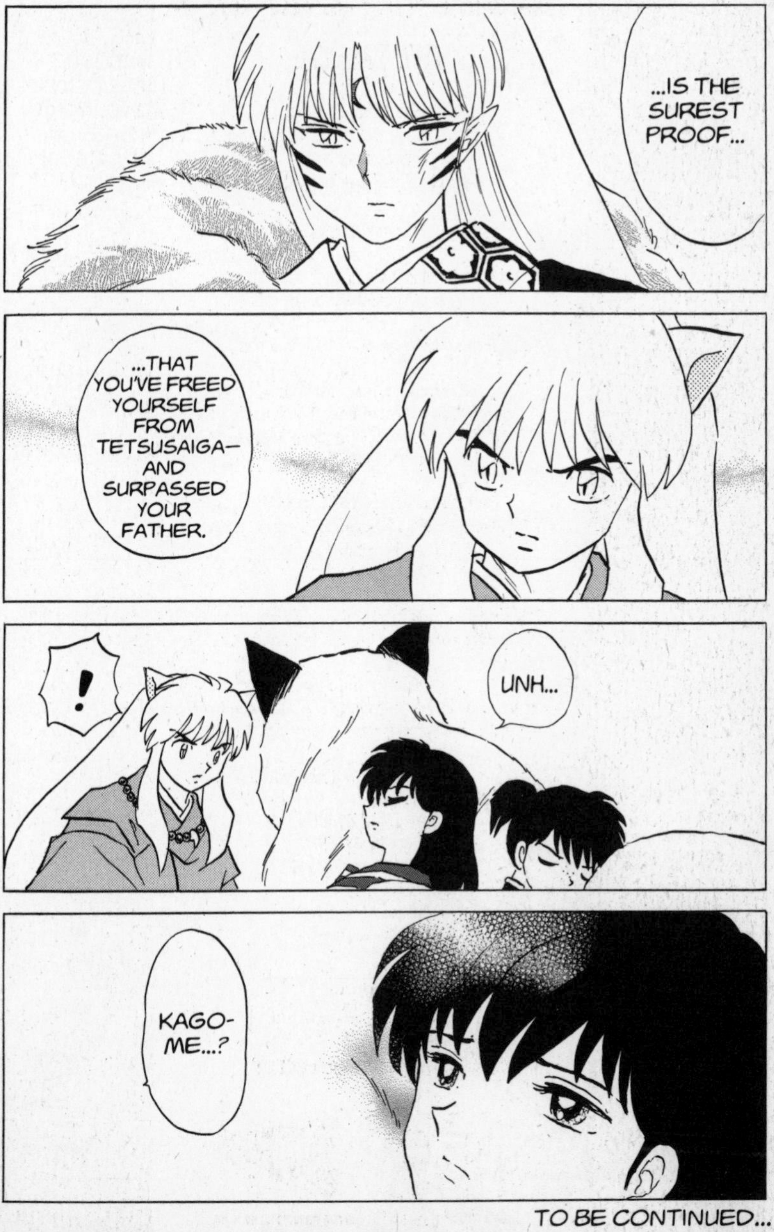
...IS THE SUREST PROOF...
...THAT YOU'VE FREED YOURSELF FROM TETSUSAIGA—AND SURPASSED YOUR FATHER.
UNH...
!
KAGO-ME...?

TO BE CONTINUED...

INUYASHA

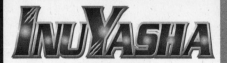

INUYASHA
VOL. 52
Shonen Sunday Edition

Story and Art by
RUMIKO TAKAHASHI

English Adaptation by Gerard Jones

Translation/Mari Morimoto
Touch-up Art & Lettering/Bill Schuch
Cover & Interior Graphic Design/Yuki Ameda
Editor/Annette Roman

VP, Production/Alvin Lu
VP, Sales & Product Marketing/Gonzalo Ferreyra
VP, Creative/Linda Espinosa
Publisher/Hyoe Narita

Printed in the U.S.A.

Published by VIZ Media, LLC
P.O. Box 77010
San Francisco, CA 94107

10 9 8 7 6 5 4 3 2 1
First printing, September 2010

RATED T+ FOR OLDER TEEN

PARENTAL ADVISORY
INUYASHA is rated T+ for Older Teen and is recommended for ages 16 and up. This volume contains violence.

ratings.viz.com

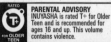

www.viz.com

WWW.SHONENSUNDAY.COM

TV SERIES & MOVIES ON DVD!

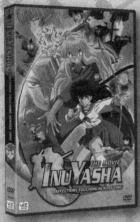
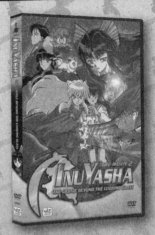
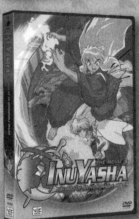
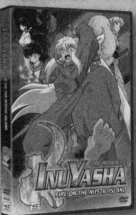

See more of the action in *Inuyasha* full-length movies

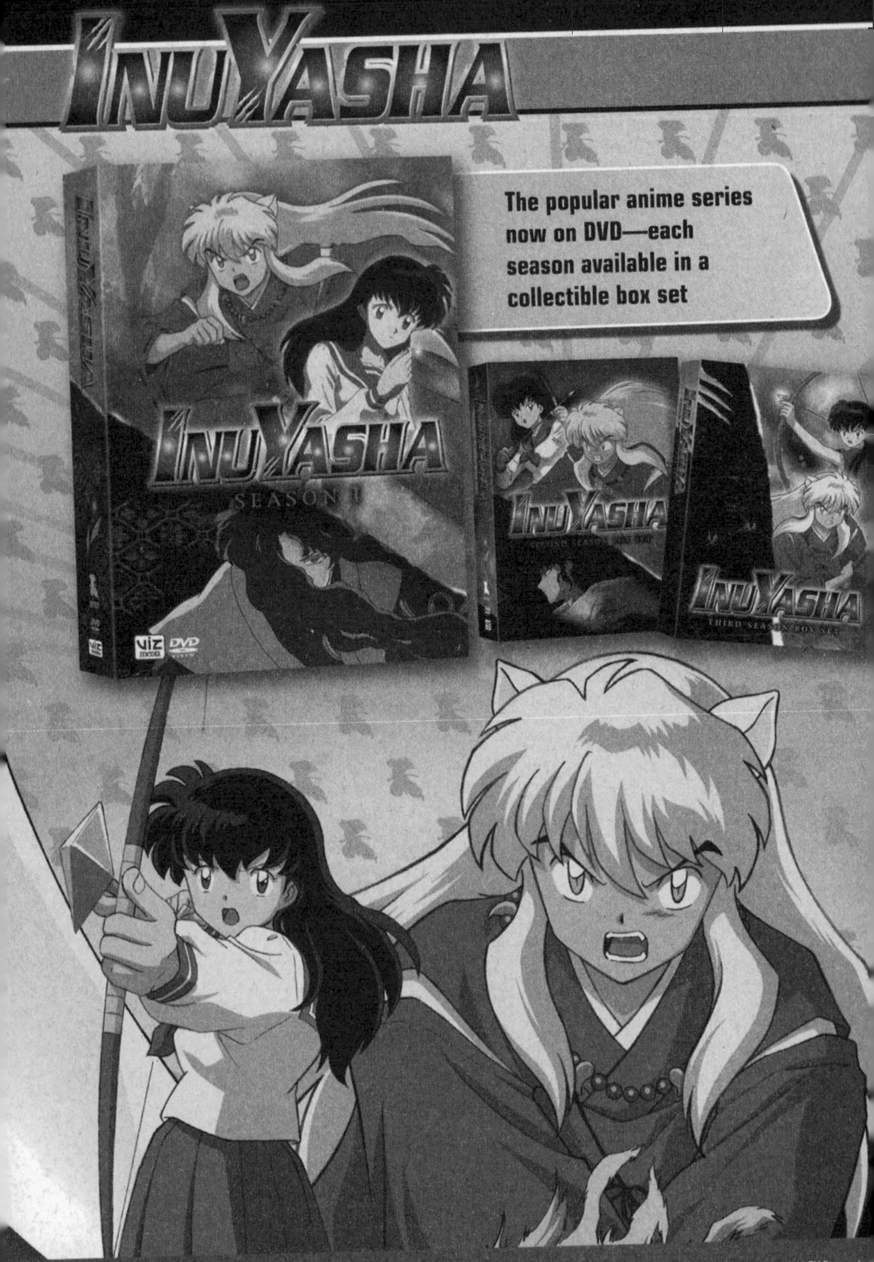
INUYASHA
The popular anime series now on DVD—each season available in a collectible box set
INUYASHA
INUYASHA
INUYASHA

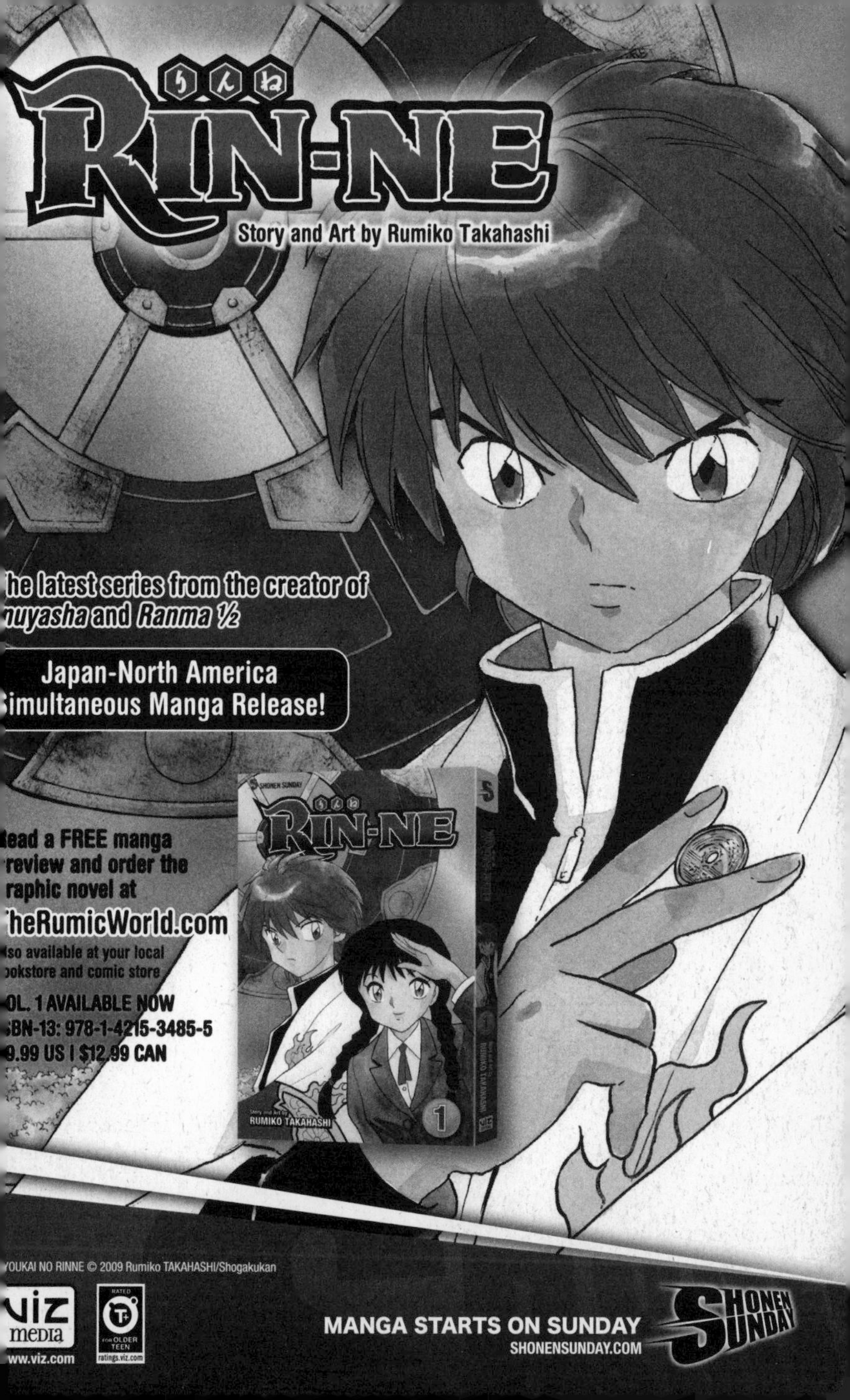
らんね
RIN-NE
Story and Art by Rumiko Takahashi
he latest series from the creator of
nuyasha and Ranma ½
Japan-North America
imultaneous Manga Release!
ead a FREE manga
review and order the
raphic novel at
heRumicWorld.com
lso available at your local
ookstore and comic store
OL. 1 AVAILABLE NOW
SBN-13: 978-1-4215-3485-5
9.99 US | $12.99 CAN
Story and Art by
RUMIKO TAKAHASHI
YOUKAI NO RINNE © 2009 Rumiko TAKAHASHI/Shogakukan
viz media
www.viz.com
RATED T+ FOR OLDER TEEN
ratings.viz.com
MANGA STARTS ON SUNDAY
SHONENSUNDAY.COM
SHONEN SUNDAY

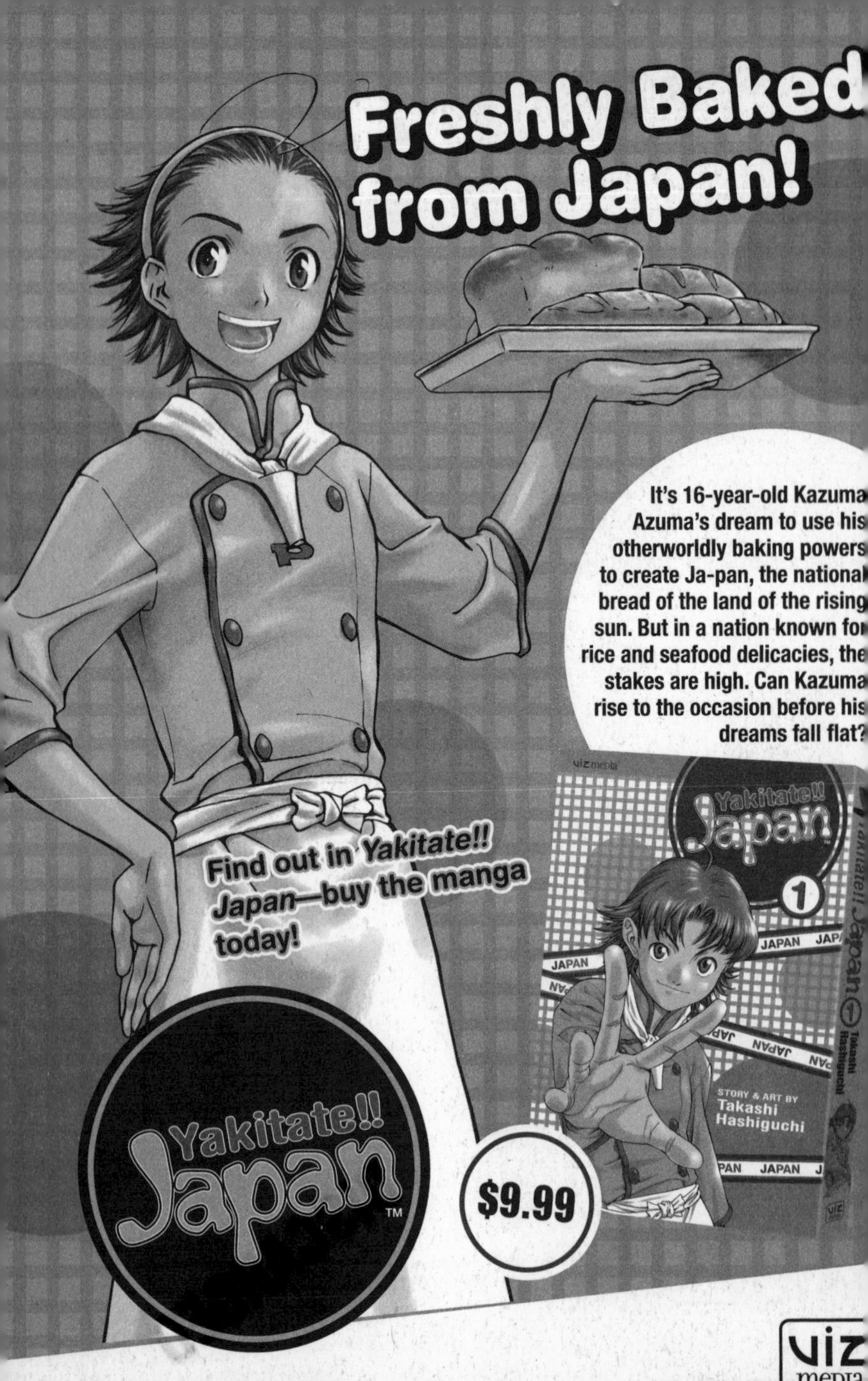
Freshly Baked from Japan!
It's 16-year-old Kazuma Azuma's dream to use his otherworldly baking powers to create Ja-pan, the national bread of the land of the rising sun. But in a nation known for rice and seafood delicacies, the stakes are high. Can Kazuma rise to the occasion before his dreams fall flat?
Find out in Yakitate!! Japan—buy the manga today!
Yakitate!! Japan™
$9.99
Yakitate!! Japan 1
STORY & ART BY Takashi Hashiguchi

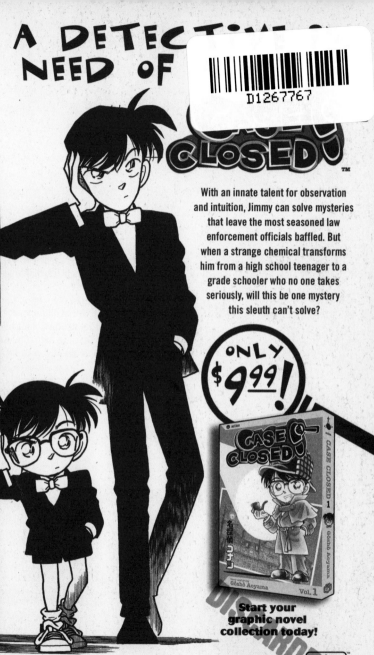

A DETECTIVE IN NEED OF

CASE CLOSED™

With an innate talent for observation and intuition, Jimmy can solve mysteries that leave the most seasoned law enforcement officials baffled. But when a strange chemical transforms him from a high school teenager to a grade schooler who no one takes seriously, will this be one mystery this sleuth can't solve?

ONLY $9.99!

Start your graphic novel collection today!

©1994 Gosho AOYAMA/Shogakukan Inc.